Russian Bureaucracy

Russian Bureaucracy

Power and Pathology

Karl W. Ryavec

ROWMAN & LITTLEFIELD PUBLISHERS, INC.
Lanham • Boulder • New York • Toronto • Oxford

ROWMAN & LITTLEFIELD PUBLISHERS, INC.

Published in the United States of America
by Rowman & Littlefield Publishers, Inc.
A Member of the Rowman & Littlefield Publishing Group
4501 Forbes Boulevard, Suite 200, Lanham, Maryland 20706
www.rowmanlittlefield.com

PO Box 317
Oxford
OX2 9RU, UK

British Library Cataloguing in Publication Information Available

Library of Congress Cataloging-in-Publication Data

Ryavec, Karl W.
  Russian bureaucracy : power and pathology / Karl W. Ryavec.
      p. cm.
Includes bibliographical references and index.
  ISBN 0-8476-9502-6 (cloth : alk. paper)
  1. Bureaucracy—Russia—History. 2. Bureaucracy—Soviet
Union—History. 3. Bureaucracy—Russia (Federation) I. Title.

  JN6531.R9 2003
  352.6'3'0947—dc21

                                                        2003002674

Printed in the United States of America

♾™ The paper used in this publication meets the minimum requirements of
American National Standard for Information Sciences—Permanence of Paper
for Printed Library Materials, ANSI/NISO Z39.48-1992.

This book is affectionately dedicated to
my wife, Isabel Mary Seaton Ryavec

Contents

Acknowledgments

I am grateful to all those colleagues, friends, and others who gave me assistance in writing this book and preparing it for publication. First of all, I am pleased to mention those who helped put me on the road to bureaucracy as a major topic of my scholarly work: Professor John N. Hazard of Columbia University, Professor Peter Juviler of Barnard College and Columbia University, and Dr. Grey Hodnett, then also of Columbia. I am particularly indebted to John Hazard for his long-term encouragement of my work. I am also grateful to those who read and commented on drafts of chapters and other related materials. They include Professors Emeritus John A. Armstrong, long of the University of Wisconsin, and Curt Tausky of the Department of Sociology of the University of Massachusetts; my former colleague Professor Fred Kramer; and Professor Robert E. Jones of the Department of History of the University of Massachusetts.

I am also indebted to several scholars who made useful comments on this project or rendered other assistance. Among them are Professor Valerie Bunce; my former colleagues Professors Craig Thomas and M. J. Peterson; Karl E. Ryavec, my son and a professor of geography at the University of Wisconsin at Stevens Point; Vladimir Zhdanov, a Ph.D. candidate at the University of Massachusetts; and several helpful librarians of the DuBois Library of the University of Massachusetts.

Well worthy of collective mention are my fellow officers and the enlisted men of my few years in the U.S. Navy as the communications officer of the *USS Falgout* (DER 324), then out of Seattle, Washington, and as an inspection officer of the reserve fleet then at Tongue Point, near Astoria, Oregon.

I am also indebted to my fellow bureaucrats of my year working on arms control and defense conversion in the U.S. government in Washington, D.C. These experiences gave me much to think about regarding bureaucracy and administration that was useful to me in formulating and writing this book.

This book is warmly dedicated to my wife, Isabel Mary Seaton Ryavec. Her continuing encouragement was fundamental to the book's completion.

Preface

$\mathcal{T}$he origins of this book lie in the 1960s and, of course, in my experiences and personality. Sometime in the mid-1960s, Professor John Hazard, that wonderful and charming man who was my academic adviser at Columbia, while talking with a confused and puzzled graduate student looking for a dissertation topic, leaned back in his chair and said, "Karl, why don't you do something on administration?" I took him up on his suggestion, and the product was a dissertation in 1968 and eventually, after additional research, a book in 1975. However, because most of the secondary literature of that time dealing with Soviet administration was by economists and concentrated on industrial administration, it caused me to write some works that were not squarely in the field of politics. Indeed, because my book had the word *economic* in the title, it was sent for review mainly to economists, some of whom did not appreciate the effort of a noneconomist to explicate the nature of the bureaucratic problem in Soviet industrial administration.

Over the years I gathered additional material on Russo-Soviet bureaucracy, wrote articles and papers on the topic, and eventually wound up the possessor of a small archive—actually piles of items, from newspaper clippings to articles, scholarly papers, and books—on it, both realizing that I ought to "do something" with it (a combined sense of scholarly "duty" and careerism) and dreading the effort it would take to put it "together." In recent years the appearance of a variety of works on administration and bureaucracy in Russia has both encouraged me and made me realize that if I did not do a book on it, then my collection efforts would never see the light of day.

Personality and experience have also played a role in my writing of this book. A most thought-provoking bureaucratic experience happened to me during my first days as an officer in the U.S. Navy, in fall 1957. My commanding officer, looking for things to keep a young officer busy and also to clear his plate of unfinished business, ordered me to look through the records of all the officers on the ship and to begin background investigations on all who had not been investigated or were not being investigated. (This was done in order to comply fully with certain requirements connected with the breaking of coded messages.) While doing this I discovered that I had never been investigated, except for a cursory and meaningless "national agency check." Accordingly, I filled out the appropriate form on myself and under "officer ordering investigation" placed my own name and signature. The stroke of an official's pen had set in motion an intrusive investigation costing thousands of dollars and also discomfiting at least one FBI agent. I later learned that an FBI investigator had had to cross treacherous and cold water in Maine in a small boat, getting drenched, just to conduct one interview in my case. The person interviewed gave the FBI agent hot coffee laced with whisky as both compensation and a bracing for the return trip.

I have always wondered if the FBI thought it odd that the person being investigated had ordered the investigation. Whether it did or not the investigation was completed, and eventually, decades later, when I obtained my files (twenty-four pages) from the FBI, the Navy, and the Department of State under the provisions of the Freedom of Information Act, I discovered that the big concern of the investigators was not communist sympathies but "pan-Slavism." This suggests that the FBI, a bureaucracy, had a mind-set or a culture of its own and a suspicion of non-Anglo-Saxons. Another example of a bureaucracy's culture was revealed in fall 1957, soon after Sputnik had been placed in orbit, when my ship received a coded message, an ALNAV to all ships and stations, which I was detailed to break. It was a short one that said, to my surprise, only, "Do not discuss Sputnik," an indication of extreme defensiveness by the U.S. Navy, a bureaucracy and a pretty good one, at least at that time.

Additional bureaucratic stimulus has come from five years at Columbia University as a student and more than thirty-five years of service at a state university. (I have also served one year as a staff person in a federal government agency located in "main state," the main State Department building.)[1] While at Columbia, no matter how I tried, I was never able to accomplish any bureaucratic task by dealing only with one administrator or office. Nothing could ever be done except by touching at least two bureaucratic bases, although I always tried to cut through the bureaucratic net. This unavoidably made me think about the bureaucratic phenomenon. Spending three decades at a state university has also made me think both bureaucratically and about bureaucracy. I have told my students that they may actually be gaining an advantage from coping with the university bureaucracy; they are thus being prepared for life in big organizations and for dealing with the IRS and other government agencies that often figure so large in our lives. At any rate, more than once I have had to fulfill one or another minor bureaucratic role, perhaps not badly. Once I was even called "the good bureaucrat" by a colleague—a compliment, I hope. I have even felt a false joy after having written a memo and thinking, only briefly of course, that I had solved a problem or actually accomplished something. It is easy to see why some officials may deceive themselves through memo writing. My experience in what President John F. Kennedy called the "great bowl of jelly" of national government in Washington showed me, again and again, that even very intelligent and highly motivated people, when working in a bureaucracy, sometimes act in ways that impede or at least retard the accomplishment of objectives.

It is not insignificant, at least to me, that I actually feel the effects of the Russian bureaucracy. My bad back resulted from my wanting to deal with Soviet officials as little as possible. When I went to Moscow in 1977 for a semester I took everything I needed with me, 96 pounds of it, and thus avoided having to go back to customs later—and activated a disc problem that has been with me ever since to remind me of bureaucracy's power and effect. But this book is not an act of revenge. Russians themselves readily admit, and even proclaim, that bureaucracy and its shenanigans are major and constant elements in Russian existence.

Last, the origins of the book lie in the "climate of the times"—the mass feeling that we are, as individuals, less than we could be, partly as a result of "the state" and "big government." As J. K. Galbraith puts it, that desire to blame someone for our troubles leads to criticism of bureaucracy—"the last racism" left to us.[2] A close analysis of any governmental actuality will unavoidably turn up much that is negative or deficient. Bismarck's statement about the way laws and sausages are made applies. Still, Russia cannot advance unless its state bureaucracy is fundamentally transformed into one that will actively support its transition to a consolidated democracy and a world-class private enterprise economy with a populace that is healthy, well educated, and at peace with itself and its sociopolitical-economic situation—and making contributions to humanity at large.

NOTES

Note on transliteration: The Library of Congress transliteration system for Russian is used here except for names and terms that have become part of established American usage in other forms or which are used in quotations.

1. I was a recipient of a William C. Foster Fellowship at the U.S. Arms Control and Disarmament Agency for one year, June 1995 to June 1996. Though "eliminated"

because of the exigencies of American domestic politics, this agency lives on as the Arms Control Bureau of the U.S. Department of State.

2. John Kenneth Galbraith writes, "The only form of discriminatory comment, racism of sorts, that is allowed these days is against bureaucrats" ("The Year of the Spy," *The New York Times*, 5 January 1986, E19).

Introduction

Purpose, Definitions, Significance

In Russia we have no classes to combat each other, one holding the power of wealth, and the other mighty with the strength of numbers. We have only an unclean bureaucracy in the face of a people as great and as incorruptible as the ocean.

—Joseph Conrad, *Under Western Eyes*

Politics has meant administration. . . .

—Richard Pipes, "Russia's Past, Russia's Future"

PURPOSE

*T*he purpose of this book is to present, examine, evaluate, and explain the role and place of the state bureaucracy in the politics, society, and public administration of Russia under three regimes—the tsarist, the Soviet, and the present or post-Soviet. A particular focus here are negative and officially undesired actual bureaucratic behavior as example and as pattern, its effects, and the problems it poses for the transformation of Russia into a modern, Western-type system. I shall present and illuminate some lasting patterns of thought and operation in Russian administration. If patterns exist in one country over a period of more than a century and under three or more very different regimes, then we may have a national variant of administration. In terms of American political science, this effort is part of "bringing the state back in" and "the new institutionalism" of again taking institutions seriously. In order not to "reinvent the wheel," the bureaucracy of the "superadministrator," the Communist Party of the Soviet Union (CPSU), is not dealt with when the Soviet period is under discussion. Coverage of the CPSU as administrator has overwhelmed or substituted for the study of the state bureaucracy during the Soviet period. The party was crucially important, yes, but most people in the Soviet population interacted with, or had to contend with, not the party as such but its powerful implemental "arm," the state bureaucracy. This body of functionaries was crucially important, for implementation masks discretion and the power derived therefrom. Those who supposedly "only serve and wait" wield power, including political power, in their own right.

To make this project manageable, certain aspects of the state bureaucracy, the military, for example, are left pretty much out of the picture. Again, as with the party, an enormous amount has been written about the Soviet military. An attempt is made to concentrate, when dealing with the Soviet period, on the economic bureaucracy. However, I draw to some degree on all manifestations of bureaucracy and administration to show as much as possible the great and overriding importance of the state bureaucracy in Russian politics and society, even in the Soviet period.

The overriding purpose of this book is to present a well-rounded and strongly documented picture of the enormous significance bureaucracy has had in any Russian society and political system, irrespective of ideology or official statements to the contrary. Indeed, it is almost impossible for anyone to contemplate Russian existence without encountering the official personage as a powerfully central figure. This book provides a good sense of the power and scope of bureaucracy in Russian government and politics. In dealing with the Soviet period this task involves presenting bureaucracy's place in a system that was ostensibly antibureaucratic. Also, this work gives us a better sense of the degree to which what we know about governmental bureaucracy's operation and power actually applies to the Soviet and Russian experience and political system and confronts the question of whether or not Russia has its "own" distinctive bureaucratic pattern. In doing this I necessarily devote considerable attention to the "negative" or formally undesired aspects of bureaucracy, informalism, and bureaucratism or "bureaupathology" as well as bureaucracy's role in politics and decision making or at least "outcome making." Completeness demands this, as do realism and the work's goals. Bureaucracy in Russia has long been both phenomenon and problem. A bureaucracy cannot be judged as good or bad without reference to the culture and society of which it is a part. Yet, because the Soviet Union and imperial Russia before it aspired and tried to match the other leading nations of the day, Russia cannot escape the standards by which leading nations are judged and by which they judge themselves. We are also concerned with the phenomenon of bureaucracy in post-Soviet Russia. The ending of the USSR has not meant the ending of its elites' power and communist-era societal strata, the introduction of a full-blown and stable democratic politics, or the start of a successful market economy. Despite postcommunist Russian society's real need for a democratic, ethical, efficient governmental administration neither feared nor hated by the populace, the former system survives in many respects.[1] Indeed, given the extent of "*nomenklatura* privatization," it is possible that the state bureaucracy is a bigger problem for many Russians now in some respects than it was in the past. The achievement of Russia's political-administrative needs still awaits its realization.

Although the state bureaucracies of Russia, imperial, Soviet, and post-Soviet, are distinctive structures of people and action, bureaucracy was omnipresent and powerful in all communist systems notwithstanding the seemingly antibureaucratic nature of the communist ideology. Possibly, Michels's iron law of oligarchy was a prediction of this result. Indeed, under what was labeled communism, bureaucracy was ensconced, entrenched, magnified, rigidified, and even ran the country after bureaucratizing the Communist Party and its ideology and achieving a certain autonomy from that party and perhaps even a sort of superiority over it. It is supremely ironic that Marxists created governments and societies powerfully at odds with Marxist principles and ideals. Marxism, in whatever variant it has taken power, has not overcome a number of issues and challenges perennially central to politics: conflict within the political elite, ethnicity and nationalism, peasants and agriculture, the military, and the self-serving state bureaucracy. It is this last challenge and failure that is examined here. Accordingly, this work is a new way of getting closer to the full nature of communist power in Russia.

The main topics are tsarist influences and continuities, Bolshevik influences and continuities, the party–state relationship, the politics of the state bureaucracy, the significance and power of bureaucrats, the bureaucratic process and its operations (including its particular culture or style), and the problems some aspects of bureaucracy have posed for the USSR and Russia. This study clarifies the nature of the Russian state and also makes a contribution to the literature on bureaucracy and the politics of bureaucracy. I am doing three main things: (1) making a case for the political and systemic importance of the state bureaucracy in Russia across three political systems, the tsarist, the Soviet, and the post-Soviet; (2) bringing together many statements and facts about the Russian state bureaucracy, particularly its problems and deficiencies, that have been made by Russian and foreign observers; and (3) suggesting that considering the Russian state bureaucracy as a factor of political and governmental significance for

Russia's present and future development would give us a more realistic and better-rounded sense of Russia and its society, politics, and government. Change over time is here sometimes minimized to a degree, which is very un-American but appropriate for Russia. We thereby become more aware of continuity and enduring patterns. We are also dredging up a great deal that is unpleasant and uninspiring—like cleaning out the basement of an old house.

To put together much that has been said about Russian bureaucracy, particularly its negative aspects, I have included many quotations from numerous sources. There is a great deal written on bureaucratism that merits inclusion because of its substantive worth or the aptness of the way it has been stated. In doing this I create a record of what has been said about Russian bureaucratism and who has said it. This provides a sense of the topic's importance and a perspective on how it has been viewed by a large number of observers over more than a century.

DEFINITIONS

By *bureaucracy* here I do not at all mean a Weberian "ideal-type" group or institution. I am concerned with "actually existing" bureaucracy. Accordingly, the definitions of bureaucracy that fit the Russian case are operations and Russian culture oriented. Still, any definitional statement regarding bureaucracy must give the "master," Max Weber, his due and also state the sort of definition that does not fit in most operational situations, particularly those in Russia. The essentials of his "characteristics of bureaucracy" as translated by Gerth and Mills are as follows:

> Bureaucrats operate in "fixed . . . jurisdictional areas . . . ordered by rules," their activities are routinized and "distributed in a fixed way as official duties," their authority to act is "strictly limited," and they become bureaucrats, in a "career" with a "fixed salary," only if qualified in an objective sense, with the qualifications usually acquired through "thorough and expert training," pertinent to their work, their official bureaucratic activity demands all their working time, and, further, a bureaucracy is internally ordered by the principle of hierarchy and of "levels of grade authority" or ranks, its work is based on written documents ("the files," as Weber called them), it follows "general rules which are more or less stable," and its offices are separate from both households and the ruler. . . .
>
> It is important to add that Weber considered bureaucracy to be "fully developed . . . only in the modern state."[2]

These criteria present us with an issue and, some would say, with a problem. Russian state administration does not generally conform, nor has it ever conformed, to Weber's characteristics of bureaucracy. What does this mean? It could mean that Russian administration is not bureaucratic, at least not in the Weberian sense. But Weber does not "own" the definition of bureaucracy, only, perhaps, the ideal-type or "what might be" definition. It could also mean that because Russia is not fully modern in the political and governmental senses (assuming that "modern" is Western Europe, Australia–New Zealand, the United States–Canada, and perhaps a few other places), its bureaucracy is not "fully developed" in the Weberian sense. It could also mean, as some among the historians of Russia have said, that Russia lacked a bureaucracy through most of its history (this is discussed in chapter 1 on the tsarist period). If we stick absolutely to Weber's set of definitional requirements, then how can this issue/problem be dealt with intelligently or "solved"? One thing to do is to turn to the interpretation of Weber's intent as given by one of his students.

Karl Loewenstein, who was Weber's longest-surviving student, says that what Weber meant by "the bureaucracy" is "the scientifically trained staff, hierarchically organized and equipped with special technological knowledge which is entrusted with the administration of the state."[3] This definition is less formal and would apply to more cases of government administrators.

Still, Loewenstein's definition is not as practical for broad application as it could be. Usage has to be given its due. Most people see bureaucracy as formalized administration (and many see it in a pejorative sense, as a nuisance flouting "red tape" or even as perverse and obstructing the "good"). The term *bureaucracy* is not used here pejoratively. When such a meaning is intended, terms such as the American *bureaupathology* or the Russian *bureaucratism* (*biurokratizm*) are used in the interests of clarity and, hopefully, of precision as well.

Another reason the Weberian model of bureaucracy need not be accepted as more than a model is that administrative behavior often deviates from it, even in "fully developed modern states." Sometimes it deviates from it quite seriously. Does this mean that such behavior is not "bureaucratic"? This answer would be untenable, for the "deviant" behavior is carried out by bureaucrats on duty.

Actual behavior by "bureaucrats at work" always includes at least some "bureaucratic informalism," a phrase encompassing both unspecified and illegal behavior. One reason for this is that all the details of administrative operation cannot be formally specified or realistically expected. Also, some informalism may be conducive to the efficient or productive operation of bureaucracy. As noted, activity that works against its official purposes is labeled "bureaupathology" in the United States and "bureaucratism" in Russia. Common examples of Soviet and perhaps Russian informalism in administration include dual channels or agencies for performing the same function, *blat* (unauthorized use of personal contacts), *shturmovshchina* (rushing to complete work), and the *tolkach* (the illegal "facilitator" and "solver" of problems and glitches).

The overall pattern of administration in both imperial and Soviet Russia was highly informalistic, personalistic, and with a tendency toward corrupt and self-aggrandizing behavior by bureaucrats—hence, definitely non-Weberian. This mode of administration may have facilitated economic development in some senses and may have been limited in extent when the political system was authoritarian, but it is incompatible with democracy and runs wild under the current Russian conditions of a weak state.[4] An important point for this definitional discussion is that informalism, even as bureaucratism, is neither fundamentally abnormal nor automatically antibureaucratic. It is often normalcy carried to excess, for example, a minor Russian official scrutinizing a university document suspiciously and at length as if it were significant for national security or a South African policeman stopping to hand out a ticket for nonuse of seatbelts during a state of national emergency and incipient rebellion (which I actually observed in 1986).

A simple definitional statement of bureaucracy comes from von Mises: "Bureaucratic management is management bound to comply with detailed rules and regulations fixed by the authority of a superior body. The task of the bureaucrat is to perform what these rules and regulations order him to do" and to be restricted in acting by personal discretion. Blau and Meyer get more detailed: "Four factors—specialization, a hierarchy of authority, a system of rules, and impersonality—are the basic characteristics of bureaucratic organization." This parallels Weber but does not include his implied idealistic values. Crozier notes that the term *bureaucratic* is "vague and lends itself to confusion" and gives three main uses of the term: First, "bureaucracy is government by bureaus. In other words, it is government by departments of the state staffed by appointed and not elected functionaries, organized hierarchically, and dependent on a sovereign authority." Importantly for politics, this implies "government without the participation of the governed." Second, bureaucracy involves "the rationalization of collective activities" and the concentration of work units and operation by impersonal rules. Third, there is unavoidably the vulgar sense of the term—"the slowness, the ponderousness, the routine, the complication of procedures, and the maladapted responses . . . and the frustrations." Downs also sees three different meanings for bureaucracy. First, what is connoted by the word *bureau*, that is, large organizations made up of full-time workers who are hired and promoted on the basis of assessment of performance as bureaucrats and whose work is not evaluated in any market. He sees as "secondary characteristics" some of the traits Weber has said are intrinsic to bureaucracy—hierarchical organization, impersonality of operations, extensive use of rules, complexity of tasks, secrecy, and use of specially trained personnel—as these traits can be logically derived from his "primary characteristics." Second, for Downs bureaucracy can also mean a "specific method of allocating resources within large organizations"; and, third, it can also mean "bureau-ness" or those secondary characteristics he lists as giving bureaucracies a certain "quality." However, even after completing this definitional exercise, Downs realistically notes that the term "is much more flexible and ambiguous" than a definition and that the context itself is important for meaning. Wilson makes a similar observation: "Bureaucracy is a complex and varied phenomenon, not a simple social category or political epithet."[5] This last point about ambiguity and complexity is key.

Bureaucracy is an organizational form, a process of action, and a body of people that are part of complex governmental administration. It can deviate from the Weberian ideal to some degree and still be bureaucracy. Even its most negative features can often still be legitimately seen as bureaucratic, though of course as deviations from the formal or intended. This study often focuses on such deviations, or bureaupathology/bureaucratism. Crozier justifies this with his work quoted here. As he announces in his introduction: "The subject to which we refer in speaking of the bureaucratic phenomenon is that of the maladaptations, the inadequacies, or, to use Merton's expression, the 'dysfunctions,' which necessarily develop within human organizations." He justifies this well but simply: "Only models of functioning at an operational level can help us progress." Weber's "ideal type . . . corresponds to an inadequate description."[6]

SIGNIFICANCE

Bureaucracy is a very old feature of government, utilized by the pharaohs of ancient Egypt, the emperors of China, the Mongols, and the Incas: "The large organizations that persisted longest in antiquity and even survived this period, the Roman Empire and the Catholic Church, were thoroughly bureaucratized." The feudalism that emerged from the breakup of the Roman Empire eventually yielded to the centralized and bureaucratized states such as France. Even the French Revolution, with all its violence, did not sweep away bureaucratic management; "it only put it on a legal and constitutional basis." The Russian Revolution did not wipe out bureaucracy either: "A government cannot do without bureaus and bureaucratic methods."[7]

There are at least four bases for bureaucracy's great political significance in any developed political system: the power of bureaucrats, the importance of their functions, their key place in government, and their elevated status in society. "A political system's higher bureaucrats are important for politics, if not politically important," but the lower-ranking administrators, as a group, are also politically important.[8] In fact, even top politicians are beholden to certain bureaucrats, who provide them with the crucial information they need to oversee government, in the form of leaks, policy drafts, and testimony to legislative committees. President Carter once found he could not discipline a senior government official because the man was a confidante of the Speaker of the House. More than one agency head has found that senior officials are freely leaking critical information to members of Congress and to reporters for their own political and policy purposes. Bureaucrats constitute what are called "resistance forces" in Japanese politics. Under modern conditions of great complexity of life and work, knowledgeable and specialized administration is crucial to existence in the style to which so many of us have become accustomed. The implementers of law and policy are as important as the lawmakers. Those who make the law and policy cannot implement it and probably would not know how to do so if they tried. Indeed, the current downgrading of politics in American culture may be a tacit recognition of this fact. There seems to be an assumption that the government runs on its own (the Social Security checks arrive on time) and that the politicians are unnecessary or actual impeders of its functioning. The lament of Mayor Skeffington, the hero of *The Last Hurrah*, is that people no longer take him as seriously as they did because the New Deal had established a system that bypassed the mayor and his machine and to which people in need went instead. The Germans, after World War II, enshrined the crucial importance of bureaucrats in the very nature and structure of their parliament. The upper house, the Bundesrat, is made up of bureaucrats from the *Länder* or states. Why pass laws if the bureaucrats are opposed to them or find them difficult to implement? "Government cannot do everything, and it often benefits from decentralizing. But to discharge many of its prime responsibilities it must be large" and, hence, possess a large bureaucracy.[9]

Leading scholars emphasize the need for powerful state bureaucracies in modern times. First, Downs strikes out at the idea that the market can run everything, pointing out that "some important social functions cannot be performed adequately by market-oriented organizations because they involve external costs or benefits. . . . Society must develop nonmarket organizations that can intervene in markets to help insure that all the relevant costs and benefits enter into the decisionmaking process." This makes especially good sense after the Enron, Andersen, and World-Com scandals. Peters notes that administration "is far from glamorous" but that it is "an integral part of the political system" and has come to have major rule-making and even judicial functions. Crozier makes the excellent point so applicable to today's ever-changing globalistic modernity—"It is only through action—i.e., by acting through institutions and by modifying those institutions themselves—that a society can transform itself." Beetham adds the primal political note that bureaucracy is now so important that it poses a "challenge to the goal-determining function" of those who stand at the heads of organizations.[10] This would include the democratically elected leaders of states.

Accordingly, because bureaucracy can undermine or destroy democracy, it is of overriding political importance. Several writers stress the importance of bureaucracy by reference to its power. For example, Rourke lists the power that bureaucrats' expertise gives to their advice, sometimes resulting in shaping the values or factual premises of decision makers; their role in the drafting of legislation ("agency bills" in U.S. parlance); the mutually advantageous linkages bureaucrats may make with policymakers; the power that implementation gives to bureaucrats to remake policy and law; their ability to put routine or standard operating procedure above formal goals; and, of course, the power inherent in agencies' or even individual bureaucrats' discretion.[11] (Bureaucratic discretion has long been very important in Russia.)

AMERICAN BUREAUCRACY

Bureaucracy is now very significant in American politics and society, notwithstanding the fact that "U.S. bureaucracy is very different from bureaucracies in other parts of the world," being, for example, more competitive, "noisy," and dynamic. This is a "paradoxical bureaucracy" with qualities usually separate elsewhere: multiplication of rules and high access and participation.[12] The power of American bureaucrats was thrust into the news with great force in 1999, when it was revealed that the Energy Department, which has custody of most nuclear weapons and does nuclear weapons research, may well have "mishandled the nation's nuclear secrets for 20 years" and also had the "bureaucratic insolence to dispute, delay and resist the implementation of a Presidential directive." Also, "plenty of evidence" of "counterintelligence failures" was found at the weapons labs of the department.[13] Here we have an excellent case of striving for a goal consistent with democratic values, that is, creating a civilian agency to control nuclear weapons, only to find that it developed a particular agency culture that did not take the protection of secrets seriously. The terrorist attack of 11 September 2001 revealed grave problems within the FBI and CIA bureaucracies.

It has been argued that "public bureaucracy is now *the core* of modern U.S. government" and that "American government, the society, and its citizens are now dependent upon vast, interconnecting webs of complicated administrative systems." In addition, "a large and increasing proportion of the American people spend their working lives as small cogs in complex organizations." A case is even made that "American bureaucracy is an independent force," can "dominate" the Congress and strongly influence the president, and is rarely reviewed by the courts. The significant result is "increased discretion vested in appointive officials whose behavior can neither be anticipated or controlled."[14] Senator Moynihan has written of a "concealed" bureaucratic regulatory regime "with patterns of self-perpetuation" that excludes the public and is not easily controlled.[15]

RUSSIAN BUREAUCRACY

If we look at Russian government and politics it is hard to either downplay or exaggerate bureaucracy's significance. To Richard Pipes, "politics has meant administration." Certainly governmental administration is one of the great and continuous themes in Russian political history, along with, for example, international expansionism and conflict, the military, nationalism and nationality, great human suffering, the intelligentsia, and personalized rule. Russia has long been rather large in population, and the old issue of "span of control" has always been very much alive, including today with rampant regionalism: "By any measure, the Russian state has failed to deliver the most basic functions in recent years." In addition, we now see "a disturbing and pervading trend in Russia: the civilian leadership's inability to control and govern its increasingly weak, fragmented and frustrated military."[16] Administration in Russia must consequently deal with the primal political task of trying to hold the country together, not only administer it. This remains so today. Accordingly, Russian bureaucracy has always had a truly fundamental challenge facing it. In Russia, the big questions are never over. To "put Russia back together again" will require, among a number of things, a powerful and effective bureaucracy and mass support from the Russian people, support that will have to be earned. Although some form of centralized "directionalism" may return, it will probably be brief. The "third wave" of democratization cannot be postponed indefinitely.

In Russia today an effective bureaucracy is lacking, even though many Russians say that the number of bureaucrats and the nuisance they cause are greater than during the Soviet period—and things were bad enough then. Part of the reason for the Soviet failure to get to the moon first may rest on administration: "The Soviets were compelled to mount this effort not with a unified team of scientists and designers but with a rocket industry riven by divisions personal, professional and bureaucratic . . . the situation was thus ripe for conflicts."[17] Interbureaucratic rivalry and politics constitute an old and big Russian story. The USSR did not escape it.

If bureaucracy is important in the West, with its

governments of limited power, it is of critical importance in the centralized and interventionist Soviet Union, a country of red tape, long lines, and the downward spiraling run-around. "It over-relies on political controls, administrative organization, and conscious manipulation and interventionism. . . ." Bureaucracies in all types of systems often have a hand in the initiation of policy, in its implementation (where it can be remade or unmade), and in affecting policy-makers through the provision of "technical advice." Although the bureaucracy rarely takes over formal leadership positions, bureaucratic requirements may over time "statize" the politicians, that is, make them over into a group that accepts the bureaucrats' outlook.[18]

This is as true of "communist" and "postcommunist" systems as it is of liberal-democratic "capitalist" ones. Any realistic study of communism and postcommunism must include an examination of the state and its bureaucracy as well as at least a well-grounded guess as to how the system's bureaucracy and its ideology and politics interact. "Communist" systems did not live up to the ideal of workers' rule; instead, they created and relied on a powerful state for much. Indeed, both capitalism and communism went through the twentieth century with heavy reliance on their state bureaucracies' intervention in social and economic processes.[19] Perhaps capitalism has had the better, or more effective and less internally troubled, state bureaucracy. If so, it behooves us to conduct a thorough examination of the problems of Soviet bureaucracy and also take a look at the functioning of the post-Soviet Russian state bureaucracy.

Bureaucracy remains important and powerful in postcommunist political systems. This attests to the truth of at least two propositions: that communism triumphed in places with a tradition or culture, a tendency, or even a propensity for the enhancement of bureaucracy and that industrial and postindustrial modernity, which was often the main goal of communist parties' policy, demands large and powerful state bureaucracies if this modernity is fostered primarily by the state.

Ironically, Marxian communism actually created one of the very things to which it was originally most opposed—the great state. And where you have a state in our times, you have bureaucracy, both formal and informal, as well as its unavoidable cousin—bureaupathology or bureaucratism.[20] "The Communist system by its very nature is bureaucratic," says Djilas. "The growing utilization of complex organizations is a means of action indispensable to modern man," correctly notes Crozier. Under what was called communism there were at least two particular reasons for large and powerful bureaucracies: industrial administration and political control. Both of these purposes require significant state intervention into society. And "in order to undertake effective interventions, the state must constitute a bureaucratic apparatus with sufficient corporate coherence"; meanwhile, "the experience of intervention builds the capacity of the state bureaucracy and enhances its ability to behave as a corporate actor."[21] There is no need to "bring the state back in" in considering Russia; the state never left, even in the first days of Soviet rule or in the ostensibly postcommunist 1990s.

The word *communism* is used here as an unavoidable term of convenience. Only the most purblind Marxist could see the USSR as a "communist" system in any general way after what Stalin did to Marxist principles—and to Marxists. Perhaps the conservatives ought to erect a great statue to Stalin for his services to their cause. Stalin wanted slaves for his helpmeets and absolute security for himself. The bureaucratic model as "Stalinized" met these desiderata. The politics of bureaucracy, even when it is oppositional, rarely involves an attempt to overthrow the system or its leaders.

Nowhere was a "communist" government substantively or fully communist, either ideologically, politically, or in terms of policy. Even during the Cultural Revolution in China the Red Guards moved about only with express authorization from the army, a military bureaucracy of the state.[22] As Obolonsky states, the Soviet ideology had two very different layers: "The external layer preached the doctrine of equality, while the internal layer condoned rampant privilege, nepotism, protectionism and caste discrimination." And it was the *internal* layer that "in fact reflected the true ideology of the regime."[23] And bureaucracy contributed greatly to this internal layer.

The Continuing Significance of Bureaucracy in Russia

The continuing importance of the state bureaucracy in postcommunist Russia is shown in many ways—by the large numbers of people who are former members of the Soviet state bureaucracy in the president's office and in the top levels of government, society, and the economy generally; by the past careers of former Prime Ministers Chernomyrdin and Stepashin and President Putin; and by the effectiveness of the claims made on government policy by bureaucratic elites such as directors of large government plants and the military officer corps, not to mention the intelligence service.[24] Even more than a decade after the end of the USSR, Russian intellectuals see the bureaucracy exercising a "parental" role over Russian society. Yury Korgunyuk speaks of bureaucracy's "dominating" role: "the state fills a vacuum left by society."[25]

The end of Sovietism as a ruling system has not meant the end of the culture or sociopolitical content of Sovietism in contemporary Russian government and society; nor could it—for the post-Soviet state necessarily has had to be staffed by functionaries of the old system. Russia has not undergone "decommunization" as Germany did "denazification." But even in defeated Germany, when the country was occupied by foreign powers strongly bent on denazification, the process went only so far, eventually being halted because of the dictates of practicality and the new requirements of the Cold War. But when the USSR came to its end, no overwhelming outside force entered to try to sweep the slate clean and start anew. There was no forced retirement of Soviet cadres—or their subordination to a new administrative and political elite. Neither option was even partially available. A mass retirement would have required an enormous sum of money, and no new elite was available. (Germany in 1945 saw the return, in American and other occupiers' uniforms, of many German expatriates and refugees, for example, Henry Kissinger, who became a "governor" of a part of the country, and Willy Brandt. Still, change went only so far. The Ministry of Foreign Affairs of the Federal Republic is organized along the same lines as agencies in Prussian times.)[26] Even if a cadre of new Russian public administrators had been available, the most radical of new leaderships could not have effected a total change in administrative mores. Patterns of organizational thinking (culture), structure, and behavior, along with much else, tend to outlast regimes. Revolutions do not "bake" totally new "loaves," only "layer cakes" containing much old dough.

We can also note another postcommunist continuity—the relative ineffectiveness, "oppressiveness," and "distance" (to the ordinary citizen) of Russian bureaucracy, indeed, of government itself. Under both the tsars and the commissars vast areas of Russia were effectively ungoverned. This problem was partly a function of Russian *prostor* or seemingly ocean-like endless space as a defining factor of existence and a serious limitation on government. Here we have another of those seeming paradoxes of Russia—a heavy-handed bureaucracy of a highly centralized state harshly imposing politically pertinent controls but not doing it either effectively or generally. This is no paradox at all when the limitations of *prostor* and bureaucracy are considered.

Russian culture, too, limited bureaucracy's effectiveness. Russians in general developed interpersonal relationships and defensive and escapist mechanisms that worked against political controls and law, while the bureaucrats too found ways to evade carrying out policy as formally or legally required. At times Russians acted defiantly against controls notwithstanding the harsh and even brutal sanctions almost unavoidably awaiting such acts. Russians can be unpredictable. Many Russian troops in Hungary in 1956 refused to fire on the Hungarians and consequently were sent to the gulag.[27]

Also, importantly, in Russia, instead of bureaucracy serving primarily as administration, it has long acted excessively as a key agent of both political control and bureaucrats' self-aggrandizement, with its administrative or governance duties ignored or downplayed. We see the continuing effects of this pattern today. The central government is collecting only some of the taxes it levies and does not even know how much chemical warfare material it possesses. Russian sources, one connected with the Russian Security Council, noted in 1994 "Russia's lack of a system that meets present-day world standards for the monitoring, inventory and physical protection of nuclear weapons."[28] An American observation of 1993 is still apt today: "Worst of all, no one seems to be in charge. The Yeltsin government issues decrees that hostile bureaucrats and enterprise managers ignore at no particular peril. Economic policy is set by committees whose power ebbs and flows with the latest skirmishes between the Office of the President and the apparatchik-dominated Parliament."[29]

Russia has long been plagued by an "Oblomovist," "sloppy," or "lackadaisical" state bureaucracy. Holding office is more important than doing work. Fear of the higher-ups and dire sanctions rarely applied have not produced, nor could they, a bureaucracy that will engage purposively in effective administration. Any Russian modernity, as does a successful transition to democracy, requires the strengthening and improving, indeed the transformation and re-creation, of this weak and self-absorbed state bureaucracy.

Is Russian Bureaucracy a Special Case?

Russian state bureaucracy is of such a specific, certainly rarified and perhaps even unusual, type that it certainly does not fit into the Weberian or "classic" definition of bureaucracy. But it also does not fit into the typical modern Western or "Euro-American" pattern of highly effective and relatively noncorrupt government bureaucracy. Present-day general usage of *bureaucracy* to mean both "actually existing" bureaucracy and, of course, Russian bureaucracy is much broader and more realistic, or "dirtier," than the Weberian model, itself derived from a particular (Prussian military?) bureaucracy at one time and place and probably also from within the confines of a specific ideological and cultural worldview, one that was semi-Victorian and full of that pre–World War I ultraconfidence that was so imbued with pride in and optimism for European ways.[30] Definitions must reflect contemporary and situational realities. But Russian bureaucracy, both under the tsars and since, may be even further removed from the Weberian conception than bureaucracy is today in Western Europe, the United States, or similar places. First, the bureaucracies of both imperial Russia and the USSR operated with extraordinary leeway and capriciousness, so much so that it can be charged that they were not, properly speaking, bureaucracies at all but, instead, some sort of secondary ruling class.

That is, the Russian bureaucracy has lacked, under all systems and ide-ologies, clear limits to its powers (in the sense of what it could attempt rather than what it could actually accomplish). Second, the issue arises in terms of imperial Russia and its legacies. John LeDonne has stated that tsarist Russia never had a civil service that was a true bureaucracy, except possibly during the late nineteenth century. LeDonne stresses that the tsarist bureaucracy lacked clearly defined protection and privileges and, hence, was not a bureaucracy but, rather, some sort of semifeudal forma-tion with corresponding functions.[31]

However, isn't this difficulty typical of any attempt to examine a so-ciopolitical "object" in Russia? As a Russian legislator has said, "Don't look for distinct boundaries in Russian politics, because there aren't any. The boundaries are very blurred."[32] For example, the Russian worker seems to be a different sociological being in some ways than the worker in France or Germany. The Russian has lacked certain rights commonly held in the West but has some rights, or at least expectations, beyond those held by Western counterparts. The Russian military offi-cer also seems a distinctive being or at least more like certain officers in the West were in earlier times. What we may have here, in general, are the effects of the common phenomenon of historical "lag." The Russian societal categories exist in a cultural or attitudinal matrix, not as distant from an earlier time as the same-named societal categories in the West are. Why shouldn't the Russian bureaucrat be similarly affected and distinctive? That is, can't the Russian be somewhat more like the me-dieval lord's bailiff, say, with powers not clearly defined or limited, than a modern Western, legally and societally limited, semi-Weberian bureaucrat?

Ozernoy correctly points out that Westerners tend to view bureau-crats as subordinate and limited beings working within strictly defined and limited confines or boundaries. This overlooks "critical differences between Russian and Western political experiences." She notes that "Russia's bureaucracy . . . enjoyed extraordinary political power, based solely on Russia's administrative system," whose un-Western institu-tions allowed the bureaucracy to limit the tsar's power (though not openly) as well as to suppress oppositional movements. And "state ser-vice in tsarist and Communist Russia was rewarded with material wealth, authority and standing in society based on one's position in the bureaucratic hierarchical ladder."[33] In addition, Russia lacked both a civil society and an independent legal system to limit bureaucrats, while the bureaucrats lacked a "public service" culture that might have formed a system of self-limitation. Accordingly, in chapter 1 I consider tsarist state bureaucracy and its possible effects on Soviet and post-Soviet administration.

AMERICAN SOVIETOLOGY AND
RUSSIAN ADMINISTRATION

American Sovietology produced only a very few books of significance on Soviet Russian administration. As Solnick correctly says, "The minimal independent role assigned by Sovietology to bureaucrats and administrators is striking." In the "traditional view" of Sovietology, "bureaucrats and administrators themselves are not independent agents of change."[34] This is odd, for American historians of Russia have written quite a bit on administration in imperial Russia. (See chapter 1.) Why is this so? There are several possible reasons.

First, American Sovietology has its origins in thinking about national security and the great concern and even fear in the United States of the newly powerful Soviet Union in 1945 and later. These origins powerfully affected Sovietology ever after. There was a basis for this concern, of course. States that had been important for limiting Russian power had been swept from the world stage or gravely weakened by the way World War II ended. And we did not know, given the secretiveness of Stalin's Russia, how weak it was as a result of the horrendous human and material losses suffered during the war.

The result of this strong American concern with national security was that an emphasis on ideological and other difference and military containment was central to American Sovietology. I call this an infatuation with "fire and brimstone" (a natural result of Puritanism?). The idea of a deadly U.S.–Soviet competition permeated thinking and dominated the selection of research topics. The big concern was: Were American values and society up to the apparently deadly challenge posed by the new and inflated Soviet power? The American academic world willingly joined in the struggle. "Government" in the usual sense was not a topic of study. Soviet governmental institutions were seen as pure facade, which was true to a degree, but the leaders' decisions still had to be communicated and implemented in day-to-day governance.

The newness of the USSR as competitor also was important, as was the fact that the United States had never had the experience of facing a big long-term opponent of differing values. This fact further emotionalized the competition, as did the "penumbra" of the recent bout with Nazism—the USSR was seen as a sort of anti-American "new Germany." World War II was not over, it seemed, a very upsetting development to many Americans who craved the return of "normalcy" after years of depression and war.

The Soviet Communist Party was a major topic of American research on Russia, as it ought to have been. It certainly was the central organization of Sovietism. However, it was also a rather large organization that included conflicting tendencies within itself and did not engage in day-to-day ordinary administration. Yet it tended to be seen as some *deus ex machina* with enormous capability, much more than it possessed. Accordingly, the number of publications on communism and the Communist Party was great. I added to them.[35] Communist Russia was seen as exotic, odd, strange, and conspiratorial (like the Masonic Order or the Catholic Church, apparent enemies of America in the past) but now with a great state and military behind it and occupying part of Europe. However, the conventional view that the CPSU was absolutely dominant as a separate entity was incorrect. Hirszowicz writes of the "emancipated bureaucracy" and points out:

> The apparent contradiction between the sovereignty of the bureaucracy and the role of the party as the ruling institution, i.e., the political master, can be easily resolved when we take into consideration that in the party state the party itself becomes the frame or backbone of the bureaucratic structure. This is a point Trotsky had reluctantly to acknowledge when he wrote: "the party was always in a state of open or disguised struggle with the bureaucracy. The historic role of Stalin's faction was to destroy this duplication, *subjecting the party to its own officialdom and merging the latter in the officialdom of the state.*"[36]

This key point can be made more directly; the Communist Party was itself part of a larger and more powerful structure of people, ideas, and action, the highly bureaucratized Soviet state.

Other images as well may have affected American study of Russia. Many Americans assumed that the entire USSR was a prison camp, that the Great Purge was still on, and that it all "could happen here." The Catholic Church published a "comic book" on a communist takeover in the United States. Masses of people were pictured being shipped to Alaska in boxcars. *Life* magazine ran a big spread on the gulag using artists' shocking drawings and also presented Russian Americans as employed mostly in demolition. The implications were obvious. I remember a friend describing how difficult it had been to grow up as a Russian American during the early years of the Cold War. The conventional wisdom, then, was that Russia and its people and government were completely unlike others.

The "Soviet threat" certainly offered careers to many in and outside of government. In 1945 perhaps no one in the entire United States taught about the government and politics of Russia. But entry into careers associated with Russian and communist studies was associated, and this is rather odd, not with the usual love of the object studied but, rather, with dislike and considerations of careerism. ("Fellow travelers" were pushed out of the academic world by McCarthyism.) This important fact, very unlike why most specialists in, say, British, French, or even Chinese politics choose their careers, was bound to drive the selection of research topics and what was said about them. Indeed, it must drive a unique ethos.[37]

Naturally, the problem of knowledge of even the subjects studied was a serious one. Much of the Soviet Union, and almost all its countryside, was closed to foreigners, and Americans had no ability to live there for lengthy periods of time. The first American graduate students arrived in 1958 for stays of only up to one academic year, and most were restricted to studying in the untypical Soviet city of Moscow and researching topics carefully approved by the Ministry of Education, no doubt with "guidance" from other institutions. In 1977 I found that an attempt at the Lenin Library in Moscow to order library books not on my topic was immediately questioned. Not without reason, then, did a prominent British political philosopher decry the study of Soviet politics. As Michael Oakeshotte has eloquently put it, "The place which the politics of contemporary Russia has come to occupy in undergraduate study is indefensible except in the irrelevant terms of a 'vocational' political education. We know incomparably less about what goes on in Russian politics than in the politics of any other country in the world, bar perhaps China."[38]

Even Alfred Meyer's defense of the study of Soviet politics, good as it is, does not fully negate Oakeshotte's objections. Meyer makes the case that despite the "relative scarcity of authoritative and verifiable factual material" on Soviet politics, we have more material on it than do historians studying Sumer, ancient Rome, and Elizabethan England. This is doubtful. Meyer is correct, however, in saying that "Western descriptions of the Soviet political system must remain impressionistic, and the line between political science and journalism in this field is tenuous."[39]

American Academic Public Administration

Another reason, perhaps, for the limited study of Soviet public administration is that the field of "PA" was long not in good odor within the larger field of American political science. Of course, there were scholarly students of Soviet PA. John N. Hazard stands out, but because he was primarily a lawyer and a scholar of Soviet law, he did not concentrate on the study of administration, though he did teach a graduate course on it. Other scholars, too, have done excellent work on aspects of Soviet administration, for example, Jerry F. Hough. More are mentioned below. However, the study of Soviet public administration was definitely a stepchild, probably for ideological and "image" reasons deriving from the effects of the origins of American Sovietology in Cold War considerations.

According to Kettl, the American study of public administration has been troubled by the conflict between the Hamiltonian and Madisonian traditions in American politics and by the excessively firm distinction between politics and administration stipulated by Woodrow Wilson in his *The Study of Administration* (1887). As Kettl puts it, "The dichotomy ultimately has led many within political science to abandon the unruly child of public administration." Further, "it is no exaggeration to say that public administration is in crisis—and that, in fact, it has been in crisis since 1950." The conflict between practice and process, on the one hand, and theory, on the other, also played a role in the near "divorce" of PA and political science in the United States.[40] This could have played a role in the "selecting out" of administration as a favored field in Russian studies. Certainly, the beginnings of U.S. Sovietology and the downgrading of the study of administration within American political science coincide in time. In any case, the picture of Russian governmental reality given by Sovietology has been a limited one.

MENTIONINGS

Strangely, although full-scale study of bureaucracy and administration in Soviet Russia was neglected, almost any published account of life in the USSR and Russia or of its government and policies, whether the author is a scholar, diplomat, traveler, dissident, or expatriate, at least mentions bureaucracy as a phenomenon of significance, often negative, in that country. This attests to the importance of the topic. In effect, the general message is that Russia is a terribly bureaucratized, if not overbureaucratized, place and that the bureaucrats are important for what happens. Below are some of the many such mentionings I have come across in a few decades of reading about the USSR and Russia. Most of the quotations or summations that follow are purposely not drawn from studies that focus on bureaucracy but, rather, from those that deal with Russian life and politics generally. This approach more effectively validates the significance of bureaucracy in Russia.

History

The people of imperial Russia endured a difficult existence plagued by bureaucrat-like harpies of the tsarist state. Szamuely sets forth this major feature that both undermines and effectuates the Russian idea:

> The bureaucracy was in complete and undivided control of the country. Russia had become a bureaucratic autocracy. "By the middle of the century," wrote Kliuchevsky, "Russia was governed by neither aristocracy nor democracy, but by the bureaucracy, i.e., by a crowd of individuals of heterogeneous origin, acting outside society and lacking any definite social complexion, and

joined together only by the table of promotion." The *chinovnik*, the government official, became the most characteristic figure of Russian life.[41]

This characterization is fundamentally correct at the cultural level. The tsars had defeated the nobility, the peasantry, and the church and did not have to fear the army. What was left as an alternative source of political power other than the revolutionaries? Only the tsar's own civil servants remained. The Russian state was opposed by only "itself." This was reality, though it flies in the face of conventional logic. Because the victorious Bolshevik Party, like the tsars, also did not allow society to have a political role, it too was limited and perhaps even brought down by its own administrative functionaries and their modus operandi. Although the revolution destroyed the royal family, the nobility, and the church, "another institution of the tsarist period, the bureaucracy, not only survived the revolution but after some major surgery transformed itself into the central nervous system of the new Soviet system." It numbered about three hundred eighty-five thousand people in the early twentieth century, having increased during the previous century at a rate seven times greater than that of the population.[42]

Wolgang Leonhard has listed "the state governmental apparatus" as one of the "five pillars of Soviet society" and one "more closely linked with the political system than are the industrial managers" and adds that its relationship with the managers and the party "is by no means always harmonious." Zbigniew Brzezinski has cited the "regularity of the encounters with brutal functionaries" and the "subordination of society to a bureaucratized hierarchy" in characterizing the former USSR. A novel about life in the former Soviet Union presents the easily recognizable uncertainty and hopelessness of late Soviet existence by recounting the Gogolesque tale of a fruitless wait in line for a railroad ticket. As a reviewer paraphrases the situation, "He waits for hours in a line at a ticket window, not even sure that he can buy the right ticket there. For long periods, the ticket seller simply closes the shutters of the window and disappears. After several more hours she closes down permanently, and Joe and the Russians who have waited with him simply turn away without a word of protest."[43]

Lenin, the "founding father" of the Soviet system, thought of excessive bureaucracy as "the most vexing legacy of his revolution." At the Tenth Party Congress Lenin declared, "Bureaucratism in our state apparatus has the significance of such a sore that it is even spoken about in our party program." And though he often considered cures for this disease, he was, as Beissinger correctly notes, "the chief bureaucrat of the Soviet state," and "almost by instinct, the Bolsheviks reached for centralist solutions to problems which, at least in part, had been caused by excessive centralization." This result was no paradox; it simply shows that even revolution-aries are constrained, and driven, by culture and situation. As early as 1920 "Lenin said that Soviet Russia was 'a workers' state with bureau-cratic excrescences; in March 1921 he spoke of the 'bureaucratic cancer' and complained that the bureaucratic apparatus was gigantic." With Stalin's later forced draft industrialization and creation of a "national se-curity state" at odds with the world, the bureaucracy and its power rap-idly and greatly increased to such an extent that what became a long line of observers, notably including Trotsky and Djilas, could discern it as a new, privileged, and even exploiting class.[44] Robert Service has taken up the issue of bureaucratic privilege: "The beneficiaries of the Soviet order were not the 'people,' not the workers, kolkhozniki and office-clerks. . . . But one group in society was certainly indebted to Stalin . . . the high and middling ranks of the bureaucracy in the ministries, the party, the armed forces and the security organs. . . . Enjoyment of life was the priority for them. . . . A new social class was in the process of formation."[45]

In such a context the party had be affected. Many in its ranks were of working-class origin and had joined the "burgeoning party apparatus and state bureaucracy where they held prestigious and powerful positions." Given the years of war and sacrifice, these functionaries naturally tended to support "those leaders who seemed able to provide the greater degree of orderly progress and material rewards." In 1923 Trotsky wrote to the Central Committee and complained of "secretarial bureaucratism" and of "the bureaucracy of the machine." This growth of bureaucracy "aided Stalin, who controlled appointments and patronage" and as "the chief of the whole Soviet bureaucracy" wielded enormous power through what Weber once called the "control of the files" and Stalin's consequent ability to pay back the new cadres for their loyalty to him and his policies, what Dunham has aptly called the "Big Deal." In this process the "fulcrum of power passed to the security police and . . . to the state bureaucracy." Togli-atti, head of the Italian Communist Party, which had escaped the Stalinist purge because of Mussolini's tender ministrations, considered that Stalin's mistakes were connected with "an excessive increase of bureaucracy." While Stalin was alive and as vigilant as the Baba Yaga of Russian folklore, though much more ruthless, the cadres could at most act like "little Stal-ins" within somewhat circumscribed areas. However, once he was gone, they could begin to enlarge their reach and magnify their power.[46]

Khrushchev, Stalin's eventual successor, by attempting to bring about change and decentralization in a number of areas, brought down on himself the anger and opposition of several key groups and was eventually re-moved. His reduction in the number of industrial ministries and their re-placement by so-called national economic councils (*sovnarkhozy*), for exam-ple, led to serious opposition, "chiefly from the administrative departments of the central planning agencies" and the "steel-eaters" lobby. Tatu refers to the Soviet government as "one of the most conservative administrative structures in the world." Khrushchev had "made the most far-reaching attempt in Soviet history to dismantle the worst institutions of Stalinism and reform the conservative, entrenched bureaucracy. . . . He succeeded in making bureaucrats uneasy and wary of losing their positions and privileges. . . . He was succeeded by a cabal of 'powerful career bureaucrats,'" for example, Brezhnev, Kosygin, Podgorny, Mikoyan, Voronov, and so on.[47]

Brezhnev's tenure could be called the "age of bureaucracy." He "was no revolutionary, only a skilled middle-level bureaucrat" with "no personal vision or program." His policy of "stability of cadres" and attempt at strengthening the existing system placed a definite limitation on change and were, in effect, pro-bureaucrat. This may have been partly a reflection of Brezhnev's personality; he had a "kindly reputation among political colleagues," and during his earlier career "his guiding aim was to avoid getting into trouble with higher authority." An administrator's personality unavoidably affects the operations being overseen. With such a "leader" and in such an atmosphere, the Big Deal was made bigger, and bureaucrats were more important than ever.

That "ingenious initial concordat between Stalinism and middleclass productivity" was embraced "fully and unequivocally" by the Brezhnev regime, "and with *it meshchanstvo* [or Babbittry] blossoms." Brezhnev's promotion of the recentralization of industrial administration and the elimination of the *sovnarkhozy* had to increase the power of the ministerial and other central state bureaucrats. And, later, with him becoming head of the Soviet state, the distinction between party and state was "virtually obliterated." Kosygin, at first almost a coruler with Brezhnev, initiated a reform of the central industrial management that "challenged the interests of the central party apparatus. If Kosygin had had his way, the premises of economic policy would stealthily have been shifted towards profit-making, managerial initiative and ministerial freedom from the party's interference." This significant attempt at economic reform was undermined and vitiated by a combination of party opposition and ministerial resistance to the rights granted to industrial managers: "By 1968, the reform had failed. For several reasons. First, once back in the picture, the ministries . . . clawed back their old powers. . . . Increasingly, they reverted to their old ways."[48] Because of Brezhnev's nature and limited goals, he never got the Soviet Union onto a new track. No significant reform was to occur until Gorbachev came to power in 1985. (True, Andropov might, if he had lived, have reinvigorated the system somewhat through his tough strategy of "acceleration.")

Gorbachev, an energetic and wordy wunderkind and a most surprising product of Sovietism, one possibly capable of being elected to public office in the United States, hustled and bustled to preserve and modernize Soviet socialism but found it beyond him. Perhaps it was an impossible quest, akin to finding the Holy Grail, albeit necessary and unavoidable if the USSR was to count for anything. Gorbachev made several errors, one of which was to underestimate the strength of the opposition, "based in the great bureaucracies of the union government." Indeed, he eventually realized that "only as president would he be able to control the executive branch," and he railroaded through constitutional amendments to create an executive presidency for himself. As chairman of the Congress he was head of state, but he "had to consult with the forty-two members of the Presidium of the Supreme Soviet and obtain the permission of the Azeri government" in order to send troops to Baku to stop interethnic violence. But his presidency did not overawe the bureaucratic establishment, which launched a coup, if a laughable and ineffective one, against him. Nothing, perhaps, shows what the Soviet bureaucracy had become—shaky-handed perpetrators of "a massive show of force without any use of force," a "comic-opera putsch which failed laughably." Still, though Gorbachev survived the putsch, he did not survive his own inadequacies and Boris Yeltsin, who contrived to bring the Soviet charade to an end.[49] As has been said, "The worst thing that can be said of a historical figure is that he meant well."

Yeltsin speaks directly to the nature of the putsch. Although the "central structures" of the government and almost all the ministers supported the imposition of the state of emergency, the coup plotters suffered from one "chief flaw": they "were not capable of appearing openly in public." Thus exposed, as it often is, the fundamental limitation of bureaucratic cryptopolitics. As Yeltsin says, bureaucrats are "ill suited to the role of political leaders." But this limitation did not prevent the bureaucratic elite from achieving a significant victory out of the ending of the Soviet Union. They got much of its, supposedly the people's, property. They "stole the state," in Steven Solnick's apt formulation. The Soviet system, destabilized by Gorbachev, a "true believer" who did not understand the nature of his own system, fell victim to "opportunism from within." Officials looked to their own futures and "defected en masse[,] and the pillars of the Soviet system crumbled." The institutions of the state fell victim to "the organizational equivalent of a colossal 'bank run,'" in which local officials rushed to claim their assets before the bureaucratic doors shut for good. Soviet institutions did not simply atrophy or dissolve but were actively pulled apart by officials at all levels seeking to extract assets that were in any way fungible."[50]

Truly, this was a *trahison des clercs*, big time. The communist system "choked on its own bureaucracy."[51] The Big Deal had created the conditions for the "Big Rip-off." The bureaucrats came out of the system with property; the poor slobs of the masses got nothing. I remember Russian academic administrators and Komsomol leaders with whom we at my university were dealing in an exchange program suddenly acquiring actual palaces that had been state property in which they set up their own profit-making "management training institutes" and "tourist centers."

Power and Politics

There is no paucity of "mentionings" attesting to the enormous power of the state bureaucracy in late Soviet Russia. For "an idea in Russia exists to be implemented by power," and implementation in the modern state means bureaucracy and its implemental power as the "permanent politicians."[52] This is not only a Russian phenomenon, of course. James Schlesinger as U.S. secretary of defense noted that American policy decisions are only nominally made by senior political figures. The capacity for resistance of "subordinate political groups" is "breathtaking," he added. Accordingly, "Actual programs and allocative decisions will consequently diverge quite sharply from those that would be predicted on the assumption of rational intelligence. Instead, they will be strongly influenced by prejudice, incompetency, and by infighting, deviousness, and bootlegging within the bureaucracies."[53]

As Yeltsin himself has noted, even after the fall of the Soviet system, "real power remained in the hands of the state nomenklatura." Even earlier, when the Communist Party was supposedly in charge, the state bureaucracy could be more powerful than the local party organs. As Hough notes, even "during the sovnarkhoz period, the local party organs still remained at somewhat of a disadvantage vis-à-vis the industrial hierarchy." He states further that the local party organs existed in a "supplicant–superior relationship" with the state bureaucracy: "A Party committee can request that a higher official follow some course of action . . . but it is in not in any sense an equal with him."[54]

A former senior staffer for a majority whip of the U.S. Senate has said, "I always found CPSU officials to be openly dependent upon civilian bureaucrats (from the Foreign Ministry) and USA/Canada think tankers in sessions with foreigners."[55] The reasons given include the bureaucrats' larger staffs and that implementation and interpretation grant some power over policy. But I wonder if Russian tradition was not also a factor as well as the "power image" of Moscow as the center of power. And certainly "a fundamental conflict of interest is inherent between the party apparatus as a monitoring agency and the operating agencies." Still, it is common in the literature to say that the party and the state bureaucracy were not in a struggle for overall power or for fundamental political change because both groups were in general agreement on the nature of the system. Rigby seems to come to an ambiguous judgment regarding the party–state relationship. He points out that the two sets of institutions had different emphases in their work—the party dealing more with "organic" and "goal rational" aspects of rule, whereas the government dealt more in "mechanistic" and "rational legal" aspects.[56] But it seems to me, based on my experience in government, that the functioning of any bureaucracy inevitably involves conflict and struggle for at least operational power within itself and with the political authorities. And operational power impinges on, undercuts, and may threaten political power. Although there was no strict dichotomy between party and state, there was one big intertwined party–state relationship. As Mary McAuley puts it, there was "no way" the party could stand aside and be in charge because the party's officials inevitably "identified with the sectors they were answerable for, and became part of a party-state apparatus."[57] Late Soviet linguistic usage often spoke of just one such ruling apparatus. But again, anything as huge as that could not avoid conflict within itself, thereby showing that in the later Soviet Union the concept of the vanguard had operationally disappeared and bureaucratic considerations and actions were very important, and sometimes dominant, in policy and politics.

White and associates point out that after Stalin "effective authority began to shift from party to state" and there developed a "substantial element of collective restraint on the leader." In 1979 Brezhnev, in perhaps the "gruffest speech" he ever made, "lashed out at do-nothing officials who would never improve, no matter how much . . . you appeal to their conscience or sense of duty." Eleven members of the Council of Ministers were actually named in this "tirade." As Colton correctly says, only significant personnel changes might have allowed administrative improvements, but this would have meant "tampering with the post-1964 pledge of semi-permanent job rights for bureaucrats," the informal but real "stability of cadres" policy. Later Gorbachev encountered strong "tooth and nail" resistance from the industrial ministries and the planning bureaucracy to his plans for decentralization and making manufacturing plants relate to consumer preferences. No wonder Gorbachev spoke of the "serious deformations" leading to the development of a "command-administrative system" and a "bloated administrative apparatus."[58]

Culture and Style

Every organization or institution, indeed, even the smallest group, has its own ways of doing things and some particular sense, however vague, of itself as special or distinctive. The eventual result is often an operational pattern of informalist activity. The informalism can come to be more important than formally specified regulations and law—and can also be illegal. One scholar sees as "the immediate, institutional cause of Russia's economic disaster the immense power and corruption of the bureaucratic-piratical complex."[59] Perhaps the most striking example in the United States of bureaucratic illegality is the "blue wall" of police disinformation concerning the illegal actions of police officers. Anyone seeking success within an organization must learn how to utilize informalism for his or her benefit.

There is no doubt that the Russian state bureaucracy is the bearer of a particular Russian cultural tradition and operational attitude and style, one that never gave in completely to either the communist ideology or party political superiority. As Hammer points out, "These [Soviet] bureaucracies have developed their own attitudes, values, and procedures. The bureaucracy's own perception of its interest does not necessarily conform to the views of the party leadership." Even the Russian language was changed with the introduction of a "new bureaucratic language" by the peculiar admixture of Leninist Marxism and revolutionary state, with their "numerous procedures and rules developed to categorize people into classes and subclasses, allocate and redistribute property . . . etc., all involving excessive paperwork, bureaucratic neologisms, euphemisms and ugly abbreviations." Andrei Sinyavsky devotes an entire chapter to this "emasculated" and "extremely standardized" language "estranged from normal human discourse," with its "very limited vocabulary" whose "principal aim is to hide the truth."[60] A similar point has often been made about the changes in the German language brought about in the "east zone" by Soviet communism, the effects of which still plague the now intra-German situation. Living in the Soviet Union was linguistically like being part of a bureaucratic formation—speaking required the common use of abbreviations and acronyms. And words in ex-communist systems often have special ironic meanings or connotations that make straightforward communication difficult. For example, one of Vietnam's leading writers says that it is ruled by a "self-satisfied, cliché-spouting Marxist bureaucracy."[61] Gorbachev was forced to try to speak in public in a new, plain language that strove to avoid compromised terms.

The culture of the Soviet bureaucracy, though it derived some of its content from the tsarist system, or, at least, ex-peasant conceptions of what a bureaucrat ought to be like, acquired other features from Stalin and his actions. Dunham presents these effects brilliantly. As she states,

> Stalin fathered a new service class, which grew into a hydrocephalic bureaucracy. . . . The vision kept receding . . . a pragmatic program was embarked on, smacking of *meshchanstvo* whatever the ideological label. . . . Stalin . . . sponsored a proliferation of bureaucratic institutions. . . . These required the parceling out of limited, yet lucrative, power to the bureaucrats. With it, something else emerged . . . anxiety. The middling bureaucrat . . . feared to

rock the precarious boat. He feared decisions, for he could neither make them nor not make them. He feared change. . . . But such power as he held was penetrated through and through by fear, which he transmitted in turn to the people. . . . Such a Stalinist drowned ideas and ideals in bureaucratese. Bowing and scraping to superiors, dealing and wheeling with peers, oppressing those below him, he ensconced himself behind the desk of local power.[62]

Murray notes that the effects were still very much in evidence in Gorbachev's time—"institutionalized paternalism—commands from above, obedience from below."[63] Hingly, referring to Chekhov's story "Fat and Thin," says that Russians in hierarchical relationships act very differently than they do in personal or friendship relationships. Gorer and Rickman state: "It would appear that Russians do not conceive of any intermediate positions: there is either complete equality [in personal relationships] or complete superordination and subordination."[64] If true, then this would account for some Russian bureaucratic haughtiness.

It is accordingly not surprising that Soviet bureaucracy had a strong air of unreality and absurdity about it. More than one Soviet writer, when able to write honestly, has tried to evoke this absurdity. See, for example, Zoshchenko's short but highly amusing satiric poke at bureaucracy in his story "The Poker" ("Kocherga"). Solnick notes that "quite obviously, logic or common sense played little role in routine decision making from the earliest days of the Soviet regime. Procedures and documentation mattered far more than any sort of Weberian rationality in guiding the behavior of policy makers."[65] Elsewhere I have referred to this commitment to sterile bureaucratic forms as a variant of "cargo-cultism."

Bureaucratic informalism and folk and other survivals from the villages, the tsarist past, and particular ethnic cultures seriously undercut official planning and policy. Service sums it up well:

New local "nests" or "family circles" were formed almost as soon as Stalin destroyed the existing ones. Wheeling and dealing occurred among the heads of party, soviet, police, army and enterprise management; local officials protected each other against the demands made by central authorities. . . . Lying to Moscow was a skill crucial for physical survival. Institutions had to fiddle the accounts so as to exaggerate achievements enough to win acclaim, but not to the point that the following year's quotas would be raised intolerably high.[66]

Many American observers have commented on Soviet bureaucratic style, sometimes from close observation. Strobe Talbott has noted the slowness and anti-improvisational nature of Soviet negotiating behavior. Writing of arms control negotiations, he states that the Soviets were "especially suspicious and resentful of the American penchant for improvisation." He adds:

> While the U.S. generally took care to give the Soviets an advance look at the American negotiating position . . . the Russians almost never reciprocated. . . . The American governmental process was more adaptable than the Russians'. The Soviets moved purposefully but slowly. The Americans were more willing to improvise. The American SALT team could adjust to a change in the Soviet position much more quickly than the other way round, and the President of the U.S. could make a decision more quickly than the Politburo.[67]

Henry Kissinger, Nixon's national security adviser and later secretary of state, who spent quite some time with Leonid Brezhnev, has described the atmosphere at one meeting: "The timetable was, as usual, enigmatic. No schedule or advance indication of subject matter was ever given, even though Brezhnev had no other visible program. Meetings occurred randomly, with little, if any, advance warning. Except for concluding the Agreement on the Prevention of Nuclear War . . . there was no definable agenda."[68] One is reminded of Oblomov, though here writ very large.

Structure, Size, Organization

Most observers have noted and commented on the vast size and seeming omnipresence of the Soviet bureaucratic establishment. This fact has often psychologically overwhelmed visitors to Russia. Words like *huge, vast,* and *large* are commonly used. Yeltsin writes of the "enormous Soviet Russian bureaucracy."

Solnick speaks of the "vast bureaucracies that came to crowd the Soviet landscape." Many governments, particularly illegitimate and dictatorial ones, have long seen the state administration as a way to buy loyalty or at least political quiescence. Marx's father converted to Protestantism to retain his position in the Prussian civil service. A graduate student from a Middle Eastern country once told me about his "service" in the state bureaucracy there; although he did no work, he did spend time at the office but took much time out for tea and cakes and long lunches. The new Soviet state bureaucracy burgeoned with "spectacular speed"; Lenin discovered with "horror" that the Council of People's Commissars had created in his absence 120 committees, when fifteen or so would have been enough. And because the new officials were often "totally untrained . . . it was necessary to staff each post with several persons, swelling the apparatus still further. In 1917 there were nearly 1 million functionaries; in 1925, 2.5 million." The number of civil servants in transportation jumped from 815,000 in 1917 to 1,229,000 as early as 1921, even though use of the system had shrunk greatly. The percentage of civil servants in the workforce more than doubled between 1913 and 1920, from 6.4 percent to 13.5 percent. Though 750,000 civil servants were dismissed after Stalin's death in 1953, the party leadership still considered the state bureaucracy "excessively large." Those removed from the central administration were often shuffled downward to republic and regional bureaucracies. Gorbachev replaced top bureaucrats, but his replacements were not much different from the people being replaced.

Bolshevism's stark increase in the size of the administration meant that control agencies also increased in a vain attempt to retain the leaders' control. "The Soviet bureaucracy is also characterized by a formidable proliferation of control agencies without parallel in the West," notes Fainsod, who goes on to point out that the attempt at control engendered informal "antidotes" that undercut it and resulted in a broad pattern of cover-ups of bureaucratic reality and resistance to policy.[69] I present these briefly below.

At first glance, in an organizational chart on Soviet government one seems to see a typical government administration divided up into ministries and subagencies. But then it becomes apparent that many of these bureaucracies deal with matters usually part of private enterprise in the West—automobile production and so forth. Soviet ministries did not just regulate, they proscribed and made things and controlled almost all economic production. Tucker calls the system of ministries "an enormous bureaucratic complex," with every ministry being "a governmental empire, a vast realm of bureaucracy . . . a gigantic monopolistic concern." This had bred, he adds, a "big-business mentality" in the top bureaucrats. Each ministry even had its own training colleges, recreational facilities, and means of transport. No wonder Alfred G. Meyer once referred to the Soviet Union as "USSR, Incorporated." Fainsod lists the peak number of ministries during Stalin's lifetime as fifty-nine in 1947. But they must have grown in number again later, because when Khrushchev virtually destroyed the ministerial system in 1957 they numbered 140. He replaced them with 105 *sovnarkhozy*. But because these were plagued with some of the same tendencies as the ministries, for example, autarkism as well as *mestnichestvo* or localism, additional levels of structure were added in a "continuing administrative adjustment." Recentralization was evident by 1962, when the USSR Council of Ministers, a "large, cumbersome body" of fifty-plus members, headed a "massively formidable" bureaucratic pyramid of fifteen ministries and thirty-one committees, commissions, councils, and administrations, not counting the republic level and the three levels below it. By 1979 these bodies had more than doubled in number. In December 1991, just before the "fall," the Russian federation's government was made up of nineteen ministries and nine state committees.[70]

Process and Problems

A fundamental problem that lay at the heart of the Soviet system has been expressed by a defector: "What was missing in my life was the ability to make my own decisions. It was simply not possible in the highly regulated, bureaucratic Soviet society." Elsewhere she has said that she had become spoiled by living in the United States, where it is often possible to resolve a problem "in a matter of minutes." But "things do not work like that in the Soviet Union . . . where everything sinks as if in quicksand." The result is that "for many Russians, getting around the law is a national game. The Soviet bureaucracy is so vast that often the only way to get anything done is to find a way around it."[71] Indeed, the U.S. consul general in Russia in 1999 said that one reason for the sharp cut in issuing U.S. visas for Russians was because "many Russians think that bureaucracy is something to be gotten around. They give us all sorts of paper that is false."[72]

Certainly the unseen but strongly felt pressure of the bureaucracy made people in Soviet Russia, even Americans, act differently than they otherwise would. While living in the USSR during 1977, I felt driven to try to avoid conforming to rules and regulations whenever possible. Victories, however, were minor and only temporary. Amusingly, when a general at the USA Institute asked me how long I had been there and I replied, "Two months," the general exclaimed in mock shock, "You are almost a Soviet man!" [Vy pochti Sovetskii chelovek!]. In other words, that oppressive net of rules and regulations that enveloped the USSR made acts of ordinary life into conspiracies, an attitude that has lived on into the present.

This was evident throughout Soviet industrial administration. Managers kept two sets of books, with true figures only for themselves. Protection from higher levels was attempted by creating so-called family circles among key figures at the local levels. Supplies were acquired outside the approved channels by the *tolkachi* or "pushers" hired by factory managers using their budgets "creatively." (Snow removal moneys were difficult to account for and could become true "slush funds.") The interstices of the seemingly monolithic and programmed regime contained many "concealed pockets of effective bureaucratic resistance." Khrushchev complained that the bureaucracy undercut his polices through "nibbling." In a vain attempt at achieving effective control, party bodies would instead rigidify the bureaucracy by taking over its work from time to time (*podmena*) and creating "petty tutelage" and "parallelism," actions that would only drive bureaucratic resistance deeper into the woodwork. Such actions by the party were doomed because party officials were "linked by *nomenklatura* with people in similar administrative offices in the state."[73]

This was not an efficient bureaucracy. John Scott saw some of the reasons during the 1920s. He suggests that the newness and large size of much of it, and the inexperience of some of its leading personnel, created problems: "It did not have a chance to grow up over a period of several decades. . . . The result was what might have been expected: tremendous enthusiasm, boundless devotion, and hard work; and unbelievable confusion, disorder, and stupidity."[74] The result was "the notoriously malfunctioning Soviet bureaucracy." In 1982 a trade official lamented, "No one is occupied with coordinating the production of the whole range of the simplest commodities, and in this lies the source of many omissions and failures." Leonhard notes that "the centralized bureaucracy stifled every creative initiative" and cites Khrushchev on the excessive paperwork and red tape, the "rigid planning with a mass of detailed, unnecessary indices" that prevented managers from making independent decisions. As early as 1931 Ordjonikidze had complained, "If we don't put a stop to the paper flow it will drown us. We defeated Denekin and Iudenich, Wrangel and every other counterrevolutionary scum, but paper of all things will smother us." Last but not least, among the problems spawned by the bureaucratized communist state was the near destruction of the environment. Many tried to stop this "pitiless destruction of natural resources, but in vain. Once a plan had been approved by the central government, it could not be changed."[75]

The Bureaucrats Themselves

Bureaucrats were stand-ins for the Russian state, the party, and its ideology and mission and so were accordingly privileged in at least two ways. First, they were "amply rewarded" and had more possessions than others. Even if their material assets were low by Western standards, they were better off materially than other Soviet citizens, though their "perks had to be enjoyed discreetly." Second, they had power over their fellow citizens. This meant that even the lowliest bureaucrat, though he or she had no car and driver or grand dacha, still had the power to make ordinary Soviets uncomfortable and perhaps even grovel. If one wanted one could even be a "little Stalin" within one's own small span of authority. Given the "overweight administrative supervisory structure" of Soviet existence, almost any administrator could be a "bureaucratic bully—the official who, browbeaten by his superiors, browbeats his subordinates in turn."[76] Despite the disappearance of the Soviet state, Russians are still concerned about their bureaucrats. In 1997, 34 percent of Russians polled said that they feared corrupt officials. In 1996, 50 percent said that they distrusted government.[77]

The number of bureaucrats increased greatly under Sovietism. Between 1926 and 1940 bureaucrats increased at least fourfold. If all institutions are considered, the increase would be much greater. Farmer, writing of the 1980s, lists a central state elite of between 510 and 680 state officials and quotes Weeks's estimate of the number of "top tier nomenklaturists" as about one hundred thousand if party and military figures are included. Farmer cites a number of about four hundred thousand state bureaucrats as a total.[78]

In sociological background and probably cultural nature as well these officials were generally Russian males of lower class and rural origin born in European Russia. Hardly any women made it to the higher ranks; Farmer's sample was only about 3 percent female. If these men had higher education, then it was specialized and from an institute, not a university, often in Moscow or Leningrad. Party membership was common. As Hirszowicz puts it, "The party state bureaucracy is based on large numbers of people from the 'lower strata' of society, in spite of the elitist character of the government." That "corruption, immorality and philistinism" were not uncommon among them is accepted by a leading historian of Russia.[79]

After Stalin's time, longevity of career was notable, often in the same ministry: "Lifelong bureaucrats stayed in their offices until they were carried out horizontally." And, toward the end of the system, membership in the Central Committee and even the Politburo itself was possible. Farmer places state functionaries into six categories: state industrial specialist (most common), state agricultural specialist, state economics specialist, state coercion specialist, state trade union and social services specialist, and miscellaneous state official. Those many who spent their lives in industry, often in Moscow, tended to be "narrowly specialized" and to have an "almost exclusively technical education, usually in engineering." Those in the state apparatus were promoted to the Central Committee faster than those in the party apparatus.

Notably absent in the background of most of these people was training in market economics and in skills such as marketing and personnel management. The Soviet bureaucracy was, to the end, "Stalinist" in the sense of being narrowly prepared to make a particular type of narrow system work. Still, it was important. Alec Nove considers state bureaucrats "players" in the Soviet economy. Sixteen, or almost half, of the biographies of principal figures in one of his books are of state administrators.[80]

REFORM AND NONREFORM

Despite various, even continual, attempts at changes and improvement in Soviet administration, no significant change ever occurred after the 1930s and the setting of the Stalinist foundations of the Soviet system. The many "tinkering changes" and "local experiments" served only to "complicate the administration of the economy without much improving it." Reform worthy of the name would have required fundamental ideological and political changes and also a large-scale purge and reconstitution of the state bureaucracy. Even Gorbachev was not heading in this direction. He was "totally committed to state ownership of industry" and to central planning.[81]

Brzezinski states the basic problem well:

> The present [ca. 1970] Soviet managerial generation, trained to operate in a highly confined, hierarchical setting, is not predisposed to assume the greater personal hazards that a more decentralized, competitive system would necessarily involve.
>
> To institutionalize an idea is to impede its capacity to adjust to change. The further evolution of the idea then becomes dependent not on the capacity of the mind to sense the speed and the significance of change but on the rate of change within the bureaucratic organization which has come to embody the idea. Vested power interests thus become more important than either ethical or intellectual imperatives.

Lawrence Summers states the reason in the language of the computer age: "Communism, planning ministries and corporate conglomerates all ran into great difficulties in the same era because with the P.C. and the microchip it became much more efficient to empower individuals, who could get more information and make more decisions themselves, rather than having a single person at the top trying to direct everything"—and rather than relying on huge, rigid, ideologized bureaucracies to make decisions.[82] Accordingly, the Soviet Union ended with its fundamental administrative problems unresolved. They would then be carried over, often in grossly exaggerated forms, into the post-Soviet era. Transsystem continuity and "déjà vu once again." Not surprisingly, Shevtsova emphasizes the need for reform: "If we fail to change the obsolete system of state administration radically, Russia will never catch up with the leading world powers."[83]

POST-SOVIET RUSSIAN BUREAUCRACY

Because post-Soviet bureaucracy is dealt with at some length in the following chapters, here I only provide some statements and quotations that indicate and highlight some of its essentials.

Continuity

There was an unavoidable continuity with the Soviet past because it ended before it was totally exhausted and before there was a conscious, organized, and majoritarian drive to push it over history's cliff. Yeltsin and Gorbachev, though they acted at cross-purposes, yet acted "together" in a way—to destroy the Soviet state. But that state had been so large and powerful and so much a part of all realities that its residue was everywhere and importantly active in many ways long after its "fall." At the moment of writing we see an attempt by a former officer of the KGB and others who served in the former state apparatus to construct a political edifice and society with which they can be comfortable. The media is being restricted, a breakaway republic has been militarily pulverized, and political officers are being assigned to the military, for example: "Russia emerged from the Soviet Union as an old and new country simultaneously."[84]

Yeltsin admits to maintaining continuity with the Soviet bureaucratic structure. "We utilized everything we could. It would have been disastrous to destroy the government administration of such an enormous state," and "the entire midlevel bureaucratic class in Russia came out of the party and government offices [of the USSR]." He later reflectively adds, "Although it's very hard to create anything in Russia, it's even harder to destroy it": "The enormous Russian state has left a peculiar mark upon us. We have grown very dependent on this wide unbounded space; we are steeped in it to the very marrow of our bones." Holmes says trenchantly, "The nameplates on the doors have changed, but the people inside are the same." And Service states the continuity directly:

> The administrative elite of the Soviet period remained in charge of factories, kolkhozes, shops and offices. . . .
>
> The political nomenklatura also endured well: three quarters of the immediate political associates and consultants of Yeltsin had held posts in the Soviet nomenklatura.
>
> And so the social structure of the new Russia was disclosing itself as a modified version of the old USSR.[85]

And, "like its Communist predecessors, the new elite seeks to monopolize both economic and political power." But this "new" elite is not new. For example, the "private sector" is really "no normal private sector" but, rather, a "more complicated form of bureaucratic ownership." This continuity exists in foreign policy and the national security apparatus as well. As Afanas'ev notes, "The fundamental directions of Russian foreign policy remain consistent with the Soviet past" in the appeal to *derzhavnost'* and the retention of a "bloated military and armed security apparatus." This last we have seen applied brutishly to much of Chechnya. The Stimson Center has noted that the Russian government has retained "holdover apparatchiks" intent on blocking Russo-American cooperation in positions of power that have kept key military biological labs and antiplague institutes closed to outside scrutiny.[86]

The Weak State

Ironically, though post-Soviet continuity is abundantly, even redundantly, in evidence, the present Russian state is far weaker than most previous Russian states. Clearly, Russia is now undergoing a crisis of the state. Vladimir Putin has stated, "If we continue like this, Russia will fall to pieces." In early 2000 he complained to his ministers that many government and presidential orders were simply being ignored or lost in a "grindingly slow bureaucracy." When Russia escaped Sovietism it also escaped governance and came to inglorious rest with a "weak state" or "undergoverned state." This has serious negative implications for the development of democracy. Linz and Stepan have pointed out that one of the requirements of democracy is a bureaucracy that is effective or usable for the government. Different observers have differing views of why this weakness of government exists. Possibly it has resulted from the end of the Communist Party's iron hold over both society and government. It may be a natural result of an understandable dash for liberty become license for many, including civil servants. Two observers look back to the Gorbachev period and say, "Perestroika weakened the centralized bureaucratic guidance system before workable market institutions were in place." They also cite the effects of "greater freedom." Another scholar claims that by 1990 state institutions were in "an advanced state of decay." The debate will continue. One result is, however, that it is often impossible to tell whether some Russian "governmental" action is indeed an act of government as policy or simply an "entrepreneurial" act by bureaucrats or businesspeople allied with particular bureaucrats. Does Russia now have a new type of political system, a "state-bureaucratic capitalism"? For example, "it is difficult, [U.S.] officials said, to determine whether the sale of technology to Iran is government policy or is yet another example of the breakdown of Government control in Russia that allows economic fiefs left over from the Communist era to do what they want."[87]

One of the most troubling issues for U.S. policy is how to act toward what is called "Minatom," the Russian Ministry of Atomic Energy, which is continually selling nuclear materials and expertise to what the United States considers "rogue states" that are anti-American. The heads of that ministry tend to argue that nuclear power is a boon for humanity and also, more pointedly and self-servingly, that the ministry must sell what it can in order to hold itself together in the face of the government's inability to maintain it. In this case the restricted capability of the Russian government to gather tax revenues is highlighted. During the mid-1990s, and perhaps after as well, the Russian government was unable to fund its customs service fully, with the result that the customs service actually levied duties on U.S. government assistance to Russia. The Yeltsin government was unable to end this practice. A letter from President Yeltsin ordering it to cease was only "good" for one shipment. It is absurd but true. What became known as the Bank of New York money-laundering scandal also revealed Russian governmental weakness. "The most rudimentary mechanisms and controls were absent" in Russian banking. Some of the banks were not banks at all but, in fact, "pocket banks" belonging to particular Russian companies or "political banks" born of the ties between businesspeople and government bureaucrats. Russian bureaucratic inefficiencies and corruption have been called "pervasive."[88]

Undoubtedly the present weakness of Russian government is a fundamental change in the Russian political pattern, at least for now. As Tucker has pointed out, historically "the Russian state organism took shape as an autonomous force acting to create or re-create its own social base, to shape and reshape the institutional pattern of society, in a series of revolutions from above." However, despite the weakness of the state, it may well remain "by far the most important story in Russian politics," and other parts of the pattern persist, for example, excessive numbers of bureaucrats. As Huskey points out, "Where the British prime minister and German chancellor govern with a support staff of no more than a hundred officials each, the Russian prime minister oversees a Government bureaucracy with approximately a thousand professional staff employees. In this, as in so many other areas of institutional life, continuity rather than change has characterized the transition from Communist rule."[89]

Elsewhere Huskey has suggested that the Russian government has more administrative staff than the Soviet one did in 1991. One Russian observer said in 1998, "The Bureaucracy will never die. The declared reduction of governmental apparatus has failed." Ironically, it is possible that the "biggest victim to fall under the cancerous weight of an ever expanding bureaucracy is the state as presently constituted." And as Goldman says, "The bureaucracy . . . continues to retain much of its influence." But the Russian public sees it as weak. For example, in one poll taken in three cities "only 6 percent . . . considered that power in fact belonged to the visible organs of government. Almost 30 percent believed that the mafia was the most powerful political force in the country." This point of view is not surprising given the pervasiveness of governmental corruption in Russia. Holmes notes "the most pathological example" of Russian soldiers' sales of weapons to Chechen fighters and adds, "The private use of public office is ubiquitous, from customs officers to tax collectors, from privatization ministers to policemen working hand-in-glove with organized crime." Shevtsova notes that, with Gaidar's second departure from government, "bureaucratic groups connected with sectoral interests, mainly with the oil and gas group, began to dominate [government]."[90]

Bureaucracy and Power

What is also striking about the bureaucracy in postcommunist Russia is that at least four prime ministers by 2000 have been ex-bureaucrats, not "party politicians" as is the rule in the United States, Western Europe, and elsewhere as well. These are, in chronological order, Chernomyrdin, Stepashin, Primakov, and Putin. Primakov has been called "a wily but amiable veteran of the Soviet bureaucracy." He hailed from the intelligence agency, as did some of the others, and naturally inserted former aides from that agency into key positions. Putin has done the same thing. "Putinburgers," or the "St. Petersburg mafia," proliferated in government positions soon after Putin's appointment as prime minister in August 1999. Almost 40 percent of the persons whom Putin appointed to high offices, some after he became acting president upon the resignation of Yeltsin, had been agents of the KGB or its successor, the Federal Security Service (Federal'naya Sluzhba Bezopasnosti).[91] Any leader seeks associates who are likely to be loyal, and that often means dipping into one's own institutional past. Rarely, however, have the bureaucrats themselves become the governors—and the guardians as well.

CONCLUSION

In this chapter I have ranged from a statement of purpose, a presentation of definitions, the case for the significance of bureaucracy in Russian history, through a series of quotations from the literature citing the importance of Soviet bureaucracy, to a brief discussion of post-Soviet bureaucratic significance. There is no need at any time to "stretch" or overargue the case. It makes itself fairly well on its own. The main problem is not one of finding sufficient sources but, rather, one of deciding which to use. We now move on by going back in time to imperial Russia to examine the foundation of attitudes, practice, and procedures, both formal and informal, that infused the Russian state bureaucracy as it became fully formed, served as one of the bases of the Soviet bureaucracy, and continues in the post-Soviet Russian state bureaucracy. The state bureaucracy appears to be one big continuing phenomenon flowing through modern Russian history from the tsars to Putin.

NOTES

1. Almost anything written on today's Russia mentions that members of the former Soviet elite still dominate all fields of activity. Even the "democrats" are

from the communist elite. See, for example, the excellent work by Lilia Shevtsova: "The Soviet Union had ceased to exist, but a substantial portion of its ruling class, including some former members of its highest echelon, found comfortable places in the new governing institutions" (*Yeltsin's Russia: Myths and Reality* [Washington, D.C.: Carnegie Endowment, 1999], 18).

2. H. H. Gerth and C. Wright Mills, *From Max Weber: Essays in Sociology* (New York: Oxford University Press, 1946), 196–199, 203.

3. Karl Loewenstein, *Max Weber's Ideas in the Perspective of Our Time* (Amherst: University of Massachusetts Press, 1966), 30. Loewenstein says that Weber identified "the untrammeled rule of bureaucracy" as "Public Enemy Number 1." This suggests that Weber recognized that bureaucracy could act in a less than "Weberian" manner. I was privileged to have met Professor Loewenstein of Amherst College on various occasions. He possessed great knowledge of political phenomena and was a delightful raconteur.

4. This paragraph is a refined version of the related statement in my *Implementation of Soviet Economic Reforms* (New York: Praeger, 1975), 9.

5. These definitions are derived from Ludwig von Mises, *Bureaucracy* (Cedar Falls, Iowa: Center for Futures Education, 1983), 45 (first published by Yale University Press, 1944); Peter M. Blau and Marshall W. Meyer, *Bureaucracy in Modern Society*, 2d ed. (New York: Random House, 1971), 9; Michel Crozier, *The Bureaucratic Phenomenon* (Chicago: University of Chicago Press, 1967), 3; Anthony Downs, *Inside Bureaucracy* (Boston: Little, Brown, 1967), 24–26; and James Q. Wilson, *Bureaucracy: What Government Agencies Do and Why They Do It* (New York: Basic Books, 1989), 10. William E. Odom (General, USA, Ret.) correctly says that "Crozier's theory of bureaucratic behavior as a 'vicious cycle' has rich applicability to Soviet political life" ("Soviet Politics and After: Old and New Concepts," *World Politics* 45, no. 1 [October 1992]: 79).

6. Crozier, *The Bureaucratic Phenomenon*, 4.

7. Von Mises, *Bureaucracy*, 15, 17–18; Blau and Meyer, *Bureaucracy in Modern Society*, 11.

8. Karl W. Ryavec, "The Soviet Bureaucratic Elite from 1964 to 1979," *Soviet Union/Union Sovietique* 12, no. 3 (1985): 323.

9. Benjamin R. Barber, "Big=Bad, Unless It Doesn't," *New York Times*, 16 September 1998, A23. Here Barber argues that privatization is about "terminating democracy" and that big government has to be "muscular and efficient" and "powerful as in 'sovereign.'"

10. Downs, *Inside Bureaucracy*, 32–33; B. Guy Peters, *The Politics of Bureaucracy*, 3d ed. (New York: Longman, 1989), 1–3; Crozier, *The Bureaucratic Phenomenon*, 8; David Beetham, *Bureaucracy* (Stony Stratford, England: Open University Press, 1987), 61.

11. Francis E. Rourke, *Bureaucracy, Politics, and Public Policy*, 2d ed. (Boston: Little, Brown, 1976), 14–38.

12. Richard D. Stillman II, *The American Bureaucracy* (Chicago: Nelson-Hall, 1987), 20. Stillman is citing Wallace Sayre, "Bureaucracies: Some Contrasts in Systems," *Indian Journal of Public Administration* 10, no. 2 (1964): 223; and James Q. Wilson, *Bureaucracy: What Government Agencies Do and Why They Do It* (New York: Basic Books, 1989), 377. My own experience working at the U.S. Arms Control and

Disarmament Agency and observing also the State Department and Pentagon bureaucracies quickly brought home to me that many if not most American civil servants are bureaucratic entrepreneurs and not at all "waiting-for-orders" types.

13. "Report Scolds Bureaucracy for U.S. Nuclear Lab Lapses," *New York Times*, 15 June 1999, A12. Another report in the same vein is the Cox Report, prepared by a congressional committee.

14. Stillman, *The American Bureaucracy*, ix; Blau and Meyer, *Bureaucracy in Modern Society*, 11; Peter Woll, *American Bureaucracy* (New York: Norton, 1963), 174; Peter Woll, *American Government: Readings and Cases*, 12th ed. (New York: Harper Collins, 1995), 334; Alan A. Altshuler, *The Politics of the Federal Bureaucracy* (New York: Dodd, Mead, 1968), 26. See also Francis E. Rourke, *Bureaucracy, Politics, and Public Policy*, 3d ed. (Boston: Little, Brown, 1984); and David Nachmias and David H. Rosenbloom, *Bureaucratic Government USA* (New York: St. Martin's, 1980).

15. Daniel Patrick Moynihan, "Secrecy as Government Regulation," *PS: Political Science and Politics* (June 1997), 165.

16. Vladimir Brovkin, "Fragmentation of Authority and Privatization of the State," *Demokratizatsiya* 6, no. 3 (summer 1998): 511; Eva Busza, "The Unpredictable Genie in the Russian Bottle," *Richmond Post-Dispatch*, 26 July 1999, from *Johnson's Russia List* (e-mail service), 27 July 1999.

17. Bill Keller, "Eclipsed," *New York Times Magazine*, 27 June 1999, 36. Keller points out that, unlike the United States, the USSR had only one bureaucracy for both the arms race and the space race. As a result, as one Soviet scientist has put it, "We could only undertake a lunar program as a sideline" (in Keller, "Eclipsed," 35).

18. Ryavec, "The Soviet Bureaucratic Elite from 1964 to 1979," 323, quoting Sewyrin Bialer, *Stalin's Successors* (Cambridge: Cambridge University Press, 1980), 285.

19. See Bruno Rizzi, *The Bureaucratization of the World*, trans. Adam Westoby (New York: Free Press, 1985).

20. *Bureaucratism* is the Russian term for what Victor Thompson has dubbed *bureaupathology*. Essentially, it is behavior by bureaucrats that is "dysfunctional from the point of view of the organization" or its leaders, though it may be functional enough from the point of view or self-interest of the bureaucrat. See Victor A. Thompson, *Modern Organization*, 2d ed. (Tuscaloosa: University of Alabama Press, 1977), 23–24.

21. Milovan Djilas, *The New Class* (New York: Praeger, 1957), 43; Crozier, *The Bureaucratic Phenomenon*, 1; Dietrich Rueschmeyer and Peter B. Evans, "The State and Economic Transformation: Toward an Analysis of the Conditions Underlying Effective Intervention," in *Bringing the State Back In*, by Dietrich Rueshmeyer, Peter B. Evans, and Theda Skocpol (Cambridge: Cambridge University Press, 1985), 68.

22. Two Yugoslav diplomats resident in China during the Cultural Revolution, personal communication.

23. A. V. Obolonsky, "Russian Politics in the Time of Troubles: Some Basic Antinomies," in *Russia in Search of Its Future*, eds. Amin Saikal and William Maley (Cambridge: Cambridge University Press, 1995), 13.

24. See Yevgenia Albats, *The State within a State: The KGB and Its Hold on Russia*, trans. Catherine A. Fitzpatrick (New York: Farrar, Straus, and Giroux, 1994). One reviewer points out that "changes of name imply virtually nothing about changes

of the organization's role" (Glenn Garelik, "The Spies Who Stayed Out in the Cold," *New York Times Book Review*, 27 November 1994, 11). Note that the chief of Russian presidential security in early 1995 was a former KGB major general. See *New York Times*, 5 January 1995, A8. Post-Soviet continuity is everywhere in Russia and in the successor states as well. There is more on this below.

25. In Gregory Feifer, "Putin's Tactics: Fatherly Love or Soviet Claptrap?" *Moscow Times*, 6 February 2002, from *Johnson's Russia List*, 5 February 2002. Korgunyuk is a political analyst at the Indem think tank.

26. My colleague Professor Ferenc Vali, who did interviewing in the ministry in the 1960s and 1970s, personal communication.

27. An American once imprisoned in the gulag during the 1960s who noticed that the next camp contained officers still wearing their uniforms and badges of rank who had refused to fire while in Hungary, personal communication.

28. Alexander Bolsunovsky and Valery Menshchikov, "Analysis: What Is Impeding the Protection of Nuclear Materials," *Moskovskie novosti*, no. 61 (4–11 December 1994): 11, translated in *The Current Digest of the Post Soviet Press* 46, no. 48 (28 December 1994): 17. About a month previously, the *New York Times* stated correctly, "Russia has a very weak system of accounting for nuclear materials" and cited a Russian government agency to the effect that Russia did not even have a nationwide system of accounting for such materials (23 November 1994, A1). This situation became apparent to me when I worked for the former U.S. Arms Control and Disarmament Agency (now part of the U.S. Department of State) during 1995 and 1996.

29. Peter Passell, "Economic Scene," *New York Times*, 18 March 1993, D2.

30. Barbara W. Tuchman, *The Proud Tower: A Portrait of the World before the War, 1890–1914* (New York: Macmillan, 1966).

31. John LeDonne, personal communication, Philadelphia, 19 November 1994.

32. Ilya V. Konstantinov, a member of the national Duma from St. Petersburg, quoted in *New York Times*, 22 June 1993, A3.

33. Maryanne Ozernoy, "A Political History of the Russian State: The Basis for Bureaucratic Power," *Soviet and Post Soviet Review* 23, no. 1 (1996): 5. For another point of view, see the presentations of Matthew Payne and Walter M. Pintner in the same issue. Still, both accept some key points of what Ozernoy says.

34. Steven L. Solnick, *Stealing the State: Control and Collapse in Soviet Institutions* (Cambridge: Harvard University Press, 1998), 15.

35. Karl W. Ryavec, ed., *Soviet Society and the Communist Party* (Amherst: University of Massachusetts Press, 1978).

36. Maria Hirszowicz, *The Bureaucratic Leviathan: A Study in the Sociology of Communism* (Oxford: Martin Robertson, 1980), 17. Here Hirszowicz is quoting Leon Trotsky's famous *The Revolution Betrayed* (New York: Merit, 1965), 279. Other editions exist.

37. As a young working-class person of Slovenian and hence Slavic background, I became a specialist on Russia on the basis of careerism and Slavic sensibility but did not then know how "un-Slavic" Russia is.

38. Michael Oakeshotte, *Rationalism in Politics* (New York: Basic Books, 1962), 332.

39. Alfred G. Meyer, *The Soviet Political System* (New York: Random House, 1965), 11.

40. Donald F. Kettl, "Public Administration: The State of the Field," in *Political Science: The State of the Discipline*, ed. Ada W. Finifter (Washington, D.C.: American Political Science Association, 1983), 407–9.

41. Tibor Szamuely, *The Russian Tradition* (New York: McGraw-Hill, 1974), 135.

42. Ronald Grigor Suny, *The Soviet Experiment* (Oxford: Oxford University Press, 1998), 14. Officials numbered only about seventy-four thousand in the middle of the nineteenth century. Suny says the tsarist state was "overly bureaucratic," of "ponderous bulk," and with an "inefficient, unruly bureaucracy" that contributed to the state's "feet of clay" (*The Soviet Experiment*, 11, 15, 28).

43. Wolfgang Leonhard, *The Kremlin since Stalin*, trans. E. Wiskemann and M. Jackson (New York: Praeger, 1962), 13–14; Zbigniew Brzezinski, *Out of Control: Global Turmoil on the Eve of the Twenty-first Century* (New York: Scribner's, 1993), 60–61; Richard Bernstein, "Love and Evil in the Last Days of the Soviet Union" (review of David Plante, *The Age of Terror* [New York: St. Martin's, 1999]), *New York Times*, 20 January 1999, B8.

44. Mark R. Beissinger, *Scientific Management, Socialist Discipline, and Soviet Power* (Cambridge: Harvard University Press, 1988), 32, 45; Leonhard, *The Kremlin since Stalin*, 9–11.

45. Robert Service, *A History of Twentieth-Century Russia* (Cambridge: Harvard University Press, 1997), 237, 320. Service explicitly says, "The promotees to administrative office were the system's main beneficiaries," and he notes that after Stalin approved the introduction of fees for the later years of secondary school and for university, "high-ranking administrators were in a better position to find the necessary finance than any other group" (*A History of Twentieth-Century Russia*, 237, 548).

46. Suny, *The Soviet Experiment*, 156, 147–48, 146; Leonhard, *The Kremlin since Stalin*, 35, 206; Vera Dunham, *In Stalin's Time: Middleclass Values in Soviet Fiction*, enlarged and updated ed. (Durham: Duke University Press, 1990); H. Gordon Skilling, "Group Conflict in Soviet Politics: Some Conclusions," in *Interest Groups in Soviet Politics*, eds. H. Gordon Skilling and Franklyn Griffiths (Princeton: Princeton University Press, 1971), 400.

47. Michel Tatu, *Power in the Kremlin*, trans. Helen Katel (New York: Viking, 1970), 116, 385, 430; Suny, *The Soviet Experiment*, 419.

48. Suny, *The Soviet Experiment*, 423; Service, *A History of Twentieth-Century Russia*, 380, 382–83; Sidney I. Ploss, "The Rise of Brezhnev," in *The Soviet Political Process* (Waltham, Mass.: Ginn, 1971), 291; Grey Hodnett, "Succession Contingencies in the Soviet Union," *Problems of Communism* 24, no. 2 (March–April 1975): 9; Dunham, *In Stalin's Time*, 244; Vernon V. Aspaturian, "Soviet Global Power and the Correlation of Forces," *Problems of Communism* 29, no. 3 (May–June 1980): 13; Mary McAuley, *Soviet Politics: 1917–1991* (Oxford: Oxford University Press, 1992), 77. See also Karl W. Ryavec, "Soviet Industrial Managers, Their Superiors and the Economic Reform," *Soviet Studies* 21, no. 2 (October 1969): 208–29.

49. Thomas F. Remington, *Politics in Russia* (New York: Longman, 1999), 41, 43; Donald Murray, *A Democracy of Despots* (Boulder: Westview, 1996), 85, 114, 118.

50. Boris Yeltsin, *The Struggle for Russia*, trans. Catherine A. Fitzpatrick (New York: Times Books, 1994), 79, 81–82; Solnick, *Stealing the State*, 3, 7. I have borrowed the term *cryptopolitics* from Ted Rigby.

51. Bill Mandel, from *Johnson's Russia List*, 28 March 1999.

52. John Bayley, review of Aileen M. Kelly, *Toward Another Shore: Russian Thinkers between Necessity and Chance* (New Haven: Yale University Press, 1998), *New York Review of Books*, 19 November 1999, 37.

53. James R. Schlesinger, "The 'Soft' Factors in System Studies," *Bulletin of the Atomic Scientists* 24, no. 9 (November 1968): 14–15, quoted in Morton Schwartz, *The Foreign Policy of the USSR: Domestic Factors* (Encino, Calif.: Dickinson, 1975), 182. This agrees with my work experience in the U.S. government.

54. Jerry F. Hough, *The Soviet Prefects* (Cambridge: Harvard University Press, 1969), 69, 102.

55. William E. Jackson Jr., personal communication, September 2001.

56. Hough, *The Soviet Prefects*, 69, 102; Darrell P. Hammer, *USSR: The Politics of Oligarchy*, 2d ed. (Boulder: Westview Press, 1986), 206; Jerry F. Hough, "The Party Apparatchiki," in *Interest Groups in Soviet Politics*, eds. H. Gordon Skilling and Franklyn Griffiths (Princeton: Princeton University Press, 1971), 70; T. H. Rigby, "The Government in the Soviet Political System," in *Executive Power and Soviet Politics*, ed. Eugene Huskey (Armonk, N.Y.: M. E. Sharpe, 1992), 38–39.

57. McAuley, *Soviet Politics*, 45.

58. Stephen White, Richard Rose, and Ian McAllister, *How Russia Votes* (Chatham, N.J.: Chatham House, 1997), 153; Timothy J. Colton, *Dilemma of Reform in the Soviet Union*, rev. ed. (New York: Council on Foreign Relations, 1986), 29–31, 145, 160; Stephen White, Alex Pravda, and Zvi Gitelman, *Developments in Soviet Politics* (Durham: Duke University Press, 1990), 23.

59. Peter Juviler, personal communication, 16 December 1998.

60. Hammer, *USSR*, 233; Ilya Lipkovich, "Russian Language and Foreign Infiltrators," from *Johnson's Russia List*, 11 November 1998. Lipkovich lists two other influences that changed Russian: "communist jargon" and the "highly informal language" of the many thousands of uneducated people "fresh from the plough" who were rapidly brought forward by the Bolsheviks to replace the "old-regime cadres." See also Andrei Sinyavsky, *Soviet Civilization* (New York: Arcade, 1990), 203, 208. When I first arrived in the USSR in 1968 people said, "You speak the old way." My first teacher of Russian was a Frenchman who learned it at the Russian high school in Paris established by upper-class émigrés from imperial Russia.

61. Richard Bernstein, review of Duong Thu Huong, *Memories of a Pure Spring*, trans. Nina McPherson and Phan Huy Duong (Westport, Conn.: Hyperion, 2000), *New York Times*, 9 February 2000, B7.

62. Dunham, *In Stalin's Time*, 132.

63. Murray, *A Democracy of Despots*, 105.

64. Ronald Hingly, *The Russian Mind* (New York: Scribner and Sons, 1977), 172; Geoffrey Gorer and John Rickman, *The People of Great Russia* (New York: Chanticleer Press, 1950), 177. Both are quoted in Raymond F. Smith, *Negotiating with the Soviets* (Bloomington: Indiana University Press, 1989), 8–9. Though Gorer's works have been derided, the observation applies well to Russian bureaucratic behavior, particularly during the imperial and Soviet periods.

65. Solnick, *Stealing the State*, 2.

66. Service, *A History of Twentieth-Century Russia*, 242, 324. For more on bureaucratic informalism, see the classic by Joseph S. Berliner, *Factory and Manager in the*

USSR (Cambridge: Harvard University Press, 1957); and my *Implementation of Soviet Economic Reforms* (New York: Praeger, 1975).

67. Strobe Talbott, *Endgame: The Inside Story of SALT II* (New York: Harper and Row, 1979), 208–9.

68. Henry Kissinger, *Years of Upheaval* (Boston: Little, Brown, 1982), 230. Elsewhere, if memory serves, Kissinger describes Brezhnev calling in a *state* official to ask *him* if a certain move could be taken. The official gave "permission" and did not hide his annoyance at being called away from his work. I discuss U.S.–Russian cultural differences at length in my *United States–Soviet Relations* (New York: Longman, 1989), 241–50.

69. Yeltsin, *The Struggle for Russia*, 19; Solnick, *Stealing the State*, 2; Mikhail Heller and Aleksandr M. Nekrich, *Utopia in Power* (New York: Summit, 1986), 149–50; Leonhard, *The Kremlin since Stalin*, 137–38, 98; Merle Fainsod, *How Russia Is Ruled*, rev. ed. (Cambridge: Harvard University Press, 1963), 388. Fainsod's chapter 12, "The Control of the Bureaucracy—Public Administration in the Soviet Union," remains an excellent overview of Soviet administration.

70. Robert C. Tucker, *The Soviet Political Mind*, rev. ed. (New York: Norton, 1971), 176–77; Fainsod, *How Russia Is Ruled*, 393, 395, 397–98, 400; Eugene Huskey, ed., *Executive Power and Soviet Politics* (Armonk, N.Y.: Sharpe, 1992), 260, table 11.3.

71. Alexandra Costa, *Stepping Down from the Star* (New York: Putnam, 1986), 15, 61, 144.

72. "Wary of Abuses, U.S. Sharply Cuts Visas for Russians," *New York Times*, 24 October 1999, 1.

73. Fainsod, *How Russia Is Ruled*, 389; Tatu, *Power in the Kremlin*, 169; Ronald J. Hill, *The Party*, in *Developments in Soviet Politics*, by Stephen White, Alex Pravda, and Zvi Gitelman (Durham: Duke University Press, 1990), 75, 83.

74. John Scott, *Behind the Urals* (Bloomington: Indiana University Press, 1973), 171, 175.

75. Sheila Fitzpatrick, review, *New York Times Book Review*, 12 September 1999, 29; Colton, *Dilemma of Reform in the Soviet Union*, 57; Leonhard, *The Kremlin since Stalin*, 34, 97; Suny, *The Soviet Experiment*, 238; Heller and Nekrich, *Utopia in Power*, 466.

76. Service, *A History of Twentieth-Century Russia*, 193, 321; William Taubman and Jane Taubman, *Moscow Spring* (New York: Summit Books, 1989), 28, 50. One taxi driver told the Taubmans that "in his garage there was one bureaucrat . . . for every two drivers."

77. Timothy J. Colton, *Transitional Citizens* (Cambridge: Harvard University Press, 2000), 177, table 6.1. Colton notes that Russians have a "lack of confidence in the fundamental integrity of the institutions of the state" (*Transitional Citizens*, 44–45).

78. Service, *A History of Twentieth-Century Russia*, 193; Kenneth C. Farmer, *The Soviet Administrative Elite* (New York: Praeger, 1992), 85, 136.

79. Karl W. Ryavec, "The Soviet Bureaucratic Elite from 1964 to 1969," *Soviet Union* 12, no. 3 (1985): 322–45; Farmer, *The Soviet Administrative Elite*, 216; Maria Hirszowicz, *The Bureaucratic Leviathan* (Oxford: Martin Robertson, 1980), 102; Suny, *The Soviet Experiment*, 405, referring to V. Dudintsev's novel, *Not by Bread Alone*.

80. Suny, *The Soviet Experiment*, 322; Farmer, *The Soviet Administrative Elite*, 204–7, 216; Alec Nove, *Stalinism and After* (London: Allen and Unwin, 1975), appendix 1, 184–90. Nove calls the thirty-four persons in his list "the principal 'actors' in the Soviet political drama" (*Stalinism and After*, 184).

81. Colton, *Dilemma of Reform in the Soviet Union*, 54–55, 158.

82. Zbigniew K. Brzezinski, *Between Two Ages* (New York: Viking, 1970), 92, 159; Lawrence Summers, quoted in Thomas L. Friedman, "Two Sick Nations, One Cure," *New York Times*, 25 July 1998, A27. Friedman does not give a source for the quotation.

83. Interview with Lilia Shevtsova, *Novaia gazeta*, no. 15 (4–6 March 2002), from *Johnson's Russia List*, 6 March 2002.

84. Steve D. Boilard, *Russia at the Twenty-first Century* (Fort Worth: Harcourt Brace, 1998), 32.

85. Yeltsin, *The Struggle for Russia*, 129, 158, 289, 291; Stephen Holmes, "Cultural Legacies or State Collapse? Probing the Postcommunist Dilemma," in *Post-Communism: Four Perspectives*, ed. Michael Mandelbaum (New York: Council on Foreign Relations, 1996), 44; Service, *A History of Twentieth-Century Russia*, 514, 542.

86. Tim McDaniel, *The Agony of the Russian Idea* (Princeton: Princeton University Press, 1996), 165; George Blazyca, "The Politics of Economic Transformation," in *Developments in Central and East European Politics 2*, eds. Stephen White, Judy Batt, and Paul G. Lewis (Durham: Duke University Press, 1998), 209; Yuri Afanas'ev, "Russian Imperial Policy: Tsars—Bolsheviks—Primakov," *Perspective* (e-mail version) 9, no. 4 (March–April 1999); *New York Times*, 10 December 1999, A14.

87. Acting President Vladimir Putin, quoted in Michael Wines, "Putin Steering to Reform: But with Soviet Discipline," *New York Times*, 20 February 2000, 1NE; Reuters dispatch from Moscow, "Russia's Putin Bewails Lack of Government Discipline," 3 February 2000; Bertram Silverman and Murray Yanowitch, *New Rich New Poor New Russia* (Armonk, N.Y.: Sharpe, 1997), 6–7; Steven M. Fish, *Democracy from Scratch* (Princeton: Princeton University Press, 1995), 1125; Jane Perlez, "Uncertainty Persists on U.S.–Moscow Dialogue," *New York Times*, 20 June 1999, 12NE. The term *state-bureaucratic capitalism* is used in *Rossiia v zerkale reform* (Moscow: Russian Independent Institute of Social and National Problems, 1995), 14.

88. In 1997 the chairman of the Russian Center for Ecological Policy stated that Minatom was "directly contributing to nuclear proliferation." See *RFE/RL Newsline*, 6 November 1997. On Minatom I am also relying on my experience working for the U.S. Arms Control and Disarmament Agency. Celestine Bohlen, "Banking Inquiry's Tangled Web Reaches Lofty Levels in Moscow," *New York Times*, 18 February 2000, A1; Silverman and Yanowitch, *New Rich New Poor New Russia*, 22.

89. Robert C. Tucker, "The Image of Dual Russia," in *The Soviet Political Mind*, rev. ed., by Robert C. Tucker (New York: Norton, 1971), 123, quoted in Eugene Huskey, *Presidential Power in Russia* (Armonk, N.Y.: M. E. Sharpe, 1999), 6.

90. Huskey, *Presidential Power in Russia*, 6, 101–2; for more on the bloat of the presidential apparatus, see White et al., *How Russia Votes*, 161; Russell Bova, "Democratization and the Crisis of the Russian State," in *State-Building in Russia*, ed.

Gordon B. Smith (Armonk, N.Y.: M. E. Sharpe, 1999), 18; a title of an article from *Segodnia*, no. 89 (1224) (1998); Association for the Study of Nationalities, *Announcement of Current Events* 7, no. 7 (March 1996), 5; Marshall I. Goldman, *Lost Opportunity: Why Economic Reforms in Russia Have Not Worked* (New York: Norton, 1994), 165 (writing about the postcommunist governmental situation generally); McDaniel, *The Agony of the Russian Idea*, 177. Although the poll was taken in 1992, its results were probably still quite applicable in 2000. Holmes, "Cultural Legacies or State Collapse?" 67; Shevtsova, *Yeltsin's Russia*, 103.

91. "Mr. Primakov Comes Calling" (editorial), *New York Times*, 22 March 1999, A24; *New York Times*, 21 March 1999, 6; Arnold Beichman, "Putin's Revealing Personnel Choices," *Washington Times*, 7 February 2000, from *Johnson's Russia List*, 8 February 2000; Giles Whittell, "Putin Lines Up Old KGB Pals to Run Kremlin," *The Times*, 14 February 2000, from *Johnson's Russia List*, 14 February 2000.

1

Origins and Development: Tsarist–Soviet Bureaucratic Continuity

[The] stunted growth [of Russian civil society] obliged the state to create a surrogate for it in the form of bureaucracy. Only by such authoritarian action . . . could the backward dynastic politics of the East become competitive internationally. . . . Politically, all power resided in the autocracy and its bureaucracy.

—Martin Malia, *Russia under Western Eyes*

CONTINUITY

Although imperial Russia is long gone, elements of its bureaucratic culture, thinking, and practice continued into Soviet government and perhaps beyond. Continuity was neither general nor total, but the Soviet system was certainly not fully or even largely new. Even revolutionaries of the most committed sort cannot avoid reproducing something of the old system in their "revolutionary" rearrangement, for they are themselves products of the old structure of assumptions, beliefs, and practices. Also, a "new" system can take on "old" forms and practices in order to facilitate its adoption. The experience of Christianity adapting traditions and rituals from paganism is well known. Gibbon even says that "under the mask of Christianity," the Greeks eventually found that "they had restored the religion of their fathers."[1] Revolutionaries may not see continuities because they refuse to see their reproduction of the old. And, no matter how one may try to reject the old, there is only a limited number of ways to do things within a specific society, particularly within the constraints of culturally acceptable processes, modernity and its legalistic routine, industrial society, and great power politics. Few revolutionaries are willing to act as the Khmer Rouge did—kill the educated and professional people en masse, desert the cities and retire into the forest, and pretend to go back in time. But even that system did not last.

The "nitty-gritty" of particular governmental actions can make the claims of distinction from the old regime seem plausible—but only until the form and context in which they exist are considered. Then it often becomes obvious that the new regime is, in fact, a continuation of the old. Although France has had twenty or so different "constitutional" arrangements since 1789, no one disputes that numerous significant bureaucratic and other political continuities exist, even from monarchical times. For example, French elites have maintained much of their former position and power in the face of the democratization of French society, and the historic institutions of the French state and the power of the state administration remain strong. The French state includes a prestigious bureaucratic institution of long duration, created by Napoleon, intended to prevent the state from violating individuals' rights, the Council of State (Conseil d'Etat).[2]

This chapter provides a historical grounding for this study. Too often works on the Soviet Union are written as if the Soviet system sprang only out of the minds of Marx and Lenin without any content derived from the Russian past. Naturally, this attempt to establish historical continuity between the Russian ancien régime and its "revolutionary" successor can be questioned by certain historians and others. Solzhenitsyn opposes any linking of tsarist and Soviet Russia. For him, the Soviet system was a decidedly un-Russian abomination. The worth of the comparison lies in the significance of the examples brought forward. Controversy may be the result, "but then, it is the nature of macro-history to be controversial," and "the role of the state and its apparatus in Russian history has always been a controversial issue."[3]

Anatol Lieven asserts correctly that contemporary American commentary on developments in today's Russia is often historicist and erroneously views Russia as in direct and full descent from imperial Russia. He suggests that it would "make more sense" to look for parallels with Russia today in the "'liberal' states of southern Europe and Latin America in the later 19th and early 20th century, and among developing countries in other parts of the world today." Agreed, such comparisons might well be useful to understanding, yet at the same time no search for the origins of political institutions and practices can ignore a country's own past. Neither Russia nor any other country can slough off its past ways completely as if they were only a temporary reptilian skin to be discarded annually or at will.[4] A nation unavoidably drags its history and its institutions and ways of doing things forward with it through time, whatever changes it undergoes. Sometimes continuity is in the form of "discontinuous continuity," a pattern of irregular or partial recurrence but one in which continuity exists nevertheless. And why shouldn't there be "legacies" from tsarism operating now? There are many legacies from the communist system in today's Russia. Yet imperial Russia was in existence far longer than the communist variant was. But not all "aftermath" is "legacy," "an enduring intergenerational transfer from the past to the present."[5]

The unavoidability of postrevolutionary continuity in general can be shown in many concrete situations. For example, the postcolonial Algerian military has accepted many Algerians who had been employees in the French colonial bureaucracy. As Ryszard Kapuscinski, who could be called the "gonzo journalist of the Third World," says, "Today members of the Algerian professional class come from the former collaborators, because only they had the opportunity to gain qualifications. Today they make up the administrative cadre: what's more, even though many of them are engaged in quiet but systematic sabotage, the government has been forced to take them back into the army."[6]

Similarly, and even more ironically, the new postapartheid government of South Africa has had to continue in place the same bureaucracy dominated by Afrikaaners that supported the former racist and antidemocratic system. A specialist on public administration says that the new government "has little choice but to make peace with the old civil service, with its secretive ways, its authoritarian style, and its penchant for manipulation." Few trained managers are available to replace it.[7] This inability of revolutionaries to make totalistic change was predicted by the great writer Joseph Conrad prior to the Bolshevik Revolution. Conrad, who had been in Siberian exile, says that the Russian revolutionaries "are unable to see that all they can effect is merely a change of names." This is because, he continues, tsardom's "autocratic rule rejecting all legality and in fact basing itself upon complete moral anarchism provokes the no less imbecile and atrocious answer of a purely Utopian revolutionism encompassing destruction by the first means to hand."[8] A similar statement can be made about the Soviet regime and the lack of principle and legality it left behind it—to the effect, so far, of "imbecile and atrocious" attempts at governance.

An examination of good secondary literature on the imperial Russian bureaucracy will give us some basis on which to see the influence of that bureaucracy on its Soviet successor—and perhaps even its "post-Soviet" successor. Is there a Russian administrative tradition or pattern that lives on today? This examination is not based on an exhaustive survey of the pertinent literature on tsarist administration. Such a survey could produce a book of its own.[9] We are fortunate that the administration of tsarist

Russia is a topic well covered by many notable scholars, both in Russia and elsewhere. Indeed, historians of Russia have paid a good deal more attention to administration than the scholars of Soviet and post-Soviet Russian politics have.

The form and content of imperial Russian regulations, the nature of procedures, the style of operation, the sociological nature of the bureaucrats and their attitudes toward work and the society, and the nature of the policies adopted and the way they were implemented in the ancien régime can provide us with a basis for historical comparison between systems. Is there continuity as well in the conduct of bureaucratic politics? Bureaucrats are not fully neutral administrators but, in fact, products of their society and act as "permanent politicians."[10]

And did the old system have a victory or victories in the "new"? Many administrators of the Soviet period, particularly the "bourgeois specialists" and others who bridged the two systems, probably carried over into the USSR prerevolutionary images and tacit understandings as to what a "normal" government is like and how it operates. V. V. Shulgin, a right-wing member of the last three Dumas of imperial Russia, wrote as early as 1921 that the "White idea" had triumphed to a degree, in that the Reds adopted some of its central tenets.[11] And remember the "change of sign-post movement" (*smenovekhi*) of non-Marxists who joined the Bolsheviks, partly because they saw them as the most "Russian" among the contenders for power?

Lenin, the "founding father" of the Soviet Union, stated unequivocally more than once that Soviet administration contained elements from that of tsarist Russia. Indeed, he could be quite caustic in noting these continuities, holdovers, and "legacies" in a political system that has been called "tsarism-Leninism." For example, in 1923 he noted that the "defects . . . rooted in the past" of the Soviet state apparatus are "so deplorable, not to say wretched," and that "the past . . . although it has been overthrown, has not been overcome." He went on to say that "so much has been left over" from the "bureaucratic capitalist state machine" of tsarist Russia and added, "We brought over from Tsarist Russia the worst, bureaucratism and Oblomovism, from which we are literally suffocating." Lenin is even said to have called the Soviet administrative apparatus "the old tsarist bureaucratic machine anointed with a little Soviet holy oil." John A. Armstrong has posited continuity between the tsarist and Soviet administrative systems. He notes that both showed "a marked rejection of legal training" and a stress on "technological backgrounds for high administrators" and that these similarities reflect "broad, underlying value assumptions in the two systems."[12] For the term *value assumptions* I would use the term *culture* in its anthropological sense. By *culture* I mean a long-term pattern of thought and action, a pattern that tends not to be questioned or examined except perhaps by some intellectuals among that people.

Even "post-Soviet" Russia is not free of influences from the imperial period. Continuities abound, some from unconscious emulation of the past and others as a result of conscious acts of will and policy. For example, to devise a ceremony for Yeltsin's inauguration in 1996 "the President's men have been poring through history books about the coronations of the tsars to infuse the event with the traditions and grandeur of the Russian empire." And in 1995 the Moscow correspondent of a leading American newspaper was only one of many noting that "the infamous Russian bureaucracy is, if anything, more bloated than ever" and that new license plates were being issued for bureaucrats' cars "to signal their immunity from traffic rules." She concludes by saying that "old habits of hierarchy . . . die hard."[13]

TRANSREGIME CONTINUITY

Continuity that transcends time and revolution is an unavoidable and very ordinary process. For example, although the U.S. political system is unique, many of its key elements can be traced back to various principles, doctrines, practices, and groups in early modern England, for example, the "Diggers" and "Levelers" of the seventeenth-century Puritan Revolution (see the Putney Debates of 1647), nonconformist Christianity, Quakerism, and the philosophy of John Locke. The U.S. Navy is in some ways a direct descendant of the British Navy. (Although this is most true of the surface or "black shoe" U.S. Navy; the submarine service borrowed from the German Navy, whereas the relatively new carrier or "flattop" navy may be the most "American.") Aspects of American regionalism may well derive from British regions.[14] The claim has even been made that the standard but odd distance between railroad rails in the United States, four feet and 8.5 inches, derives, in a rather roundabout way, from the distance between the wheels of a Roman war chariot.

That imperial Russian governmental forms and practices were derived from those of several other states and political systems is well known and not questioned. There are at least three non-Russian general sources for the culture and practices of Russian administration: Byzantium, the Mongol Empire, and Sweden. Kievan Rus may also have been a source as well as Prussia, and in particular areas of administration we might add other states as sources, for example, Holland for naval administration and terminology.

Byzantium provided the Russians with "the beginnings of their statecraft," according to Jaroslav Pelikan.[15] John Lawrence goes further, asserting that "the influence of Byzantine ideas taught the Russians by degrees to look for their political ideal in a mighty unified state under an absolute ruler served by a faithful bureaucracy."[16] Malia writes of "Mongol–Byzantine tsarism." Hosking notes of the Russian Empire, "In its administrative structures, it has been an Asian empire, building upon or adapting the practices of China and the ancient steppe empires." Russian schoolbooks are now presenting the Tatars as laying "the groundwork for the modern Russian state."[17] Byzantium may also have given the Russians a sense of imperial mission. As for the Mongols' effect, one is reminded of Kozyrev, in 1992 when he was the Russian foreign minister, immediately getting the full attention of his Western audience when he began a talk by saying, "Our traditions come mostly, if not altogether, from Asia." Hingley points out that "Moscovite Grand Princes continued to rule on principles absorbed from the Tatars."[18] Charles J. Halperin, relying partly on the work of George Vernadsky, states that "the Mongols had . . . a profound effect on Russian social and political institutions" and that "the Russians absorbed many features of Mongol government." He goes on to say that "the Russians borrowed extensively from Mongol fiscal, military, diplomatic, and administrative institutions" and that there was a living bridge between the Mongol and Muscovite systems in the "assimilated descendants of the Mongols who entered the Muscovite aristocracy" and "made significant contributions to Russian history." (Edward Keenan, a historian at Harvard, once discussed a Russian aristocratic extended family of Mongol origin in a panel discussion during the 1990s.) Although Joseph Fletcher suggests that little of a structured bureaucracy could have come from the Mongols, a reading of Fletcher reveals that Mongol rule was a personalistic one by a supreme leader served by retinues of "slaves and companions" who derived their powers only from him, a style of rule that one can easily recognize in various periods of Russian history.[19] (Some might even see it in Yeltsin's presidency.)

It is likely that Peter I borrowed a great deal in administrative structure and terminology from Sweden because it provided a model of "effective absolutist administration."[20] Sweden was effective. It thwarted Peter's territorial ambitions for many years and defeated him once. Perhaps Peter and other Russian rulers believed that "reform" and "modernization" required maintaining special features of the Russian state, including its relative isolation from society and its capacity to dominate all levels of society, even the nobility. The consequences for the nature of the state's bureaucracy are both obvious and profound. As Yaney puts it,

> For all practical purposes the Russian state evolved apart from Russian society. Its needs and purposes were quite beyond the conscious needs of its subjects, and thus the unity it imposed on them possessed no other institutional form than what the central government itself established. . . . The government

has taken form primarily as an instrument for the tsar (and later, the party secretary) to use in order to direct the energies of the people toward the goals he and his supporters have selected for them.[21]

Clearly, then, the bureaucrats of Russia could not be "civil servants" but had to be "state servants" above all else. As Anisimov points out, "In the absence of institutions of civil society, . . . the state . . . considered the people and the lands of the empire as property of the state."[22]

This formulation is represented well in the Soviet film of the 1970s, *The Chairman (Predsedatel')*, about a collective farm chairman who had performed heroic deeds in reviving his farm after the devastation of war. The film ends with the chairman's funeral, during which a voice proclaims proudly, "He was a man of the state" [*On byl gosudarstvennyi chelovek*], not, significantly, "a man of the party" or "a man of the people." Obviously, the prestige of the Russian state and its servants was still great in the late Soviet period. Hough has pointed out that state bureaucrats sometimes were more important than their comparable figures in the party.[23] It is also worth noting that in the early 1980s some state bureaucrats were admitted to the Politburo, for example, Gromyko, the long-term minister of foreign affairs.

As for bureaucratic continuity in general, Weber has noted that "bureaucracy is among those social structures which are the hardest to destroy," and La Palombara has emphasized the long-term continuity of political and administrative forms and practices, noting that "traditional ways have amazing survival power; they are capable of adapting to even the most radical changes in formal organizational structure."[24] Skocpol shows that the fundamental changes brought about by the Russian and Chinese revolutions "recapitulated certain structural patterns of the old regimes." For example, the "Soviets could build upon economic conditions continuing from the prerevolutionary era" such as the state-dominated "substantial existing heavy-industrial base" to which were applied "direct bureaucratic controls by the Soviet state."[25] It may be facile to say, "From the Tsars to Stalin there is a clear line of continuity. And it has yet to be broken."[26] But particular attitudes and practices can survive even the most disruptive changes. And all states are similar structures, whatever the ideological differences among them. Even the modern, democratic state is not as new as is often thought. Its main features—the army, the police, the judiciary, the prisons, the administration, and the government—were all present under monarchic government and were inherited and adapted in the transition to the liberal democratic system.[27]

But, as Orlovsky has said, surface similarities should not be construed as explanations and, in any case, *continuity* is a "very slippery term." The revolution of 1917 significantly changed the terms in which the Russian state functioned. Accordingly, any claim of continuity must have a sharp focus.[28] Discontinuity, too, exists between the two systems. Malle states, "Continuity between Tsarist and Soviet institutions, however, should not conceal some innovations." Armstrong notes, for example, that the tsarist administrative elite was much more military in background than the Soviet elite was.[29] Yes, discontinuity exists, but institutions have lives and values of their own, irrespective of the ideology or system they serve. In 1996 a book was published in Russia that considers the Ministry of Internal Affairs as one institution from its founding in 1802 into the "post-Soviet" present.[30]

Still, any attempt to establish a relationship of continuity between tsarist and Soviet or post-Soviet administration will be somewhat speculative because seeing such a linkage is an intellectual act of recognition that necessarily chances error while it strives to show a hidden reality. What appears similar and possibly connected may have been borrowed from elsewhere or developed ahistorically. However, having said this, it is at the same time obvious that some tsarist administrative content must have survived the Russian Revolution. Why? For one thing, all the Soviet population in the early days of the new system had lived under the empire. Indeed, as Armstrong says, as late as the 1970s, "about nine-tenths of the . . . present Soviet generation had four generations of ancestors who lived under tsarist rule."[31] Accordingly, many people who served the former system continued their functions under the new, and, after all, people when faced with the challenges of work tend to take the easy way out and copy the old ways. As Weber says, "Destroying public documents overlooks the settled orientation of *man* for keeping to the habitual rules and regulations that continue to exist independently of the documents."[32] Why write a law *de novo* when one can copy an old one on the same topic and make only a few changes? This was actually done by the Soviets, according to various scholars. There is more on this below when the "means of transmittal" are presented. Here it is enough to raise the possibility that nations as well as other human systems, once established, live on within cultural, societal, and intellectual frameworks and boundaries, invisible, that limit change and force generation after generation to act in roughly similar ways with similar means. Arthur Hartman, a former U.S. ambassador to the Soviet Union, tells the story of asking George Kennan, one of the first four American diplomats trained as Russian specialists, for advice prior to taking up his duties in 1981. According to Hartman, Kennan said, "Don't worry about any studies of what has happened since 1917 and the Russian Revolution. Go get yourself a couple of good 19th-century memoirs. . . . You will get more insights into the current situation by reading that material than you will by studying what happened in 1917."[33]

Much of the scholarly writing on Russo-Soviet bureaucracy explicitly emphasizes continuity, even from the Muscovite period. But first we need to lay out some fundamentals of the governance of imperial Russia. This reveals similarities between the tsarist and Soviet systems and their bureaucracies.

FUNDAMENTALS OF TSARIST BUREAUCRACY

Controversy still surrounds this topic, despite the passage of more than eighty years since the end of tsarism.[34] Realism demands recognition of this fact and the fact that a certain imprecision, even "messiness," affects the topic strongly. But this is to be expected in a system of administration with origins in old Muscovy, the Mongol conquest of Russia, and the connections of Russia with Byzantium.[35] Russian reality cannot escape looking "messy" in terms of a "Western" desire to impose order and logic on it. Governmental administration in imperial Russia embodied a number of qualities, or at least raised issues, that would not seem to go together if either logic or conscious and rational design were to apply. First, to what degree was the Russian "bureaucracy" "bureaucratic" in the Weberian sense or even in terms of ordinary European administrative reality? Raeff says that "a better term" is needed for the Russian imperial administration.[36] Agreed, but no obvious or generally agreed-on replacement exits. Hence, *bureaucracy* is used here as a term of convenience for a system of state administration and its members, recognizing that the administration of imperial Russia does not fully fit into our meaning of "bureaucracy."

If it was not Weberian (but which bureaucracy is?), then how "un-Weberian" was it, and in what ways did this manifest itself? The old and difficult question of distinguishing the "politicos" from the "specialists" also applies.[37] To what degree was administration "personalized," that is, not carried out by permanent "bureaucrats" or according to set norms or stable law? And how did the different types of administrators divide their work? What was the particular mix of different administrative traditions—the Muscovite, the Mongol, the Byzantine, the Petrine, and the post-Petrine? Did this produce a particularly "Russian" administration? If so, how did this "sift out" in day-to-day activity? What was the sociological makeup or background of the administrators, and what did this mean for administration and the governmental and social systems? What sort of divisions of thinking (and ideology?) among the administrators existed, and what were their effects? What was the power and "reach" of the bureaucracy, and what did it try to do and not do? Was it content mainly to occupy a societal niche and reap the benefits and perquisites of that position, or did it act on its own and in favor of its own interests? These are all important questions about which the historians are in disagreement.

Some eminent historians of Russia have tried to clarify the less-than-clear nature of imperial Russian bureaucracy. Russia never had a bureaucracy approximating the Weberian model, except possibly during the late nineteenth and early twentieth centuries. According to John LeDonne, there was no state bureaucracy in the full or even partial sense in Russia until perhaps 1830. At that time promotions began to be made on the "bureaucratic" basis of seniority (one reason for the high average age of Russian generals during the Crimean War of the mid-1850s).[38] Marc Raeff points out that the "very nature of autocratic power" and its need to prevent the development of a competing or limiting authority, as well as the desire of the tsar's entourage to preserve his power, long prevented the emergence of any institution that could "bureaucratize" or "regularize" the administration of the empire. Raeff goes on to say that the term *bureaucracy* is inadequate; "a better term is needed to cover the complexity of the imperial government." He later cites the American historian T. Taranovski on the division of tsarist "functionaries" into two rival groups, "liberal reformers" and "conservatives." (Is this sort of bifurcation, with the term *liberal* taken in its European sense only, still present?) The special nature of Russian imperial administration is evident from a reading of Pipes. He emphasizes the wide latitude of action enjoyed by bureaucrats and the confused overlapping of different agencies' areas of competence, as well as what in the West would be called arbitrariness and corruption.[39]

Some reasons for this unusual bureaucracy are given by historians. Pipes mentions the "insignificant" size of the bureaucracy in relation to the number of inhabitants and points out that "the obstacles to bureaucratization were formidable: the size of the country, the thin distribution of the population, difficulties of communication, and, perhaps most of all, lack of money." Yaney emphasizes the "simple fact" that governing Russia in the 1861–1917 period "was a colossally difficult task involving a number of utterly unprecedented problems, the solution of which demanded contradictory policies."[40] (This can also be said of the immediate postcommunist period in Russia.)

Claims of post-tsarist Russian continuity are common. One that sticks in my mind comes from a Polish-born shoe repairman in Amherst, Massachusetts, who once asked me why I was in such a hurry to have some shoes reheeled. When I said that I was going to Russia in a few days, the cobbler looked at me and said with emphasis, "If I you, I not go." When asked why he felt that way, he replied, "Russians don't like educated people." The harsh history of Polish–Russian relations, notably the harsh Russian treatment of Polish intellectuals in both tsarist and Soviet times, gave him good reason for his opinion. Think of Joseph Conrad's family in exile in Siberia. This tsarist–Soviet continuity exists in administration as well. Pintner and Rowney say, "One can think of the history of Russian officialdom as a rope that spans the 350-year period" from "the early seventeenth century to our own times." They point out that under the Bolsheviks "with the governmental reorganization of 1917–18, Imperial Ministries and their functions were not so much abolished as they were broken up into their specialized—and often technical—positions." For example, the Imperial Ministry of the Interior was transformed into a number of specialized agencies. Pintner and Rowney add that this "reorganization" (perhaps an excessively neutral term for the Bolshevik Revolution) expanded the role of the administrator, who became an "engineer bureaucrat" under Soviet rule.[41] That is, a sort of discontinuous continuity can be seen as having been at work between the tsarist and Soviet and post-Soviet periods. Not everything flows smoothly from the past; yet continuity there was, nevertheless. Pipes is in company with many scholars when he notes the continuities in dictatorial means:

> The techniques of police rule, introduced piecemeal by the Russian imperial regime, were first utilized to their fullest potential by their one-time victims, the revolutionaries. . . . Their vision of a proper government was a mirror image of the imperial regime's to the extent that what the latter called "subversion" (*kramola*) they labeled "counter-revolution." . . .
>
> So it was not in the least surprising that almost the instant they took power, the Bolsheviks began to put together the pieces of the imperial proto-police apparatus.[42]

Venturi suggests that because the struggle between the imperial Russian government and the revolutionaries was so bitter and played for unlimited stakes, any middle ground was unable to develop and the revolutionaries became just like the regime in some political values.[43] Pipes goes further: The Bolshevik regime "was mainly shaped by the institutions it inherited from the czarist regime—the autocracy, the secret police, the Siberian exile system, and so forth." The reasons were obvious: "Marxism fell on a soil devoid of traditions of self-rule, observance of law and respect for private property." The result was that some of the features of imperial Russia were also present in the revolutionary successor state: "the urge to empire, economic backwardness, . . . lack of social structure, alienation of society from the state, the weakness of the principles of individualism and entrepreneurship."[44] And certainly Soviet existence became extremely bureaucratized—in the sense of the inescapability of petty bureaucrats and their manipulation of the population, often in the bureaucrats' own interests, through the arbitrary wielding of the power of granting permissions of all sorts in the form of countless little pieces of paper. (As a visiting scholar in Russia in 1977 I felt driven by the immensity of the bureaucracy to avoid bureaucratic regulations, trying to dodge the system whenever I could. As a retired general said to me, "You are almost a Soviet person" [*Vy pochti Sovetskii chelovek*].) The present-day Russian weak state is partly the result of its inhabitants having been forced over the centuries to become "avoiders." As Marshall Goldman notes, "Even in tsarist times, the Russians felt a certain mixed pride in their ability to mislead their governments."[45]

In contrast to the cautions concerning the applicability of the term *bureaucracy* made by LeDonne and Raeff, Dominic Lieven does not hesitate to use it, saying that the later "Russian Empire was governed by a largely bureaucratic elite" and that "the path to political power lay through the civil service in the last decades of the Old Regime." Florinsky quotes a provincial marshal of the nobility, who said in 1859, "The entire life of the people is under governmental tutelage. No question, however trifling, can be dealt with by the people themselves." Nicholas I even said, "Russia is really ruled not by the Emperor, but by the departmental chiefs."[46] Florinsky's statement reflects the fact that the tsarist system was rooted in the borrowing of "the practices of the well-ordered *Polizeistaat*," including the initiation and implementation of legislation by the "central political authority" and "the tentacular spread of the sovereign's power and competence to all areas of public life" through "the constantly expanding administrative apparatus."[47] How else to try to accomplish this exalted aim except through a bureaucracy or a bureaucratic-like body? The aristocracy and the landed gentry could not provide the required "reach" and expertise without both supplementation and transformation. But the older elites of the monarchy were never totally transformed, which is probably one reason that the tsarist civil service was never a Weberian bureaucracy.

This lack of development does not undercut the importance of administrators to tsarist Russia, and it does not preclude a Russian non-Weberian bureaucracy, under a different ideology, continuing to be of crucial importance for Soviet government. Orlovsky says, "Bureaucracy had a centuries-long history in pre-revolutionary Russia during which it functioned as one of the state's principal political and social institutions."[48] The importance of bureaucracy to tsarism, or at least to its "developmental sector" (in contrast to its "traditional sector"), is suggested by Mosse, who notes that it produced for the ancien régime "its economic success, its partial modernization, and the fear it inspired in Germany." Yet the struggle between the developmental and traditional sectors of the bureaucracy also produced "the inherent instability" and the "paradox" of that regime. Taranovski points out that even the "liberal" or "developmental" bureaucrats held many traditional values and viewed themselves "still as dynastic, not public servants" and, therefore, could not produce an alternative to, or oppose, government policy.[49] Elsewhere Taranovski suggests, citing Zaionchkovskii, that the tsar was nevertheless limited to a degree by his top bureaucrats.[50]

PROBLEMS

The significance of imperial Russian bureaucracy was politically great, but the governmental system was negatively affected by several problems of that bureaucracy. Taranovski refers to the Russian bureaucrat as almost a Russian archetype: "The ubiquitous official, uniformed, epauletted, bursting with authoritarian self-esteem, and combining ignorance and stupidity in equal measure with venality and incompetence, looms over the Russian scene as a fugitive from the asylum of Gogol's imagination."[51] This picture works well for the "Soviettime" as well, when all sorts of nonbureaucrats, for example, salespeople, took on the supercilious airs of Russian bureaucrats. Once a salesgirl in a Moscow bookstore rudely snatched back a book I had dared to pick up, and she returned it to the shelves and orderly safety. And remember, Stalin, very much a man of the Russian nineteenth century (born 1879), dressed all sorts of state employees in uniforms.[52] A marshal of nobility said, "The whole of our administration is a vast system of malfeasance raised to the dignity of state government." The nobility of Tver even wrote to the tsar of the "patent bankruptcy of the bureaucratic government." The Table of Ranks, the "very foundation" of Russia's bureaucracy, was a "dead weight and handicap to good administration, for it put a premium on length of service rather than ability . . . [and] killed all incentive for learning and self-improvement," for promotions depended more on titular rank than on ability. And finally, despite its occasional impressive accomplishments, notably under outstanding and exceptional bureaucrats, the bureaucracy "could not generally function as a responsible force for social and economic transformation," a necessity for the survival of the system.[53] In addition to its many other problems, it may have been understaffed.

LINKAGES AND MECHANISMS OF TRANSMITTAL

There has always been continuity in Russian administration. The Bolshevik Revolution was a horrific and decisive change in many ways, but because the tsarist and Bolshevik systems were both Russian there had to be similarities between them. The culture of a people does not change at once with revolution. For example, when Islam went beyond Arabia it achieved some significant and lasting victories, but it did not turn its converts into Arabs.[54] And the Catholic Church, although almost universal in its expansion, is not the same thing in all countries or even neighborhoods in one country. Accordingly, we speak of the "French" Church and so forth.

Prior to the Bolsheviks, Ivan IV and Peter I, each in his own time, had tried to change the Russians, and although each had some success, each also failed to achieve a cultural transformation. Remember what Maxim Gorky said in response to the question asking whether the Whites or the Reds were the cruelest during the Civil War. Both were equally cruel, he replied, because both were Russian. Orlovsky sees in Russian administrative history "a continuum of institutional development—a long process beneath the surface of formal change" and adds that "the growing ennobled bureaucracy of the eighteenth century was an expanded but direct descendant of the various service groups of earlier centuries."[55] This continuum lengthened into the Soviet period—and beyond: "The Bolsheviks were forced to maintain much of the bureaucratic structure after their seizure of power."[56] Waller notes correctly that the issue of continuity is "extremely contentious" and goes on to say,

> The new elite . . . contained not only well-traveled and highly literate Marxist theoreticians, but also very many often totally unlettered cadres. . . . No doubt those cadres were alive to the new ideas and receptive to some extent to new patterns of administrative behaviour that were being enjoined on them. But those new ideas and expectations must at least to some extent have coexisted in their minds with more familiar perceptions of authority, and were presumably all too often influenced by them.[57]

But let us be specific. Lenin said clearly that administrative borrowing from imperial Russia had occurred: "We took over the old machinery of the state and that was our misfortune. . . . Down below there are hundreds of thousands of old officials we got from the tsar." He added that the Bolsheviks lacked the means to exercise effective control over them. He also wrote: "Our State apparatus, with the exception of the People's Commissariat for Foreign Affairs, represents in the highest degree a hangover of the old one, subjected to only the slightest extent to any serious change."[58]

People from the old regime kept on in the new were a major linkage between the two governments. Rigby explicitly states that the Bolsheviks "acquired a functioning bureaucracy, largely inherited *via* the Provisional Government from the Imperial Regime." This bureaucracy included, first, "the 'proletarian' employees—guards, cleaners, office messengers and so on"; second, "many of the junior office staff"; and, third, a "few senior officials." Then, as often happens in reorganizations, "the general run of officials got their old jobs back, and those with specialist qualifications were made particularly welcome." The almost predictable result was "the emergence of structural and operating characteristics similar to those existing in the pre-revolutionary government" and, of course, "less tangible behavior patterns and attitudes" that could have had a "major influence" on Bolshevik governance. Rigby later explains that the takeover of the old ministries meant that certain "models" of government were also acquired, particularly because the Bolsheviks lacked any concrete "blueprints of their own": "Thus it was natural to slip into patterns which were well entrenched in Russian 'political culture.'"[59] Barrington Moore notes that so-called bourgeois specialists "remained an important element in the Soviet industrial establishment throughout the 1930's" and retained "virtually monopolistic control over many of the most fundamental 'premises' of policy decisions."[60] Even instances of Soviet decrees being patterned on tsarist decrees are noted. Edeen is particularly definite on the Bolsheviks' "reliance on the 'capitalist' civil servants," citing a Soviet journal of 1957: "During the course of nearly *two decades'* development of the Soviet state, persons who originated in the petty-bourgeois group . . . comprised the dominant element in the composition of the civil-service corps."[61] Heinzen, in an excellent study of early Soviet agricultural administration, states plainly, "The Bolsheviks did not create a new state in 1917; rather, they inherited one across the revolutionary divide . . . a huge state administration populated by many people whom the Bolsheviks considered to be 'class enemies.'" For example, in 1918 "a full 57 percent" of specialists in one commissariat's central apparatus were "holdovers." In some cases this percentage had actually increased by 1923, six years after the takeover. Holdovers included former White Army officers; gentry; priests and their children; functionaries from the former *zemstva*, known as the "third element"; and members of revolutionary parties opposed to the Bolsheviks such as the Socialist Revolutionaries.[62]

The ending of the USSR enabled Russian scholars to be more explicit on the negative aspects of tsarist–Soviet bureaucratic continuity. Komarov charges that former tsarist bureaucrats transmitted "typical bureaucratic vices of the past" such as red tape, bribery, and "muddleheadedness" to the new administrative cadres as a "social legacy." The holdovers are also charged with having "consciously spread bureaucratism," which was, it is noted, part of the "legacy of previous forms and methods of work." Komarov says that ex-tsarist functionaries were once quite numerous in Soviet agencies in percentage terms—in 1918 in the People's Commissariat of Health they made up 60.9 percent of the employees, and even in the Cheka they made up a striking 16.1 percent, one out of every seven employees.[63] This continuity strongly suggests that the Bolsheviks were not ready to govern.

Continuity can also be attributed to situational and historical factors, not only to people. First, as one Russian scholar says, "From the very outset the authority of the Russian bureaucracy was far broader than it had been in the West. Peter left behind a vast, overcentralized and inefficient bureaucracy. The breakup of the old state machinery in 1917 failed to sever the bureaucracy's roots."[64] The times, or societal conditions, too, were not propitious for a new administrative start. The new regime began in crisis, as a political, ideological, and cultural minority with a fear of Western attack and facing the beginning of Civil War. Top administrators had fled, were being imprisoned or executed, or were joining the White Army. The practical study of administration had only begun. The "militaristic underground" culture of Bolshevism and the "commandist" thinking and behavior of Lenin and other Bolshevik leaders were not conducive to neutral administration. The situation was made worse by the Civil War, at the end of which half the Bolshevik Party had served in the Red Army. The resultant militaristic siege mentality tended to turn administration into authoritarian rule in which the questioning of state administration was branded "counterrevolutionary" activity and was proscribed and punished. Again Russia had a "punitive . . . all-powerful bureaucratic Power."[65]

EXAMPLES OF CONTINUITY

Culture and Style

Culture and style are equated here. By *culture* is meant what a people routinely thinks and does when it is not being introspective or self-analytical. We do not deal here with the "high culture" or the great intellectual accomplishments of Russian civilization. More pointedly, we deal with the assumptions and unconscious patterns of thinking and acting of the Russian imperial administrators. We do realize, however, that there always exist people who are, for some reason, "outside" or "above" the culture surrounding them in their society or place of work. But such people are few. It may even be possible for two or more cultures to coexist within the same societal group. But one will tend to dominate. We need not argue the case that bodies of people who work together come to have shared sets of attitudes and actions, particularly in routine work activity and in dealing with "outsiders," including clients. This has been proven to be so in many places and is one of the bases of the concept of interest group. For example, the sociologist Blau shows, in a wonderful little book based on his close observation within a particular bureaucratic group in the United States, that work culture can be so strong that it leads to ostracism of a member of the group if he or she chooses to act against or outside the group's work culture. Blau noted this when a welfare caseworker treated clients decently. Apparently, this violated some informal norm of the particular bureaucratic work group.[66] Anyone who has worked within a group comes to realize, sometimes as early as the first day on the job, that the other members of the work group, or certainly the "old-timers," share a set of assumptions, values, and routine, even automatic, responses to particular situations. Sometimes the newcomer even has the feeling that he or she has entered an "unreal" or "absurd" world. I myself and my replacement a year later both felt this way only a few days after coming on board a particular U.S. Navy warship. The novel *Catch 22*, however "fictional," catches this situation in a memorable way.

And culture becomes policy as well. Any work group produces its own set of job-connected actions and the justifications for them. This is called "informalism" in the literature. The term means that a set of beliefs, norms, and actions exists in addition to the formal, often written rules for the work organization. Some of the informalism may be illegal, even going against the formal or legal rules. An example from the old U.S. Marine Corps is the sentencing of guards who allowed a prisoner to escape to serve out the escapee's term. A humorous U.S. Navy example of legal informalism is the granting of an extra day's liberty to the sailor who first sights and reports a Coast Guard vessel attempting to ascertain the Navy vessel's speed. My experience in the U.S. government in 1995–96 revealed a great deal of informalism, for example, intra- and interbureaucratic struggle, including withholding of information and even lying between agencies. Absurdist behavior occurred; for example, a group in the State Department had to get information required to do its job from another agency because its superiors had cut it out of the "loop." Looking at the culture of bureaucracy is to a degree an anthropological approach to the state, including, in the realistic words of Gregory Freeze, considering what an institution really means in people's lives. Culture is a determiner of governmental process: "Scholars such as Howard Wiarda, Daniel Bell, and Clifford Geertz have all made the point that cultural factors are as important in shaping political development as technology, modernization, economic development, or institutional change."[67]

What can we say about the culture of the tsarist bureaucracy? Although the state was nominally all-powerful, its effective reach was often limited and even weak, but the state could act with great energy and oppressiveness if it chose and could also find the occasional outstanding bureaucrat to implement its policies well, so long as the bureaucrat stayed on top of the continual bureaucratic and political infighting. (One thinks of Chubais during a good part of the Yeltsin presidency.) Milosz notes "the Russian cult of energy that always emanates from a center of supreme power and breaks through barriers with complete disregard for spontaneous growth." Accordingly, we find in connection with tsarist state administration the frequent use of terminology such as *centralization, oppressive police control*, and *administrative tutelage*, but at the same time we encounter "counterterminology" such as *personalized bureaucratic rule, lack of institutionalization, politicization, lack of supervision of local administration*, and *Oblomovism*.[68] In other words, the tsarist central administration was supposed to be all-powerful, but in reality it was not and often and in many ways simply did not operate in any routinized or effective manner. And it often operated with glacial slowness. Indeed, as a Russian engineer lamented to an American in 1913, "Everything is very slow here, full of formalities, red tape."[69] This was also true during the late Soviet period.

And, in addition, individual administrators at all levels of the system could and did act autonomously and in terms of their personal interests, including pecuniary ones. Gogol's play *The Inspector General* portrays this anomalous situation well both humorously and powerfully. The state was often not "there," only some bureaucrat who acted on the basis of a personal whim—if the bureaucrat even chose to act. The reasons for this situation are various, and certainly the huge size of the country and the weakness of communications had a role. Barbara Tuchman in her classic *The Guns of August* quotes a Russian grand duke who points out that in Russia a state order might never even be received by its intended recipients. But factors beyond the structural also had a role. The lack of an effective legal system and any semblance of a *Rechsstaat* was also a factor. Raeff writes of the "chaos" caused by Russia's lack of an "up-to-date, complete, and easily accessible collection of laws and regulations to direct the functionaries in the performance of their duties." Armstrong even speaks of "the rejection of law." LeDonne says, "Russian justice has always been political justice." Yaney points out that Russia lacked a societal basis for the compilation of a law that would guide its officials.[70] The commonness of cultural factors such as what Westerners would call corruption and a tendency by many bureaucrats to assume administrative work was only paper shuffling, and the rigid observation of narrow rules also played a big role in making Russian administration what it was. This "Russian" administration was not unique to Russia; many underdeveloped countries today have similar administrative systems, and even the First World is not free of such features.

Russian autocracy was not in practice the "well-ordered police state" that may have been the ideal of Russian tsars and their ideologues and top aides. Its operation was heavily affected by personalized decision making, lack of supervision, and political patronage. The result was an unpredictability and arbitrariness that were two of its hallmarks. This does not mean that its actions were always arbitrary or unjust by the standards of Russian culture of the time. Political patronage exists in all political systems. Yet rule by the band of underlings and cronies of the tsar, the *druzhina*, had been a feature of Russian rule for centuries.[71] (The later *nomenklatura*, part of which initiated the new capitalism through theft of state assets, was the Soviet equivalent.) The idea of a social contract was lacking because there had been no feudalism in the Western sense, says LeDonne, who goes on to say that the Russian rulers never accepted the idea of a general good and that for a long time the internal constitution of the ruling class was military, as was that of the *druzhina* of old. As a result,

Russian society and government were long pervaded by "police attitudes and run by police methods."[72] Government's purpose was exploitation. Accordingly, no legalistic, neutral "Weberian" bureaucracy was possible, and nothing close to a "textbook"-type bureaucracy existed until the nineteenth century; even then the Russian "bureaucracy" was still permeated by prebureaucratic, that is, non-Weberian, attitudes and practices.

This fact is exemplified by the "essentially unfettered" local administrative agencies during the reign of Peter I. Local administrators' whims "took precedence over rules and laws," administrative bodies "were a long way from achieving institutionalization," and "cliques based on kinship and mutual services seized control." This pattern had not ended even 200 years later. According to Lincoln, arbitrariness of administration was still common in the mid–nineteenth century and even Russia's bureaucratic reformers acted autocratically. (Again one thinks of key figures in the Yeltsin government at the post-Soviet end of the twentieth century.) And in the late nineteenth century political expediency and politicization were endemic features of the Russian bureaucracy.[73]

Informalism

Informalism was common, as it is in all bureaucracies. Thinking and activity by members of an organization that are unspecified by law or the formal regulations of that organization are unavoidable. As Barnard said, bureaucratic informalism is "indispensable" in fostering communication, maintaining organizational cohesiveness, and giving members of the group a "feeling of personal integrity, of self-respect, of independent choice," that is, informalism allows a bureaucrat to feel that he or she is not just a "cog" but still a human being with the power of choice.[74] However, informalism can go further and make the bureaucracy drift away from its official standards and purposes—even to corruption and other illegalities. The bureaucrat can even become primarily an independent operator serving personal interests. Yaney correctly says that Russian officials, both tsarist and communist, "had" to disrupt the rules, including violating their own decrees, to get their work done.[75] This suggests that the formal rules inhibited performance of functions.

A significant long-term cultural feature of Russian bureaucracy has been what could be called "bureaucratic fetishism"—bureaucracy became a quasi-religious, that is, "sacred," aspect of government. Particularly noticeable in this regard is a ruling assumption in Russia that bureaucratic forms must be observed and the bureaucrat must be highly honored. In other words, in Russia there is a tendency for the bureaucrat to become an acolyte and symbol of the governmental system and its ideology instead of merely a servant of the system performing certain formally set and legally limited functions. Indeed, under both the tsarist and the post-Soviet systems, bureaucrats were so important that elected officials either were equated with them or were quite willing to give up their elected positions to become bureaucrats.[76] Sometimes this approach to bureaucratic activity took on aspects of "cargo-cultism," that is, if the bureaucrat acted out his role in a rigid and undeviating manner, a necessary system-strengthening "ceremony" had been performed that demonstrated the great power of the overall system. A Russian scholar writing in the post-Soviet period says that the "paper-fetishism" that existed under the tsars was continued by the Bolsheviks, as was a culture of talking and philosophizing about work ("Oblomovism") instead of one of stressing actual performance of the work. He goes so far as to blame this pattern on the "habits of the Russian" (*privichki rossiskogo cheloveka*).[77]

Aspects of tsarist bureaucratic informalism are often noted in the literature. Low-level bureaucrats were independent enough to "block orders from above," a sign of "absence of supervision," as well as of a rampant and rule-negating informalism (at least one example of this in the late twentieth century stopped an order of Gorbachev, the general secretary): "The government took action only when the need had become crying; it acted by fits and starts, with little sense of continuity and responsibility." In addition, "precise orders were issued and blindly obeyed throughout the Empire," and the monarch's representatives governed in accordance with their "own notions."[78]

Corruption

Corruption is informalism become illegality, as well as informalism divorced from the formal purposes and rules of the bureaucracy. Florinsky writes of the "self-seeking, corrupt, and inefficient bureaucracy," while Pushkarev says, "In addition to the usual bureaucratic vices, the Russian bureaucratic class . . . was renowned for its money-grubbing and extortionism," partly, he adds, because of that class's "very modest salary." In 1998 Russia's procurator-general said, "The officialdom in Russia never was very law-abiding" and added that today "corruption has spread to all levels of the state mechanism." Kavelin saw the source of the problem in the nature of the Russians, "ourselves." The Russian pattern of illegal informalism lives on.[79] It is apparent not only in the state bureaucracy but also in the new entrepreneurial class and in how that class deals with government and law.

The Bureaucrats Themselves

A reading of Zaionchkovskii suggests a Russian state bureaucracy of mixed composition toward the end of the nineteenth century. Though it was growing, an "insignificant" number of bureaucrats with bourgeois backgrounds worked within it. This suggests that Pintner's data on the early part of the century was still pertinent at century's end. Nobles and former military officers were common, with sons of churchmen not uncommon in the provinces. And although men of the lower class were entering the bureaucracy even in the late eighteenth century, these were mostly sons of the urban lower class, not of peasants. Men of foreign birth were no longer conspicuous. Germans of Russian citizenship could be important at the top; Armstrong has said that they were "especially important." Pintner found that "in the central agencies Lutherans filled 15 percent of the top posts." (This may have been the result of the tsars' search for honest and efficient servitors who were culturally oriented toward performing the official goals of the bureaucracy.) Nobles dominated the top ranks, and "really substantial wealth" (500 serfs or more) was "apparently helpful" in reaching the top. The noble marshals of the nobility "played a vital role in provincial administration until the fall of the old regime," being second in power to the governors, though roughly half the marshals had mortgaged estates and were, as were the nobles as a class, an economically endangered species. (Chekhov's plays present the situation well.)

By mid-century this civil bureaucracy was "an essentially self-perpetuating group." Even earlier, according to Torke, the bureaucracy had become "a caste independent of the *dvorianstvo*" or nobility. By the end of the imperial regime "top bureaucrats were no longer recruited predominantly from either the aristocracy or the landed gentry." A substantial and growing proportion was of non-noble origin, and "another large group consisted of the offspring of senior officials." This is supported by Lincoln's study of Miliutin. Career structures had become differentiated. Mosse writes of three sectors: the "law and order," the "developmental," and the "legal," with a "heavy preponderance" of landless commoners in the developmental sector.[80] A "considerable element of 'meritocracy'" now existed, as shown by the careers of many outstanding bureaucrats, for example, Witte, Stolypin, and others.[81] And the nobility had long been somewhat open to new blood, including non-Russians. As LeDonne points out, "The ticket of entrance into the [aristocratic] ruling class . . . was also given to stable hands, cooks and barbers, riding masters (*bereiter*) and valets, who . . . passed on their noble status to their children."[82] The bureaucracy was a power in its own right toward the end. Taranovski writes of the existence of "two camps" within the bureaucracy, the conservatives and the legalistic reformers, with a "symbiotic relationship of the tsar and his agents." Although Alexander III had "no intention of establishing a united bureaucracy," he was limited in what he could do against the bureaucracy he had. The last tsar was just as limited. But there was a "bottom line"; even "Russia's bureaucratic reformers . . . remained autocratic servants of an autocratic master," Lincoln reminds us.[83]

But how did these very important men act, and what does this tell us about their attitudes and beliefs? Here "answers" can be only guesses and even prejudice. Certainly there were always some bureaucrats who had a true sense of service and strove to be honest and to do a good job. And the outstanding administrators who stood out at the top may well have been matched by others at lower levels. Yet they have had "bad press" overall. Raeff's characterization of ordinary officials of the early nineteenth century persists throughout the century and beyond:

> The majority of the officials were ignorant, timorous clerks without either the power or the ability to make decisions. The circumstances of these clerks . . . were simply appalling. Under such conditions, the clerks were only too willing to accept bribes and gifts. Venality started at the lowest rung where it weighed most heavily on those who needed the protection of the government the most. Their vices, in addition to their inadequate education and training, made it impossible to entrust to the ordinary officials important or responsible tasks. They could only copy papers and file reports. As a result, the governor had to do almost everything himself.[84]

This is not an isolated view. Pushkarev, writing of the same time period, says, "In addition to the usual bureaucratic vices, the Russian bureaucratic class, which received a very modest salary at this time, was renowned for its money-grubbing and extortionism." And Velychenko, writing of the later years of the empire, notes that the tsar's subjects were faced with "administrative unpredictability, arbitrariness and languor" and accordingly interacted in corruption with the bureaucrats and developed "little if any sense of civil morality as understood in western Europe." Possibly many men (there were no women among them) entered on a bureaucratic career "in order to acquire personal advantage, remuneration, rank and benefits." Pipes says that "the idea of office-holding as a public service was entirely alien to the Russian bureaucracy; it was something imported from the west." Near the empire's end "a tendency toward gerontocracy" existed because there was no upper age limit. The worst aspects of the bureaucrats' behavior have been summarized by Pipes. Even the "good-natured and gentle," he says, were "living off the land as if they were foreign conquerors among a subjugated race. Their society resembled a closed order. They tended to associate only with their own kind, fawning on superiors (*nachal'stvo*) and bullying inferiors. . . . They instinctively ejected from their midst the overzealous and scrupulous." Honest officials existed only in the center, in some ministerial offices. Bukharin writes of the behavior of the officials in Bessarabia (Moldavia) during his boyhood: "The 'chinovniks' . . . were all Russians, and usually Russians of a rather specific kind: thick-headed, arrogant, and 'patriotic,' the kind who threw the word Yid around contemptuously and scorned the Moldavians too." Pipes makes the significant point that between 1878 and 1881 the regime, overreacting to the threat of terrorism, began to lay part of the basis for a "bureaucratic-police regime with total-itarian tendencies" by giving officials judicial powers and the ability to sentence Russian citizens to exile on the mere suspicion of subversion.[85]

STRUCTURE, SIZE, DUALITY

As Rigby points out, the Bolsheviks inherited "certain structures" of ad-ministration. Although the word *structure* tends to suggest coherence and solidity, some minimization of these connotations applies here. The struc-ture of the imperial Russian bureaucracy was not at all as logical or clear as it might have been. Another issue is that of size. McClellan says that in 1914 Russia had six hundred thousand civilian bureaucrats representing one official for every fifty-six inhabitants, a figure twice that in Germany, three times that in Britain, and nearly five times that in the United States. The regime was also overcentralized and inefficient, he says. However, some recent research suggests that the Russian bureaucracy "was smaller than its continental counterparts." Velychenko, using a particular methodology, says that the official population ratio was 1:552, one closer to those of European colonies than those of European states themselves. If this is true, why does the tsarist bureaucracy have the image of great size? Velychenko suggests that, given the bureaucracy's behavioral tendencies, the intelligentsia, who produced most of the writers and revolutionaries, would have written of the bureaucracy as large and powerful. Also, says Velychenko, its relatively small size vis-à-vis the great size of the country made it "weaker in formal-legal terms" than its European counterparts and thereby more subject to corruption and other informalist behavior.[86] A "tsar-first" derivative ideology that bureaucrats may well have tended to display to the populace could also have been a factor. Also, the bu-reaucrats may well have taken advantage of the lack of rule of law. In ad-dition, because the opposition was excluded from the recruitment "pool," resentment resulted. And once an image is set, later writers accept and propagate it as if it were "gospel."

Another issue is that of the duality or parallelism of Russian bureau-cratic structure, even in the "post-Soviet" 1990s. Russia has long had a tendency to have two administrative structures routinely and "officially" dealing with one task. It does often happen in administration that two or even more agencies "overlap" in their functioning. However, this is usu-ally either informal or undesired or proscribed behavior. In Russia this tendency has been normal, common, or routine. Yaney puts it well when he says: "Russian administrators have tended to organize themselves into a 'formal-irrational' system even though the terms and ideals of the written laws have been largely 'formal-rational.'" The continuing pattern of parallelism in Russian structures and functions has a Russian historical origin, perhaps originally stemming from the great dualism of Tatar and Russian rule. Ostrowski notes that both Muscovy and the Kipchak Khanate set up dual administrative structures and claims that "the major institutions of Muscovite secular administration in the fourteenth century can be seen as direct cognates of those in the Kipchak Khanate." But Langer speaks of "the dual administration of prince and mayor" in Novgorod, expressed in a number of statutes. Billington, however, emphasizes the *oprichnina* of Ivan the Terrible. Before 1917, Pares wrote of the bureaucracy, "There is overlapping of every kind." In any case, Yeltsin was following a very old tradition when he tried to set up in the regions administrative bodies appointed by him parallel to those led by elected governors. Raeff has argued that imperial Russia came to have two parallel legal systems, one a combination of popular customary tradition and the bureaucratic practice introduced by the Petrine state and the other a foreign-based model introduced in the 1860s.[87]

If we look at an organization chart of the imperial bureaucracy for the period from 1905 to 1914 we find that it is relatively straightforward. There were ten bodies called ministries plus four bodies of the same rank, for example, the Main Administration of the General Staff, all subordinated to the Council of Ministers, its chairman, and above all the lonely eminence of the emperor or tsar. The ten ministries were Internal Affairs, Justice, Finances, Communications, Trade and Industry (new at the time), Education, Defense ("military"), the Navy, Foreign Affairs, and the Imperial Household.[88]

PROCESS AND PROBLEMS—"THE WAY THINGS WORKED"

Much about this process could be derived from the preceding discussion. Perhaps the fundamental point about process is that because "from the very outset the authority of the Russian bureaucracy was far broader" than that of bureaucracies in the West, it was not regularized and was often inefficient with a tendency to excessive personalization. Even Russians could lose patience with the process and curse it—though there was nothing they could do to improve it. In a letter just before the start of World War I a Russian engineer relates how difficult it was for him just to retrieve a letter from the post office: "When I happen to get a notice from our post office about a registered letter addressed to the firm of which I am a manager I have to hunt after three of our partners to secure their signatures, to go to the post office personally and to present that notice together with my passport and only then may I get that letter, very often a foolish, good for nothing one."[89] This letter indicates the Russian tendency to overformalization and fetishization of the administrative process. The phenomenon is long-standing.

Raeff notes that during the eighteenth century local administration was "subject to arbitrary and fantastic interpretation. The whim of local administrators and the personal authority of influential figures in the region took precedence over rules and laws." Cliques "based on kinship and mutual services" could take over the administrative apparatus. Later, says Crankshaw, Nicholas I used to indulge his "exaggerated passion for ad hoc committees . . . cutting clean across the usual ministerial channels and reporting directly to him" and elevated his own chancery into a "formidable center of power." Yeltsin did the same. (No doubt it is "Russian" practices like these that gave rise to the term *czar* in American administration, for example, *drug czar* and so on.) The center was formidable in a way, but Yaney, writing of the eighteenth and nineteenth centuries, notes that "there was a general lack of systematic communication between the central offices and the countryside" and that, given "the absence of an operational system outside the capital cities, then, a minister's orders were likely to produce unforeseen and unintended results when they were carried out." As noted, Tuchman quotes a grand duke who said that in Russia an order might never even be delivered. Yaney also points out that for a variety of reasons Russian administration "was manifestly incapable of operating on a systematic basis," and, accordingly, "arbitrary authority . . . remained a vital element in government operations at all levels." The reasons were several. Russian administration did not operate within a formalistic legal framework, and without arbitrariness as routine the "system could not exist." In addition, because "for Russian servitors . . . the government organization was itself their salvation," they "conceived of the state as an agency of their ministry" and acted in self-serving ways that produced "profound disharmony" within the tsarist government. Daniels sees in the late nineteenth and early twentieth centuries a great reluctance of bureaucrats to make decisions, a tendency to push responsibility up the hierarchy, even to the tsar, and a pattern of corruption on a "mass scale." Decisions could be taken with great slowness, and "delays of many years were not unusual." As McClellan puts it so well, "There were too many bureaucrats, too many procedures, too little incentive to perform efficiently. Such a system bred corruption, fear, suspicion, caution, and above all inertia." Russians, confronted with such a government, "had little choice but to persist in time-honored practices like denunciation, petitioning, bribery, influence peddling even in routine affairs," notes Velychenko. In other words, arbitrariness and corruption from the bureaucracy produced hostility toward government and public life and inhibited the development of civil society.[90] This tended to lead to more arbitrariness from above in government's attempt to encompass the sea of incoherence and opposition below. The revolutions of 1905 and 1917 were the results. The bureaucratic process was disruptive of the tsarist system itself.

CONCLUSION

Although no one can blame the fall of the Romanov dynasty and of the imperial system just on poor administration alone, it played a crucial role. The empire had adequate stocks of grain, but the state bureaucracy could not get it in the necessary quantity to the places where large groups of people lived—St. Petersburg (then Petrograd), for example. The result is well known. Women took to the streets in protest at the shortages of bread, and the rest is history. Yes, revolutionaries were actively involved, but without the grievances built up over the years by the tsarist system, as strengthened by the quagmire of war and other problems, including those resulting from poor governance, the empire might have survived. It is possible that imperial Russia was doomed by her inability to adapt to the requirements of that modernity she was seeking and by that demanding international political game in which her leaders insisted she compete.

But even here administration was a factor. As Crankshaw writes, "Yet how could a society of obedient functionaries form a suitable stock on which to graft artificially the technological profusion of the West . . . ?" He notes that near the end Russia had some extremely and energetically competent men in government, Stolypin and Witte, for example. Indeed, "Stolypin may well have been 'the most notable figure in Europe' of his day." But these extraordinary bureaucrats could not do what had to be done on their own and within the only partially reformed tsarist system: "Russia was not yet ready for Stolypin. . . . A single man left to dominate or to fight alone is liable to go mad." Stolypin was saved from madness by being assassinated by a double agent. Raeff also ends a book with reference to the systemic limitations favored by the modernizing bureaucrats. Because "Russian society was not yet sufficiently organized to provide an independent power base" to the modernizing bureaucrats—or "liberals," as he calls them—the conservative bureaucrats got the crucial support of the monarch, who "remained the final arbiter." There was "no escape" short of violence, concludes Raeff.[91] "Holy Russia" triumphed over "good government" only to be undone by war, societal change, and evil but attractive utopian ideas and their henchmen. This utopia, too, was to be taken over by the Russian way.

This chapter has dealt with a number of aspects of the state bureaucracy of imperial Russia and also with several issues of importance to this book: the nature of the tsarist bureaucrats, the structure of their bureaucracy and how it operated, and, implicitly, its policies or "outputs." I have also tackled the important topic of transregime continuity, in terms of both politico-historical issues and the Russian twentieth-century specifics. We return to the theme of continuity later in the book, for it cannot be avoided in any discussion of the late Soviet bureaucracy, the main subject here, or of the post-Soviet governmental arrangement of Russia.

NOTES

1. Edward Gibbon, *Gibbon's Decline and Fall of the Roman Empire*, ed. Moses Hadas (New York: Fawcett Premier, 1962), 248.

2. See Ezra N. Suleiman, *Elites in French Society: The Politics of Survival* (Princeton: Princeton University Press, 1978); and Government of France, *News from France*, 17 September 1993.

3. Rasma Karklins, book review, *Slavic Review* (winter 1994): 1156; Daniel T. Orlovsky, "Recent Studies on the Russian Bureaucracy," *Russian Review* 35, no. 4 (October 1976): 448.

4. See Anatol Lieven's introduction to his *Chechnya: Tombstone of Russian Power* (New Haven: Yale University Press, 1998). I have used the version Lieven placed on *Johnson's Russia List*, 14 July 1998.

5. James R. Millar and Sharon L. Wolchik, "Introduction: The Social Legacies and the Aftermath of Communism," in *The Social Legacy of Communism* (Cambridge: Cambridge University Press, 1997 [1994]), 1–2.

6. Ryszard Kapuscinski, *The Soccer War* (New York: Vintage, 1992), 103.

7. *New York Times*, 4 June 1994, 1. Unbelievable as it may seem, when I was in a South African government office building in 1986, another academic (who had also lived in the Soviet Union) and I both remarked on how similar the offices seemed to Soviet government offices. Why? No obvious answer suggests itself. Were we noting some sort of common continuity derived from northern European (Dutch?) administrative style—or was the similarity based on the administration of dictatorship? Or was there another explanation that escaped us?

8. Joseph Conrad, "Author's Note," in *Under Western Eyes* (Garden City, N.Y.: Anchor Books, 1963), xi. This semi-Dostoyevskyan novel is also a study in Russian culture.

9. Possibly the field could use a new summational review article on the secondary literature in Russian, English, and other languages on the bureaucracy and administration of imperial Russia.

10. Antony Jay, *Management and Machiavelli* (London: Hodder and Stoughton, 1967).

11. V. V. Shulgin, *1920 God* (Sofia, 1921), cited in Leslie Milne, "The Image of the White Guard in the Works of Marina Tsvetaeva and Mikhail Bulgakov," *Sbornik*

(Leeds, England), no. 2 (summer 1976): 12. For information on Shulgin, see the entry in S. V. Utechin, *A Concise Encyclopaedia of Russia* (New York: Dutton, 1964).

12. Ye. I. Komarov, *Biurokratizm—na sud glasnosti!* (Moscow: Political Literature, 1989), 26; V. I. Lenin, "Better Fewer, but Better," *Pravda*, 4 March 1923 (also in *Collected Works*, vol. 33, 487–502), cited in V. I. Lenin, *On the Soviet State Apparatus* (Moscow: Progress, 1977), 412, 426; John A. Armstrong, "Tsarist and Soviet Elite Administrators," *Slavic Review* 31, no. 1 (March 1972): 27.

13. Two columns by Alessandra Stanley in the *New York Times*, 3 August 1996 and 23 May 1995, A1.

14. See David Hackett Fischer, *Albion's Seed: Four British Folkways in North America*, vol. 1 of *America: A Cultural History* (New York: Oxford University Press, 1989); and Roger Thompson, *Mobility and Migration: East Anglian Founders of New England, 1629–1640* (Amherst: University of Massachusetts Press, 1994). Fischer makes a strong case that "folkways" from four British regions were carried over into North America, for example, that the American religious camp meeting is an old institution from the British borderlands and that even such apparently "American" words as *redneck, leather stocking*, and *cracker* are imports from Britain.

15. Jaroslav Pelikan, review of John Julius Norwich, *Byzantium: The Apogee* (New York: Knopf, 1992), *New York Review of Books*, 16 February 1992, 9.

16. John Lawrence, *A History of Russia* (New York: Mentor [New American Library], 1962), 35.

17. Martin Malia, *Russia under Western Eyes* (Cambridge: Harvard University Press, Belknap Press, 1999), 183; Geoffrey Hosking, *Russia and the Russians: A History* (Cambridge: Harvard University Press, Belknap Press, 2001), chap. 1, from *Johnson's Russia List*, 9 July 2001; Judith Matloff, "Russia Revisits History in Its School Textbooks," *Christian Science Monitor*, 28 March 2000, from *Johnson's Russia List*, 28 March 2002. For an interpretation of pre-Petrine Russia as a Eurasian civilization, see Irina B. Orlova, *Evraziiskaia tsivilizatsiia* (Moscow: Norma, 1998).

18. Andrei Kozyrev, speaking to the meeting of the Commission on Security and Cooperation in Europe, December 1992, in Jerrold L. Schecter, *Russian Negotiating Behavior: Continuity and Transition* (Washington, D.C.: U.S. Institute of Peace Press, 1998), 49. Schecter also quotes (in *Russian Negotiating Behavior*, 19) from Ronald Hingley, *The Russian Mind* (New York: Charles Scribner's Sons, 1977), 197.

19. Charles J. Halperin, "George Vernadsky, Eurasianism, the Mongols, and Russia," *Slavic Review* 41, no. 3 (fall 1982): 489–90; Joseph Fletcher, "The Mongols: Ecological and Social Perspectives," *Harvard Journal of Asiatic Studies* 46, no. 1 (June 1986): 17, 20, 22.

20. Max J. Okenfuss, review of Claes Peterson, *Peter the Great's Administrative and Judicial Reforms: Swedish Antecedents and the Process of Reception* (Stockholm: Juridska Fakulteten, 1979), *Slavic Review* 40, no. 1 (spring 1981): 105–6.

21. George L. Yaney, "Law, Society and the Domestic Regime in Russia, in Historical Perspective," *American Political Science Review* 59, no. 2 (June 1965): 381, 383.

22. Evgenii Anisimov, lecture at the Kennan Institute for Advanced Russian Studies, Washington, D.C., 14 May 1991, quoted in Kennan Institute for Advanced Russian Studies, *Meeting Report* 8, no. 16. Anisimov was then a senior researcher at the Institute of History of the Academy of Sciences of the USSR in Leningrad.

23. See Jerry F. Hough, *The Soviet Prefects: The Local Party Organs in Industrial Decision-Making* (Cambridge: Harvard University Press, 1969).

24. Max Weber, *From Max Weber: Essays in Sociology*, eds. H. H. Gerth and C. Wright Mills (New York: Oxford University Press, 1946), quoted in Max Weber, "Bureaucracy and Revolution," in *Revolutions: Theoretical, Comparative, and Historical Studies*, 2d ed., ed. Jack A. Goldstone (Fort Worth: Harcourt Brace, 1994), 35; Joseph La Palombara, ed., *Bureaucracy and Political Development* (Princeton: Princeton University Press, 1963), 13.

25. Theda Skocpol, "Old Regime Legacies and Communist Revolutions in Russia and China," in *Revolutions: Theoretical, Comparative, and Historical Studies*, 2d ed., ed. Jack A. Goldstone (Fort Worth: Harcourt Brace, 1994), 251, 250 (originally published in *Social Forces* 55, no. 2 [December 1976]: 284–315).

26. Roger Draper, "Russia's Impermanent Revolution," *The New Leader*, 11–25 April 1994, 16.

27. Tony Bunyan, *The History and Practice of the Political Police in Britain* (London: Quartet Books, 1977), 301.

28. Daniel T. Orlovsky, comments at a panel of the American Association for the Advancement of Slavic Studies (AAASS). I regret that the notes lack a date.

29. Silvana Malle, *The Economic Organization of War Communism, 1918–1921*, unpublished manuscript (ca. 1982), 271; Armstrong, "Tsarist and Soviet Elite Administrators," 26–27.

30. V. F. Nekrasov, V. I. Vorontsov, and A. G. Gorlov, *Organy I voiska MVD Rossii: Kratkii istoricheskii ocherk* (Moscow: Ob"edinennaia redaktsia MVD Rossii, 1996). This reminds me of the Soviet radio announcer in the 1970s who referred to a military unit marching past Lenin's Tomb as one founded in the 1700s.

31. Armstrong, "Tsarist and Soviet Elite Administrators," 2.

32. Weber, *From Max Weber*, 36.

33. "A Conversation with Arthur Hartman," *Harvard University Gazette* (spring 1993): 12. Another story, perhaps apocryphal, that illustrates Russian continuity is the claim that the first American ambassador to the USSR sent as his initial cable to Washington a copy of the final cable of the last American ambassador to imperial Russia (Alexander Dallin, personal communication, January 1964).

34. Russian books on the imperial bureaucracy include A. A. Dorskaia, *Istoriia gosudarstvennykh uchrezhdenii Rossii do 1917g.* (St. Petersburg: RGPU, 1998); and P. A. Zaionchkovskii, *Pravitel'stvennyi apparat samoderzhavnoi Rossii v XIX v.* (Moscow: "Mysl'," 1978).

35. Marc Raeff once said, apropos this topic, "As an old *pomeshchnik* [landowner], I like messiness" (national meeting of the AAASS, Philadelphia, 19 November 1994). The Mongol origins of the Russian bureaucracy are specified by both Donald Ostrowski and George L. Yaney. The former says that "the forms of civil and military institutions in fourteenth century Muscovy were overwhelmingly Mongol in origin" (see Donald Ostrowski, "The Mongol Origins of Muscovite Political Institutions," *Slavic Review* 49, no. 4 [winter 1990]: 541); whereas the latter points out that "the chief functions" of Russian princes at one time were "the collection of the Tatar horde's tribute and the recruiting of its armed forces" (see George L. Yaney, *The Systemization of Russian Government* [Urbana: University of Illinois Press, 1973], 22). However, Russian administration was not purged of all pre-Mongol practices by the "Tartar yoke."

36. Marc Raeff, *Understanding Imperial Russia*, trans. from French by Arthur Goldhammer (New York: Columbia University Press, 1984), 197.

37. This is the question that Professor Wallace Sayre of Columbia University suggested in 1964 ought always to be asked first in examining bureaucracy.

38. John LeDonne, personal communication, Philadelphia, 19 November 1994. And see his *Ruling Russia* (Princeton: Princeton University Press, 1984). Here LeDonne often notes the antibureaucratic nature of some of Catherine I's reforms and sees the beginnings of a true bureaucratic class only after the passage of two generations. He states, for example, that "the vast increase in the number of administrative personnel" in the reign of Catherine "was certainly no part of a process of bureaucratization" but, rather, "a division of the spoils on a grand scale and benefited chiefly the rank-and-file nobility" (*Ruling Russia*, 101). Yet he also says, "However, there already existed an incipient bureaucracy" in the clerks, scribes, and noncommissioned officers who made up a "political world of their own" with their own interests in "stable impersonal and non-political norms and procedures" (*Ruling Russia*, 15).

39. Raeff, *Understanding Imperial Russia*, 65, 197–98; Richard Pipes, *Russia under the Old Regime* (New York: Scribner's, 1974), chap. 11, "Towards the Police State."

40. Pipes, *Russia under the Old Regime*, 281; Yaney, *The Systemization of Russian Government*, 243.

41. Walter M. Pintner and Don Karl Rowney, "Officialdom and Bureaucratization: Conclusion," in *Russian Officialdom: The Bureaucratization of Russian Society from the Seventeenth to the Twentieth Century*, eds. Walter M. Pintner and Don Karl Rowney (Chapel Hill: University of North Carolina Press, 1980), 369–70, 379.

42. Pipes, *Russia under the Old Regime*, 317.

43. See Franco Venturi, *Roots of Revolution: A History of the Populist and Socialist Movements in Nineteenth Century Russia* (New York: Grosset and Dunlap, 1960).

44. Richard Pipes, *Russia under the Bolshevik Regime* (New York: Knopf, 1994), 29–30, quoted in Marshall D. Shulman, book review, *New York Times Book Review*, 17 April 1994, 3; Cynthia Hyla Whittaker, review of Marc Raeff, *Political Ideas and Institutions in Imperial Russia*, *Slavic Review* 54, no. 3 (fall 1995): 765.

45. Marshall I. Goldman, "Loans Keep Crisis Alive," *Moscow News*, 21 July 1998, from *Johnson's Russia List*, 21 July 1998.

46. Dominic Lieven, *Russia's Rulers under the Old Regime* (New Haven: Yale University Press, 1989), 29, 121; Michael T. Florinsky, *Russia: A History and an Interpretation*, vol. 2 (New York: Macmillan, 1960), 896–97; V. O. Kliuchevsky, *Kurs Russkoi istorii*, vol. 3 (Ann Arbor: J. W. Edwards, 1948), 8, quoted in Tibor Szamuely, *The Russian Tradition* (New York: McGraw-Hill, 1974), 135.

47. Marc Raeff, "Seventeenth-Century Europe in Eighteenth-Century Russia?" *Slavic Review* 41, no. 4 (winter 1988): 613, 615.

48. Orlovsky, "Recent Studies on the Russian Bureaucracy," 467.

49. Werner E. Mosse, "Russian Bureaucracy at the End of the *Ancien Régime*: The Imperial State Council, 1897–1915," *Slavic Review* 39, no. 4 (December 1980): 632; Theodore Taranovski, "The Imperial Bureaucracy in the Reign of Alexander III," mimeographed paper prepared for the Central Slavic Conference of the AAASS, St. Louis, Mo., November 1971, 16–17.

50. Theodore Taranovski, "Alexander III and His Bureaucracy: The Limitations on Autocratic Power," *Canadian Slavonic Papers* 26, nos. 2–3 (June–September 1984): 213–14.

51. Taranovski, "The Imperial Bureaucracy in the Reign of Alexander III," 1.

52. President Nixon had similar tendencies, once dressing up the White House guards in ornate German-type police uniforms (which later wound up on a high school band in the Midwest).

53. Florinsky, *Russia*, 897, 1066; Boris Mironov, "Bureaucratic- or Self-Government: The Early Nineteenth Century Russian City," *Slavic Review* 52, no. 2 (summer 1993): 255; Marc Raeff, *Michael Speransky: Statesman of Imperial Russia, 1772–1839* (The Hague: Martinus Nijhoff, 1969), 63–64; W. Bruce Lincoln, *Nikolai Miliutin: An Enlightened Bureaucrat of the 19th Century* (Newtonville, Mass.: Oriental Research Partners, 1977), 103.

54. This is suggested in Richard Bernstein, review of V. S. Naipaul, *Beyond Belief: Islamic Excursions among the Converted Peoples* (New York: Random House, 1998), *New York Times*, 8 July 1998, B9. According to Bernstein, the book is "a portrait of a group of societies that turned to Islam partly to reject pasts . . . that were deemed inauthentic by local revolutionaries. But in so doing, these societies adopted a foreign creed that was also inauthentic and that replicated the injustices that had motivated the revolutionaries in the first place" (review, B9).

55. Orlovsky, "Recent Studies on the Russian Bureaucracy," 454, 462.

56. Jonathan R. Adelman, *Torrents of Spring: Soviet and Post-Soviet Politics* (New York: McGraw-Hill, 1995), 89.

57. Michael Waller, *The End of the Communist Power Monopoly* (Manchester: Manchester University Press, 1993), 24. Waller then says "an acceptance of leadership roles and a tendency to pass responsibility upwards" were particularly strong in Russian traditional behavior (*The End of the Communist Power Monopoly*, 25).

58. V. I. Lenin, *Collected Works*, vol. 33 (Moscow, 1965), 430, quoted in Mary Kaldor, *The Disintegrating West* (New York: Hill and Wang, 1978), 32. Lenin was speaking to the 4th Congress of the Comintern in 1922. See V. I. Lenin, *Polnoe Sobranie Sochinenii*, 5th ed., 45, 383, quoted in T. H. Rigby, *Lenin's Government: Sovnarkom, 1917–1922* (London: Cambridge University Press, 1979), 51. Rigby writes of a "high level of continuity in the central administrative machinery of the Russian state" (*Lenin's Government*, 51).

59. Rigby, *Lenin's Government*, 40, 47, 50–51, 64, 234–35. Even a critical review of this book accepts as fact the "curious fusion of Bolshevik ideas and existing governmental practices" (*Soviet Studies* 32, no. 4 [October 1980]: 599).

60. Barrington Moore, *Soviet Politics* (Cambridge: Harvard University Press, 1951), 163, quoted in Karl W. Ryavec, *Implementation of Soviet Economic Reforms* (New York: Praeger, 1975), 11–12. Moore is citing Alimov and Studenikin in Ye. B. Pashukanis, ed., *15 let Sovetskogo stroitel'stva* (Moscow, 1932).

61. Alf Edeen, "The Soviet Civil Service: Its Composition and Status," in *Revolutions: Theoretical, Comparative, and Historical Studies*, 2d ed., ed. Jack A. Goldstone (Fort Worth: Harcourt Brace, 1994), 208. Unfortunately, Edeen does not provide additional information on the source he quotes. Other works that emphasize tsarist–Soviet continuity include, on industry, Bruno Grancelli, *Soviet Management*

and Labor Relations (London: Allen and Unwin, 1987); and, on the military, Mark von Hagen, *Soldiers in the Proletarian Dictatorship: The Red Army and the Soviet Socialist State, 1917–1930* (Ithaca: Cornell University Press, 1990).

62. James W. Heinzen, "'Alien' Personnel in the Soviet State: The People's Commissariat of Agriculture under Proletarian Dictatorship, 1918–1929," *Slavic Review* 56, no. 1 (spring 1997): 80, 81, 91, 98.

63. Komarov, *Biurokratizm*, 24, 26, 42, 52. Komarov gives no source for the statistics. Some holdovers had been not in the tsarist government but in "private and social agencies." One negative side of continuity, bureaucratism or bureaupathology, is discussed in my "Russo-Soviet Bureaucratism: Recent Russian Views," *The Soviet and Post-Soviet Review* 23, no. 1 (1996): 67–69.

64. Vasily Selunin, "Istoki," *Novyi mir*, no. 5 (May 1988); *Current Digest of the Soviet Press* 40, no. 40 (2 November 1988): 17.

65. R. I. Khasbulatov, *Biurokraticheskoe gosudarstvo* (Moscow: Megapolis-Takom, 1991), 13. The author, a Chechen, was sent into internal exile with his family by this "Power." Alexander Bogdanov, who may have invented the term *war communism*, has said that by 1918 Bolshevism was a movement with "the logic, the culture, and the methods of the army barrack" (*Voprosy sotsialisma* [Moscow: Izdatel'stvo politicheskoi literatury, 1980], 342, quoted in Alec Nove, "The Soviet System in Retrospect: An Obituary Notice," the Fourth Annual W. Averell Harriman Lecture, 17 February 1993 [New York: Columbia University Press, 1993], 12).

66. Peter M. Blau, *The Dynamics of Bureaucracy*, rev. (2d) ed. (Chicago: University of Chicago Press, 1963 [1955]).

67. See the conference report by Jane Burbank, "Revisioning Imperial Russia," *Slavic Review* 52, no. 3 (fall 1993): particularly 562, 566. Nicolai N. Petro, *Russian Democracy: An Interpretation of Political Culture* (Cambridge: Harvard University Press, 1995), 4. Petro advocates utilizing the "symbolist" or "interpretive" approach to culture instead of the "behavioral" or "subjectivist" civic culture model (see *Russian Democracy*, 20).

68. Czeslaw Milosz, *Native Realm: A Search for Self-Definition*, trans. from Polish by Catherine S. Leach (New York: Doubleday, 1968), 146. For some good, brief, conventional characterizations of tsarist administration, see Florinsky, *Russia*, 765, 769, 880, 1087. Florinsky writes of the government and its "marked tendencies towards centralization, bureaucratism, and oppressive police control, hardly novel departures in Russian administrative practice" (*Russia*, 765).

69. Pskov, letter, 26 August/8 September 1913 (a four-page English-language letter in my possession).

70. Raeff, *Michael Speransky*, 65; Armstrong, "Tsarist and Soviet Elite Administrators," 27; John LeDonne, speaking at the Russian Research Center, Harvard University, 12 May 1989 (my notes); Yaney, "Law, Society and the Domestic Regime in Russia, in Historical Perspective," 380.

71. Lawrence sees this pattern as early as the reign of Andrew of Bogolyubovo, the son of Georgyi Dolgoruki, perhaps the founder of Moscow, who "governed through his own creatures," a practice to be seen again and again in later Russian history (see *A History of Russia*, 44). LeDonne also has referred to the ruler governing with a *druzhina*. He says that the *druzhina* expanded into "the ruling class" (speaking at the Russian Research Center, Harvard University, 12 May 1989). Fi-

nally, Lieven mentions the politicization of the bureaucracy (see *Russia's Rulers under the Old Regime*, 365n22).

72. LeDonne, speaking at the Russian Research Center, Harvard University, 12 May 1989.

73. Raeff, *Understanding Imperial Russia*, 82–83; Daniel Brower, review of W. Bruce Lincoln, *The Great Reforms: Autocracy, Bureaucracy, and the Politics of Change in Imperial Russia* (DeKalb: Northern Illinois University Press, 1990), *Slavic Review* 52, no. 1 (spring 1993): 175–76; Yaney, *The Systemization of Russian Government*, 293, citing P. A. Valuev, minister of internal affairs 1861–68.

74. Chester I. Barnard, "Informal Organizations and Their Relation to Formal Organizations," a chapter from his classic book, *The Functions of the Executive* (Cambridge: Harvard University Press, 1938), reproduced in Jay M. Shafritz and Albert C. Hyde, eds., *Classics of Public Administration* (Oak Park, Ill.: Moore Publishing Co., 1978), 52. Barnard points out that "when formal organizations come into operation, they create and require informal organizations" ("Informal Organizations and Their Relation to Formal Organizations," 51).

75. Yaney, "Law, Society and the Domestic Regime in Russia, in Historical Perspective," 386.

76. See Mironov, "Bureaucratic- or Self-Government," 233–55. In the nineteenth century "elected officials were equated with state functionaries (*chinovniki*) and were given ranks according to their positions" (Mironov, "Bureaucratic- or Self-Government," 242).

77. Komarov, *Biurokratizm*, 11, 43.

78. Mironov, "Bureaucratic- or Self-Government," 245, 249; Raeff, *Michael Speransky*, 230–31.

79. Florinsky, *Russia*, 1088; Sergei Pushkarev, *The Emergence of Modern Russia: 1801–1917*, trans. Robert H. McNeal and Tova Yedlin (New York: Holt, Rinehart and Winston, 1963), 27; Procurator-General Yuriy Skuratov, at a press conference in Moscow, 2 July 1998, from *Johnson's Russia List*, 8 July 1998; Kavelin, quoted in W. Bruce Lincoln, *The Great Reforms: Autocracy, Bureaucracy, and the Politics of Change in Imperial Russia* (DeKalb: Northern Illinois University Press, 1990), 171. Vietnam also is plagued by corruption as "part of day-to-day life" (see *New York Times*, 25 May 1999, A5).

80. Zaionchkovskii, *Pravitel'stvennyi apparat samoderzhavnoi Rossii v XIX v.*, 223–24; John A. Armstrong, "Toward a Framework for Considering Nationalism in East Europe," *East European Politics and Society* 2, no. 2 (spring 1988): 296; Walter M. Pintner, "The Social Characteristics of the Early Nineteenth-Century Russian Bureaucracy," *Slavic Review* 29, no. 3 (September 1970): 431, 434, 436, 438, 442; G. M. Hamburg, "Portrait of an Elite: Russian Marshals of the Nobility, 1861–1917," *Slavic Review* 40, no. 4 (winter 1981): 585–86, 593; Hans-Joachim Torke, quoted in Mosse, "Russian Bureaucracy at the End of the *Ancien Régime*," 617n11 (exact writing quoted by Torke is not clear); Lincoln, *Nikolai Miliutin*, 103; Mosse, "Russian Bureaucracy at the End of the *Ancien Régime*," 630, 628.

81. A recent Russian book on Witte is Sergei Iul'evich, *Vitte: Gosudarstvennyi deiatel'* (Moscow: Institut Ekonomiki RAN, 1999). Recent books on Stolypin include Viacheslav Khotulev, *Petr Stolypin: Tragediia Rossii* (Moscow: Olimp, 1998); and Peter Waldron, *Between Two Revolutions: Stolypin and the Politics of Renewal in*

Russia (DeKalb: Northern Illinois University Press, 1998). Putin has been likened to Stolypin in the Russian press. See, for example, *Russia Business List*, no. 402 (20 September 2002).

82. John P. LeDonne, "Outlines of Russian Military Administration 1762–1796," *Jahrbücher für Geschichte Osteuropas* 33 (1985): 192, 194. A recent richly illustrated, fact-filled book on the imperial bureaucracy is L. E. Shepelev, *Chinovnyi mir Rossii: XVIII-nachalo XX v.* (St. Petersburg: Iskusstvo-SPB, 1999).

83. Taranovski, "Alexander III and His Bureaucracy," 207, 215–16; Brower, review, 172.

84. Raeff, *Michael Speransky*, 235–36.

85. Pushkarev, *The Emergence of Modern Russia*, 27; Stephen Velychenko, personal communication, 12 March 1999; Mironov, "Bureaucratic- or Self-Government," 244, citing an imperial Russian state archive; Lieven, *Russia's Rulers under the Old Regime*, 147; Pipes, *Russia under the Old Regime*, 286–87, 298–99; Richard Bernstein, review, quoting Nikolai Bukharin, *How It All Began*, trans. Stephen F. Cohen (New York: Columbia University Press, 1998), *New York Times*, 25 May 1998, B10.

86. Rigby, *Lenin's Government*, 234; Woodford McClellan, *Russia: A History of the Soviet Period*, unpublished manuscript, 10 (I have not been able to find this material in the published version [Englewood Cliffs, N.J.: Prentice-Hall, 1986]); Stephen Velychenko, personal communication, 12 March 1999.

87. Yaney, "Law, Society and the Domestic Regime in Russia in Historical Perspective," 385n24; Ostrowski, "The Mongol Origins of Muscovite Political Institutions," 530; James H. Billington, *The Icon and the Axe* (New York: Vintage, 1970), 67; Bernard Pares, *Russia: Between Reform and Revolution* (New York: Schocken, 1962), 136, quoted in Ryavec, *Implementation of Soviet Economic Reforms*, 12; *Obshchaia gazeta*, no. 27 (10 July 1997), from *Johnson's Russia List*, 17 July 1997; Marc Raeff, comments at the Kennan Institute for Advanced Russian Studies, *Meeting Report* 11, no. 12.

88. N. P. Yeroshkin, supplement to *Istoriia gosudarstvennykh uchreshdenii dorevoli-utsionnoi Rossii* (Moscow: Tretii Rim, 1997).

89. Vasily Selunin, article in *Novyi mir*, abstracted in *Current Digest of the Soviet Press* 40, no. 40 (1988): 17; Pskov, letter, 26 August/8 September 1913.

90. Raeff, *Understanding Imperial Russia*, 82–83; Edward Crankshaw, *The Shadow of the Winter Palace* (New York: Viking Press, 1976), 60; Yaney, *The Systemization of Russian Government*, 198–99, citing D. P. Troshchinskii, "Zapiska ob uchrezhdenii ministerstv," *SIRIO* 3 (1986): 228–29, 398; R. V. Daniels, *A History of Russia and the Soviet Union*, unpublished proofs, 58; McClellan, *Russia*, 11; Stephen Velychenko, personal communication, 12 March 1999.

91. Crankshaw, *The Shadow of the Winter Palace*, 368, 373, 390; Raeff, *Understanding Imperial Russia*, 200–201. A book on one of the key "conservative" bureaucrats is Edward H. Judge, *Plehve: Repression and Reform in Imperial Russia, 1902–1904* (Syracuse: Syracuse University Press, 1983). Plehve strove to reform Russia while at the same time repressing dissidents, activist workers, and minorities.

2

Power and Problems

One understands there are problems. It is so with all bureaucracies. Bureaucracies are the most evil of man's institutions, Herr Ned. They enshrine the worst of us and bring low the best of us.

—John le Carré, *The Secret Pilgrim*

For this is the invariable way of Russian evolution: the state swells, while the people wither.

—Vitaly Tretyakov

A bureaucracy has powers of its own. It is not just a dutiful servant of the state or its leaders. A bureaucracy's ways of doing things may well conflict with a government's goals, priorities, or intended pace of work. This can be true even if the bureaucrats are political or ideological supporters of a particular government or administration. During the Cuban missile crisis in 1962, President Kennedy found that the U.S. Navy would not implement certain orders he gave. The admirals' first priority was the safety of their ships and crews. The ancient "law of the sea" came first. At the extreme, a bureaucracy may instigate or support a coup. A less extreme but still important action is conscious opposition to a government's will. There are many ways for bureaucrats to do this. In Washington the leak to the media or to lobbyists is a favorite method. During the Ford administration the State Department held an informal session between young diplomats and the department's inspector general over the issue of leaks. But, said one foreign service officer, "it's the generals in the Pentagon" who are doing it, "not us."[1] In another case, in 1996, the director of a federal agency vowed to stop all leaking and called together his top ten people and confronted them about the issue. They all denied it to his face. The leaking went on.[2]

More routinely, bureaucracies influence policy by their nondramatic regard for routine and simple resistance to change. This low-key but still effective process challenges the notion that even in communist times all power was held at the top or the center. And then there is the bureaucrats' power over implementation, particularly if results are not continually and closely monitored by superiors. Here the bureaucrats are truly the "permanent politicians." Their struggle for power and place among themselves also unavoidably affects the course and results of policy. Representatives of U.S. government agencies can lie to officials of other agencies. Sometimes people from one agency have to go to another for information necessary for their work because their own superiors are keeping them in the dark.[3] (Military officers assigned to a civilian agency can go to the Pentagon and get the facts from their own kind.) Russian bureaucrats cannot avoid similar practices.

Although bureaucracy poses problems for Russia, bureaucracy is not only a problem. It is an essential and unavoidable part of any large organization or political system, even large-scale private enterprise. Structure must be made rational and effective. For example, the Tibetan "authority" in Dharmsala, India, has a "Department of Security, Central Tibetan Administration of H.H. the Dalai Lama."[4] Even the "revolutionary" Students for a Democratic Society stated on its handouts that they were prepared by a propaganda "section." And, of course, the Catholic Church has had a large and powerful bureaucracy in its Curia for centuries.[5] Business or "capitalism" finds that the state bureaucracy can be a benefit to it. Business needs government to set the "rules of the game" and to provide it with crucial infrastructure, educated workers, and a secure environment.

It is likely that "Russia's crisis is not the result of overharsh shock therapy or of a deficient national character or mingy western aid. It is, in the end, a failure of government" and, indeed, the collapse of what we called communism and the failure of Russian elites and politicians to replace it with a stabilizing system of rule.[6] In Russia, a failure of government has also been a failure of its state bureaucracy, for in some countries systems may fall, but the bureaucrats, out of *esprit de corps*, a devotion to duty, or a sense of civic consciousness, hold things together on their own until another system can be formally established. France is a prime example; "governments change, but the bureaucracy remains."

Where once leaders led, today they can often only coordinate and guide. Those whom they "supervise" can be the real movers and shakers, even though they usually work anonymously in the background. This has long been true in Russia as well. Two leading specialists on Russia see it as a country ruled by bureaucrats of various kinds.[7] Hollander writes, "The study of Soviet bureaucracy is important and challenging because it is a type of bureaucracy largely undreamed of in the philosophy of Western sociologists and students of bureaucracy, a type which defies many of our major preconceptions about bureaucracy." Galbraith too has written of the general usefulness of studying Russian bureaucracy: "In Russia much can be learned about one of the basic tendencies of the modern economy and polity, West or East. That is the present-day commitment to vast organization: in the West, to the great modern public agency and the large, inevitably bureaucratic corporation; in the Soviet Union, to the even more enormous socialist apparatus that combines the structures of government, industry, and commerce."[8]

But in Soviet Russia the "vast" organizations were elitist and often operating against the best interests of society. As Raeff points out, "'Administration is the foundation of [a structured] society'—but only on condition that the administration is actually involved with the life of society at the grass roots and shares in the crucial activities of the people and the nation." Its operations also need to be somewhat visible or "transparent" to the populace. In 1977 Andrei Kokoshin, then of the USA Institute, replied to my question of how Soviet agencies worked by saying only, "What looks complicated is simple and what looks simple is complicated." This was not much help. Still, problems of study aside, it is clear today that although "the [Russian] state apparatus is only one part of a much larger political system that no Russian government, . . . can summon into being from on high. . . . [a]t this stage the most urgent need is for action by capable administrators."[9] One of Russia's biggest present problems is that, though such people exist, they have not been able to act consequentially.

Bureaucracies have many "meanings." They can be refuges for their "denizens." For example, those who leave the military can find that they feel a loss of camaraderie and of societal "place." le Carré, however "fictionally," states the pleasantness of a bureaucracy well: "It provided shelter from the complexities of modern life. . . . For its servants, the Department had a religious quality. Like monks, they endowed it with a mystical identity far away from the hesitant, sinful band which made up its ranks."[10] I have seen this feeling of almost ethnic "departmental meaning" several times: in the U.S. Navy, in the federal government, and in the university. The other, negative side of bureaucracy, that is, the idea of bloat and dehumanization, of cog-like existence in a "machine," is also found expressed. Kafka may have presented this conception best.

But bureaucracies may be different things to different people. Both le Carré and Kafka can be right—though not for the same reasons. Bureaucracies can also be quite distant, even alienated, from society at large.

They can be the equivalent of classes and perhaps more powerful than purely economic groupings and thus more exploitative as well. They can do great harm and even engage in genocide. The Holocaust is the worst and most inhuman thing done by a bureaucracy. There has been mass murder before and since, for example, Armenia in 1915 and Rwanda in the 1990s, but not accomplished on such a large scale and so "efficiently." Standing on a tower at Auschwitz in 1994 I quickly realized that the death camp spread out before me was consciously and effectively constructed to kill using the techniques of "Fordism," of mass production, a sobering thought that led to another even more sobering one—if it was done there, it could conceivably be done again.

The anonymous but real power of bureaucracy is suggested by the comments on the Holocaust by Raul Hilberg, author of the classic *The Destruction of the European Jews*, apropos of the letter Göring sent to Heydrich on 31 July 1941 authorizing the "final solution." Hilberg discovered that Eichmann, not a top-level person in the Nazi hierarchy, had drafted it. What this suggests, Hilberg said in 1985, is that "even under a totalitarian regime, any number of people make decisions." Earlier, for the Bolsheviks "killing simply became a bureaucratic function, both for the leaders commanding it and for the executioners performing it. In that respect, the mass murder of the Jews by the Nazis or of class enemies by the Communists had much in common." The anonymous but real power, and horror, of bureaucracy is also suggested by the fact that documents reporting the existence of the Nazi extermination process were routinely filed away by American government agencies without action. And note that the American government did not protect its citizens from the negative effects of nuclear testing and development.[11]

The problems and power of communist bureaucracy were not confined to the Russian variant. Almost a half century ago, Milovan Djilas, once one of the top five leaders of Yugoslavia, declared, "The communist system by its very nature is bureaucratic."[12] Agreed, all twentieth-century communisms have been highly bureaucratized. This outcome flowed inexorably from Lenin's fixation on organization, power, and industrialization.[13] Twentieth-century leaders were often preoccupied with the "masses" and their controlled integration into a single, industrialized economy. In Yugoslavia the League of Communists was, according to the party leader himself, in a "bureaucratic alliance with state agencies." When the German Democratic Republic came apart in 1989 the government took over, briefly, from the party as the "sole source of authority" before the final crash. In postcommunist Hungary in 1990 the new government had some difficulty achieving some sort of *modus vivendi* with the bureaucracy it had "inherited from the departing Communist government."[14]

Democratic governments often have powerful and semi-independent bureaucracies. France, Sweden, and Japan are good examples. Much has been written about the Japanese case. For example, Wassily Leontief says, "The Japanese government has fostered the exceptionally rapid growth of its free-enterprise economy, using a well-educated and greatly respected civil service"—how un-Russian a result. One commentator even argues that in Japan "bureaucrats had long ago seized control of the policy-making apparatus from politicians."[15]

THE STATE

Here we run into the issue of the "state." The concept is much discussed but not as often defined. Some books on the state include no definition. By the term I mean all the persons and institutions, as well as the practices and justifying ideas, associated with the governmental system. I would include even those only psychologically supportive of the prevailing system. A more restricted definition is Pierre's: "the public organizations constituting the system of governmental institutions. This, of course, includes public administration."[16] A standard Soviet definition is "a system of special organs and agencies which are engaged in exercising power" that possesses a "special administrative apparatus."[17] A recent definition used in the survey "Developing Measures of State Capacity," developed by the Task Force on State Failure, is "all political and judicial institutions, as well as any administrative or bureaucratic institutions and organizations whose budgetary and decision-making authority derives directly from the government." A classic definition is Weber's: "a human community that (successfully) claims the *monopoly of the legitimate use of physical force within a given territory.*"[18]

Although Marx and Lenin were opposed to the state, communists never allowed it to wither as called for by their ideology. There are many reasons for this: the protective power of the state, particularly in a non-communist world; the fact that the state gave top communists the power and status they might have lost with a true communist system of organization; the organizational capability of the modern state; and the capitalist and traditionalist world's requirement that only states may be legitimate players in international affairs. Marx recognized that if the state exists so must its bureaucracy—and with significance and power: "Bureaucracy has the state in its power . . . it is its private property." Elsewhere he says that bureaucracy "is the 'state's consciousness,' the 'state's will,' the 'state's power' as a corporation and thus a particular, closed society within the state . . . a web of 'practical illusions' or the 'illusion of the state.' . . . The bureaucrats are the Jesuits and theologians of the state."[19] It is widely recognized that the state has some degree of independence and capacity for arbitrariness even if it is democratic.[20]

In Russia the state, long being particularly autocratic and not facing a true civil society, was bound to have a particularly powerful and semi-independent bureaucracy. (Or, in Marx's terms, that great state was possessed by a strong and nonresponsible bureaucracy.) Putin has stated the situation clearly: "Russia has from the very start developed as a super-centralized state. It is part of its genetic code, its tradition, and the mentality of its people."[21] Perry Anderson sees the Russian tsarist state as a particular type of absolutist formation, one with a "feudal cast . . . blunt and manifest," resting on serfdom. He notes that even up to 1917, "while the Russian *social formation* was dominated by the capitalist mode of production, the Russian *State* remained a feudal absolutism." Some elements of its feudal nature may exist to this day. Anderson points out that the state long owned two-fifths of the serfs in Russia, treated priests as functionaries owing duties to the government, and controlled the educational system through a "colossal" and "vast and proliferating bureaucracy." The Russian state "was in certain decisive respects far more powerful than any western absolutism had ever been" because it survived to use the technology offered by industrialization for its purposes of control.[22] Many historians have suggested that it would not have fallen absent World War I.

Any successor regime in Russia would have been permeated by the inheritance of this great state. We have already gone into the continuities between it and the Bolshevik system. Although Lenin often spoke against the bureaucratic distortions in the Soviet state and recognized that it was not free of its Russian past, he was often "unstylishly, humorously bureaucratic." Indeed, despite his stated recognition that "the state is a machine for the oppression of one class by another," he almost crows with pride over the fact that the Bolsheviks have "taken it over." He goes on to trumpet, "With this machine, or bludgeon, we shall destroy all exploitation," and he adds that it would be cast aside only when capitalism no longer exists. Because that outcome never materialized, the Russian state never underwent fundamental modification. It remained a "bludgeon" for one class and was for politicians and bureaucrats to use against others. True, Lenin did write *State and Revolution*, with its transformative humanistic goals for the Soviet state, but, as has been said, it was "the most un-Leninist thing he wrote." Lenin's nature contained at least as big a Tkachevian strain as a Marxist one. Still, he was aware of the dangers of a semi-independent bureaucracy. He once wrote, "The class character of the tsarist monarchy in no way militates against the vast independence and self-sufficiency of the tsarist authorities and of the 'bureaucracy.'" Perhaps, given his realistic recognition of the "bureaucratic distortions" and "bureaucratic twist" of his "workers' state," he might have moved for some reform if he had lived longer.[23] Instead, the Russians got Stalin and an intensified absolutism, if not a despotism.

Stalin and his goals and motivations will forever remain somewhat a mystery. Yet it is clear that he built a great state and state bureaucracy, one connected both sociologically and culturally with the mass of the Russian people. This is a great achievement. The Russian state was not an oppressive "other" to tens of thousands of bureaucrats who had risen from the mud of the village to responsible state positions with perks and power. The Stalinist state and its "unchallenged central bureaucracy" have been called his "most significant legacy." Alexander Nekrich once recounted that one of Stalin's security chiefs expressed regret at not being able to make a file on everyone. (China keeps a file on "virtually everyone except peasants." They are opened on each urban resident at entry into elementary school. The German Democratic Republic's *Stasi* maintained files on a great many persons and ran a large informer network.) Some have said that Stalin was a "victim of his own bureaucracy," and Moshe Lewin has said that Stalin was an "anti-bureaucrat" in some senses. When Stalin held meetings, the participants did not know what body was meeting until Stalin told them at the end what to prepare a report of. But this only means that Stalin was one cagey bureaucrat. McDougal has suggested that Stalin undermined his own system by raising up a new class based on expertise, similar to Lewin ironically saying that eventually bureaucracy, a form of tenure, "eliminated the worst aspect of Stalinism."[24] Yet, although the Soviet communists always maintained that their state was not a problem for humanity, Stalin's effects on it decidedly undercut the claim.[25]

BUREAUCRATIZED SOCIETY

"The type of society that Stalinism produced differed dramatically from the Marxist vision of a proletarian dictatorship," notes Daniels. This led to an entire literature of critical examination of Soviet society, perhaps beginning with Trotsky's *Revolution Betrayed*. Even if the new ruling class was not the bureaucracy, it could, in Gramsci's terms, have been the "dominant class," the societal force that defines the system and "keeps it running." Various observers of the USSR, for example, Leonhard in the 1950s and Reddaway in the 1980s, have seen the top state bureaucrats as one of the four "pillars" of the Soviet system. By the late 1980s, for some Soviet writers, White notes, their society was best understood as one "with a bureaucratic 'class' exploiting the labour of ordinary workers." Zaslavskaya sees the "bureaucrats who run the Communist Party and Government" as the top stratum of Soviet society. By 1989 and the famous

19th Party Conference, she was speaking of a "redistribution of a significant part of existing powers—from Party to state agencies." Stratification and bureaucratization had begun much earlier. In his memoirs, George Kennan writes of two changes that struck him "sharply" in the 1950s: "One was the growing inner detachment of the people from the ostensible purposes of a revolutionary regime. . . . The second was the growing extent and rigidity of stratification, both social and bureaucratic."[26] Anyone who lived in the Soviet Union could not fail to note what could be called a "bureaucratic [or bureaucratized], semi-bourgeois society." I once characterized that society as one of "many little pieces of paper" and innumerable bureaucratic hurdles, most of which existed, it seems, only to stifle spontaneity and creativity and, of course, prevent societal "events" undesired by the ruling groups.

CONTINUITY

It seemed, in August 1991, that perhaps St. George, Russia's patron saint, had given strength and guidance and that the "dragon" of oppressive communism was slain. However, although that huge beast was indeed killed, its tentacles, mentality, and urges live on in the form of elites, bureaus, and other structures and their actions.

As Vladimir Bukovsky has stated,

> Yeltsin was unprepared to take power. . . . He lost momentum and got bogged down in the daily routine of government, having no government to speak about. As usually happens, the vacuum of power was quickly filled by the bureaucracy. . . .
> The old regime is still very much alive.

He also notes that "Yeltsin overstretched his human resources."[27] Putting it differently, Russia was not Poland or another country where communism was only superimposed relatively recently on a resistant people; it had been part and parcel of Russian life for decades and had melded into it. The state apparatus had become a "popular bureaucracy". As Lewin has put it,

> To an historian, it appears as if we are watching the latest remake of an old Russian classic. The forms are new each time, of course. But the country is still struggling under the same burden. . . .
> Once again an energetic Russian state intent on modernizing the country has turned into a parasitic excrescence.[28]

The Russian intelligence service, the Federal Security Bureau, is made up largely of KGB functionaries. And consider the heights to which Putin, an ex-KGB operative, has risen. Note that there is continuity within continuity. Putin left some of Yeltsin's "gatekeepers" in place in the Kremlin apparatus. Former KGB officials run the Security Council and serve as aides to Putin. Another force maintaining bureaucratic continuity is the cultural proclivity of Russians to opt for bureaucratic positions over others.[29]

SOME WESTERN VIEWS

Here is only a sampling of the views of a wide variety of Westerners who deal with Russia. Many of them have noted the problems associated with bureaucracy there. Jeffrey Sachs says that, for Russians, the point is whether they will ever rid themselves of communist-minded officials and run their country in a normal way.[30] The economist Robert Solow, speaking of the ex-communist economy, notes that it is "half market-driven and half-controlled by bureaucrats" and that most Western economists do not know how it works or how to model it.[31]

Many in the West have noted the capacity of bureaucrats in the ex-communist countries to block reforms. A former U.S. ambassador says that the bureaucrats work "through shallow execution of orders and Oblomov-like passivity." In 1993 the United States was pressing the other countries of the G7 to set up an office in Moscow to coordinate Western aid, but Britain and France were resistant because they maintained that Moscow is "already too bureaucratic." Marshall Goldman has spoken of the "ossified institutions" impeding change in Russia.[32]

POWER

It is an unquestioned principle of the study and practice of administration that bureaucrats have and exercise power. By *power* I mean the ability of bureaucrats and their agencies to take consequential governmental actions. Bureaucratic "power can neither be suppressed nor ignored."[33] Certainly top bureaucrats are close to the political leaders and thus can influence them. And they are "housed" within the buildings and institutions of the state, are protected by the state, and wield the state's symbols and imagery. The BBC made a very successful TV series out of *Yes, Minister*, a show in which the politician heading the department was continually manipulated by the permanent secretary. The bureaucrats' powers are many and have to be contended with by the "policy makers." Bureaucrats are the "permanent politicians" who are in charge of implementation of policy and the determination of "routine." In implementing policy they may change it or resist its full intent. They may also disobey and not implement policy as it was designed. And more and more they are the initiators of policy. Their powers are based in the ideology and purposes of the state, in their group interests and even their individual wills, and in the processes of government that they oversee and run.

The formal theory of bureaucracy as a "neutral executor of plans made by others . . . is of course a myth. . . . The fact is that in all countries the bureaucracy is one of the important actors in the making of governmental decisions; in some systems the bureaucrats are the leading actors, and in most systems their power as decision-maker would seem to be increasing."[34] Accordingly, they are "at the table" of policy making even when they are not in the room. In this section we delve into the nature of their power. The problems they cause we shall leave to later.

Bureaucratic Power in Other Systems

The power of bureaucracy has been cited by so many that it is almost a truism of government today: "It is now the bureaucracy, not the parties, that grants critical grace and favors." The president of the United States cannot get anywhere as commander in chief unless the military's Joint Chiefs are "on board." The "enduring force of the bureaucracy in American life" reasserted itself in the midst of the Reagan administration. Its "'anything goes' ethos" was "set back" by civil servants. The tax reform law of 1986, the "most devastating assault on the privileges of big business and big investors since the New Deal," was the product of career professionals in the Treasury Department. And the Occupational Safety and Health Administration and the Environmental Protection Agency both exerted their power; the former slapped a big fine on Union Carbide, whereas the latter persuaded the president not to veto the "Superfund" environmental cleanup bill. Sometime during Reagan's administration, I saw that Reagan was losing, especially when the local fish and wildlife office got twenty new vehicles all at once. Although the civilian bureaucracy suffered some reductions in funding during the Reagan years, it continued to function much as before because it had constituencies that included Republicans. Is the bureaucracy a negative "third culture" that never discovers and tells the truth but, instead, is always making the "most acceptable temporary statement, and then hoping against hope that it might all turn out to be correct"? A book on the McCarthy period states: "The F.B.I. was the single most important component of the anti-Communist crusade and the institution most responsible for its successes—and iniquities." Possibly public employees in the United States constitute one-sixth of the nation's employees and vote heavily, and, because of low turnout by others, accordingly are one-half of the electorate in congressional elections and so limit cutbacks in the bureaucracy.[35]

The bureaucracies of many countries are noted for their power. The French bureaucracy "was forged according to a model . . . which corresponded closely to the ideas and prejudices of Napoleon Bonaparte." This model "is deeply embedded in the political culture and both cause and consequence of a style of authority often found inappropriate to modernity." Although it does bargain with interest groups, "the bureaucracy usually has the upper hand." Luckily for the general interest, the French bureaucracy tends to be "honest, well-trained, efficient and politically neutral."[36] In Germany the top bureaucrats of the states or *Länder* have a hand, collectively, in legislating, through "their" upper house, the Bundesrat. An Indian member of parliament has said that "if a villager has to go before a Government official . . . he is completely filled with terror." In 1992 low-level Japanese bureaucrats had issued "guidance" on their own to leading private trading companies to reduce imports of (U.S.?) beef. Japanese bureaucrats have even been called "the central pillar of Japanese society" and an essential part of the infamous collusive "iron triangle" of corporations, politicians, and bureaucrats. They even tend to draft the laws. They are increasingly the children of bureaucrats and sometimes even speak for politicians during debates in Parliament, where former bureaucrats constitute one of the largest groups of members, 15 percent in 1993.[37]

Although the U.S. government may limit the bureaucracy's powers fairly well, due heavily to Congress's investigatory and budgetary powers, the U.S. bureaucracy still has a real ability to operate in pursuit of its interests and desires. For example, when Secretary of State Shultz was kept in the dark on Iranian issues by a U.S. ambassador, a former National Security Council (NSC) staffer said, "It happens all the time." American bureaucrats play a dominant role in the policy process and strive to be "proactive, not reactive," masters of their fates and not mere "corks in the ocean." Indeed, "recent developments in public choice theory have demonstrated the limits of legislative control over the discretionary powers of the [U.S.] bureaucracy." Representative Hamilton (D-IN), chairman of the House Iran–Contra Committee, addressing Admiral Poindexter, the national security adviser to President Reagan (who resurfaced in George W. Bush's Defense Department), said, "You have testified that you withheld information from the president that denied him the opportunity to make the most fateful decision of his presidency." Senator Boren (D-OK) noted, "If you have non-elected bureaucrats making decisions, what you're really doing is taking power away from the people themselves." At the same hearings, when he was asked, "Are you in charge now?" Secretary Shultz replied, "It's a fight all the way all the time." To another query, he replied that the operation was run by "a staff group" that was "unaccountable to anybody." Senator Sarbanes (D-MD) said at the time that a "junta" existed inside the U.S. government. Congressman Jack Brooks

(D-TX) spoke of a covert "government within a government." It was revealed that the CIA was the first agency to propose keeping Congress and the Defense and State Departments in the dark about the sale of arms to Iran. It has even been claimed that State Department officials have run "surveillance" operations against presidential appointees. Several years ago a Foreign Service officer in Moscow said to me glumly, apropos of the State Department's internal policy not to tell its employees about Soviet use of microwave transmissions against them, "They never tell you anything." And remember the members of the CIA who violated directives and saved the poison that was to be destroyed? Of course, bureaucratic discretion may sometimes be justified. During the 1930s some Foreign Service officers went against Congress's will and saved the department's books on Russia by hiding them in the attic of the building. Congress had ordered that they all be destroyed.[38]

The increasing role of military officers serving in key bureaucratic positions throughout Washington also raises interesting questions of bureaucratic power. In 1986 over one-third of the NSC staff was active-duty military. During 1995 and 1996 about twenty-five military officers worked for the U.S. Arms Control and Disarmament Agency. They are attractive to administrations because they are "hard workers and come cheap."[39] Sometime in the mid-1990s an active-duty military officer wrote a war college paper on a future U.S. military coup as an outgrowth of the military's position in government.

If bureaucracies can run off on their own in a democracy, then they can really "fly" in a communist system. For here the bureaucrats are safe from exposure, questioning, and criticism unless the leaders of the party apparatus turn against them. However, most antibureaucratic campaigns in the USSR were only that—campaigns—and they were short-term and limited at that. For, as Drakulic has pointed out, the "gigantic government bureaucracy" was "a system that was built just to keep communists in power and that perceives every spontaneous movement . . . as a threat to their rule." Why should the party deal harshly with this basis of its power? In the GDR, according to an East German scholar, the bureaucracy had a degree of independence from all classes of society. By 1987 in Hungary the government structure seemed to be in ascendancy over the party.[40] Much has been written about the power of the bureaucracy of Communist China. China probably has the longest bureaucratic tradition in the world and one in which the "bureaucrat has exercised more discretion, and played a more significant role in the formation of policy, than has been usual in the West." Given the country's large population and strong central state, the bureaucracy also has had to be large, "the largest the world has ever known." Possibly, however, the Chinese administrative system has been less centralized and less technocratic than the Soviet system has been. And although the Chinese bureaucracy seems to be more subject to political pressures than the Soviet one is, "the 'emperor' may set the policy, . . . [but] the bureaucracy below often puts up countermeasures. . . . [E]vasion from below is resourceful and not unavailing." Lieberthal and Oksenberg note that Chinese central leaders' "decisions" are really "steps in a process of mobilizing bureaucratic resources" that require "protracted bureaucratic negotiations."[41]

An Outline "History" of Soviet Russian Bureaucratic Power

Although the power of the Russian state and its bureaucracy was downplayed because of the dominance of the "party ideology" model, it was recognized by some astute observers. Rosa Luxemberg warned Lenin in 1903 that his vision of the party would lead to the triumph of organization over the political party. In about 1940 Max Eastman wrote of "the new holders of [Russian] totalitarian power, the class of bureaucrats"; and in 1993 an American professor of constitutional law realistically noted, "The Russian background of the past 70 years has exalted administrative decrees over all else," and he added that much that passed for law in the USSR was in the form of such decrees. Tarschys documents a shift in *Pravda* editorials on the policy process during the 1950–70 period away from the centrality of the party to the government ministries. Dunmore, in his study of the state apparatus and economic policy between 1945 and 1953, attributes the distortion between the enunciation of policy and the outcome to the ministries' ability to pursue their own interests significantly. And, of course, Stalin's remaking of the party and the destruction of the Old Bolsheviks magnified the power of the state apparatus. Did this lead the surviving state bureaucrats to assume that, whatever thunder and lightning occurred in politics, they could go on running the country? At Stalin's death it was widely assumed by Western observers that his successor would be a primarily state, and not party, figure. Lukacs perceptively notes that "what the purges meant was the rise of a state, rather than party, bureaucracy," the introduction of the respectful Stalinistic usage now accorded the word *state*, and "the evolution of . . . the supremacy of a state bureaucracy." The radicalism of 1917 was not abandoned, but it was bureaucratized. The main Russian military newspaper once referred to "the times when the Big Boss appeared on top the mausoleum once a year, while in reality the country was ruled by the nameless and faceless army of bureaucrats." Dudintsev's famous novel has the hero's bureaucratic tormentors, even after he succeeds, all remaining in power with their rare luxuries and privileges.[42]

Yanov has detailed the power of even low-level administrators to stymie reform during the Khrushchev period. Soon after Khrushchev's removal the number of government agencies that could impose punishments on their own increased, even though an ukase of 1961 had ordered the decrease of agencies having such powers. Blackwell notes that under Brezhnev the state bureaucracy was "increasingly independent" of Moscow. Hough writes of a "major devolution of power from the Politburo to the ministries in the Brezhnev era," with the ministries acting like "independent baronies, operating under a weak king."[43]

Although Gorbachev perhaps intended to launch a "major attack on the central state apparatus," he never did. Top-level bureaucrats maintained their power and were not removed. A Russian academic even went so far as to say that the bureaucracy that Gorbachev was trying to tame had exercised its "third power" to "strangle" the basic goals of the Russian Revolution. Even Yeltsin wound up depending on state bureaucrats like Korzhakov and Putin. Finally, in asking what led Russia into its present crisis, Strokanov answers by citing two factors: "brainless privatization" and "the power of the bureaucracy—the major Russian evil, both historically and presently."[44] He is right on target.

Russian Bureaucratic Power Basics

Power in Russia is not just an American social science concept: "Since the state in Russia is almost coeval with the world itself, those who have the power of the state behind them, the *vlasti* [the 'powers that be'], are really of a different order of magnitude than mere 'authorities,' which always in America has a vaguely municipal ring to it." Imagine a country in which there are large numbers of intellectuals in conscious support of a strong state and for whom there is a special word, the *gosudarstvenniki*. The United States knows no such sociopolitical formation. American conservatives are antistate, while Democrats value the state for what it can do for their constituencies and ideas, not for itself. Lewin has expressed puzzlement that such a highly bureaucratized system did not attract studies of bureaucracy. For "it *was* the Russian state, no one else was." This "administrative-bureaucratic apparat" successfully defended its "monopoly position" all through the Gorbachev period and beyond. Near the end of the Soviet era a member of the Soviet Academy of Sciences said, "My country has the strongest bureaucracy in the world . . . the most powerful force against perestroika. . . . Not a single [other] country in the world has such a bureaucracy." At about the same time a leading Russian intellectual stated that "the nomenklatura bureaucracy remains the only unified force in society . . . the most organized, the most stable and the most politically conscious force in society."[45]

Interestingly, a Russian editor said in 1993 that Yeltsin's successor as president might well be from the state bureaucracy. By 2000 we see that the guess was correct. He added, "In the absence of strong political parties, effective representative institutions and a powerful private sector, the bureaucracy will become the leading political force." Paul Goble has said, "I think the bureaucracy's going to play a big role in that country [Russia] for a long time to come. Vastly larger than even the bureaucracy plays here. And that will slow things down." This is naturally so: consider the central place of bureaucracy in the tsarist and Soviet systems. During the late Soviet period there were extant an estimated ten thousand "sublegal acts" having the force of law issued by bureaucrats, even by heads of lowly sections. And if one of these directives conflicted with a law, then the directive took precedence.[46]

A former British ambassador to Moscow emphasized the power of Soviet state bureaucrats, saying it was "essential" to see the top personnel of a number of ministries in order to get things done. They were "strong on expertise" and had "disproportionate influence" based on their "political ties" and being the "repository of power to get things done" as well as the links between the executive and the units of work. (He also said that the bureaucracy is insufficiently studied.) Lane and Ross speak of the "institutional autonomy of the state bureaucracy and its power of self recruitment and renewal." Further, "the government bureaucracy has been a systemic force which has undermined the nomenklatura and circumscribed the power of the Communist Party."[47]

Russian Bureaucracy in Post-Soviet Russia

The power of bureaucrats remains significant in post-Soviet Russia. One observer notes that the bureaucracy is now playing an "even more important role," particularly by abusing its power, and that while Gorbachev had a staff of 400, Yeltsin's was 3,000. General Lebed said that enterprises are at the mercy of government functionaries and that "these bureaucrats have more power now than they did in Soviet times," partly because of the absence of party supervision. Persons desiring to open businesses legally have some difficulty getting the requisite permissions. Sergei Rogov has stated that "bureaucrats do what they like, without fear." As he says, "There is no real government in Russia" today. Kagarlitsky has written of the Russian government's "inability to seize control of anything." Yes, but the individual bureaucrats and their agencies can now act on their own. As Gavriil Popov says, "As soon as the controlling system had been destroyed . . . the bureaucracy . . . split into bureaucratic sectors" along both vertical and horizontal planes.[48] And because the Russian bureaucracy has been neither renewed nor replaced in a democratic direction, it holds a definite place of "reserve power" within the present weak governmental arrangement and awaits the return of Russian "normalcy" to resume its full power and role. Putin's presidency may well be crucial for this.

The Bureaucracy and Political Power

The bureaucracy has its defenders. Zyuganov, the chairman of the main Communist Party, still defending the Soviet way, has said that those who speak of "omnipotent officials" and "bureaucratic piratization" are "creating and peddling myths" and pursuing their "own personal objectives," for example, shifting responsibility for problems from the political elite to state officials and making the population hostile toward the state apparatus as a whole. "No sociopolitical structure can exist without a state apparatus," he concludes. His points are well taken in the abstract, but the weight of evidence underscores the covert but significant political power of the state bureaucracy. As Stephen Cohen has stated about the Soviet bureaucracy:

> No Soviet leader since Stalin has had dictatorial power inside the top leadership. Nor has any leader been able to impose policy on the hundreds of high officials who actually run the vast centralized bureaucracies of the Soviet party-state. . . .
> That bureaucratic officialdom occupies the essential arena of Soviet politics, where important conflicts over power and policy are resolved.

The same judgment was made by Grey Hodnett a decade earlier, when he noted the "'cabinet'-like composition of the current Politburo," with the inclusion of the minister of defense and the chairman of the KGB.[49]

Lewin speaks of the "interminable battles" the Soviet leaders had with the bureaucracy. And the "bureaucracy won," he adds. Major decisions could not be taken without the approval of the various bureaucracies affected. In other words, the agencies of the government had policy-affecting institutional representation at the top party levels. In the post-Soviet period the bureaucracy has not been monitored by Parliament and not much by the president's or prime minister's offices either. Huskey says that "Yeltsin was never able to impose discipline" on the ministries, partly because he lacked loyal executive agencies willing to implement his will. Accordingly, the ministries, and regional leaders as well, were able to "expand their own domains at the expense of the state." The fact that there was "at times intense competition and even conflict" between the presidency and government did not help matters. The lack of a unified state policy was evident in the contretemps associated with the reappointment of Boris Fyodorov as finance minister in 1994, for example. The politics of state and bureaucracy were complicated further by what Solzhenitsyn calls the "dirty hybrid" of the former *nomenklatura*: serving bureaucrats, "sharks of the financial underworld," "false democrats," and the KGB. In addition to the interests of the new capitalists, Yeltsin was "forced to take into account . . . the interests of the central and regional bureaucracy." Boris Nemtsov points out that in a presidential election the support of the bureaucrats could be a "decisive factor."[50]

Some Uses of Bureaucratic Power

Now it is time to look at a few of the many ways Russian bureaucrats have used their powers. The attempt at reforms of the administration of the economy begun by Kosygin in 1965 ran into massive resistance by the ministerial bureaucracy that gutted the reform. The ministries used their power of implementation to violate both the spirit and letter of the reform. They changed enterprise plans frequently and applied the old "ratchet principle" to them, and they added newly invented "additional conditions" for the success of industrial enterprises and thereby kept industrial administration about where it had been prior to the reform. They generally interfered in the enterprises' fields of activity, breaking the law when it suited them, and resurrected the "established routine" of autarkic ministerial dominance. As a result, Schroeder has said, "the bureaucracy is stronger than ever."[51]

"Bureaucratism" or "bureaupathology," that is, the formally unspecified and officially undesired behavior that impedes or distorts official work goals, existed in many forms. As a member of the Central Committee put it in 1989, "And bureaucratism—it is everywhere . . . wherever exist our native bureaucrats—invisible 'snowmen,' who leave only their traces behind." Specific forms include "inertness, red-tape and paper creation," "localism, departmentalism," "pedantic execution of directives," "over-insuring," and passing the buck.[52]

Bureaucratic resistance and inaction also existed. For example, Gorbachev's reforms "barely moved due to the resistance of the mid-level bureaucrats." A bit later, the U.S. ambassador said to Yeltsin's first prime minister, "I thought we in America had done a pretty good job inventing a bureaucracy where very little could be accomplished, but you Russians have beat us cold. You've got a bureaucracy where nothing can happen." Gaidar answered, "Yah, Bob. You are right about that. It is very difficult here. Impossible!" An order of Gorbachev's was once "sat upon" for almost a month by a functionary in the Council of Ministers' Administrative Office and then returned unexecuted. The head of a subsection of Gosplan (itself adept at blocking change) commented, "It's really amazing how the good intentions of thousands of people can run aground on one single bureaucrat's desk." In another case from Gorbachev's time the 2,000 employees of an institute tried to elect a new director in tune with the new atmosphere, but all the candidates withdrew under pressure from higher-ups, 85 percent of the employees were declared ineligible to vote, and in the end the ministry, "just as it has always done," picked the new director. The "stand patism" of the bureaucracy was legendary. Even the appointment of a new minister could not produce much change in a Soviet ministry's work.[53]

The post-Soviet period has seen a continuation of such self-serving uses of bureaucratic power. Viktor Chernomyrdin, when he was prime minister, complained that "the bureaucrats remain a state unto themselves." His particular objection was to the "bizarre" tax rates imposed on business, up to 80 percent of profits, a deadly deterrent to honesty, success, and foreign investment. Indeed, the bureaucracy seems to have a novel idea of success, for example, Rosugol taxed profitable mines highly in order to support the many losers. Bureaucracies can also disobey. For example, even though Yeltsin ordered the termination of research on biological weapons, the State Technical Commission (GosTech Kommissiia) has engaged in a program of denial and deception regarding bioweapons research and production. In 1995 U.S.–Russian relations were adversely affected by the commission's refusal to allow procedures approved in agreement with the Ministry of Foreign Affairs (MFA) to be followed in an American examination of a particular missile. The MFA was powerless because one Russian colonel stood firm.[54]

Problems of Bureaucratic Power and Action

The great problem posed by the state bureaucracy for today's Russia was raised by no less a personage than Yeltsin, in his "State of the Nation Address" of 1995. Here he made several references to the state bureaucracy. He ascribed the lack of economic development and various problems to the "low effectiveness" and the "inefficiency of the state authorities" and went so far as to say that the bureaucratic apparatus had tried to "subjugate" the state and had "disregarded" the law.[55]

In 1997 Alexander Bovin, the political commentator, wrote of the "strangling of nascent democracy by the giant, monstrous bureaucratic machinery, incomparable even to what we had during the stagnation period. A machinery driven by old-time engineers. A machinery which, in accordance with Parkinson's Law, is working not to the benefit of Russia, but to the benefit of bureaucrats. Bureaucracy, uncontrollable and corrupt, is the real power which has risen above us and is managing us."[56] The advent of Putin to the presidency soon saw in 2000 the bureaucracy regaining even more of its old powers. He granted forty ministries and other officials the right to classify information as secret.[57] Was Putin to some degree a product of the bureaucracy's resurgence?

There are those who argue that Russia's problem lies not in its bureaucracy but in its people's mentality or culture or in its "system," its guiding idea or ideology or its official purposes or goals. For some, the nature and culture of its political class are seen as decisive in defining Russia. It is also said that it is individuals who make mistakes and wrong decisions and that blaming institutions is a "cop-out" and even a sort of racism. It is pointed out as well that Soviet and post-Soviet leaders have often struck out at the bureaucracy or tried to reform it and that the relative lack of effect proves that the problem is something more systemic, something more fundamental, than just the nature of the bureaucracy. Various observers have noted the growth of professionalism in Russian administrators and an improvement in their functioning. Some have even called the USSR as a whole a giant bureaucracy. And the number of bureaucrats is up everywhere, it is said; so why single out Russian bureaucrats for criticism?

The vast size of the country and the consequent difficulties of assuring a high nationwide standard of administrative behavior have been cited more than once. In 1998 Hochschild repeated the story cited by Barbara Tuchman in *The Guns of August*: a Russian grand duke explained "that in an empire as vast as Russia when an order was given no one was ever sure whether it had been delivered." Hochschild says that the "anarchic nature of Russia" remains; no one in Irkutsk pays much attention to orders from Moscow. Galleotti says, "The USSR was just too huge and varied a nation for centralization to be anything more than a crude instrument."[58] Russia is smaller but not all that much smaller. These are all good points to keep in mind.

Some commentators see Russia's administrative difficulties as inherent in the nature of communism and its unavoidable heritage, particularly because in Russia communism became, with Stalin's contrived and violent urging, very much a Russian cultural construction that also lasted so long that it outlived most people who remembered other ways of doing things. Tony Judt has eloquently denounced communism: "Communism was indeed monstrous, a dysfunctional inversion of social and human values. . . . The claims of politics reigned supreme. In the ideological calculus, doctrinal projects took precedence; personal and familial relations meant nothing."[59]

No form of Leninist communism in power has avoided being highly bureaucratized. For example, even the Khmer Rouge retained "voluminous archives" of the confessions, some of them hundreds of pages long, of those killed in its nationwide terror.[60] The Sandinista Front of Nicaragua, after its electoral defeat in 1990, blamed its failures partly on "the reproduction of the practices of socialist countries that led us toward one-party forms of political leadership, and toward excessive emphasis on the control and centralization of public administration. The implementation of those policies was often carried out in a bureaucratic and coercive manner."[61]

Poland's party indulged a "swollen bureaucracy rife with mismanagement, incompetence and outright corruption and bent on sabotaging every reform that might cut its power and privileges."[62] The daily paper of the Cuban communists recognized that a bureaucratic "tendency" and "morass" developed in Cuba as a "special stratum" consolidated itself in the state. "Hanoi Battles against Bureaucracy," said a Vietnamese headline of 1975, but this "hidebound communist bureaucracy" was still there in 1996. Even as it was coming to an end, the GDR was still "regimented by a system of government bureaucracy." Ukraine had still not escaped the bureaucratic problem and its corruption by 1998.[63] Why did this happen?

Communism suffered from a big initial problem that was never overcome: it was built putting control first, above good government and administration. Because of this, Hollander once called Soviet bureaucracy a new type and one with scope and functions that are not entirely rational.[64] Control retained its priority until the end of the system, although it could not avoid that end. A Polish scholar says, with that irony characteristic of the Polish intelligentsia, that state socialism (a better appellation than *communism*) was "a fundamentally defective idea that was well carried out."[65] Brzezinski has said that "the communist system tends to rigidify its doctrinal orientation. Bureaucratic conservatism and dogmatic orthodoxy tend to reinforce each other, with dogma legitimizing established power and power protecting the established dogma."[66] Despite the claim that "it's the system" that is the problem, the system was unavoidably bureaucratized in a special way that was itself a big problem for communist states.

Certain fundamental issues connected with bureaucracy always exist. Kafka's emphasis on the faceless power and emotional suffocation a bureaucracy can produce reveals one such issue. Also there is the question of whether bureaucracy survives because no replacement model has been developed or applied. Can a bureaucracy become "obsolete" and turn into "a major threat" to the welfare and standing of a country? Parkinson's Law must never be ruled out. For example, in the U.S. Department of Defense, as in the British Admiralty that Parkinson used as his example, there has been an astounding proliferation of bureaucratic berths. The Joint Staff, which originally was to be no more than 100 people, numbered 2,000 by 1985. There are eleven defense agencies and nine joint commands with thousands of personnel each. A Marine colonel who worked in the Defense Intelligence Agency described it emphatically as the biggest bureaucratic boondoggle he had ever seen. Remember the building of a new HQ building by one intelligence agency without reference to Congress? There may be fourteen intelligence agencies in the U.S. government.[67]

Another issue is that of the possible "bureaucratization" of controlling agencies, for which the French use the apt term *colonization*. Was the Communist Party of the Soviet Union "statized" by the state bureaucracy? One Soviet academic points out that sometimes party officials "introduce the administrative methods used in economic management into the work of Party agencies." Lane states, "There can be no doubt that the state administration was the dominant political body under Stalin." Bureaucrats can become "careerists." A retired Vatican official has written that "he and many others within the church were disgusted by the rampant careerism and corruption of some officials." Corruption, too, is always a possibility, and control is an issue. As Lane says, "The major political problem facing the leadership of the Soviet state is how to control . . . this large, complex, differentiated administrative structure." Lewin says that effective control over the bureaucracy had disappeared in the USSR by the 1970s.[68]

The bureaucrats' relationship with people always arises. Does the bureaucracy deal correctly with people, or does it cause them gratuitous difficulties or demand payment for services? Sayre asks, What "boundaries," "restraining rules," and "arrangements" to ensure that bureaucrats are "responsible actors" exist? Is the bureaucrats' own culture conducive to society's goals, or is it contributing only to the bureaucrats' convenience, power, or privilege? Does the bureaucracy facilitate the general well-being and technological and economic development, or does it hobble innovation and adaptability? As Cocks notes, "Increasingly, organization is seen to be the decisive element that links technology and development." There is a special issue in the Soviet case: Did the state bureaucracy violate the norms of socialism or make it more difficult to achieve? Odom calls for the application of "middle-range" theories of organizational behavior to the Russian system: Merton's "goal displacement," Crozier's recognition that an institution's goal seeking may be "destroyed by all the individual voluntarism by bureaucrats and employees," and the effects on organizations of the way they obtain their resources. These issues must be resolved for bureaucracies to run well.[69]

The Soviet Period

Perhaps the most generally significant problem of Soviet bureaucracy involves the negative effects it had on the ideal of socialism. As Djilas has said, "The greatest and most significant revolution of our era had got stuck in the ruts of bureaucracy and, unlike the earlier 'bourgeois' revolutions, had thereby become more intolerant and aggressive." The intractability of the problem was humorously dramatized in a Moscow Puppet Theater production in 1968; every time a bureaucrat puppet was eliminated, it split and reappeared as two bureaucrats roaring orders. The bureaucratization of socialism has spawned a series of critical socialist writings, beginning with Trotsky's *Revolution Betrayed*. As Urban says, even the ideology of administration in the USSR "has not been particularly kind to the philosophy of Karl Marx" in terms of the state, the division of labor, and the continuation of administration into communism. Gorbachev himself said that the Soviet system was a betrayal of "October" and the "socialist idea." Hodges specifies the repression of revolutionary intellectuals and the violent antagonisms among socialist states.[70]

Although bureaucracy cannot be directly blamed for the end of the USSR, Gorbachev's destabilization of the Soviet system was closely related to his attempt to solve its rigidity and "stagnation" (*zastoi*) to cope with the overall problem bequeathed by Brezhnev, a "swollen state and spent society." Once Gorbachev's reforms began, the bureaucrats, already enjoying power and latitude, seized the assets of the organizations they controlled, and the state was doomed.[71]

Bureaucracy was rough on Soviet society and the Soviet people in several respects. A Soviet professor of psychology has suggested that the bureaucracy was one of the forces driving some educated people into typically Soviet "sub-employment," that is, "dropping out" to employment below skill level. Favorite menial jobs for graduates of higher educational institutions were night watchman and lift operator. The USSR actually had a statistic for workers with M.D. degrees. The professor has said that people "drop out of the game only after having run up against 'routine, bureaucratism and formalism,'" and he denounces "the functionaries, the human automatons whose faces have grown masks" and who stifle initiative. Gogol's Russia outlived him. One is reminded of Rosa Luxemburg's warning that "without . . . unrestricted freedom of the press and assembly, without a free struggle of opinion, life . . . becomes a mere semblance of life, in which only the bureaucracy remains as the active element." Perhaps the harshest Russian bureaucracy is the military, which, with its unrestricted hazing of first-year conscripts and poor food, kills some, drives others to desert, and leaves many others with lifelong health problems. Bureaucratic factors also had a role in the deterioration of public health. The national health care system, like factories, operated on the principle of sheer volume. As one doctor has put it, "Physicians' work is evaluated primarily according to statistical indicators. . . . Numbers determine our way of working." Patients who could afford it tried to get better care by "thanking" doctors with bribes. Gorbachev's minister of health said that one-third of the institutes in the health care system could be shut down without adverse effects on the nation's health.[72]

Waste is high on the list of the Soviet bureaucracy's problems. John Armstrong says that it "encumbers" the Soviet "bureaucracies" and "indeed their entire society." *Pravda* received "many" letters about the "wasteful" use of resources of all kinds. John Hazard has emphasized that "coordination is a major problem." General "overbureaucratization" was one of the major reasons for the economic stagnation. In agriculture there was a "huge and overlapping bureaucracy that poked into everything and had to be placated and bribed at every level." But nevertheless, new agencies were always being created, to absurd lengths: "In the towns, each mode of public transport is under a different administrative body." No wonder the USSR had a "bloated administrative class." Environmental degradation was significant and readily noticeable.[73]

Despite highly developed theory, science suffered. Roald Sagdeev, the director of the Soviet Space Research Institute, says that bureaucracy "stifled Soviet scientific research." Almost all advanced equipment had to be purchased from the West with precious foreign currency. Innovation showed weak prospects. Gustafson says, "Soviet science is terribly hampered by its administration, which allows subordinate scientists virtually no initiative. Support and funds are awarded to institutions, not specific research projects." Academician Trapeznikov writes that the inefficiency of the Soviet economy was closely linked to the quality of management, which needed improving "at all levels." Various economic problems were attributed to "bureaucratic clumsiness." A big general problem was the oppressive and stifling climate brought about by the bureaucracy. It was difficult to work with, and it tended to degrade ordinary people. The leading economist Aganbegyan has cited ministries for exercising excessively close supervision of economic associations and enterprises.[74]

A high-level German diplomat with long experience in Russia wrote of the "formidable obstacles to accomplishing anything in Russia" and the "virtually insurmountable" difficulties of dealing with its bureaucrats. Bureaucratism was deep and prevalent, with its "devotion to process, not results." The excessive privileges of the bureaucracy were often decried. The Soviet government spent as much on cars and drivers for bureaucrats as it did on all public transport. Zaslavskaya saw the bureaucracy as only a "stratum" but has said that it was "confidently" moving in the direction of becoming a new class. The use of a large slice of the bureaucracy for military purposes did little to fulfill the needs of society at large. Even "civilian industry" had enormous and draining military responsibilities. However, the USSR still had to import large amounts of militarily-relevant goods from Japan and NATO countries. In 1989 Barrington Moore suggested that this "series of huge bureaucratic apparatuses" had become "obsolete" and also a "major threat to the welfare of the Soviet population as well as to the international standing of the Soviet Union."[75]

The Post-Soviet Period

The post-Soviet period has not seen an improvement in the operation of the Russian state bureaucracy. The fundamental problem is that of a "weak state that cannot perform the most basic administrative tasks, such as tax collection." The Russian state is unable, as Malia points out, "to collect taxes, to pay wages, to regulate the banks and to finance its debt." He could have added a number of other "inabilities," for example, to conscript soldiers, to fight wars well, to control its administrators, to minimize corruption, and to provide a modicum of social welfare and that relative security and predictability that populations everywhere deserve from the state. Himmelfarb points out that "good government is the precondition of civil society, providing a safe space within which individuals, families, communities, churches and voluntary associations can effectively function." Malia cites the "legacy of the leviathan Soviet state, which when it collapsed left behind only administrative and economic rubble, devoid of the judicial, accounting and police procedures necessary for a modern society—an institutional abyss."[76] Nevertheless, as Shevtsova points out, "while the old state has been destroyed, its backbone, the bureaucracy, has been preserved and revitalized . . . even as it remains the repository of old habits and traditions. Russia's bureaucracy quickly privatized all the functions of the state."[77]

This is seemingly paradoxical, yes, but Russia is a living paradox. Simply put, Russia now has a state bureaucracy that often serves its own interests, not those of the state or its people. Sergei Markov, a Russian political analyst, puts it well with the power of the macabre: the state seems to move, but it is really dead. Its movements are those of the "worms," the bureaucrats, who are feeding off it. Alton puts it less dramatically. Russia's near-anarchy is caused not by lack of regulations but by "a lack of enforcement . . . of laws and regulations that really matter." Politics, then, is "distinguished by the weakness and incoherence of institutions" of this "failed and bankrupt state," with its near "absence of governance." It will be extremely difficult to reestablish a true state in Russia, for, as Michel Tatu has pointed out, the Russians are determined "never to obey anyone again." Ex-General Alexander Lebed, as the governor of Krasnoyarsk, has blasted the Moscow-centered state. "We are sick and tired of Moscow's control," he rumbled in the gruff voice of the "man who looks like his own bodyguard." He talked of Moscow as the "tiny brainless head of a huge dinosaur country" and added, "It takes a very long time for signals to travel from the head . . . to the tail. By that time the tail has been bitten and swallowed. There is no way back, no signal from the tail to the head."[78]

Yeltsin stated some of the basic problems: "There is still no orderly system of civil service. There is no clear division of functions between various power branches . . . [and there is] no well-founded vertical division of powers between the federal level and the component parts of the federation." In addition, he said, "there is no system for attracting young people into the civil service in a consistent and organized way." Indeed, he added, "on the whole the civil service . . . continues to be in a state of crisis," and "the degree of corruption within the state apparatus is growing." Huskey points out that Russia has "lacked an institution common to Western democracies—a permanent civil service." The proliferation of overlapping bureaucratic structures, a chronic Russian problem, never stopped. For example, by 1995 there were at least fifteen security agencies and twenty-eight major directorates and departments within the Federal Security Bureau (FSB), the successor to an important part of the KGB.[79] One of the major problems of post-Soviet Russia is its health situation. Infectious diseases are spreading at an "alarming rate." This is partly because of the breakdown in the national health care system. But, as one American consultant for a U.S. Information Agency–sponsored health assessment project in Russia told me, if a city has a highly competent and motivated top health official in charge of its hospitals, then the health situation there will "not be too bad."

Bureaucratic overstaffing persists. In 1997 Russia had "far too many generals," almost three thousand on active service, with 400 colonel-generals. And the Russian military is still treating its recruits terribly. Poor coordination was still a serious military problem, in the second Chechen War as well as the first one, where clashes occurred between Russian forces themselves, with troops of two ministries sometimes shooting at each other. Perhaps the saddest bureaucratic problem has been stated by Evgenia Albats in testimony in the United States: "Hannah Arendt . . . used to say that nothing is more dangerous for any country than when it starts to be run by 'nobody,' by unseen faces, unidentified persons, who represent nobody and are under nobody's control. Right now Russia is run by such 'nobodies' who have come from the old Soviet Union's . . . institutions and are ready to put the country over the edge even though not necessarily under the Red banner." Some social workers and human rights activists say that crime could be reduced by eliminating the officials whose negligence, theft, and greed tend to create crime among their charges in the grim state institutions such as orphanages.[80]

A particularly serious problem of Russian administration is that of controlling both nuclear power and weapons and their fissile material. Here, just as in industry as a whole, production, quantity, and secrecy have been put above accounting, regulation, and control. For example, right after the 1986 Chernobyl disaster local Soviet officials sent their own children to safety but did not inform local residents about the radiation danger. And even after the accident employees of nuclear power plants continued to receive inadequate training. Top Soviet nuclear officials themselves have said that the Soviet administrative system could not ensure that tasks were performed well or even adequately. In addition, there was "no governmental body responsible for regulating the full panorama of safety issues

in the nuclear industry." Indeed, the administrative system's "fragmentation" did not even allow objective safety analysis.

There is no evidence of significant improvement during the post-Soviet
period. For example, in 1996 a Russian source said that the operation of
Gosatomnadzor, a regulatory agency, was "paralyzed" and that the pre-
Chernobyl situation regarding the control over nuclear power plants was
returning. The present underfunding of the Ministry of Atomic Energy
(Minatom), for example, has led its top officials to seek money above
safety and sell nuclear knowledge and capabilities to states that are unlikely to be safety conscious or have peaceful foreign policies. Its minister
in the mid-1990s has been characterized as "always on the lookout for
sources of hard-currency income to shore up his obsolete empire." It is not
clear that his successors are different. Minatom tried to sell gas centrifuges
to Iran without informing the Ministry of Foreign Affairs and despite the
opposition of the Ministry of Foreign Economic Relations. Unfortunately,
because Russia lacks an effective system for preventing illegal exports of
nuclear materials, such shipments may have taken place.

When we turn to accounting for and control of nuclear weapons and
other weapons of mass destruction the situation is not qualitatively better. True, in this area there are fewer bureaucracies involved, and the military, with its potential for firm discipline, may be a better guardian than
civilian agencies. The fundamental question is: Does the military high
command care about and want to control its nukes? Perhaps the answer
is a mild affirmative—so far. Even if high-tech means of control are lacking, as they have been in the Russian case, highly motivated armed sentries with the willingness to shoot do constitute an effective deterrent to
theft. At this moment we have no evidence that any nuclear weapons
have been stolen. The same cannot be said for fissile material and other
materials associated with nuclear weapons production, however. A Russian source says that "Russia has no state system for monitoring and taking stock of nuclear materials," and reports from Americans who have
toured Russian nuclear storage sites suggest that accounting and control
would need to be improved considerably just to match Western standards. Another problem is that Russian bureaucrats who deal with nuclear matters tend to diverge widely in attitude and decision making.
Last, according to the U.S. Sandia National Laboratories, the problems
facing the Russian railway system, on which nukes are transported, are
serious and worsening by the day. The provision by the United States and
Britain of special railway cars and containers for nukes could not solve
this systemic problem.[81]

Post-Soviet Russia speaks with different bureaucratic voices in its foreign policy. A former foreign policy analyst in the Soviet government, later
an ambassador to the United States from a "newly independent state," told

me that Russian diplomats working in the same office in the Foreign Ministry each may well present different versions of what Russia's foreign policy is. Adam Ulam has referred to the limitations that bureaucratic practices impose on Soviet foreign policy. And one American business executive with extensive experience in the USSR has said that he was never successful in linking deals made with one ministry with another. "Bureaucratic separatism" is also a serious problem among Soviet academic institutions, according to an American archaeologist. Certainly, this has been a problem in my university's exchange program with Russian academic institutions. When Russia joined the Partnership for Peace, Chernomyrdin, Kozyrev, and Grachev all made different statements of Russia's intentions within a period of only several weeks. One U.S. diplomat found the lack of coordination among the members of a Russian negotiating team "striking." Is this a cultural trait or simply post-Soviet lack of coordination? A Russian composer once expressed surprise that an American orchestra was willing to follow his direction; not so a Russian orchestra, he said. Another American diplomat says that Churchill's famous statement about the nature of Russia ("a riddle inside a puzzle inside an enigma") remains "frustratingly accurate." He noted a great deal of confusion among Russian diplomats as to what Russian policy on U.S.–Russian relations is. Also, sometimes Russian texts of U.S.–Russian approved agreements do not match the U.S. texts. Other American diplomats have complained of the "lethargy" of Russian ministries, for example, the Ministry of Defense, Minatom, and so on, in their relations with the United States, namely, lack of response to American messages. American governmental assistance to certain Russian companies would only be released to the companies by Russian customs offices on an individual shipment basis; no general or continuing agreement was possible. And it turns out that Russian diplomats or delegates to conferences were often without instructions or guidance, an old problem of many years' duration. Unlike the United States, with its NSC staff, the Russian government often lacks an arbiter, and accordingly the Russian interagency process can be most confused and even collapse, at least during the mid-1990s. As one American governmental source put it in 1996, "The Russians have very limited interagency communication; their vertical communication is relatively poor. And there's the fiefdom problem," an allusion to Minatom in this case.[82] I have watched telephones in Russian government offices go unanswered by people at adjacent desks. Is the reason fear of getting involved or a simple lack of concern for others? Or is it an unwillingness to "take one step forward"?

Bureaucracy has also posed serious problems for the Russian economy, as it did for the Soviet one.[83] Although bureaucracy was never the only reason for the inefficiency and many other problems of the Soviet economy, bureaucratic inertia, resistance to reform, and general disjointedness caused real difficulties for the Soviet economy, which fundamentally was, in Hanson's words, an "administrative economy." Factory directors were not managers concerned with profits and costs but, in fact, bureaucrats driven to produce (or pretending to do so) in accordance with the state plan, a law. The bureaucrats enjoyed the power of implementation and the power to misinform their superiors. As Arbatov has said, "Soviet leaders . . . did not know the whole truth about the economic condition of their country. This was largely because they were constantly misled by their own bureaucracy." The bureaucrats' power continued beyond the "fall" into the post-Soviet period. A U.S. government source has said that Prime Minister Chernomyrdin was not adequately advised on economic issues. And as Afanasyev puts it, "The real winners in the October 1993 showdown between Yeltsin and the . . . parliament was the military-industrial complex, acting in unison with the bureaucracy."[84]

Although ministries and other state agencies now call themselves "holding companies," "concerns," and other such private enterprise terms, they still "suppress all market-oriented competition." For example, Agroprom, a huge state monopoly, is the "main social brake on the development of agricultural production." One observer says that a key to success in today's Russian economy is "strong connections with the government" and that "the state remains the prevailing force in the economy." In 1997 Yeltsin said that "hundreds" of factories were still run by bureaucrats from the Soviet era "who have no sense of competition and no interest in learning." Aslund has pointed out that incomplete liberalization has allowed "an excessive role for state intervention," even through "arbitrary administrative action." But even with incomplete liberalization the government does not always receive its share of a state industry's profits, for example, with Gazprom in 1997. And state-owned industry is deteriorating; the railroads are only one example.[85] This set of problems has still not been solved today.

BUREAUCRATISM/BUREAUPATHOLOGY

Examining the major problem of Russian bureaucratism will provide a good sense of Russia's present governmental and political situation.[86]

Significance and Definition

Unless the postcommunist Russian state and privatized industrial and other enterprises are able to employ an efficient administrative process in which behavior that undercuts policy, productivity, and goals is minimal, the Westernization and modernization of Russia will be severely hampered and unduly prolonged, possibly even arrested for some time. Accordingly, the creation of a truly post-Soviet, effective civil service purged of bureaucratism "is a prerequisite for the establishment of democratic government in Russia."[87] It is also a prerequisite for the reestablishment of "governability" and governance itself.

Definition

Bureaucratism is on-the-job behavior by administrative personnel that is both formally unspecified and officially undesired and which impedes or distorts an administrative unit's officially designated work or goals. Not all informalist bureaucratic behavior is bureaucratism or, as it is sometimes called in Western literature on public administration, bureaupathology. The phenomenon need not be conscious or planned. Continual activity by an administrator that obstructs, subverts, or distorts the unit's work or goals that is a result of cultural or personality traits, poor training, or deeply held beliefs fits the definition. Merely "sloughing off" or wasting time is not bureaucratism unless it is inordinate in amount and truly obstructionist of work and policy.

In Victor Thompson's *Modern Organization* administrative "behavior patterns which are dysfunctional from the point of view of the organization, though functional from that of the . . . official" are bureaupathic. In other words, behavior that is uncalled for or even proscribed but which is "personal rather than organizational," that is, "a function of an individual's personality . . . is of no concern to organization theory." Put differently, "the appropriation of major aspects of bureaucratic organization as means for the satisfaction of personal needs is pathological" for the organization because "it is a form of behavior which is functional for less than the system as a whole."[88]

A more specific sense of bureaucratism's nature is presented in Harry Cohen's *Demonics of Bureaucracy*. He lists the following examples: protection of career above performance of duties, working to rule, ritualistic behavior, the "runaround" to avoid taking action and risk, inflation (or minimization) of figures, performance of useless and nonsense work, violation of law, informal modification of procedures, fabrication of information or documentation, providing misinformation, avoidance of solutions or the end game by shunning conflict or unpleasantness, pretending to work, and being rigid and inflexible.[89] How "Russian" much of this sounds, although it is not exclusively Russian.

Russia and Bureaucratism

Any observer of Russo-Soviet administration will easily find examples of bureaucratism. Common ones include interagency conflict, Parkinson's

Law (uncontrolled and unnecessary growth of staff), "passing the buck" or the inability to make decisions except at the highest levels, and outright corruption such as embezzlement or taking bribes. The latest important Russian examples include seizure of state assets by bureaucrats, that is, "nomenklatura privatization," also called "insider privatization" or "wild privatization," and the financial alliance of bureaucrats with business-people. This latest illegality reminds us that illegal activity was routinely necessary for Soviet industrial administrators and is extremely well documented. One Soviet factory manager said that he had "earned" at least two hundred years in jail without ever having done anything for personal gain, an admission showing that some bureaucratism was ingrained in the system itself.[90]

Definitions—Russian

Russian definitions of *bureaucratism/bureaupathology* appeared even before the Soviet system, suggesting that Russia could be rather "modern" in various ways despite its general underdevelopment and also that the phenomenon has Russian, and perhaps even pre-Russian, roots. As early as 1905 Lenin wrote about it and defined it with words like *red tape, procrastination*, and *answers for form only (otpiski)*. Lenin also seems to have used the word *bureaucracy*, often a neutral term in academic discourse in the West, as a synonym for *bureaucratism*. Lenin may have held the Marxist assumption that administration is an activity for everyone, a position expressed at length in his "un-Leninist" work, *State and Revolution* of 1917. (Of course, a Marxist could see even the best bureaucracy as an antihumanist formation.) In early 1920 Lenin wrote of the "greatest disgrace" of the "astonishing red tape, carelessness, bureaucracy and helplessness" in "our commissariats, in all of them." For Trotsky, "bureaucratism meant the Party's increasing alienation from the masses, and the tendency for political leadership to give way to mere administration." He also expressed concern with the drain on the economy of the "swollen privileged apparatus," which, he said, "in all its different forms, centered around Stalin," his nemesis.[91]

Contemporary Russian definitional statements are common. Komarov defines bureaucratism as a "paper carousel, red-tape, inability to decide the essence of the question, formalistic answers, haughty inattention, confusion and excess complexity in work . . . and the deficiencies and distortions caused by this in the style, forms and methods of work of the administrative apparatus and its leaders." Khasbulatov sees it as characterized by "irrationality and . . . parasitism . . . founded on the sum total of formal and informal ties of officialdom (*chinovnichestvo*). . . . These ties form an all-powerful, secretive, acting-by-law hierarchical, rigid mechanism of power, standing above the law and the will of the members of society." The "Russianness" of this definition lies in its emphasis on politics and political and state power.[92]

Another Russian definition uses Merton's displacement of goals and sees bureaucratism as the turning of goals and norms into goals in themselves (*samotsel'*). G. Popov, the first post-Soviet mayor of Moscow, sees it as an administrative "subsystem" with so much independence from the larger system that it lives "its own life, in accordance with its own laws and in accordance with its own interests," becoming superior to the nominal rulers and all of society. Accordingly, he designates it with capital letters as the "Administrative System." Khudokormov defines it as an administrative apparatus "working for itself" to the "detriment of the ruled" and "isolating itself from them while preserving its own privileges." A particularly lengthy definition adds "pedantic execution" of directives, "humoring higher-ups," careerism, and "over-insuring." Another defines it in broad sociopolitical terms as "an anti-social means of administration through formal-conservative relations toward official duties, the result of which is the infringement of the constitutional rights of the citizen and the causing of economic and political harm to societal interests and values."[93]

The variety and yet similarity of these definitions shows that bureaucratism is commonly recognized in Russia as a serious, widespread, concrete phenomenon. We can also see that Russian bureaucratism is definitely the same phenomenon that American writers call bureaupathology. This administrative peculiarity is a major factor impeding modern governance and full democratization. As a Russian analyst states: "No one negative phenomenon . . . in this country has received and receives now as much required attention as does bureaucratism. . . . Practice has shown that bureaucratism is a tenacious and dangerous enemy of the economy and society as a whole . . . one of the most difficult obstacles on the paths of development . . . of renewal, democratization."[94]

A former aide to Gorbachev notes that bureaucracy and bureaucratic power have played an "even more important role" in post-Soviet Russia than they did previously. He adds that Yeltsin had a much larger staff than Gorbachev did and that the number of ministries is almost double the former number. An American correspondent with experience in Soviet Russia has noted that bureaucratic abuse is worse than it had been.[95]

Soviet Examples

Perhaps the most harmful instance of Soviet bureaucratism is the Chernobyl disaster. Officials have justifiably been condemned for negligence, excessive risk taking (the safety features were turned off to run a test), disregard for people's safety, and rampant nepotism and careerism: "They spent the day after the accident debating, instead of taking decisive action." Only on the ninth day after the catastrophe were the workers on the scene given protective equipment—but only because the media people were about to arrive. (And the fact that Gorbachev did not speak publicly on the incident for two weeks could not have helped.) Anyone who has seen the radiation fallout pattern on a map, from Ukraine through Poland all the way to Lapland, cannot but be impressed by the enormity of this failure of administration and common sense. "Absurd" bureaucratism was a serious impediment to relief and rescue operations after the Armenian earthquake the next year. Relief was not delivered to certain needy areas because the officials who had to sign for it were dead.[96]

The Chechen War of 1994–96 with its thirty thousand dead also has "bureaucratistic" ramifications, as does the genocidal second "edition" of 1999–2003. A silly example of bureaucratism in Russia is the ending of the new business of a young entrepreneur by a Russian border guard in 1993. "Are these wood?" asked the guard about some toys. "Yes, they're wooden." "Then you need a special permit," said the guard. "The government has decreed wood a strategic export." The old Soviet "runaround" continued in the 1990s. As late as 1993, despite the democratization that had occurred, leaving the country still required permission from the security service, obtainable, perhaps, after filing an "objective data form" with an attached photograph plus three official seals and waiting longer than such a process formerly took, even two months or more.[97]

Passing the buck up the chain of command was institutionalized during the Soviet period. The classic historical, if not historic, example may have been the ordinary boxcar that, stuck on a siding during World War II, was finally moved by the personal order of Molotov, one of the top five people in the country. An amusing example is that of an American tourist receiving compensation for a samovar wrongly seized by Soviet customs only after the tourist had written to Brezhnev himself. Another case involving bureaucratism and a foreign tourist was cleared up only after a Russian newspaper had taken the matter to the head of a department of the USSR Ministry of Finance.[98]

Only a few additional examples need be cited. During the Soviet period it was common for decisions made by one official to be canceled by another official at the same, not a higher, level. In science there were "so many obstacles and forms of petty and humiliating control" that it could take a new scientific finding "not months but even years" to hurdle the barriers to publication. And publishing in general suffered from "the rigid, bureaucratic structure of the industry" and served the interests of particular groups only. Environmental efforts too were severely hampered by bureaucratic constraints. Even the display of works of art was determined by bureaucrats. And the process of ending the Soviet Union, as the former mayor of Moscow has noted, "was dominated not by the democrats, but by Russian bureaucrats who used it as a pretext for moving into more prestigious buildings, larger offices and better clinics." Not surprisingly, the post-Soviet Russian government is also experiencing the operation of Parkinson's Law, "an unparalleled growth . . . as competing centers of power create their own turf."[99] Clearly, bureaucratism was a severe and distorting brake on the operation of the Soviet system and has continued into the post-Soviet period.

SOURCES

Looking at what Russians say are the sources of bureaucratism gives us a sense of whether they are intellectually prepared to overcome it and also a better sense of the nature of the phenomenon and its manner of development as well as its power and hold on Russian administration. Certainly Russians have the best knowledge of the problem because they have lived under it and still have to contend with it. The etiology here is in two parts: one, sources associated with historical events, stages, and personages; and two, causal factors connected with bureaucratic processes themselves.

Historical Sources

The historical sources begin with imperial Russian government. Tsarist bureaucratism continued into the Soviet period. The Bolshevik Revolution was not a clean break with the past, and Lenin was not granted a tabula rasa on which to build his "new" system. Lenin himself is criticized, at least for not fully understanding the difficulties facing the new enterprise, although it may well be that he eventually understood it better than many other Old Bolsheviks. Stalin, of course, comes in for major criticism as a magnifier of bureaucratism and an originator of much of it. Khrushchev is not much mentioned, but Brezhnev is seen as having allowed many negative bureaucratic phenomena to continue unabated.

Tsarist Legacies

Tsarist legacies are recognized by many. As Popov says, the nature of a government does not change just because it is led by people from the underground, particularly when they did not refound it on a true socialist base. And what sort of effects will it have even on ex-workers serving in it? he asks.[100] The heritage of Russian administration was a powerful one. As Selunin notes, "The legacy of the prerevolutionary Russian bureaucracy continues to be the chief obstacle to reforms . . . from the very outset the authority of the Russian bureaucracy was far broader than that of government bureaucracies in the West. Peter left behind a vast, overcentralized and inefficient bureaucracy. The breakup of the old state machinery in 1917 failed to sever the bureaucracy's roots."[101] Former tsarist bureaucrats taken into Soviet administration are charged with having transmitted "typical bureaucratic vices of the past" such as red tape, bribery, and "muddle-headedness" to the new administrative cadres as their "social legacy." They are also condemned for having "consciously spread bureaucratism," which was, it is claimed, part of the "legacy of previous forms and methods of work." Functionaries from the former system were once quite numerous in Soviet agencies in percentage terms—in 1918 in the People's Commissariat of Health they made up 60.9 percent of the employees, and in the Cheka, 16.1 percent.[102]

In 1922 Lenin lamented, "We brought over from Tsarist Russia the worst, bureaucratism and oblomovism, from which we are literally suffocating." It may have been at that time that Lenin trenchantly commented that the Soviet state apparatus was the tsarist bureaucratic machine anointed with a little "Soviet holy oil." This comment reflects a tendency, by both Lenin and present-day Russian commentators, to blame others and a refusal to accept their share of responsibility for bureaucratism. And this tsarist–Soviet continuity suggests that the Bolsheviks were not fully ready to govern in accordance with their expressed beliefs. This continuity "did . . . greatly influence the way the government operated," says Rigby.[103] Continuity there must have been, very possibly with effects still with us.

Revolutionary Sources

"The times" surrounding the Bolshevik takeover, the confused and disruptive social conditions, were not at all conducive to the minimization of bureaucratism. The Bolsheviks were desperately trying to seize and hold onto power. For a while, said Trotsky, no one knew which way the Civil War was going. There was also a general "lack of knowledge and experience of administrative work" during the period; advanced study of administration had only just begun, with Russia not a main locale for it. And the flight, execution, and imprisonment of top tsarist administrators only made a poor and deprived situation worse.

Marxist and Leninist Sources

Lenin and Marxism itself are not blameless. To pin bureaucratism entirely on the tsars would be an easy and contrived way out. Despite Marxism's antigovernmental bias in thought and verbiage, it is not antibureaucratic in actual policy. Milovan Djilas, once a leading practitioner of Marxist revolution and rule, has noted approvingly, "It was Bakunin, with the intuition of an anarchic utopian, who observed first that Marx's doctrines lead inevitably toward the creation of monstrous, oppressive state machinery." Perhaps Bakunin's unsatisfactory meeting with Marx made him realize that Karl Marx had a somewhat bureaucratic personality. When Bakunin requested to see the minutes of the meetings of the International, Marx refused. When Bakunin asked for the reason, Marx replied, "Because you're not a member."[104] Djilas also notes that in Yugoslavia "the bureaucracy proliferated incessantly. Only when one held a bureaucratic post was one offered stability and perspective." I have heard the same from several other citizens of the former Yugoslavia, including relatives. This suggests that bureaucracy in a communist system was a sort of substitute for the structures of civil society. It was the only possible "aboveground" civil society in a communist system. This is a continuation of tsarism in a way. Malia has pointed out that the "stunted growth" of civil society in Russia "obliged the state to create a surrogate for it in the form of bureaucracy."[105]

Lenin, despite his high intelligence, strong realism in many respects, pronounced revolutionary drive, and undoubtable leadership ability, had harshly authoritarian or at least what could be called "commandist" tendencies. Yet he lacked a typical "bureaucratic personality." Most bureaucrats tend to decide things through committee meetings, consensus among at least their own kind, and to favor low-risk and limited decisions. Of course, there do exist "leader bureaucrats" who decide things on their own and become quasi politicians, for example, Admiral Rickover, Chancellor Bismarck, Count Witte, and the "master builder," Robert Moses. Lenin when in power forgot, it seems, his Marxist proletarianism and issued orders on anything and at a machine-like pace: "Power tends to corrupt." In some other system he would have been a general or top corporate executive. Although Solzhenitsyn's *Lenin in Zürich* is a construct of the imagination, the psychologically rigid Lenin presented therein nevertheless seems the true, "inner" one. Lenin's forceful personality and strong organizational abilities enabled him to bring off a coup, but, at the same time, these abilities undercut and pushed into the background Marxist sensibility, inclination, and vision. Lenin's rush to rule supplanted principled purpose.

Bolshevism in Power

Bolshevism, "undergroundism," and civil war provided poor soil for socialist and communitarian idealism. Aleksandr Bogdanov, who may have coined the term *war communism*, said that by 1918 Bolshevism was transformed into a movement with "the logic, the culture, and the methods of the army barrack." Because all armies, even revolutionary ones, are organizations that rest on discipline, rank, special procedures, and separation from society at large, they inevitably have bureaucratic tendencies. By the end of the Civil War half the Bolshevik Party had served in the Red Army. Because the revolution did not take hold elsewhere, except briefly in Hungary, a minority siege mentality developed further. This led to the confusing of opposition to the Bolsheviks with counterrevolutionary activity and the turning of administration into authoritarian and suppressive societal supervision and policing by means of, notes Khasbulatov, "unlimited . . . development of the punitive parts of the state apparatus, and on this basis the formation of an all-powerful bureaucratic Power. The Power suppressed the spirit, will and the very physical existence of the individual."[106]

The lack of real differentiation among the various branches of government, the merging of the party with the state apparatus, the shortage of administratively trained cadres, the absence of the habits required of effective administrators, and the turning of the party and state apparatus into an elite all exacerbated the problems of Bolshevik bureaucracy and its bureaucratism, according to contemporary Russian commentators. More fundamentally, the party's "underground" and conspiratorial culture did not give it "any kind of understanding of legal political and societal activity."[107] The running of a conspiracy is not suited to producing a dispassionate administration and the rule of law. And it was the lack of an independent judiciary and the inability to sue bureaucrats that protected and locked in bureaucratism.

The establishment of Soviet power did not allow either control or reduction of the problem. The "administrative command system" then forming accepted only harsh measures for coping with bureaucratism, which could not be studied or approached coolly or scientifically. It was not supposed to exist. In addition, the "bureaucratic centralism and on-paper-only-for-show democratism of the time put a powerful brake on societal development." And later, the "struggle against bureaucratism" was never realistic because the omnipresence of the problem was never acknowledged.[108]

Stalin

The Stalin era produced a great, even overwhelming, increase in bureaucratism. There is disagreement as to what degree Stalin himself was responsible. One Russian commentator says, "It was the bureaucrats who usurped power prior to the emergence of the personality cult." Nevertheless, it is strongly likely that Stalin's totalitarian ethos, goals, and practices confirmed, encouraged, and rigidified bureaucratism. Stalin also put an end to the serious study of organization and management that had come into existence during the 1920s. Popov emphasizes that for Stalin the "main source of development was power—state power" and that under Stalin "bureaucratism acquired unprecedented strength not only in the power of the giant apparatus of repression (the 'subsystem of Fear') . . . but . . . in the power of the right to distribute enormous material resources . . . [and] material benefits" and to "exclude the very capability of having resources from any societal group."[109]

Khrushchev

Khrushchev, like Lenin, admitted the problem's existence and took steps against it. He eliminated the ministries. Their cores remained, however, in Gosplan and the secretariat. Like Lenin, he failed to either control bureaucratism or reduce it significantly. He had too many "irons in the fire" simultaneously and was undone by the failure to prioritize and maintain a sufficient political base for self-protection. "Father was isolated," writes his son. But making real headway against bureaucratism would have required a "root and branch" approach that Khrushchev, a believer in the socialist experiment, could not adopt: "His successors quickly curtailed all his innovations and experiments, especially in the country's administrative structure—the ones most hated by the bureaucrats."[110]

The Later Soviet Period

Brezhnev's chances of significant progress were almost nonexistent because his "stability of cadres" policy in his "regime of the clerks" (Brzezinski's phrase) precluded any action other than tinkering on the "treadmill of reforms" (an apt coinage by Gertrude Schroeder): "Now it took many months and sometimes years to receive approval of documents."[111] Significantly, Gorbachev, although he fired half or more of the higher-ups in most bureaucracies, did nothing serious against bureaucratism. As one Russian observer states, even the many Soviet antibureaucratic campaigns of the late Soviet era were themselves forms of bureaucratism in a "new wave of bureaucracy unknown to Weber."[112] Yeltsin never gained control of the problem for several reasons. Bureaucrats achieved semi-independence from the state, and Yeltsin relied too much on cronies in key bureaucratic positions and changed bureaucrats purely for reasons of his political survival. The result was a "bizarre structure."[113]

Clearly, the obstacles facing a minimization of bureaucratism are formidable. This is particularly so in the post-Soviet environment of societal impoverishment and degradation, when observers see the appearance of "gangocracy, the combination of organized crime and bureaucracy," and bureaucrats tending to seek "minimal freedom and maximum social protection" and displaying a "hostility toward innovation."[114] Accordingly, it is highly unlikely that bureaucratism will be reduced significantly in the near future.

RUSSIA'S WEAK STATE

One of the biggest problems facing Russia today is the weakness of the state, government, and its institutions. Here we shall deal with this problem mainly as it is connected with bureaucracy and its difficulties.[115]

"Upper Volta with missiles" is a famous characterization of the Soviet Union, reputedly coined by then Chancellor Helmut Schmidt of Germany. Interestingly, several observers see the weakness of the Russian state as already existing in the late Soviet period. Hoffman notes, "Moscow's once-all-powerful authority had been eroding for years, even before the breakup of the Soviet Union." As Wettig puts it, "A problem of ungovernability emerged which increasingly manifested itself . . . as a growing feudalization, i.e., as the formation of largely particularist powers resembling the development of medieval feudal systems." Today it is not uncommon to see Russia placed with highly decentralized developing countries whose central governments cannot carry out their core functions. Contemporary Mexico and China after 1911 come to mind. I have already quoted Huskey on Russia's current inability to carry out "the most basic administrative tasks." However, it may be going too far, as Jensen does, to equate Russia with countries such as Somalia, Haiti, and Liberia, for there we have continual violent internal conflict as well, with foreign military intervention in Liberia. Russia is amazingly quiescent for a country in deep and fundamental difficulties, a feature often ascribed to popular disinterest in, and even a fatigue with, politics and the general need of people to spend their time trying to fulfill basic human needs.[116]

Russians seem to know that the state is now unable to help them. When Russians were polled in 1998 as to who they relied on in a crisis, only 12 percent said the state; 61 percent said that they would rely "only on myself." As a prominent Russian has stated: "We live today in a weak state. . . . Our state's weakness does not lie in the absence of a 'firm hand.' Its weakness lies in total indifference to the fate of living people, for whose sake law and order are supposedly established. . . . [T]he Russian state demonstrates impotence most clearly."[117]

Where once great nations feared the power of Russia, today many fear its weakness—"the atrophying of state authority . . . and the questionable control over its instruments of mass destruction and its territory." A former U.S. ambassador to Russia has spoken of the significance of Russia's geographical space for U.S. security. Some commentators speak of Russia as a "failed state" and even one that might disappear.[118] The specter of Chinese-type "warlordism" has been raised by some, though that would require a drive for independent power among Russian generals that their bureaucratic nature prevents. Each country gets its "own" kind of weak state. That old Greek word *chaos* is being used, though Russia lacks the rampant disorder, unpredictability, and utter confusion that the word implies. Russian weakness is calm and resigned, like the proverbial long-suffering Russian peasant. The country has been "anaesthetized," said one Russian newspaper. Still, many Russians are concerned and even aghast and angry at the present weakness of the state, though others accept it in a way because they view the state not as theirs but as the plaything of an elite engaged in its own games. As Kagarlitsky puts it, "Power goes to whoever can grab it first and property issues are decided by political campaigns and bureaucratic shuffles . . . everything else is handled by PR and propaganda [and] . . . the brush strokes of image makers. . . . Backstage, though, you can see the puppeteers squabbling over who gets to pull the strings."[119]

One of former Prime Minister Primakov's advisers exclaimed that Russia was looking to become no more than a "shape on a map." The economy is in deplorable condition, yes, but the "state is in a more archaic condition than the economy," says one leading academic. Lynch's "chronic incompetence" of the state is apt. As Thomas Graham stated in 1998, "For more than a decade, the centralized Russian state has been growing weaker in a complex process of devolution, fragmentation, decentralization, erosion, and degeneration of power, both political and economic." The loyalty of even elite security forces is "dubious," the national financial system is "in a shambles," wage and pension arrears is a persistent and widespread problem, and "for the first extended period in modern Russian history, the Center is neither feared nor respected." Witness the pervasive draft and tax evasion: "In short, the Center has only a minimal capacity to mobilize—or extract—resources for national purposes. . . . Indeed, for the first time in Russian history, the bulk of power and authority lies outside the Center." Russia, then, does not have a state in the proper sense.[120]

It could well have what Brubaker calls an "incipient state," a possible "state in the making." Accordingly, "there are many signs of state dysfunctionality—the perpetual and dramatic changes in economic policy, volatility in the distribution of power among political factions, and the absence of a stable and effective governing system that could mediate political struggles" as well as the "loss of ability to use the armed forces to promote state goals" (still true despite Chechen War "II").[121]

Graham gives some of the main reasons for this weakening: attempts at transforming the country's economy, elite struggles, the acquisition of

power by regional leaders, and globalization and its diffusion of governmental powers. He could also have mentioned the end of the Communist
Party. Sperling notes that state rebuilding has been deficient. Russia's new
political leaders allowed the transition to proceed "without building in a
strong place for state regulation." She suggests, with a reference to Reno
and Migdal and the "politics of survival" among "strongmen," that such
politicians do not want to create strong institutions for fear of rivals "cap-
turing" the state and using it against them.[122] The result can be a confusing parallelism of competing agencies. It existed under "strongman"
Stalin, and it existed under pseudo"strongman" Yeltsin as well. But in
Russia some of the power has simply dissipated, and some has been taken
by criminal groups, the so-called *mafiya*, while much of it has gone to two
related groups, both resembling ministates: the rich big businessmen (the
"oligarchs") and the regional political elites. Some of this may eventually
be a plus. A new civil society could develop out of the oligarchs, and the
regional elites may produce, here and there, good variants of government
that work and that serve as models for the rest of Russia, including the
center.[123]

Now to bureaucracy's place in this Russian "weak state." Put briefly,
the state bureaucracy does not carry out state policies well because it is
linked with the oligarchs, the criminals, and the regional leaders and
also suffers from incompetence, understaffing, underpayment, and consequent demoralization. In addition, "wild privatization," confusion at
the policy-maker level, and the current culture of "anything goes" restrict the bureaucracy's capabilities. The commentary on the unfortu-
nate relationship of the state bureaucracy to Russia's governmental decline is almost endless. McFaul says that an effective bureaucracy
simply does not exist in Russia today and that "given the weakness of
the state, Russian entrepreneurs are compelled to turn to the only force
that can protect their property—the mafia."[124] And often the bureaucracy and the mafia are interrelated. Solzhenitsyn says that "bureaucracy has doubled and tripled in size, and it feeds itself at the expense
of the people. As a result we have got state authority that is powerless
to manage the country effectively but which is very tenacious in defending its own prerogatives."[125]

All pertinent sources claim that Russia's state bureaucracy has increased in numbers. One source says that the number of state officials increased by 14 percent between 1994 and 1997. Another says that instead
of replacing Soviet institutions with more functional organs, Russia is seeing the superimposition of new nonproductive agencies with no-show
functionaries on top of Soviet institutions. Sergei Rogov says that Russia
possesses "democracy for the bureaucracy," whereas Ariel Cohen says
that "Russia's problem today is too much incompetent government, too

many bureaucrats, and too much regulation and corruption." (I discuss corruption in the next chapter.) This curious debility is summed up by Sperling as "Russia's blend of state weakness and elite abuse of power." Grzegorz Kolodko, one of the architects of Poland's economic success, says that "the core of Russia's troubles is . . . mismanagement," whereas Arch Getty goes so far as to say that Russia is "a country run by incompetents and crooks." Others say that the "best cadres" have been dismissed from the bureaucracy, even from the "power" ministries. And the inability of these ministries to coordinate their statements and action has been noted by U.S. government sources.[126]

It has also been noted by various observers that Russian bureaucracies did not often follow President Yeltsin's orders and were also engaged in open rivalries and conflicts. An ambassador from one of the "Newly Independent States" says that even Russian diplomats are at loggerheads over what Russian foreign policy is. In 1996 Prime Minister Chernomyrdin harshly criticized the Finance Ministry and the State Property Committee for not fulfilling numerous presidential decrees. Perhaps 50 percent of Yeltsin's decrees were fulfilled late. Many ministries are offenders. The Ministry of Foreign Trade has claimed that the Ministry of Agriculture's decision in 1996 to ban imports of chickens from the United States was taken without consulting it. Absurdities abound, for example, "several tens of thousands" of diplomatic passports have been issued, most for nondiplomatic purposes such as private business and tourism. Visas stamped "USSR" were issued to foreigners as late as 1996. In an incident in 1995, FSB staffers and police shot at each other. As late as 1999 the infant and flawed court system was forced almost to a halt of operations because of a lack of appropriations.[127]

Given this sort of situation, it is not surprising that Russia's state institutions are mere shadows of what they once were. At least two former recent U.S. ambassadors to Russia have noted Russia's bureaucratic difficulties. Robert S. Strauss has said that Russia's bureaucracy is too unwieldy to absorb aid and that it is in decay, and Thomas Pickering has spoken of "terrifying" bureaucratic delays in Russia.[128]

The bureaucratic problem of Russia's weak state has many ramifications. One of the variables impeding foreign investment in Russia is the "incapacity of government structures," including the unfair, "highly complex and ineffective taxation system." *The Economist* notes that a "damaging" problem for Russian economic development is "a customs bureaucracy cumbersome enough to frighten away legitimate trade." Small business people have a myriad of difficulties with the bureaucracy. Some officials, many "from the old school," are unalterably opposed to anything that small business does. Some want bribes. Others "find" all sorts of violations, for example, a can of instant coffee lacking instructions on use. Regionalism may have gone too far. Governors intercept money from the central government and use it for their pet projects and investments. The government has had to use questionable private banks for its own funds. Some of them have sent tax revenues to postboxes in the Cayman Islands and elsewhere. Foreign policy is negatively affected. At times it seems that there is no one Russian central government. The U.S. government has had to deal with Russian officials who do not obey general orders of their own government and insist on dealing with each matter on an ad hoc basis. A NATO adviser has pointed to the Russian government's inability to implement its policies because of "a serious lack of administrative competence and trained managers."[129]

President Vladimir Putin, Yeltsin's successor in early 2000, apparently recognizes that for Russia to arrest its decline and start up the road to normalcy and a better situation for most of its citizens the state and its bureaucracy must be revived and improved. In May 2000, just before he formally became president, he said, "When a person comes to work the first thing he does is check and tune the tool he works with. This is the presidential administration, the government, the other tools of governance." Because he has a background in the bureaucracy, he has some of the requisite experience for the job. But it is a most difficult one. "For the foreseeable future, the most important task of the desperately sick [Russian] central state will be simply to survive," notes Anatol Lieven. Still, much, perhaps all, depends on the reconstitution of the state and at the same time making it one that will serve both democracy and a free enterprise economy. It was Napoleon who said, "Men are powerless to secure the future; institutions alone fix the destinies of nations." Although there were once good reasons to "shrink the state" in Russia, given the sort of state it became under Stalin's "tender" ministrations, in many important respects it is now necessary to strengthen the Russian state and make it work in support of a free and fair market, according to a former high official of the U.S. Treasury. As Himmelfarb has said, "A delicate balancing act is required" to diminish the state in some respects while "retaining a healthy respect for the state itself" and making it do what a modern economy and democracy require: "There can be no 'new' Russia, one geared structurally to the 21st century and one integratable into Western (modern) alliance systems unless it sheds itself of both Soviet and post-Soviet Soviet-like bureaucracies." Also important is the answer to the question of "where power will finally be concentrated, both geographically and within the state bureaucracy." A former U.S. State Department official has suggested that the new Russian central state will have to be a "minimal Center, focused on a few core responsibilities," that would downsize itself in deference to the requirements of democracy, a market economy, and the realization of what powers it can "reasonably defend." We shall see if President Putin follows such a course or one more in the Russian tradition.[130]

Taxes

An important example of the great weakness of the post-Soviet Russian state and its bureaucracy has been that of tax collection or the relative lack thereof. This is not to say that Russia's inadequate tax collection is caused only by the nature of the state administration. The high tax rates, the way taxes are levied, and the nature of Russia's federalism also have a role, as does its "wild" privatization and its political-administrative aspects. The tax system has been highly complex and highly ineffective.[131]

The problem with Russian taxation during the 1990s, in a nutshell, is that it collected too little money to pay for the state and its necessary expenses and that it encouraged evasion of payment by a large percentage of potential taxpayers. In addition, it cast a negative light on Russia's image internationally in several respects—as a military power, as a place for investment, and even as a modern state. If a state cannot acquire the resources it requires to exist and operate as such, then it comes to be seen as a failed state: "Russia's state institutions responsible for taxation provide a striking illustration of incapacity." One specialist even said in 1998 that "Russia's inability to collect taxes is rapidly becoming the greatest threat to its economic and political stability. The current government cannot raise the revenues needed to run a modern state." A leading Russian state banker has said that Russia's economic crisis "is largely rooted in the inability of the state to perform . . . tax collection." In 1998 then Prime Minister Kiriyenko said, "If the state does not learn to collect taxes it will cease to exist." Yergin and Gustafson have suggested that "it is the struggle over taxes that will, in large measure, determine how this Russian crisis comes out."[132]

Aslund goes so far as to say that "Russia has no actual tax system." Elsewhere, he has called that system "hopeless" and says that "in practice, taxation is a free negotiation . . . meaning that the strong win and small entrepreneurs are chased out of business." Another observer has labeled Russia "a nation of tax deadbeats" after noting that only one million of 147 million Russians filed tax returns in 1997. The result is a "monstrous budget crisis, the scale of which calls into question the ability of the state to perform its functions," says Anatoly Chubais. "Tax revenue is collected only to be stolen," says the director of Russia's Chamber of Accounts. The *New York Times* has editorialized that "the Russian tax system is riddled with corruption, loopholes and atrocious administration" and "has left government coffers half empty." Certainly, taxation in Russia does "not resemble that known in the West." For some years the mafia was able to collect its "taxes" better than the state did, encouraging tax evasion to make up for the mafia "take."[133]

M. Kasyanov, Putin's first prime minister, has stated, "The main headache for producers today is the tax burden." Taxes were simply set way too high for making profits. One hotel executive to whom I spoke in the early 1990s said that his St. Petersburg hotel's taxes were 70 percent of profits. President Putin has expressed the view, most probably correct, that "high taxes had contributed to industrial decline." Russia literally could not finance government or pay its officials, even many of its most important ones. Accordingly, the best bureaucrats left for better-paying jobs in the private sector. The health service and the system of social protection just broke down. Corruption went unpunished, government was further undermined, and democracy became further discredited. The "insane" tax system encouraged some entrepreneurs to hide their capital abroad and in general to "go underground." For some time perhaps as much as $2 billion left Russia every month. This forced a "barterization" of the money-starved economy (similar to the rural economy of the United States during its early history). In addition, the tax system drove away desperately needed foreign investment. And then there has been the absurdity of the Russian government lacking a mechanism for implementing a permanent exemption from taxation for U.S. aid to Russia.[134]

What are the specifically bureaucratic reasons for the tax crisis? Despite cultural and structural reasons, it is possible that "government inefficiency and lassitude are primarily responsible." *The Economist* has stated that "the tax service is simply not equal to the job of collecting taxes in any comprehensive fashion." Part of the problem may be low expectations. In 1996 a group of Russian officials told visiting Americans that they were achieving 34 percent compliance in tax collection. When they asked the Americans how they were doing in this regard an American scholar replied that at the federal level it was assumed that the compliance rate was about 90 percent. "Too high," exclaimed the Russians, and they went on to suggest that the United States must use draconian measures to reach such a high rate. Here we may have very different political cultures and views of what government can do. Although Americans grumble about taxes and make them a perennial political issue, they do tend to pay up. Russians may simply not pay whatever is done. Yavlinsky has said, "What will they pay? . . . About ten percent, not more." Sergei Shtarev, the deputy head of the tax service in 1998, has said that "in general, less than half pay taxes." This may still be so in 2003. The head of the Moscow office of the tax police said in early 2002 that 60 percent of Russian business entities do not pay taxes. One is reminded of the French government's difficulty in collecting taxes on actual income and its "solution" of taxing on the basis of appearances of income, the *forfait* method.[135]

Although there is an enormous amount of statistics on the deficiencies of Russian tax collection during the 1990s, very little of it need be cited because all statistics in Russia today are suspect. It is as if the deceptive practices of the Soviet period reached their full development in an obscene apotheosis of false numbers. Not until early 2000, with Putin as acting president, were there claims of significant increases in tax collection.[136]

Certainly what is needed is a sea change in tax laws and tax collection agencies and their actions and procedures, but to make a real difference there will have to be structural changes in the economy and big cultural changes among politicians, bureaucrats, and the population at large. Vladimir Putin has recognized that some such change is needed. He has said that the government needs to stimulate business. There are no secrets in how to do this. As two Russians state: "The burden of currently excessive taxation on private enterprises should be reduced to a level common for developed market economies." Prime Minister Kasyanov says, "The tax regime must be simplified" and "the main headache today for producers is the tax burden."[137] Putin has taken steps in this direction and has called tax reform one of the key priorities of the new government.[138]

Putin, with the approval of Parliament, has instituted what could be called a "bold experiment," a 13 percent flat-rate income tax that might delight American right-wingers. It increased revenues from income tax by 47 percent. However, the other taxes, which produce most of the government's revenues, are still high.[139] According to Gaidar in June 2002, Russian tax revenues have risen by 70 percent and the government expected to collect $7 billion in taxes in 2003.[140] But any improvement in tax collection may last only as long as higher oil and natural gas prices. The story of Russia's war with itself over tax collection is still not over. Winning it is still problematic and awaits a number of battles over considerable time.

CONCLUSION

The central and sometimes overriding importance of bureaucracy to Russia has been demonstrated by the contents of this chapter. Everywhere in Russia bureaucracy has power, sometimes decisive or at least important power, and making it fulfill the goals of the "policy makers" can be a very big problem with no easy or obvious solution. In Russia the state almost fell apart, and bureaucracy, sometimes in league with newly released social forces, often has had its own way, much to the detriment of anyone's conception of the national interest. Putting Humpty Dumpty back together again, with due regard for the requirements of democracy, will be a task for the next few generations of Russian leaders. But even when this goal has been achieved, the leaders and the body politic, too, will have to be continually cognizant of bureaucracy's powers and problems. Only with fundamental socioeconomic and political change and improvement, as well as a change of ruling generations, might this bureaucratic "lock" lose its grip. This is a matter of luck, hard work, political drive, and at least a few decades. However, we have seen that there is real agreement on the phenomenon by those who write about it and that many commentators have a good intellectual grasp of it, although a lot of these writers may lack political clout and may be unrepresentative of those professionally concerned with public administration in Russia. Still, any ruling group, even nationalists who want Russia again to be a great power, will have to tackle and reduce bureaucratism. And what if a new Count Witte or Premier Stolypin comes to power? (Could Putin be that figure?) Then this literature and its authors may finally have a chance to have an influence on Russian administration and, over time, to reduce the role of bureaucratism within it: "Eternal vigilance."

NOTES

1. Personal observation, November 1976.
2. This occurred at the U.S. Arms Control and Disarmament Agency, 1996.
3. Personal observation, U.S. Department of State, 1996.
4. This is from a return address on a letter.
5. Reputedly, Pope Pius XII, who had long served in the Curia, exclaimed on his deathbed: "To work! Files! Documents! To work!" (quoted in Gerald Renner, "Lingering Questions Remain in 'Hitler's Pope,'" review of John Cornwell, *Hartford Courant*, reprinted in *Daily Hampshire Gazette* [Northampton, Mass.], 22 March 2000, C4).
6. Marcus Gee, "Understanding Russia's Collapse," *The Globe and Mail* (Toronto), 10 February 1999, from *Johnson's Russia List*, 10 February 1999.
7. Daniel Yergin and Thane Gustafson, *Russia 2010* (New York: Random House, 1993). The authors foresee a Russia ruled by defense industrialists, managers of government industries, and members of the police and the army.
8. Paul Hollander, "Politicized Bureaucracy: The Soviet Case," *Newsletter on Comparative Studies of Communism* 4, no. 3 (May 1971): 13; John Kenneth Galbraith, "Reflections: A Visit to Russia," *The New Yorker*, 3 September 1984, 54. Galbraith adds, "It may, indeed, be that a certain stability is provided by the huge bureaucratic apparatus and its own inertia" ("Reflections," 61). This "stability" is something many in Russia want to return to.
9. Marc Raeff, *Understanding Imperial Russia*, trans. from French by Arthur Goldhammer (New York: Columbia University Press, 1984), 54 (the phrase he quotes is from Maurice Hauriou); Moshe Lewin, "The Collapse of the Russian State," *Le Monde Diplomatique*, March 1998, from *Johnson's Russia List*, 11 November 1998. A recent Russian book on political science begins with a section on administration (*upravlenie*); see *Aktual'nye problemy politiki i politologii v Rossii* (Moscow: RAGS, 1999).

10. John le Carré, *The Looking Glass War* (New York: Dell, 1965), 73. The rest of the quotation goes, "While they might be cynical of the qualities of one another, contemptuous of their own hierarchical preoccupations, their faith in the Department burned in some separate chapel and they called it patriotism" (le Carré, *The Looking Glass War*, 73, see also 30).

11. *New York Times*, 30 May 1985, C19; Zbigniew K. Brzezinski, *Out of Control: Global Turmoil on the Eve of the Twenty-first Century* (New York: Scribner's, 1993), 12–13. Some say that the American development and use of the atomic bomb is another example of bureaucracy's dangerous power.

12. Milovan Djilas, *The New Class* (New York: Praeger, 1957), 43; Svetozar Stojanovic, *Between Ideals and Reality* (New York: Oxford University Press, 1973), 79.

13. As the Flerons say, Lenin's "remedy took on bureaucratic forms" (Frederic J. Fleron and Lou Jean Fleron, "Administration Theory as Repressive Political Theory: The Communist Experience," *Newsletter on Comparative Study of Communism* 6, no. 1 [November 1972]: 18).

14. See, for example, Henry Kamm, "Opening Is Glum at Party Congress in Yugoslavia," *New York Times*, 26 June 1986, A6; Serge Schmemann, "East German Out as Chief of State," *New York Times*, 7 December 1989, A1; Celestine Bohlen, "Democratic Hungary Nibbles on Political Fringes," *New York Times*, 9 July 1990, A7.

15. Wassily Leontief, "Forget the Free Market," *New York Times*, 3 March 1992, 25; James Sterngold, "Thinking the Unthinkable, Japan May Curb Its Bureaucrats' Power," *New York Times*, 13 September 1993, A1. See also James Sterngold, "The Men Who Really Run Fortress Japan," *New York Times*, 10 April 1994, F1, F8. As he points out, "Politicians have often thrown up their hands when confronted with the power of the bureaucracy" ("The Men Who Really Run Fortress Japan," F8).

16. Jon Pierre, "Comparative Public Administration: The State of the Art," in *Bureaucracy in the Modern State: An Introduction to Comparative Public Administration*, ed. Jon Pierre (Aldershot, England: Edward Elgar, 1995), 9.

17. *What Is the State?* (Moscow: Progress Publishers, 1986), 26, 30.

18. The survey was carried out by the Task Force on State Failure, based at the Center for International Earth Science Information Network at Columbia University. The quotation from Max Weber is from his "Politics as a Vocation," in *From Max Weber: Essays in Sociology*, eds. H. H. Gerth and C. Wright Mills (New York: Oxford University Press, 1958), 78.

19. Karl Marx, quoted in Anatolii Sobchak, *Khozhdenia vo vlast'* (Moscow: Novosti, 1991), 159, my translation; Karl Marx, "On Bureaucracy," in *Karl Marx: Selected Writings*, ed. David McClellan (London: Oxford University Press, 1977), 30–31. McClellan notes that Marx wrote a "brilliant analysis of bureaucracy's tendency to form a state within a state."

20. See, for example, Symon Chodok, *The New State: Etatization of Western Societies* (Boulder: Lynne Rienner, 1989). Also, Jean Blondel, in his *Government Ministers in the Contemporary World* (Beverly Hills: SAGE, 1985), writes of "rule by a political class of ministers."

21. From Vladimir Putin, *First Person: An Astonishingly Frank Self-Portrait by Russia's President Vladimir Putin*, trans. Catherine A. Fitzpatrick (New York: Public Affairs, 2000), 186, a "book" of interviews. The translation used here differs slightly from that printed.

22. Perry Anderson, *Lineages of the Absolutist State* (London: Verso, 1979), 346–47, 353, 356, 430. This impressive, erudite, illuminating, and thought-provoking "history from above" ought to be read by all with an interest in the state.

23. Richard Bernstein, "Lenin Paints Himself Black with His Own Words," review of Richard Pipes, *The Unknown Lenin* (New Haven: Yale University Press, 1996), *New York Times*, 30 October 1998, C19; V. I. Lenin, *The State* (Peking: Foreign Languages Press, 1970), 14, 24–25 (lecture at Sverdlov University, 11 July 1919, first printed in *Pravda*, 18 January 1929); V. I. Lenin, *Collected Works*, vol. 17 (Moscow, 1965), 363, quoted in Anderson, *Lineages of the Absolutist State*, 355; Max Gordon, a former editor of the *Daily Worker*, citing Lenin in a letter to the editor, "How Lenin Felt about Independent Unions," *New York Times*, 5 October 1980. Also see V. I. Lenin, *On the Soviet State Apparatus* (Moscow: Progress Publishers, 1977) (this collection does not contain the speech of July 1919 cited above).

24. Editorial, *New York Times*, 22 December 1979 (on the centennial of Stalin's birth); my recollection of Alexander Nekrich, lecture at Harvard University, sometime in the late 1980s or early 1990s; "Beiching Journal," *New York Times*, 16 March 1999, A4; Vyacheslav Gorbachev, *Molodaia gvardiia*, July 1987, 10, cited in *RL Report 1/88*, 5 January 1988; Moshe Lewin, "Working on Bureaucracy," lecture at Harvard University, 8 April 1997 (from my notes). The argument that Stalin was a sort of prisoner of his own security forces is also made by his daughter. See Walter A. McDougal, *The Heavens and the Earth: A Political History of the Space Age* (New York: Basic Books, 1985), quoted in Alex Roland, review, *New York Times Book Review*, 7 April 1985, 1.

25. For the claim, see, for example, *What Is the State?* One chapter, "The State's Creative Role," is itself a Stalinist concept.

26. Robert V. Daniels, "Stalin: Revolutionary or Counterrevolutionary?" *Problems of Communism* 38, no. 5 (September–October 1989): 86; Peter Reddaway, "Gorbachev the Bold," *New York Review of Books*, 28 May 1987, 26; Stephen White, *Gorbachev and After* (Cambridge: Cambridge University Press, 1991), 137; Andrew Rosenthal, interview with Tatyana Zaslavskaya, "A Soviet Voice of Innovation Comes to Fore," *New York Times*, 28 August 1987, A6; interview with Tatyana Zaslavskaya, "Restructuring as a Social Revolution," *Izvestia*, 24 December 1988, trans. in *Current Digest of the Soviet Press* 40, no. 51 (18 January 1989): 1; George F. Kennan, *Memoirs: 1950–1963* (Boston: Little, Brown, 1972), 132.

27. Vladimir Bukovsky, "Tumbling Back to the Future," *New York Times Magazine*, 12 January 1992, 34, 39.

28. Lewin, "The Collapse of the Russian State."

29. A panelist, conference on issues of U.S.–Russian intelligence, the Heritage Foundation, Washington, D.C., 28 March 1994, on C-Span 2; Yevgenia Albats, quoted in *New York Times*, 19 March 2000, 3; Alexander Rahr, "Yeltsin's New Team," *RFE/RL Research Report* 2, no. 2 (28 May 1993): 21. On former KGB officials working for Putin, see Michael R. Gordon, "Putin Will Use Ex-K.G.B. Men to Battle Graft," *New York Times*, 24 March 2000, A1.

30. Jeffrey D. Sachs, quoted in Steven Erlanger, "Wrestling for Rubles," *New York Times*, 28 July 1993, A8.

31. Robert M. Solow, quoted in Louis Uchitelle, "No Economic Model Fits East Bloc," *New York Times*, 30 December 1989, 33.

32. William H. Luers, "A Glossary of Russia's Third Revolution," *New York Times*, 7 July 1987; Steven Greenhouse, "Call for Moscow Aid Office Splits Wealthy Nations," *New York Times*, 20 June 1993, 14.

33. Michel Crozier, *The Bureaucratic Phenomenon* (Chicago: University of Chicago Press, 1967), 158.

34. Wallace S. Sayre, "Bureaucracies: Some Contrasts in Systems," *Indian Journal of Public Administration* 10, no. 2: 8.

35. Russell Baker, "The Spreading Decline," *New York Times*, 31 December 1977, 17; Lance Compa, "In Washington, Revenge of the Nitpickers," *New York Times*, 9 December 1986, A35; John Herbers, "How 43 Agencies Keep Surviving the Reagan Ax," *New York Times*, 9 September 1986, A20; Francis D. Moore, "The Third Culture," *New York Times*, 17 April 1979; Ellen Schrecker, *Many Are the Crimes: McCarthyism in America* (Boston: Little, Brown, 1998), quoted in Thomas C. Reeves, review, *New York Times Book Review*, 14 June 1998, 22; Richard L. Strout, "Why Don't Americans Vote?" *Christian Science Monitor*, 11 January 1985, 14.

36. Vincent Wright, "The Administrative Machine: Old Problems and New Dilemmas," in *Developments in French Politics*, eds. Peter A. Hall, Jack Hayward, and Howard Machin (New York: St. Martin's, 1994), 115; Henry W. Ehrmann, *Politics in France*, 4th ed. (Boston: Little, Brown, 1983), 340; Mark Kesselman, "France," in *European Politics in Transition*, 3d ed., ed. Mark Kesselman et al. (Boston: Houghton Mifflin, 1997), 195. See also Crozier, *The Bureaucratic Phenomenon*; and Philip G. Cerny and Martin A. Schain, eds., *French Politics and Public Policy* (New York: Methuen, 1981).

37. The quotation on India is from "As India Approaches 40, Bitterness Replaces Pride," *New York Times*, 14 August 1987, A6. On Japan, see, for example, Steven R. Weisman, "U.S. Says It Foiled Japan on Beef Sales Curb," *New York Times*, 23 January 1992, D8; Nicholas D. Kristof, "Status of Elite Bureaucrats Declines as Japan Does," *New York Times*, 17 April 1998, A1; David E. Sanger, "Japan's Bureaucracy: No Sign It's Losing Any Power," *New York Times*, 27 February 1994, 3; James Sterngold, "Who Really Runs Japan? Stay Tuned," *New York Times*, 24 December 1993, A3.

38. Associated Press, "Bypassing Shultz—'It Happens All the Time,'" *Daily Hampshire Gazette* (Northampton, Mass.), 12 December 1986, 16; Daniel S. Matlay, lecture at the University of Massachusetts at Amherst, 5 February 1988; James M. Buchanan, "Why Governments 'Got Out of Hand,'" *New York Times*, 26 October 1986; Associated Press, "Iran–Contra Hearing: Conflicting Testimony Rules," *Daily Hampshire Gazette* (Northampton, Mass.), 22 July 1987, 7; public TV and radio reports on 23, 24, and 31 July 1987; "Panel Members Recount the Moments They Won't Forget," *New York Times*, 9 August 1987, E5; Stephen Engelberg, "Order to Bypass Congress Called C.I.A. Idea," *New York Times*, 12 December 1986, A1; William Safire, "Foreign Service Scandal," *New York Times*, 23 December 1992, A17.

39. Bernard E. Trainor, "Role of Officers Growing in N.S.C.," *New York Times* 15 December 1986, A13; personal observation, U.S. Arms Control and Disarmament Agency, 1995–96.

40. Slavenka Drakulic, *How We Survived Communism and Even Laughed* (New York: Norton, 1991), 88–89; Deputy Director Karl-Heinz Roder, Institute for the Theory of State and Law, Academy of Sciences, German Democratic Republic,

lecture at the University of Massachusetts at Amherst, 21 October 1985; *New York Times*, 26 December 1987, A24.

41. H. G. Creel, "Chinese Bureaucracy and the Modern State," paper prepared for the Annual Meeting of the American Political Science Association, Washington, D.C., 8–11 September 1965, 1; Ezra F. Vogel, "Politicized Bureaucracy: Communist China," in *Communist Systems in Comparative Perspective*, eds. Leonard J. Cohen and Jane P. Shapiro (Garden City, N.Y.: Anchor Books, 1974), 168. On Chinese–Soviet bureaucratic differences, see Yasheng Huang, "The Statistical Agency in China's Bureaucratic System," *Communist and Post-Communist Studies* 29, no. 1 (1996): 59–75; Parris H. Chang, book review, *American Political Science Review* 87, no. 2 (June 1993): 509 (in 2000 Chang was an official of the Government of Taiwan); and Kenneth Lieberthal and Michel Oksenberg, *Policy Making in China* (Princeton: Princeton University Press, 1988), 27. Other books on the bureaucracy of the People's Republic of China include David Bachman, *Bureaucracy, Economy, and Leadership in China* (New York: Cambridge University Press, 1991); A. Doak Barnett, *Cadres, Bureaucracy, and Political Power in Communist China* (New York: Columbia University Press, 1967); Harry Harding, *Organizing China: The Problem of Bureaucracy* (Stanford: Stanford University Press, 1981); Hong Yung Lee, *From Revolutionary Cadres to Party Technocrats in Socialist China* (Berkeley: Center for Chinese Studies, 1990); and Kenneth G. Lieberthal and David M. Lampton, *Bureaucracy, Politics and Decision-Making in Post-Mao China* (Berkeley: Studies on China, 1992). See also Franz Schurmann, *Ideology and Organization in Communist China*, 2d ed. enlarged (Berkeley: University of California Press, 1968).

42. Max Eastman, "Stalin's Russia and the Crisis in Socialism" (1940), partially reprinted in *The American Image of Russia: 1917–1977*, ed. Benson Lee Grayson (New York: Frederick Ungar, 1978), 149; Herman Schwartz, lecture at the Kennan Institute for Advanced Russian Studies, Washington, D.C., 3 January 1993, on C-Span 2, 4 January 1993; on Tarschys, see Valerie Bunce, letter, 6 November 1979; Susan Linz, review of Timothy Dunmore, *The Stalinist Command Economy* (London: Macmillan, 1980), *Slavic Review* 40, no. 4 (winter 1981): 147; John Lukacs, "The Soviet State at 65," *Foreign Affairs* 65, no. 1 (fall 1986): 25, 29; *Krasnaia zvezda*, 10 September 1996, from *Johnson's Russia List*, 11 September 1996; obituary of Vladimir Dudintsev, *New York Times*, 30 July 1998, D19.

43. Alexander Yanov, *The Drama of the Soviet 1960s: A Lost Reform* (Berkeley: University of California Press, 1984); V. I. Popova, "Nasushchie zadachi sovershenstvovaniia zakonodatel'stva ob administrativnoi otvetstvennosti," *Sovetskoe gosudarstvo I pravo*, no. 12 (1965): 63; Robert Blackwell, "Gorbachev: How Much New Thinking in Soviet Domestic and Foreign Policy?" lecture at Hampshire College, 1 June 1987; Jerry F. Hough, "Gorbachev's Strategy," *Foreign Affairs* 64, no. 1 (fall 1985): 42–43.

44. Dmitri Simes, "Gorbachev: A New Foreign and Domestic Policy?" lecture at Hampshire College, 1 June 1987; Reuters, 8 December 1987, quoting Professor S. Dzarasov, reprinted in *RL Report 503/87*, 11 December 1987; Alessandra Stanley, "The Man at Yeltsin's Side," *New York Times*, 5 January 1995, A8; Alexander Strokanov, "What Led Russia into This Crisis?" *Charlotte Observer* (N.C.), 2 September 1998.

45. Richard Lourie and Aleksei Mikhelev, "Why You'll Never Have Fun in Russia," *New York Times Book Review*, 18 June 1989, 1; Lewin, "Working on Bureau-

cracy"; White, *Gorbachev and After*, 137; Robert Ivanov, lecture at Middlebury College, 28 September 1990; Boris Kagarlitsky, lecture at the University of Massachusetts at Amherst, 19 November 1991.

46. Aleksei K. Pushkov, "Can the Demolition Man Also Build" (op-ed), *New York Times*, 2 December 1993, A27; Paul Goble, testimony before the Commission on Security and Cooperation in Europe, in *The Situation in Russia*, October 1993, 18; *RFE/RL Research Report* 4, no. 5 (20 November 1986): 2, based on Julia Wishnevsky, *RL 409/86*.

47. Sir Iain Sutherland, former British ambassador to Moscow, lecture at Harvard University, 11 March 1986 (the most impressive lecture I have ever heard); David Lane and Cameron Ross, "The Non-nomenklatura: The Personnel of the Government Bureaucracy in the USSR," unpublished paper (ca. 1992), 1, 10. Lane and Ross say, "It was the state bureaucracy, and its aging and technocratic leadership, which dominated Soviet society and precipitated the collapse of communism" ("The Non-nomenklatura," 2).

48. Sergei A. Grigoriev, lecture at Harvard University, 15 April 1994; interview with General Alexander Lebed, *Nezavisimaia gazeta*, 23 May 1996, in *OMRI Presidential Election Survey*, no. 5 (29 May 1996); Sergei Rogov, quoted in "Russia's Army," *New York Times*, 28 November 1993, 18; Boris Kagarlitsky, quoted in *Moscow News*, 21 September 1998, from *Johnson's Russia List*, 21 September 1998; interview with Gavriil Popov, *Rabochaia tribuna*, 4 November 1995, in *FBIS-SOV-95-216*, 8 November 1995, 7.

49. Gennady Zyuganov, "On the CPRF's Attitude toward State Apparatus Officials," *Pravda Rossii*, 9 November 1995, 2, in *FBIS-SOV-95-219*, 5–6; Stephen F. Cohen, "Brezhnev and the Reign of Conservatism," in *Sovieticus* (New York: Norton, 1985), 54; Grey Hodnett, "Soviet Succession Contingencies," *Problems of Communism* 24, no. 2 (March–April 1975): 21.

50. Lewin, "Working on Bureaucracy"; Eugene Huskey, *Presidential Power in Russia* (Armonk, N.Y.: M. E. Sharpe, 1999), 41, 45, 100; Steven Erlanger, "Ruble Sinks Further," *New York Times*, 20 January 1994, A3; Alexander Solzhenitsyn, quoted in *RFE/RL* 2, no. 3 (15 January 1993): 7; Alex Buzgalin and Andrei Kolganov, Jamestown Foundation *Prism*, no. 13, pt. 2 (26 June 1998); Boris Nemtsov, quoted in *RFE/RL*, 21 January 1998.

51. Karl W. Ryavec, *Implementation of Soviet Economic Reforms* (New York: Praeger, 1975), 80–81; Gertrude Schroeder, "Soviet Economic Reform at an Impasse," *Problems of Communism* 20, no. 4 (July–August 1971): 46.

52. Karl W. Ryavec, "Russo-Soviet Bureaucratism: Recent Russian Views," *The Soviet and Post-Soviet Review* 23, no. 1 (1996): 68, 74–75; *Pravda*, 27 April 1989, 6.

53. "The Diplomatic Life: Ambassador Bob Strauss Comes Home," *The New Yorker*, 4 January 1993, 148; Alex Goldfarb, "Testing Glasnost: An Exile Visits His Homeland," *New York Times Magazine*, 6 December 1987, 49; V. Romanyuk, "How an Ordinary Bureaucrat Blocked a Decision of the USSR President," *Izvestia*, 5 July 1990, 1, in *Current Digest of the Soviet Press* 42, no. 27 (1990): 26; Philip Taubman, "Election Is Snuffed Out at Institute in Moscow," *New York Times*, 29 May 1987, A3; Elizabeth Teague, "*Pravda* Editorial Testifies to Strength of Opposition to Change," *RFE/RL 192/86*, 15 May 1986, based on *Pravda*, 3 March and 12 April 1986.

54. Steven Erlanger, "End of Russia's Economic Slide Brings Eerie Calm," *New York Times*, 22 August 1994, A1, and 29 October 1994, 6. The facts about the State Technical Commission were well known in U.S. government circles during 1995.

55. Boris Yeltsin, "State of the Nation Address," 16 February 1995, on C-Span.

56. Alexander Bovin, "Power Crisis," *Izvestia*, 30 December 1997, from *Johnson's Russia List*, 30 December 1997.

57. Masha Gessen, "Lockstep to Putin's New Military Order," *New York Times*, 29 February 2000, A27.

58. Recent improvement in Russian bureaucratic behavior is suggested by Vlad Ivanenko of the University of Western Ontario (*Johnson's Russia List*, 1 April 2000); the statements about size and administration are from Adam Hochschild, book review, *New York Times Book Review*, 28 June 1998, 20; and Mark Galeotti, *The Age of Anxiety: Security and Politics in Soviet and Post-Soviet Russia* (London: Longman, 1995), 4.

59. Tony Judt, "Extremism, without the Virtue," *New York Times*, 30 January 2000, WK15.

60. Judith Shapiro, review of David Chandler, *Voices from S-21: Terror and History in Pol Pot's Secret Prison* (Berkeley: University of California Press, 2000), *New York Times Book Review*, 30 January 2000, 15.

61. Mark A. Uhlig, "Sandinista Leadership: Rethinking Its Ideology," *New York Times*, 10 August 1990, A4.

62. Sarah M. Terry, "What the West Should Demand of Poland" (letter to the editor), *New York Times*, 21 December 1980, 16E.

63. "Hanoi Battles against Bureaucracy," *New York Times*, 2 September 1975, 4; Keith B. Richberg, "U.S.–Vietnam Talks Turn Out Knotty," *Washington Post*, 30 January 1996, A10; Ulrich Schreyer, "Portrait of an Economy Gagged by Central-Planning Bureaucrats," *Stuttgarter Zeitung*, trans. in *The German Tribune*, 26 November 1989, 7; "Ukraine's Dangerous Decline," *New York Times*, 14 April 1998, A24.

64. Paul Hollander, comments on Soviet bureaucracy at the Annual Meeting of the American Political Science Association, New York, 9 September 1966.

65. An advertisement for Bartlomiej Kaminski, *The Collapse of State Socialism: The Case of Poland* (Princeton: Princeton University Press, 1991).

66. Zbigniew K. Brzezinski, *The Grand Failure* (New York: Scribner's, 1989), 164.

67. The terms associated with Kafka's works are suggested by John Tagliabue, "K. Makes His Way into the Castle," *New York Times*, 12 April 1989, C19; review of James P. Pinkerton, *What Comes Next: The End of Big Government and the New Paradigm Ahead* (Westport, Conn.: Hyperion, 1995), *Washington Post Book World* 25, no. 48 (26 November 1995): 1; Barrington Moore Jr., *Liberal Prospects under State Socialism: A Comparative Historical Perspective*, the First Annual W. Averell Harriman Lecture, 15 November 1989 (New York: Columbia University Press, Harriman Institute, 1989), 25; (then) Secretary of the Navy John F. Lehman, speech, 3 April 1985, excerpted in *New York Times*, 6 April 1985, 6.

68. V. Bondar, "Questions of Theory: The Political Nature of Party Leadership," *Pravda*, 4 May 1984, in *Current Digest of the Soviet Press* 36, no. 18 (30 May 1984): 9; Alessandra Stanley, "Tell-All Book Creates Furor at Vatican," *New York Times*, 17 July 1999, A4; David Lane, "Soviet Elites, Monolithic or Polyarchic?" in *Russia in*

Flux, ed. David Lane (Aldershot, England: Edward Elgar, 1992), 11, 8; Lewin, "Working on Bureaucracy."

69. Sayre, "Bureaucracies"; Paul Cocks, "Rethinking the Organizational Weapon," *World Politics* 32, no. 2 (January 1980): 229; William E. Odom, "Soviet Politics and After," *World Politics* 45, no. 1 (October 1992): 79–80. Here Odom is referring to Robert Merton, *Social Theory and Social Structure* (New York: Free Press, 1968), 39; Crozier, *The Bureaucratic Phenomenon*; and James Q. Wilson, *Political Organizations* (New York: Basic Books, 1973).

70. Milovan Djilas, *Rise and Fall*, trans. John Fiske Lord (New York: Harcourt Brace Jovanovich, 1985), 87 (the original title in Serbo-Croatian is *Vlast* [*Power*]); Donald C. Hodges, *The Bureaucratization of Socialism* (Amherst: University of Massachusetts Press, 1981); Michael E. Urban, *The Ideology of Administration: American and Soviet Cases* (Albany: State University of New York Press, 1982), 113–14. And see Ronald M. Glassman, William H. Swatos Jr., and Paul L. Rosen, eds., *Bureaucracy against Democracy and Socialism* (New York: Greenwood Press, 1987). The quotation from Gorbachev is from his *Gorbachev: On My Country and the World* (New York: Columbia University Press, 1999), quoted in Jack F. Matlock Jr., review, *Foreign Affairs* (January–February 2000): 169.

71. Robert C. Tucker, "The Last Leninist," *New York Times*, 29 December 1991, 9; Steven L. Solnick, *Stealing the State: Control and Collapse in Soviet Institutions* (Cambridge: Harvard University Press, 1998).

72. Aaron Trehub, "The New Oblomovs," *RL 19/86*, 8 January 1986, 1–2; Luxemburg's statement is quoted in Wolfgang Leonhard, *Three Faces of Marxism* (New York: Holt, Rinehart and Winston, 1974), 91; *RFE/RL Soviet–East European Report* 3, no. 32 (20 August 1986): 3; *RL 149/87*, 17 April 1987, 3.

73. On waste, see John A. Armstrong, "Gorbachev: Limits of the Fox in Soviet Politics," *Soviet and Post-Soviet Review* 19, nos. 1–3 (1992): 190; and "Khoziaisvovat' ekonomno," *Pravda*, 13 February 1981, 1. John N. Hazard stressed the lack of coordination in a letter to me dated 2 April 1985; overbureaucratization was cited by Sergei Rogov in a lecture at Hampshire College, 5 June 1985, and by Mark Kramer in his *Travels with a Hungry Bear: Journey to the Russian Heartland* (Boston: Houghton Mifflin, 1995), quoted in John Lloyd, review, *New York Times Book Review*, 23 June 1995, 25. See also David Marples, "The Last Bus to Minsk," *RL 4/85*, 7 January 1985, 3; White, *Gorbachev and After*; and *RL 323/88*, 22 July 1988, 3.

74. "Russian Says Leaders Have Stifled Scientists," *New York Times*, 19 July 1988, C11; Malcolm W. Browne, "Soviet Science Assessed as Flawed but Powerful," *New York Times*, 20 May 1980, C3; *RL 281/82*, 12 July 1982, 1; *New York Times*, 1 February 1982, D6; A.G. Aganbegyan, comments at an EKO Round Table, *Ekonomika I organizatsiia promyshlennogo proizvodstva*, no. 8 (August 1983), trans. in *Current Digest of the Soviet Press* 35, no. 48 (28 December 1983): 1.

75. Hans von Herwarth with S. Frederick Starr, *Against Two Evils* (New York: Random House, 1981), 66; T. S. Bondarenko, *Sindrom nepogreshimosti: Kak s nim borot'sia?* (Moscow: Politizdat, 1989), 101; *Sotsialisticheskaia industriia*, cited in *RL 271/85*, 16 August 1985, 3; Zaslavskaia, "Restructuring as a Social Revolution," 2; U.S. Department of Defense, *Soviet Military Power*, 2d ed. (Washington, D.C.: U.S. Government Printing Office, 1983), 76; Moore, *Liberal Prospects under State Socialism*, 25.

76. Eugene Huskey, *Presidential Power in Russia* (Armonk, N.Y.: M. E. Sharpe, 1999), 220; Gertrude Himmelfarb, "Kind, yet Tough," *New York Times*, 28 July 1999, A23; Martin Malia, "Russia's Retreat from the West," *New York Times*, 3 September 1998, A29.

77. Lilia Shevtsova, *Yeltsin's Russia* (Washington, D.C.: Carnegie Endowment, 1999), 280.

78. Sergei Markov, quoted in Thomas L. Friedman, "BizCzarism," *New York Times*, 18 April 2000, A31; Greg Alton, an American resident in Moscow, "Jerry Hough and the 'American Model,'" from *Johnson's Russia List*, 5 November 1997 (he also notes that "the bureaucracy is by some measures larger and more powerful than ever"); Timothy J. Colton and Robert Legvold, eds., *After the Soviet Union* (New York: Norton, 1992), 18; Fred Hiatt, "Russia in Trouble," reprinted from the *Washington Post* in *Daily Hampshire Gazette* (Northampton, Mass.), 2 September 1999, A10; Michel Tatu, *The Independent* (U.K.), quoted in Keith Bush, "Light at the End of the Tunnel," *RFE/RL Research Report* 2, no. 20 (14 May 1993): 67; interview with Alexander Lebed, *The Globe and Mail* (Toronto), 27 October 1998, from *Johnson's Russia List*, 27 October 1998.

79. Boris Yeltsin, address to the Civil Service Academy, 6 September 1995, *FBIS-SOV-95-173*, 7 September 1995; Eugene Huskey, "Institutional Design in Russia," unpublished paper, 10; *RFE/RL*, 16 March 2000; Pavel Felgengauer, quoted in *Johnson's Russia List*, 23 May 1997.

80. Evgenia Albats, testimony before the Commission on Security and Cooperation in Europe, "Hearing on Chechnya," 1 May 1995 (Washington, D.C.: U.S. Government Printing Office, 1995), 15–16; Vanora Bennett, "Russia's Harvest of Have-Nots," *Los Angeles Times*, 22 September 1998.

81. *RL 223/87*, 12 June 1987, 5; *RL 366/87*, 11 September 1987, 11; O. M. Kovalevich, V. A. Sidorenko, and N. A Shteinberg, "Soviet Bureaucracy and Nuclear Safety" (based on an article in the Soviet journal *Atomic Energy* 68 [May 1990]), *Forum for Applied Research and Public Policy* (summer 1991): 92; *Nezavisimaia gazeta*, 17 October 1996; Thomas W. Lippman, "Russia Close to Selling Enriched Uranium," *Washington Post*, 14 January 1996, A29; report, *OMRI* (Prague), 19 May 1995; Norwegian and U.S. government sources, 1995. Strobe Talbott has emphasized the independent power of Minatom in his *The Russia Hand* (New York: Random House, 2002), 65–66.

82. A remark by the ambassador of Georgia to the United States, ca. 1994; Adam Ulam, "The Historical Background of U.S.–USSR Negotiating Experience," lecture at Harvard University, 5 May 1986; Robert Schmidt, Earth Energy Systems, lecture at Harvard University, 5 May 1986; the archaeologist quoted is C. C. Lamberg Karlovsky of Harvard University, 1986; various U.S. government sources, 1995–96; unclassified message, U.S. embassy, Moscow, 22 November 1995; Thomas W. Lippman, "Russia Balks at Arms Control," *Washington Post*, 21 January 1996, A24.

83. Two books on the bureaucratic aspects of the Soviet economy are Paul R. Gregory, *Restructuring the Soviet Economic Bureaucracy* (Cambridge: Cambridge University Press, 1990); and Ryavec, *Implementation of Soviet Economic Reforms*.

84. Philip Hanson, "Foreign Economic Relations," in *Soviet Policy for the 1980s*, eds. Archie Brown and Michael Kaser (Bloomington: Indiana University Press,

1982), 68; Georgi Arbatov, "Foreword," in *Re-viewing the Cold War*, eds. Patrick M. Morgan and Keith L. Nelson (Westport, Conn.: Praeger, 2000), xiii; a U.S. government source, 1995; Yuri N. Afanasyev, "Russian Reform Is Dead," *Foreign Affairs* 73, no. 2 (March–April 1994): 23, 25.

85. Julia Smith, "Obstacles to Economic Reform in Russia," *The Woodrow Wilson Center Report* 7, no. 2 (September 1995): 12–13; Michael Specter, "Yeltsin Declares Economic Decline Has Been Stopped," *New York Times*, 5 July 1997, 2; Anders Aslund, speech at the Carnegie Endowment, September 1996, partial text; interview with Boris Nemtsov, NTV, 13 April 1997, in *RFE/RL*, 14 April 1997; "Railway Ministry Performance Report to Government," *Gudok*, 16 June 1995, 1, in *FBIS-SOV-95-141-S*, 24 July 1995, 36–40.

86. This section draws on my article "Russo-Soviet Bureaucratism," 67–84. I am indebted to John A. Armstrong, Lewis C. Mainzer, and Curt Tausky for their comments.

87. Victor Yasmann, "The Russian Civil Service: Corruption and Reform," *RFE/RL* 2, no. 16 (16 April 1993): 18.

88. Victor A. Thompson, *Modern Organization*, 2d ed. (Tuscaloosa: University of Alabama Press, 1977), 23–24, 153, 170. What Crozier calls "ritualistic" attitudes and behavior caused by the "displacement of goals" noted by Merton are similar to Thompson's "bureaupathology" (see Crozier, *The Bureaucratic Phenomenon*, 179). Elsewhere in this book I suggest that for some Russians administrative tasks are more ritual than work.

89. Harry Cohen, *The Demonics of Bureaucracy: Problems of Change in a Government Agency* (Ames: Iowa State University Press, 1965), 15, 21, 68, 172, 225–27, 231.

90. C. Northcote Parkinson, *Parkinson: The Law* (Boston: Houghton Mifflin, 1980 [1957]). The term *insider privatization* is used in Peter Rutland, "Privatization in Russia: True and False," paper presented at the 25th National Convention of the American Association for the Advancement of Slavic Studies (AAASS), Honolulu, 21 November 1993, cited in "Two Years after the Collapse of the USSR: A Panel of Specialists," *Post-Soviet Affairs* 9, no. 4 (October–December 1993): 283. The term *wild privatization* is used in Richard E. Ericson, "Economics," in *After the Soviet Union*, eds. Timothy J. Colton and Robert Legvold (New York: Norton, 1992), 83. On routine illegality, see Joseph S. Berliner, *Factory and Manager in the USSR* (Cambridge: Harvard University Press, 1957); and Leonid Khotin, "The Soviet Enterprise Director," Kennan Institute for Advanced Russian Studies, *Meeting Report*, 2 May 1988.

91. E. I. Komarov, *Biurokratizm—na sud glasnosti!* (Moscow: Politicheskaia literatura, 1989), 22, citing V. I. Lenin, "S bol'noi golovy na zdorovuiu," in *Polnoe sobranie sochinenii*, vol. 10, 5th ed. (Moscow: Gos. isd-vo polit. lit-ry, 1958–65), 36; V. I. Lenin, "To the All-Russia Central Council of Trade Unions, 16 January 1920," in *On the Soviet State Apparatus: Articles and Speeches* (Moscow: Progress, 1977), 233; David W. Lovell, *Trotsky's Analysis of Soviet Bureaucratization* (London: Croom Helm, 1985), 15; Michael W. Lustig, *Trotsky and Djilas: Critics of Communist Bureaucracy* (New York: Greenwood, 1989), 9, 14.

92. Komarov, *Biurokratizm*, 21; R. I. Khasbulatov, *Biurokraticheskoe gosudarstvo* (Moscow: Megapolis-Takom, 1991), 11. Although Khasbulatov is not ethnically Russian, he has had a long career in Russia.

93. A. F. Zverev, "Biurokratiia v zerkale sotsiologii," *Gosudarstvo i pravo*, no. 8 (1992): 121; Gavriil Popov, *Blesk I nishcheta administrativnoi sistemy* (Moscow: PIK, 1990), 79, 102; A. G. Khudokormov, *Ekonomicheskie korni biurokratizma* (Moscow: Ekonomika, 1988), 41–42; A. V. Obolonskii, "Biurokraticheskaia deformatsiia soznanii i bor'ba s biurokratizmom," *Sovetskoe gosudarstvo i pravo*, no. 1 (1987): 55; V. M. Kosiakov and O. A. Mitroshenkov, "Biurokraticheskie proiavleniia i metody bor'by s nimi," *Sovetskoe gosudarstvo I pravo*, no. 6 (1985): 21. The journal *Gosudarstvo i pravo*, formerly *Sovetskoe gosudarstvo i pravo*, is particularly useful for this topic. See also A. F. Zverev, "Teoriia biurokratii: Ot M. Vebera k L. fon Misesu," *Gosudarstvo i pravo*, no. 1 (1992): 91; and D. N. Bakhrakh, "Administrativnaia vlast' kak gosudarstvennoi vlasti," *Gosudarstvo i pravo*, no. 3 (1992): 17.

94. Komarov, *Biurokratizm*, 4, 8.

95. Sergei A. Grigoriev, "Is the Yeltsin Era Over?" address at the Annual Meeting of the New England Slavic Association, Harvard University, 15 April 1994. Grigoriev says that whereas Gorbachev had a staff of 400, Yeltsin's numbered 3,000 and that whereas eighty-five ministries once ran the Soviet Union, in 1994 there were 137 different ministries and state committees in Russia, though with less real power. See Michael Dobbs, "What the Russians Call Democracy," *Washington Post*, 16 June 1996, C2.

96. *RL 351/87*, 31 August 1987, citing an article in *Iunost'*, no. 6 (1987). See also Murray Feshbach and Alfred Friendly Jr., *Ecocide in the USSR* (New York: Basic Books, 1992), 151–52; *New York Times*, 13 December 1988, A8, citing *Pravda*.

97. Serge Schmemann, "A New Capitalist Goes Foreign Shopping for Profit," *New York Times*, 21 June 1993, A4; Aleksandr Kiselyov, "Free Exit and Clarifications of It," *Nezavisimaia gazeta*, 19 January 1993, in *Current Digest of the Post-Soviet Press* 45, no. 3 (17 February 1993): 19–20. For a piece on obtaining a Soviet exit visa, see Julia Wishnevsky, "Twenty Reasons for Not Granting an Exit Visa," *RFE/RL*, 10 November 1986. Among the "reasons" given were "You don't have to know why you have been refused; it is enough that we know," and "No one has ever been able to leave the Soviet Union easily or quickly."

98. *RL 298/78*, 27 December 1978, 2; *Boston Globe*, 21 February 1978; *Moscow News*, 28 August–4 September 1988, 2.

99. *Sovetskii trud*, 12 February 1971, in *U.S. Joint Publications Research Service* 52574, 10 March 1971, 2; B. Rakitsky, "Problems of Restructuring the Political Economy," *Voprosy ekonomiki*, no. 12 (1987): 14–23, in *Problems of Economics* 31, no. 4 (August 1988): 35; Donald B. Kelley, "Environmental Problems as a New Policy Issue," in *Soviet Society and the Communist Party*, ed. Karl W. Ryavec (Amherst: University of Massachusetts Press, 1978), 102–3; Nikolai V. Zlobin, "Perestroika versus the Command-Administrative System," *Demokratizatsiya* 1, no. 2 (n.d.): 62; Barbara Jancar, *Environmental Management in the Soviet Union* (Durham: Duke University Press, 1987), 140; Yasmann, "The Russian Civil Service," 18.

100. Popov, *Blesk I nishcheta administrativnoi sistemy*, 103.

101. Vasily Selunin, "Istoki," *Novy mir*, no. 5 (May 1988), in *Current Digest of the Soviet Press* 40, no. 40 (2 November 1988): 17.

102. Komarov, *Biurokratizm*, 24, 26, 42, 52. Komarov gives no source for the statistics. Not all "holdovers" had been tsarist employees; some had worked for "private and social agencies."

103. Komarov, *Biurokratizm*, 26; T. H. Rigby, *Lenin's Government: Sovnarkom, 1917–1922* (Cambridge: Cambridge University Press, 1979), chap. 4, "Acquiring a Bureaucracy," 51.

104. Milovan Djilas, *Tito: The Story from Inside* (New York: Harcourt, Brace, Jovanovich, 1980), 43–44, 71. The story about the Bakunin–Marx meeting was presented by a female former member of the Polish Worker's Party at a seminar at Harvard in about 1971.

105. Martin Malia, *Russia under Western Eyes* (Cambridge: Harvard University Press, Belknap Press, 1999), 70.

106. A. Bogdanov, *Voprosy sotsializma* (Moscow: Izdatel'stvo politicheskoi literatury, 1980), 342, quoted in Alec Nove, *The Soviet System in Retrospect*, the Fourth Annual Harriman Lecture, 17 February 1993 (New York: Columbia University Press, 1993), 12; Khasbulatov, *Biurokraticheskoe gosudarstvo*, 13—the author, a Chechen, was sent into internal exile with his family and has personal experience of this "Power."

107. Komarov, *Biurokratizm*, 24; Khasbulatov, *Biurokraticheskoe gosudarstvo*, 34, 39, 50.

108. Komarov, *Biurokratizm*, 9–11.

109. V. Gorbachev, "Arendatory glasnosti: O perestroike i podstroike," *Molodaia gvardiia*, no. 1 (1989): 229, Abstract 636 in *Economic and Political Reform in the USSR*, pt. 1 (Berkeley: Informatics and Prognostics, 1990), 109; Popov, *Blesk I nishcheta administrativnoi sistemy*, 104–5.

110. Sergei N. Khrushchev, *Nikita Khrushchev and the Creation of a Superpower* (University Park: Pennsylvania State University Press, 2000), 737.

111. Khrushchev, *Nikita Khrushchev*, 749.

112. Khrushchev, *Nikita Khrushchev*, 705; Zverev, "Teoriia biurokratii," citing P. P. Gaidenko and Iu. N. Davydov, "Problema biurokratii u Maksa Webera," *Voprosy filosofii*, no. 3 (1991): 182.

113. Gennadi Barbulis, quoted in *New York Times*, 18 July 1996, A3.

114. "Bandokratiia v zerkale politicheskoi ekonomii," *Obshchestvennye nauki*, no. 4 (1990): 66–70, 81–82, Abstract 97 in *Economic and Political Reform in the USSR, 1990–1992* (Berkeley: Informatics and Prognostics, 1992), 18; V. A. Polikarpov, "Sotsiokul'turnye obshchosti molodezhi v usloviiakh perestroiki," *Vestnik Belorusskogo Gosudarstvenogo Universiteta*, seriia 3 (Minsk: Byelorussian State University, 1990): 38–40, Abstract 934 in *Economic and Political Reform in the USSR* (Berkeley: Informatics and Prognostics, 1990), 176.

115. See, for example, Valerie Sperling, ed., *Building the Russian State* (Boulder: Westview Press, 2000), for example, the chapters by Louise Shelly on the state and crime and corruption, by Eva Busza on dysfunctionality in the military, and by Pamela Jordan on the courts. See also Piroska Mohacsi Nagy, *The Meltdown of the Russian State: The Deformation and Collapse of the State in Russia* (Williston, Vt.: Edward Elgar, 2000).

116. David Hoffman, "Yeltsin's Absentee Rule Raises Specter of a 'Failed State,'" *Washington Post*, 26 February 1999, from *Johnson's Russia List*, 3 March 1999; Gerhard Wettig, "The Transformation from the Cold War to Today's Challenges," *Aussenpolitik* (English ed.), September 1997, 110; Huskey, *Presidential Power in Russia*, 220; Donald N. Jensen, "Is Russia Another Somalia?" End Note, *RFE/RL Newsline* 3, no. 18 (27 January 1999).

117. *New York Times*, 8 October 1998, A12; Otto Latsis, "Brutality Breeds Nothing but Brutality," *Izvestia*, 20 June 1995, 1–2, in *FBIS-SOV-95-118*, 20 June 1995, 21.

118. Jack Matlock, lecture at Mount Holyoke College, 11 April 2002; Joerg Kastl, "European Security without Russia?" *Aussenpolitik* (English ed.), January 1997, 32.

119. Boris Kagarlitsky, "Putin Is a Nobody," *Moscow Times*, 28 January 2000.

120. *Financial Times*, 23 March 1999, from *Johnson's Russia List*, 24 March 1999; interview with German Gref, *Itogi*, 8 February 2000, in *RFE/RL*, 16 February 2000; Allen Lynch, "The Crisis of the Russian State," *The International Spectator* (Rome), April–June 1995, quoted in Association for the Study of Nationalities, "The Institutionalization of the Mismanagement of the Russian State," *Analysis of Current Events* (of the Association for the Study of Nationalities) 7, no. 7 (March 1996): 5; Thomas Graham, testimony before the U.S. Senate Foreign Relations Committee, 15 September 1998, from *Johnson's Russia List*, 17 September 1998.

121. Rogers Brubaker, *Nationalism Reframed* (Cambridge: Cambridge University Press, 1996), 43, quoted in Valerie Sperling, "Introduction: The Domestic and International Obstacles to State-Building in Russia," in *Building the Russian State*, ed. Valerie Sperling (Boulder: Westview Press, 2000), 15; Eva Busza, "State Dysfunctionality, Institutional Decay, and the Russian Military," in *Building the Russian State*, ed. Valerie Sperling (Boulder: Westview Press, 2000), 113.

122. Graham, testimony before the U.S. Senate Foreign Relations Committee; Valerie Sperling, "Introduction: The Domestic and International Obstacles to State-Building in Russia," in *Building the Russian State*, ed. Valerie Sperling (Boulder: Westview Press, 2000), 8, 12, citing William Reno, *Warlord Politics and African States* (Boulder: Lynne Rienner, 1998), 19; Joel Migdal, "Strong States, Weak States: Power and Accommodation," in *Understanding Political Development*, eds. Myron Wiener and Samuel P. Huntington (Boston: Little, Brown, 1987), 396–97.

123. Graham, testimony before the U.S. Senate Foreign Relations Committee.

124. Michael McFaul, "Why Russia's Politics Matter," *Foreign Affairs* 74, no. 1 (January–February 1995): 91, 96.

125. Alexander Solzhenitsyn, quoted in *Obshchaia gazeta* and *Johnson's Russia List*, sometime in 1996.

126. *Izvestia*, no. 68 (25168) (1998); Association for the Study of Nationalities, "The Institutionalization of the Mismanagement of the Russian State," 5, referring to Timothy J. Colton, *Moscow: Governing the Soviet Metropolis* (Cambridge: Harvard University Press, Belknap Press, 1995); Sergei Rogov, quoted in Jim Hoagland, "Memo to the Vice-President," *Washington Post*, 28 June 1996, A21; Ariel Cohen, "Competing Visions," *RFE/RL Research Report* 2, no. 38 (24 September 1993): 55–56; Valerie Sperling, quoted in Davis Center of Harvard University, *Novosti* 6, no. 3 (spring 1998–99): 4; Grzegorz W. Kolodko, "Russia Should Put Its People First," *New York Times*, 7 July 1998, A23; Arch Getty from Moscow, quoted in *Johnson's Russia List*, 12 July 1997; Vladimir Klimov, "The Power People Have No Power," *Rossiiskaia gazeta*, 23 June 1995, 2, in *FBIS-SOV-95-121*, 23 June 1995, 32; a U.S. government source, 1996.

127. Bill Geertz, "Fear Destroys U.S.–Russia Cooperation," *Washington Times*; Chernomyrdin's criticism reported in *Ekho Moskvy* and *Rossiiskie vesti*, 25–26 July 1996; a U.S. government source, 1996; *FBIS-SOV-95-186-S*, 26 September 1995, 12; Hoffman, "Yeltsin's Absentee Rule Raises Specter of a 'Failed State'"; Klimov, "The Power People Have No Power."

128. Clifford Krauss, "Strauss Opposes Broad Soviet Aid," *New York Times*, 17 July 1991, A9; "Pickering Comments on Elections," *Moscow Interfax* (in English), 4 November 1995.

129. S. Kashlev, "Tax Reforms in Russia," *Nezavisimaia gazeta*, 17 October 1995, 4, *FBIS-SOV-95-214-S*, 6 November 1995, 26; "Russia's Far East: Rotten to the Core," *The Economist*, 18 October 1997, 54; Celestine Bohlen, "Small Entrepreneurs Tired of Russian Politicians," *New York Times*, 16 December 1999, A3; Lynn D. Nelson, presentation at the National Meeting of the AAASS, Boston, November 1996; Stephen Kotkin, "Disappearing Rubles, Omnipresent Rust Belt," *New York Times*, 5 October 1998, A23; reports in *RFE/RL*, 18 June 1997, and *Johnson's Russia List*, 12 June 1997; personal observations while in a U.S. government position, 1995–96; a U.S. government source, 1995.

130. Vladimir Putin, quoted in *RFE/RL*, 9 May 2000; Anatol Lieven, "Why We Shouldn't Write Off Russia," *New York Times*, 17 March 1999, A29; Mark Medish, deputy assistant secretary of the Treasury for International Affairs, "Building the New Russian State," lecture at the Kennedy School of Government, 9 January 1998, text from the U.S. Information Agency; Himmelfarb, "Kind, yet Tough"; Association for the Study of Nationalities, "The Institutionalization of the Mismanagement of the Russian State," 5; Jensen, "Is Russia Another Somalia?"; Graham, testimony before the U.S. Senate Foreign Relations Committee.

131. S. Kashlev, "Tax Reforms in Russia," *Nezavisimaia gazeta*, 17 October 1995, 4; *FBIS-SOV-95-214-S*, 6 November 1995, 26.

132. Sperling, "Introduction," 12; Daniel Treisman, "Russia's Taxing Problem," *Foreign Policy* (fall 1998): 55; Sergei Alexashenko, quoted in Hoffman, "Yeltsin's Absentee Rule Raises Specter of a 'Failed State'"; Minister Kiriyenko, quoted in Treisman, "Russia's Taxing Problem," 56; Daniel Yergin and Thane Gustafson, "Waiting for the Taxman," *Washington Post*, 2 August 1998, from *Johnson's Russia List*, 3 August 1998.

133. Anders Aslund, "Sanity in Russia," *New York Times*, 25 April 1998, A25, and remarks at the Carnegie Endowment, September 1996; Michael R. Gordon, "Brash Russian Tax Chief Takes on Land of Evasion," *New York Times*, 4 July 1998, A1; Anatoly Chubais, quoted in *The Hindustan Times*, from *Johnson's Russia List*, 17 April 1997; Venyamin Sokolov, "The Virus in Russia," *New York Times*, 1 June 1998, A19; "A Polite Warning to Mr. Yeltsin" (editorial), *New York Times*, 24 July 1996, A24; Jerry F. Hough, in *Johnson's Russia List*, 1 May 1997; Yergin and Gustafson, *Russia 2010*, 105.

134. M. Kasyanov, summary of speech to the Duma, quoted in Reuters, Moscow, 17 May 2000, from *Johnson's Russia List*, 17 May 2000; V. Putin, speech to workers in Ivanovo, quoted in Michael R. Gordon, "Putin Running 'Uncampaign' on the Way to Election," *New York Times*, 8 March 2000, A5; Michael Specter, "Rudderless Russia," *New York Times*, 20 January 1997, A3; a U.S. government source, 1995; Alexander Yakovlev, "Continuation of the Theme: Insane Taxes Are Expanding the Shadow Sector," *Rossiiskie vesti*, 22 October 1997, from *Johnson's Russia List*, 10 November 1997; Yergin and Gustafson, "Waiting for the Taxman"; a scope paper of the Gore–Chernomyrdin Commission, 11 January 1996, 3.

135. "Russia's Tax Crisis" (editorial), *New York Times*, 17 October 1996, A26; my letter to the editor, *New York Times*, 20 October 1996, commenting on the basis of

personal experience on the editorial of 17 October, "Russia's Tax Crisis"; "A Hope and a Prayer;" *The Economist*, 23 May 1998, 66; Gregory Yavlinsky, speech at Harvard University, from *Johnson's Russia List*, 22 March 2002; Reuters, Moscow, 23 July 1998, from *Johnson's Russia List*, 23 July 1998; Victor Vasiliev, quoted in *Ros-Balt*, 8 January 2002, in *RFE/RL Newsline*, 9 January 2002.

136. *RFE/RL*, 26 January 2000.

137. Putin, speech to workers in Ivanovo; Galina V. Starovoitova and Eugene N. Gurenko, "Russia: A Chance for Improvement," *The Brown Journal of World Affairs* 2, no. 2 (summer 1995): 114; Kasyanov, summary of speech to the Duma and his speech on NTV, *BBC Monitoring*, 17 May 2000, from *Johnson's Russia List*, 17 May 2000; Treisman, "Russia's Taxing Problem," 64.

138. President-elect Putin's statement in London, *Moscow Times*, 18 April 2000, from *Johnson's Russia List*, 18 April 2000.

139. Sabrina Tavernese, "Russia Imposes Flat Tax on Income, and Its Coffers Swell," *New York Times*, 23 March 2002, A3. A new tax code, effective in 2001, was signed into law by President Putin on 6 August 2000 (*RFE/RL*, 8 August 2000).

140. Yegor Gaidar, speech at the University of California at Los Angeles, 14 June 2002, text from the UCLA International Institute via e-mail.

3

Process, Culture, and Style or "The Way Things Work"

But your rituals and your hierarchy are even more rigid than the Church's!

—Paolo Garimberti, interview in Florence with a functionary of the Communist Party of the Soviet Central Committee, 1986

In our blessed country, our so-called "enlightened" elite always strived toward Western models and standards. But, they also always succeeded in transforming these models and standards into the exact opposites of themselves.

—*Nezavisimaia gazeta*

[In Russia] Montesquieu's separation of powers became a mere division of bureaucratic functions.

—Martin Malia, *Russia under Western Eyes*

Russians have always had a propensity to squirrel away every piece of paper.

—Sergei Schmemann, *Echoes of a Native Land: Two Centuries of a Russian Village*

INFORMALISM

*T*he way things actually work" in any organization is always somewhat different from the way they are officially supposed to. This
is most apparent to long-term employees or members, some of whom become adept at using the informal system to their or their departments' advantage. At times the person who can "get things done" informally is
worth a great deal. I am reminded of the proverbial U.S. Navy engineering chief who can arrange to take on fuel oil when the temperature is
warm, or, better yet, hot, when more oil can be acquired than is indicated
by the gauge. This will later be to the advantage of the engineering officer
in preparing the quarterly report on fuel usage, a document manipulable
to the ship's advantage. My students enjoy the Soviet story of the factory
director interviewing for an accountant. He asks only one question of the
applicants: "How much is two and two?" He rejects all who answer the
question mathematically. Finally, he interviews a rather shady character
who has done time. When he asks this applicant the question, the latter
shuts the door and asks in a loud whisper, "How many do you need?" He,
of course, gets the job.

Sometimes the gap between officially, formally, and legally specified
rules, procedures, and processes can be wide indeed. A CIA station chief
involved in the Iran–Contra affair, bewildered at being blamed for the
agency's actions, said, referring to unwritten understandings between operatives and superiors, "In the clandestine service, there are rules that are
absolutely inviolable."[1] In any case, every organization is run partly, if not
in the main, by informalism, the aspects of which every long-term member of the organization comes to know, understand, accept, and sometimes manipulate to his or her advantage. At times informal procedures
actually improve an organization's functioning by making up for deficiencies in its formal rules.[2] Often they do the opposite. It can be difficult
for newcomers and outsiders to learn what actual procedures are because
insiders may consider them to be too important to themselves and their
power to reveal. Informalism has long been recognized in Russian work-
places. For example, Yaney says that Russian officials, both tsarist and
communist, "had" to disrupt the rules, including violating the government's own decrees, to get their work done—if they wanted to get it done.
And a Russian source speaks of "unofficial social structures," "unofficial
leaders," and "situations of social conflict" in Soviet work organizations.[3]

Reasons for Informalism

The reasons for informalism are many. Over time any organization devel-
ops its own "supplementary" or informal understandings and proce-

dures. Misunderstandings can become institutionalized into long-term informalisms. The culture of the larger society can penetrate and sometimes even overcome an organization's formal rules. Individuals may, for a variety of reasons, withhold commitment to the organization's goals and standards. As Selznick recognizes, "Individuals have a propensity to resist depersonalization, to spill over the boundaries of their segmentary roles [formally required by organizations], to participate as wholes and let their full personalities guide them in their work. . . . In large organizations, deviations from the formal system tend to become institutionalized, so that 'unwritten laws' and informal associations are established . . . a persistent structural aspect of formal organizations."[4] Accordingly, the actually functioning organization is an amalgam of firmly fused formal and informal rules, goals, and procedures. Although attempts can be made to mitigate or change informalism, some of it will always be present in an organization's internal life and functioning. In 1999–2000 the U.S. federal government was troubled by the informalisms of the Energy Department. Its civil servants had a willingness, if not a propensity, to fail to inform their superiors of nuclear security problems. In 1999 the president's Foreign Intelligence Advisory Board repeatedly faulted the Energy Department's bureaucratic culture for putting administrative convenience before security considerations. One knowledgeable analyst has said that even after an investigation the secretary running the department "will still be hard pressed to point a finger at any one person who can be held ultimately responsible for what goes right or wrong on nuclear security."[5] After 11 September 2001 the informal "rules" inhibiting FBI–CIA communication came into the open.

It is important for new members to learn the informalities of their organization as quickly as possible. American corporate culture recognizes this and even speaks of "taking out" and "putting in" company cultures from and into employees. Ethnic and elite cultures will also be a factor in the functioning of organizations, particularly in the functioning of the Russian state bureaucracy, long without the countervailing powers of civil society or law operating independently of the ruling elites.

THE RUSSIAN BUREAUCRATIC PROCESS

Although we focus on problems of the Russian bureaucracy in this book, it must be recognized that that bureaucracy built a great industry, military, and science with many real achievements to their credit. As Sternheimer puts it, work got done in the USSR: "Cities are built, . . . garbage collected, transportation provided, and so on." And as Kuchment has noted, the Soviets could have "enormous flexibility" when a project was high in priority.[6] However, much of the work done was not done well, and only projects that seemed to enhance national power in conventional heavy industrial or military ways received priority. Accordingly, much that ought to have been done to make the Soviet Union truly modern and keep it that way was left undone.

A few anecdotes indicate the basic problems with the Russo-Soviet bureaucratic process, even at the highest levels. President Nasser of Egypt was meeting with Brezhnev, Kosygin, and Gromyko in June 1970. He noted that a telegram to General Siad in Somalia had to be signed by all three in a process that took all of five minutes. Nasser later said to one of his aides, "Did you see that? If a telegram to General Siad needs the signatures of all those three, we are in trouble. Now I understand why our requests take such a long time to produce results."[7] Here we seem to have an example of that "fetishization" of paperwork not uncommon in government organizations. An amusing example of this is the stamping of photocopies I had made while living in the Soviet Union with the stamp of the government place doing the copying. Every page was so stamped. Taking paper very seriously goes well back in Russian history (the word for paper, and also for document, *bumaga*, is of Mongol origin). As Schmemann found in researching his family's history, "The [imperial] state took record-keeping seriously: official records were fastidiously copied, stamped, notarized, cross-referenced, and filed, and the bureaucracy prescribed the quality of paper for each level of communication. Important documents . . . were on stock that even now feels new."[8] "Seeming to get things done" can be very important in all governments. As an investment banker who served in the U.S. Treasury puts it, "The tempo of life in government is frenetic, but there is no result—process is everything."[9]

Certainly the Russian bureaucracy's operations have often deviated from official prescriptions. For example, as Vlachoutsicos has noted, there was a "striking discrepancy" between what was decided at the top levels of a Soviet trade organization and what actually happened below. He has suggested that this divergence was because of the power of *edinonachalie* (one-person management or control) in Soviet management. The top leader at every level operated as if he were a "commander" of all within his sphere. But that top "authority" was more like a "cloud" than anything definite. Bureaucratic complexity, too, leads to informalism. This can include middle levels following orders too strictly in order not to deal with problems. Elsewhere Vlachoutsicos has elaborated on his findings by pointing out that higher level managers can take over the work of those at lower levels and that "structural task units" or work collectives in Soviet industry are usually quite separate from each other and create "excessive centralization" and the lack of even "simple acts of coordination."[10]

Sternheimer gives several instances of informalist bureaucratic activity and suggests reasons for it. He states that "informal communications play a critical role" in and, indeed, serve as the "grease" for the better operation of local administrative agencies. He suggest that overcentralization, overly taut plan targets, information and communication distortion, and "extremely long bureaucratic chains of command" are some of the reasons for the informalism. "Personal contacts are everything" was a unanimous view of his respondents. (The same point was made to me by a senior staffer of a U.S. Senate majority whip.) Significantly, there was a "male bias in the informal network," a reason why women had difficulty getting ahead, and also a Russian or at least Russian republic bias. New developments could take years to reach non-Russian areas. However, overall Sternheimer concludes that informalism facilitated the operation of a "quite cumbersome administrative machine."[11]

Problems of the Process

Problems of administrative process exist everywhere. For example, in 1999 a Massachusetts Turnpike official required a convoy of fire trucks racing to a fire to stop and pay tolls, even though such emergency vehicles can legally use the turnpike without charge. The U.S. Department of State may have engaged in a bit of overreaction in issuing notices on such things as "burn bag disposal restrictions" and on how people and paper delivery vehicles are to avoid each other in the corridors.[12] (The department uses a lot of paper.)

Process problems of Russo-Soviet administration have long existed. An American engineer working in the USSR during the 1930s found only one agency that was efficient, the security police. He was also never able to find a person who would take clear responsibility. He has described the "bureaucratic inertia, corruption, duplicity and inefficiency" of Soviet administration as well as the hidebound planners who refused to accept new methods and construction bosses who covered up serious disasters. One leading scholar of the Soviet system has listed the following management practices as "remarkably persistent" from Stalin to Gorbachev: excessive tautness, the "ratchet," the maintenance of hidden production reserves, barter and resale, hoarding of labor, enterprise autarky, failure to innovate, subquality output, "storming," and "equality-mongering" in wage policy. Although the Russian economy has changed greatly since 1992, governmental administration has continued to suffer from problems analogous to those of Soviet governmental and economic institutions. A U.S. government source has referred to the "good old-fashioned bureaucratic sloth, lack of interagency coordination, and exclusive focus on the short term that characterizes much of the GOR's [Government of Russia's] current activities."[13]

Waste and a general loss of control of the work process are also often cited as general features of Russo-Soviet administration. Since the mid-1960s the USSR reinvested only about one-third of its output to achieve a growth rate of only 3 percent, whereas South Korea managed a 9 percent rate of growth during the same period with roughly the same rate of investment. Agriculture was almost a disaster. During the harvest every sixth combine was inactive, and large amounts of the harvest were lost every year. Significant losses of livestock also occurred annually. Deficiencies existed at all levels and sectors of economic management during the Soviet period.[14]

Russian writers since Gogol have satirized "their" government's administration. Vladimir Voinovich wrote several worthy satires in the Gogolian tradition, for example, *The Ivankiad*, which focuses on the struggle for an apartment between the author and one Ivanko, a "Soviet bureaucrat from that gray half-world where the secret police and literature meet." To one emigrating writer who asked, "Who needs this system?" Voinovich replies, "Ivanko, he needs it!" Bukovsky says reflectively, "Truly we were born to make Kafka live."[15]

The newspaper *Kommersant-Daily* has satirized the process that produced President Yeltsin's edicts, suggesting that "in the majority of cases the specific path taken by any given edict remains unknown." In any case, "initiators of controversial drafts do their best to keep their intentions secret and not let their potential enemies get prepared." (Secrecy is also a game much played within the U.S. government bureaucracy. For example, a group that is able to obtain a briefing by another agency may try to exclude others from the briefing, often by booking a small room, claiming, "You can't come; the room is too small.") In a satire on Russian bureaucracy the daily *Segodnia* published a supposed draft law: "On the Regulation of Activities Related to the Preparation and Utilization of Cabbage Soup." The head of the Cabbage Soup Commission is to receive the rank of minister, and the apparatus is to consist of exactly 218 people with a working space of at least 7,000 square meters and the corresponding number of vehicles and other equipment.[16]

Such satire is a sign of some healthiness in Russia; Russians at all levels know that they have a real problem in their bureaucracy. "Our officials are used to doing things their own way without asking what the people think. Our needs are lost in thick layers of bureaucracy," exclaimed one local council member, speaking of Moscow's attempt to take over his village after Moscow had cut off its water for ten days. Even Viktor Chernomyrdin, while prime minister, said in 1998, "The most serious thing today is the decline of confidence of ordinary people in the actions taken by Russian authorities." In 1996 a poll by the Academy of Civil Service found that 77 percent of those surveyed agreed that the organs of state administration are unconcerned with ordinary people, while 35 percent thought that the bureaucrats are "incompetent." Perhaps more importantly, 43 percent had had their civil rights and freedoms infringed by government bodies. More than half felt that the central organs of the state had lost control over the train of events. Among the "most characteristic" responses were the following: "Our regime is less like a government than an ephemeral 'cloud in trousers,'" and "Our ship of state . . . bumbles along."[17]

This situation is not just the result of the failures of the ineffectual post-Soviet government. It is the culmination of decades of bureaucratic mismanagement, which existed, and flourished, in all the communist states. Entrepreneurship, in the only sense in which it existed, was bureaucratic and "mainly geared to the establishment of big enterprises producing low quality mass produced products for protected domestic markets." In addition, Taylorism, or "scientific management," to the extent it was followed, had created a "dichotomy between those who were in command [in enterprises] . . . and those who were responsible to carry out assigned tasks," which did not facilitate high-quality production. The top directing agencies of the bureaucratized economy came to face a serious management problem that could not be solved with the existing system and methods. Many in this system recognized aspects of its deficiencies. One minister noted that "the highest links generally strive to accumulate surplus information that does not pertain directly to their competence and hence is unneeded." In 1970 as many as four million pages of administrative documentation were produced daily, one Soviet source says. (And in a national security apparatus, such as that of the United States, many of the pages produced are very soon shredded.) Even in the 1970s there was still no standard system of Russian state administrative documentation. Although the work of financial agencies in checking on the work of industrial enterprises was judged as inadequate, that work found "frequent" instances of "illegal and uneconomical" expenditures.[18]

Slowness, confusion, and bad decisions were commonplace in the operation of the Soviet industrial bureaucracy. Ministries were often cited for dragging out the completion of plans. Different ministries and agencies pursued contradictory aims and also engaged in various forms of interagency conflict. Bukovsky writes: "Bureaucrats are . . . always at loggerheads with one another, and often enough your complaints become weapons in internecine wars between bureaucrat and bureaucrat, department and department. This goes on for months and months." The Soviets might have won the space race, one commentator says, "if only they had acted like good communists" and the aerospace effort had not been put into parallel industrial complexes in a situation "ripe for conflicts." (Of course, interagency conflicts exist in any government; that between the

Secret Intelligence Service and the Special Operations Executive in Britain during World War II is said to have been "a legendary bureaucratic war." Mutual suspicion was so high that people in one agency did not allow people of the other to pack their parachutes.)[19]

Poor decisions and nondecisions were not uncommon. "Owing to red tape" in one ministry, a machine for which there was a high demand was not being produced. Despite the Russian familiarity with the problems of winter, more than forty ships were allowed to be trapped in Arctic ice early one autumn. Gossnab was blamed for "procrastination," and all the agencies involved were said to be "totally uncoordinated." In 1990 more than half of the cigarette plants were shut down for maintenance at the same time. This worked to the advantage of American companies, which sold the USSR 34 billion cigarettes for hard currency that could well have been better spent.[20]

A lack of a drive for success, the proliferation of bureaucracy, and peculiar and self-defeating planning are also to be noted. The Soviet oil bureaucracy did not drill nearly as many wells as American companies did in their search for oil—only 1,100 versus 12,000 in 1983, for example. One particular kolkhoz was subordinated to three agencies on the *raion* level alone, as well as more at the oblast and ministerial levels—about one administrator for every head of cattle, said the director. The Ministry of the Fruit and Vegetable Industry was shipping tomatoes from Moldavia to the Urals and Siberia while tomatoes for Byelorussia and the Ukraine came from the Central Asian republics. A look at the map might have given someone a sense of relative distance and relative cost.[21]

For most white-collar workers meetings are an inescapable and rather frequent part of the work process. But meetings, at best intended to facilitate the process, can create problems for it. They can be time wasters, ranting places for some, and ways of avoiding actual work in one way or another. Meetings to steer clear of, if possible, are those harboring persons who like meetings so much that they prolong them for their enjoyment or research interest. Russian workplace meetings can be harsh. More than once I sat waiting outside someone's padded door, listened to the chief's shouting tirade, and then felt sorry for the dejected and crestfallen creatures who eventually emerged. Russian bureaucratic meetings can be rather lengthy and frequent occurrences.

During the early 1970s meetings involving the minister and deputy ministers of one ministry took place two to three times per month. Each meeting dealt with three or four questions, but "often" the number increased to six to nine when rapid decisions were required. Meetings sometimes lasted as long as six to eight hours. "Additional questions" could be put on the agenda, or removed, only with the approval of the minister. This place seems a model of order and reticence. Another source says that "as many as 40 problems are discussed at some meetings of the collegia" of ministries. Another source notes that the chiefs of one division of a planning agency "spend 30 percent of their time on various conferences and meetings, on the performance of functions not inherent in their jobs—the search for material resources, personnel and so forth." Vlachoutsicos found in 1990 that "his" factory manager, who arrived at the plant at 7:15 A.M. and did not leave until 8 P.M., attended at least *five* separate meetings daily.[22] (The factor of Russian culture may apply here and will be discussed below.)

We know fairly little about meetings of the topmost body of the Soviet state bureaucracy, the Council of Ministers. Doder says that it was "so unwieldy that it has never met to decide anything." This is probably not so. In 1988 *Izvestiia* disclosed that the full government met once every three months in the Oval Room of the Kremlin and that the latest session had met for six hours. A few former ministers, for example, the former head of Gosplan and a former member of the Politburo, attended. This gibes with a statement made by van den Berg in the 1970s, that is, that the council, the state's "highest administrative agency," met four times each year, normally on matters of planning.[23]

The bureaucratic process in the Soviet military-industrial complex was complicated and difficult to manage. The Defense Industry Ministry, eight other production ministries, the Military-Industrial Commission, the Central Committee secretariat's Defense Industry Department, and the Defense Ministry and general staff were all key players in this process. Although the high output of weaponry gave the West pause and even great concern, the Soviet military establishment was never able to produce really high-quality weapons and instead relied on quantity: "Mistakes were made." The MIG-25 was designed to meet a threat that never materialized, the never-built U.S. B-70 bomber, and was virtually helpless at low altitudes. The MIG-25 remained in long-term production only to keep people employed and as a gift for Third World allies such as India. The problem of defense industry coordination continued into the post-Soviet period. Yeltsin created a State Military Inspectorate that was to coordinate defense policy and appointed a key civilian military expert to head it, Andrei Kokoshin.[24]

Management of nuclear components, nuclear power plants, and weapons of mass destruction ("WMD" in Washingtonese) also has been, and remains, less than satisfactory. However, I am not an alarmist on these matters. So far as is known, Russia has not lost sufficient fissile material for a nuclear bomb. Gen. Eugene Habiger, head of the U.S. Strategic Command, said in 1998, after touring Russian weapons storage sites, "I want to put to bed this concern that there are loose nukes in Russia." Still, post-Soviet Russia does not know how many chemical weapons or how much material for them it has and relies excessively on sentries alone to protect its nukes.

Certainly the Chernobyl nuclear disaster of 1986, not the first one in Soviet history, shows that the USSR's control and safety system for nuclear power plants was inadequate, although no doubt the political leadership ought to share some of the blame, perhaps for pushing a too-rapid expansion of nuclear power. American scientists also lay some blame on the excessive complexity and difficulty of operating Soviet nuclear power plants. The fact that the disaster occurred because operators running a test shut off key emergency equipment suggests that there was a serious and ramified management problem in the nuclear power industry. Was the "center" informed immediately? And did it have to follow certain set and time-consuming procedures internal to itself before acting and giving out information? Why were residents of the zone immediately around the power station not moved until thirty-six hours after the incident? And why did Gorbachev, then the general secretary, wait almost two weeks before speaking publicly on the accident? (A Swedish monitoring facility began asking about new radiation soon after the incident but could get no response from the USSR.) A number of key bureaucrats were eventually sacked, including the head of the State Committee for Safety in the Atomic Power Industry. Another related problem is Russia's "severely underfinanced and understaffed" export controls. Barely fifty persons made up the full-time staff in this area recently. In addition, the enforcement side of export control is weak, as one would expect in a weak state. Two close students of Russian export control had seen no evidence of prosecutions by 1996.[25]

The natural environment of Russia has not fared well under communism. Criticism of pollution by state factories could be seen as an ideological assault on the ideology and the state itself. Any visitor to Russia, and indeed most ex-communist countries, cannot avoid noting the multitude of dumps of waste material in the countryside and the wide-scale pollution that has been wreaked by industry. In certain areas it was painfully difficult to breathe. Clearly the industrial ministries and their plants and operations were not under any operative system of pollution control, although certain showcase areas may have enjoyed some special consideration.[26] Both Jancar and Ziegler list the same administrative limitations on restricting pollution in the USSR. Jancar stresses the problems of administrative fragmentation and the difficulties of coordination in a "complex, segmented system" that "merges the environmental agent with the polluter" and notes that "multiple and partial administrative authority undermines efficient land-use regulation and monitoring and enforcement activities." Ziegler notes that Soviet environmental administration had a "fragmented, uncoordinated character" and was hindered by "narrow . . . bureaucratic interests" with economic and administrative structures "inextricably intertwined" and inspectors "intimidated by the close collusion of Party and government officials" protecting growth.[27]

This less-than-satisfactory bureaucratic process has had a definite negative effect on Russians' views of government and the state. Putin himself has stated that "the people of Russia have always preferred to curse the government, to fear it, also expecting nothing good from it." In a 1999 poll on people's attitudes toward the Russian state, fully 75 percent had a critical attitude, 38 percent chose the option "the state gives us so little that we owe it nothing," and 37 percent chose "we should become a free people and make the state serve our interests." Amazingly, only 1 percent had a totally accepting and favorable view of the Russian state, and this in a society often said to harbor strong authoritarian sentiments. In mid-2002 a poll showed that the public had a very low opinion of all ministries and ministers except one. (This negative image of the state will make any great changes attempted through the state impossible.) It takes a citation of only one shocking fact to begin to explain such antistate attitudes: Almost half of HIV infections in the USSR occurred in state-run medical facilities, and most of those infected were children. In addition, underlying this public attitude is the near certainty of being given the runaround by what one Russian play presents as an "inane and sometimes depraved bureaucracy" in almost any approach to the state machine. Politics made the runaround extreme. When Andrei Sakharov applied for an exit visa in 1977 he was told to complete two eight-page questionnaires and provide six photos, a certified translation of the invitation, a written statement of no objections from his wife, and a reference from his place of work.[28]

Attempts at Reform

Attempts at solutions to problems of administrative process are numerous in Soviet history. The 1920s saw much research on "scientific management" and Taylorism. Khrushchev's decentralization through *sovnarkhozy* of the 1950s must be mentioned. *Libermanism* as adapted by Premier A. N. Kosygin in 1965 contained good ideas but was not implemented because of ministerial and other opposition. Later, General Secretary Brezhnev seems to have been taken with computerization as a way of improving the economic administration. Gorbachev put much faith in glasnost and raised again the old socialist ideal of workers' participation. And, of course, the recurrent standby, as it is everywhere, was the personnel cut. None of these attempts eliminated the problems in the process. No try was "revolutionary" enough in its drive and source. All came from "inside" and accordingly were limited in intent and became entangled in the

Russo-Soviet mentality and the "standard operating procedure" so comfortable for so many state and party bureaucrats.[29]

Causes of Problems in the Administrative Process

There is wide agreement on some of what made the Soviet administrative process as poor as it was. First was the Soviet bureaucracy's sheer size. It administered and operated the economy through, in 1971, 50,000 industrial enterprises, 34,000 kolkhozes, and 15,000 sovkhozes. This was an operational, not a purely regulatory, state bureaucracy, as normal in noncommunist countries. As Spulber puts it, the position of command is "held by a vast and sprawling bureaucracy" and any claims that it will wither away "can be dismissed as self-serving blather." Every plant and other governmental unit in the USSR was strapped to a huge and overcentralized bureaucracy that had acquired an almost sacred place as part of the dictatorial communist ruling elite. Berliner has listed major problems of the economic bureaucracy: the imposition on enterprises of unrealistic and excessively "taut" production plans, including the tendency to "ratchet" goals even higher; enterprises' self-protective maintenance of concealed production reserves against supply shortages; the unauthorized but widespread barter and resale of equipment by enterprises; the hiring of excess labor as a safety factor; the maintenance of autarky at all levels; low levels of innovation and low quality; "storming" to fulfill the plan; and "equality-mongering" or *uravnilovka in pay*. Gregory also lists a number of causal factors negatively affecting the Soviet economic bureaucracy: the relative insignificance of bonuses, the acceptance of low-quality production, the harm done by too-powerful and overprivileged apparatchiks, the lack of realism of plans, and, stressed by him, the overloading of bureaucrats with unnecessary functions and the commonness of principal–agent problems, that is, those who give orders often are not responsible for the negative effects of those orders.[30] (This has often been cited by Soviet sources as a severe problem. For example, in 1973 a Soviet writer pointed out that "there is as yet no special system of [success] indicators . . . for the higher elements—the ministries." Peter F. Drucker once made a similar point.)[31] A host of other causal factors for Soviet administrative difficulties are also cited in the literature, both Russian and foreign. Here are some of them.

The system and its bureaucratic denizens were working under great and perturbational burdens. Plans were often unrealistic and continually changing. (An employee of Poland's state planning commission once said that its primary work was "correcting" plans.) Indeed, plans were often simply unworkable and sometimes served as a type of punitive "insurance policy" set by higher authority to squeeze out as much production as possible—just in case "hidden reserves" could be coerced into production. And, of course, the reports that higher-ups received from the operating entities below required "decoding" and "additional information" because the reports were only partial and misleading. Good information was difficult to come by, even though possibly 90 percent of administrative personnel were engaged in collecting it. One editor has even claimed that central administration was in such "chaos" that lower level administrators were forced to engage in illegal activities in order to meet plan targets. It was often said that the influence of executive organs on subordinate agencies was "excessive" and that the latter had insufficient freedom and authority. Even the associations or amalgamations created in Brezhnev's time to take advantage of economies of scale never had sufficient authority to change this situation.[32]

Autarky was forced on enterprises by the autarky of their ministerial superiors. "Most . . . industrial enterprises manufacture their own instruments and technical equipment," said one Soviet source. This was a great burden to scientists as well, according to a Finnish physicist who worked in the USSR whom I have interviewed. Scientists had no catalogs of equipment and either had to make their own or band together with a number of other scientists with similar wants and thereby make a winning case to the ministry. And even the Western equipment obtained with such difficulty and with scarce foreign exchange was often kept by the ministry that acquired it from all other ministries. Last, higher level administration was negatively affected by nepotism and the employment of failed "party hacks" from the party apparatus. The most famous case of nepotism in the later USSR may be the appointment of Brezhnev's son-in-law as first deputy minister of internal affairs in 1979. Even the KGB had to take such people. Putin says, "People who joined the intelligence service after being full-time party officials invariably turned out to be good for nothings, loafers and careerists . . . [with] overblown egos."[33]

Soviet state bureaucracy was ramified and bloated, in both powers and numbers of personnel. This may be continuing. As early as 1992 a number of bodies in addition to the then new Federal Security Bureau (FSB) were endowed with state security functions: the Ministry of Internal Affairs, the armed forces, the Foreign Intelligence Service (like the FSB from the KGB), the civil defense force, the tax collection service, the internal and border troops, the security departments of state enterprises and nuclear power stations, and still others.[34] (By 2003 Putin was initiating a recentralization of security agencies, but this by itself will not solve problems.)

The Communist Party was itself a major source of problems. True, the party, that "iron net over society," did keep the state bureaucracy from pursuing solely its own interests, but at the same time the party created through its "petty tutelage" within the state apparatus a fear of acting.

This was routinely inveighed against by higher party figures and organs, but it was never effectively quashed. Some bureaucrats may have liked this, for it gave them an easy "out." As one Russian diplomat said in 1995, it used to be much easier to be a diplomat abroad during the Soviet period when the "CC" provided definite decisions and guidance. The "disorganized" post-Soviet interagency process (sounds like the United States) made him uncomfortable.[35]

CULTURE AND STYLE: MIND-SET AND PRACTICE

Causal factors of Russian bureaucratic problems include culture or mindset, a force that has not vanished despite the passage of a decade since the end of Sovietism. This is a sensitive and difficult but absolutely necessary topic to cover. Because of the tendency to see any attribution of cultural traits to people as prejudiced, it is difficult to deal with the issue of culture and the behavior stemming from it without seeming controversial or nonscholarly. Robert D. Putnam has tried to counter the cultural approach to political phenomena: "I think Russia has had such a difficult time not because of some ineffable Russianness or Slavicness but because of specific social structures and networks that have inhibited the emergence of a modern state."[36] But there is no contradiction. Russian culture today is different than it was before the victory of Lenin and Stalin and very different from those of other Slavic countries such as Poland and Slovenia. Variables such as geography, leadership, and natural resources have also been seen as crucial for political behavior. Lawrence E. Harrison notes that "the conclusion that culture matters goes down hard. It clashes with cultural relativism, widely subscribed to in the academic world, which argues that cultures can be assessed only on their own terms and that value judgments by outsiders are taboo."[37] However, it would be unscholarly not to at least grapple with the topic of culture. Some contemporary scholars have explored the cultural approach as a possible metadiscipline that would make better sense of the modern world.[38]

To me culture is the basis for the way we think and act when we are not being consciously introspective or self-conscious. The topic here is not the impressive literary and philosophical "high" culture of the Russian intelligentsia but, rather, that of politics and administration. The poet Czeslaw Milosz stated the dichotomous problem of Russian culture quite well when he referred to "their whole eternally ambiguous civilization, so powerful, human, hungry for justice in literature, and so miserable and cruel in worldly affairs."

Everyone thinks and acts on the basis of some set of culturally based attitudes. This is not to say that individual psychology may not sometimes be more important than culture. Indeed, in each group of people some have not been socialized into the dominant culture or have rejected it. And, of course, subcultures exist. No stereotyping "national character" explanation of bureaucratic behavior, with all administrators tarred with the same brush to the same degree, is being attempted here.[39] This has been applied at times. Leibnitz has said that Russians were "intolerant, not amenable to reason, sunk in stupor and ignorance; worse than the Turks." The Marquis de Custine also read the Russians out of Europe, saying that "Russian civilization . . . is masked barbarism, nothing more." Maxim Gorky once mused, "I think the Russians have a unique sense of particular cruelty in the same way that the English have a unique sense of humor: a cold sort of cruelty that seeks to explore the limits of human resistance to suffering and to study the persistence and stability of life."[40]

Definitions

Culture may be defined as that complex of feelings and attitudes that the members of an ethnic group or national community share and act on unthinkingly and automatically. It is a totality of "social usages" or ways of thinking and behaving that are questioned by few in any society and followed even by members of opposing political parties. Once established, a culture has a life of its own and has effects throughout social life—in the family, in work, and in politics. People can even be puppets of their cultures.[41] When I lived in Moscow I noticed that American diplomats took the concept of culture very seriously. They spoke of it often. Indeed, it may be their ruling operational concept. Some recent research by psychologists seems to show that "people who grow up in different cultures do not just think about different things: they think differently."[42]

Political Culture

When applying the concept to bureaucratic behavior we are emphasizing that part of it known as political culture. Though perhaps used first by Herder in the late eighteenth century, it became a concept of modern political science only in the 1950s. (Was it a scaled back reintroduction of the controversial concept of national character?) Archie Brown has defined political culture as "the subjective perception of history and politics, the fundamental beliefs and values, the foci of identification and loyalty, and the political knowledge and expectations which are the product of the specific historical experience of nations and groups."[43] Brown has written at length on the considerations involved in applying the concept of political culture to Russian politics. He has pointed out, for example, that political behavior is based not only on "basic beliefs" but also on interest, the threat of

sanctions, and "more subtle social pressures."[44] Yes, but once such influences have been in effect they can create a culture that will last until conditions are radically changed. Brown has also noted that just as the an-
thropologists disagree greatly on many questions related to the concept of
culture, students of politics are not in agreement on how the concept of political culture "should best be delineated." A big issue is whether political
culture ought to be considered just a matter of belief or a matter of behavior as well. Still, whatever may be the best way to view the concept,
Brown's quotation from Huntington and Dominguez is apt for our purposes: "Political culture tends to resist change, and when it changes, it does
so more slowly than ideologues may desire." Equally important, he recognizes that there is a strong element of transregime continuity in political
culture: "A Stalin could at a stroke make concessions to 'traditional' elements in Russian political culture which had remained part of the dominant, though not hitherto of the official, Soviet political culture."[45] No
doubt the present Russian state bureaucracy has a culture that is still partly
both traditional and Soviet. Among the traditional and mass political cultural elements in the elite Russo-Soviet political culture Brown lists fear of
chaos and the consequent emphasis on order, patriotism and pride in superpower status, and agreement on the identity of national heroes.[46]

Continuities with the Past

Continuities in culture with the past are easy to find in today's Russia, as
they are in all countries, Japan, for example. Here, too, as in Russia, there
has been the forced challenge of adapting Western ideas and forms to traditional ways. As Takako Kishima has said, the experience of Japan since
1945 and its conquest by the United States show that cultures reconstruct
themselves in their own ways. Japan has adapted to its "Japanness" three
elements of Western modernization that would have caused Japan problems if adopted directly, without modification: capitalism, democracy
based on individualism, and humanism. But Japan may well have retained a national administrative style.[47] Still, despite its "Japanese Westernization," some observers have suggested that Japan still lacks a civil
society, often cited in the West as a necessary precondition for democracy.
Different communist parties have borrowed from their own national cultures. For example, Alexander Leyfell once told me of a communist pro-
cession in Naples in the 1940s that used the same colors as the Church,
reds and violets. And a Yugoslav (Croatian) cultural attaché in the United
States said that the Yugoslav Communist Party copied methods of the
Catholic youth organization when starting its own.[48]

Two Russian political analysts note that "during the 1990s Russia has
returned to many pre-1917, pre-Communist behavioral patterns. Among

them is a tendency to oscillate between extremes, including patience and rebellion and messianism and self-doubt." They go on to point out that the 1999 dash by a Russian battalion to Pristina in Kosovo cannot be explained solely by rationalistic or strategic calculations: "It also has a strong cultural-psychological component." Further, "the military initiative represented a . . . consensus about the need for Russia to reclaim its rightful place in the sun." Significantly, the action "united almost everyone" in Russia, a sure sign that it was cultural, for one test of the applicability of culture is its support by opposing political parties and factions.[49] Culture is shared across the political spectrum.

Another Russian cultural continuity is the alcohol-centered culture that has remained prevalent in Russia despite initial efforts of the Bolsheviks and later Gorbachev to end it. Huskey notes that "an obvious cultural vestige in Russia is the personalization of authority," which encourages "fealty to bosses" instead of Weberian loyalty to offices and law-specified duties and thus spawns an "intricate web of 'family circles'" over a hierarchical network of offices and a tendency to "privatize" state power and wealth for the bureaucrats' own benefit.[50] I am reminded of a Russian friend proudly showing me a photograph of himself at the birthday party for the governor of a Russian region.

Stavrakis points to bureaucratic cultural continuity when he discusses a post-Soviet agency that "came to resemble in many respects the style and substance of earlier Soviet bureaucracies," a "resurrected Gosplan" that looks "like a typical Soviet bureaucracy that seeks to control as many resources as possible" and is designed to defend itself and to make it difficult for outsiders and ostensible controllers to discern lines of accountability. Multiplicity of bureaucratic forms and procedures is typical in Russia. Another Soviet bureaucratic legacy is the "thin pyramid" or "vertical" in government and business structures, "where all decisions and actions emanate from the top." Apparently, "none of the country's big companies have yet conquered the 'thin pyramid.'" Another continuing problem is the government's decree that the railroads must carry about forty categories of freight for next to nothing, with the "power" and some other ministries not paying. "It's a psychology formed during the Soviet period," said a spokesperson for the Railway Ministry. In many ways, then, the culture of the bureaucracy remains much as it was. This is not surprising because as many as three-fourths of the present civil servants worked for the USSR and "a considerable number of officials value their government work mainly because of the privileges they receive, which allow them to fulfill their personal interests."[51]

Whatever we take culture to be, it is undeniable that history lays a burden of experience on a people that is passed on from one generation to another. Russia endured a harsh revolution. Yet, while it underwent outward

industrial transformation, old concerns and patterns of behavior were re-
inforced. The Russian sense of uniqueness and the fear of foreigners were
given support and even strengthened by Stalin's "socialism in one country." Stalin may well have understood Russians' cultural needs and manipulated them to his advantage. The "new, revolutionary institutions carried the signs of an ancient heritage."[52] And once institutions were carried
over, the thinking characteristic of them earlier was given a new lease on
life. This is still true. The term *post-Soviet* is more often a term of sarcasm
or irony than one of definite meaning.

The Mongol and Byzantine sources of the Russian state, and centuries
of autocratic practice by the tsars in "Mongol-Byzantine tsarism," prevented the rise of an effective civil society, as did the lack of a Renaissance
or a Reformation, two of the cardinal creative events of Western history.[53]
Merchants and cities in Russia lacked the semiautonomous status they acquired in Europe. The peasantry remained enslaved and subject to sale by
their masters until 1861 and even after being freed did not develop significant political power by the time of the Bolshevik Revolution. The administrators of this overcentralized and bloated state never had to face either a law or a society that limited their actions. Only a rare peasant
uprising or the occasional inspector from St. Petersburg might bring some
of them to account now and then, an unlikely outcome humorously presented in *The Inspector General* (*Revizor*). Despite the harsh treatment of
Russians by their governments over the centuries, many Russians today
still accept extremely centralized, arbitrary, and bureaucratized rule as
normal and perhaps even necessary to avoid disorder, that common fear
of Russians. (It is often said that the French accept a powerful central state
because they feel that they need one to protect themselves from each
other.) President Putin's moves against the governors, the wealthy businesspeople, and the upper house of Parliament have been highly popular,
as is he. There are cultural reasons for this popularity. One Russian says
that Putin fits perfectly into the old Russian myth of "a tsar fighting the
boyars" as well as into the classical Russian historical cycle or rhythm,
"attention–rest–attention."[54]

There is an old saying that "every people deserves the government it
gets." Despite the hard times most Russians have faced in the post-Soviet
period, there has been no significant mass unrest. Such quiescence only
encourages bureaucrats to be arbitrary and difficult. Why this Russian political passivity? The repressiveness of the imperial and particularly the
Soviet systems may well have had a long-term effect on society, with it being "genetically purged" of "troublemakers." The lack of a believable
"counterexample" must also play a role. Many Russians seem to have
thought that Westernization was mainly a plenitude of inexpensive consumer goods. Malia suggests that because Russia was long "the last and

rawest plateau on the West–East cultural gradient," it faced "models of achievement too complex to be readily imitated." In addition, as Albats points out, Russian libraries did not contain books about the realities of bureaucracy.[55] And then there may be the old "peasantish" general assumption that bad or unjust sociopolitical life can only be endured, not changed. As a Russian writer put it only a few years ago, "Everyone says the same thing. Things are going poorly for us; today is worse than yesterday, and tomorrow we can expect a complete catastrophe."[56] Yet society organizes no movement to solve its problems. Last, there may be a general feeling among Russians that administration, like so much else, ought to be left to the "experts." Of course, Russians have long been adept at avoidance and minimization of authority and also at petitioning it through "groveling" and wheedling, an approach that some bureaucrats may enjoy and which perpetuates their power.

Does culture affect bureaucracy? Yes. How can the way a government works and relates to its people, even in a dictatorship, not be shaped by that people's culture? Even the most rational bureaucrats must sometimes act according to the norms and assumptions imbedded in the dominant culture (unless the bureaucrats were all foreigners). Still, "it is not obvious what are the precise incompatibilities between particular cultures, or aspects of culture, and particular forms or levels of organization."[57]

Another issue arises. A bureaucracy cannot be adjudged "good" or "bad" solely in accordance with some standard foreign to its cultural context. A bureaucracy's worth depends at least partly on the degree to which it upholds the values of the culture it serves. The Japanese ministry that deals with foreign trade would seem despotic in American culture. Even the British military would seem "too military" for most Americans' taste. (I once saw a Scottish army sergeant gathering together his squad of soldiers in a railway station. He loudly excoriated them in picturesque language while they moved ever so quickly and fearfully, as if a fire had been lit under them. An Oxford-trained British academic once said to me, "How can you people march without leather soles?" Another asked, "How can you let soldiers get so heavy? What will they do in a war?") Unavoidably, "the nature of a particular bureaucracy is linked to the system of government and the society in which it operates."[58] Accordingly, we must cut Russian bureaucracy some slack. There are good cultural reasons for it being the way it is. That does not mean that foreigners will not sometimes be repelled by it. As a Polish communist has noted, for him "it was better to sit and teach in Polish prisons than to vegetate in Soviet bureaucracy."[59]

Still, even Russians often disapprove of the ways in which their bureaucracy works. Komarov faces up to the sensitive (and "politically incorrect") issue of culture and its problems. He says that Russian culture supports and favors "bureaupathology" or "bureaucratism," saying that its "paper fetishism" is based on a culture of talking and philosophizing about work ("Oblomovism") instead of actually doing the work in a straightforward manner, a culture based on the "habits of the Russian" (*privichki Rossiiskogo cheloveka*).[60] An imperial Russian diplomat said that he understood the Russian Foreign Office's preference for non-Russian "Baltic barons" because of the dislike for "the contradictions which are in the character of every Russian" and the fear of "willful and capricious Russians with a tendency to consider themselves more clever than their superiors" who would alter reports and correspondence in tune with their personal preferences.[61]

Organizational Culture

Service in the U.S. Navy first brought home to me the special culture of an organization. Navy life is replete with particular ways of doing things that are nowhere in Navy regulations. A humorous example involves the offering of an extra day's liberty in port to the lookout who first sighted and reported the U.S. Coast Guard cutter as we neared port. The ship then reduced speed below the legal limit and avoided trouble with the admiral commanding the district. But as soon as we had passed the cutter we speeded up again, to an illegal and dangerous speed that made the entire ship shudder. Once, when the main radar antenna had broken partially loose from the mast while we were in rough North Pacific seas, I was told by my chief that a man could not be ordered to do something as dangerous as climbing up to fasten it down. Volunteers had to be called for, with the volunteer who did the work rewarded informally and off the books in some way. Officers also learned that they were not to use the lavatories or "heads" of the enlisted men. These were for the men only. The Boatswains' Mates always had the best-looking spaces, perhaps because they used English, and not the regulation U.S. Navy, brass polish and floor wax. Those enlisted men were pressured by their enlisted superiors to contribute cash for these items because it was generally advantageous in terms of informal rewards to have the cleanest spaces. Sailors who got into mild trouble were often informally given the probably illegal option of either going through the judicial process (Captain's Mast, etc.) or giving up their liberty cards for a few weeks. In such ways is an organization ordered. Navy regulations and the Uniform Code of Military Justice passed by Congress, voluminous as they are, are apparently insufficient for the Navy's "good order and discipline." Of course, the life of the sea has always seen many informal arrangements, for example, working on Sundays and holidays, "deep-sixing" ballast (and much else) in harbors, and so on. As Richard Henry Dana put it in the early nineteenth century,

"There has grown up . . . a series of customs, which have become a well-understood system, and have almost the force of prescriptive law."[62]

Every organization of any length of existence has its own informal ways and rules. An institution not only carries and reflects societal values; it creates and shapes them. It may even change some values to a pathological extent and reject or discard others. Accordingly, there is an organizational culture perspective in the scholarly literature on bureaucracy and organization: "A culture is not something an organization has; a culture is something an organization is."[63]

Definitions

Many definitions of organizational culture exist. A convenient functional definition is: "a social force that controls . . . organizational behavior by shaping members' cognitions and perceptions of meanings and realities, providing affective energy for mobilization, and identifying who belongs and who does not."[64] It is useful to see organizational culture as existing in three levels, from the foundation of basic underlying assumptions, to values and beliefs, to material artifacts. The specific elements can fill a page, from anecdotes, to shared expectations, heroes, jargon, myths, rituals, symbols, and worldviews. The culture of an organization is taught and learned, often unconsciously, through work and its cues, practices, and communications, and is held unconsciously. Nevertheless, the culture of an organization can be comprehensive and highly potent.[65] It is also possible for an organization to harbor two, or perhaps even more, cultures. For example, one high-tech American company found that it needed both more discipline and, at the same time, to retain its free-wheeling drive in experimentation and development. Accordingly, two cultures were allowed, and big gains came from getting employees in the two into interactive teams. However, sometimes cultures can clash within an organization and impair its functioning. This can occur, for example, when companies merge.[66] Academic departments in universities can suffer from excessive friction among their subfields.

Organizational Climate

Although organizational climate may not be, as Ott maintains, a part of the organizational culture, it cannot but affect it. Ott defines it as "an amalgamation of feeling tones, or a transient organizational mood."[67] One feels it immediately, for example, when dealing with an American professional diplomat or a career Marine Corps officer. An amusing example was quite evident at an academic conference on Russian themes when members of the Central Intelligence Agency and the Defense Intelligence Agency on the same panel exhibited very different points of view on the same topic. They also dressed differently and even exhibited hostility toward each other. Clearly they had been formed within different organizational cultures, the CIA, that is, the analysis branches, more "academic," and the DIA, more "military." Clothing and haircuts were very different. The British novelist le Carré plays with the theme of conflict between MI5 and MI6. In trying to state what this is in a Russian government we may be on shaky ground. Still, the phenomenon can be "bracketed" to a degree.

It seems, for example, that Russian government agencies are fairly isolated from each other. Top Soviet ministerial officials tended to work their whole lives within a single ministry, whereas imperial Russian bureaucrats did not interact easily or informally with bureaucrats of other ministries or chains of command, even if they worked in the same building. They would correspond with each other instead of walking across the hall to talk.[68] This is very unlike American practice, in which bureaucrats maintain long-standing contacts in other agencies. Also notable is that there was a strong tendency for Russian officials to see their work in terms of their own self-interest. According to Lincoln, Russians have tended to lack a "sense of civic responsibility" and to divide into "petty-minded, self-serving interest groups, upon which reform and change have never been imposed successfully except by autocratic rulers."[69] Below I deal with an extreme expression of bureaucrats' self-interest—corruption.

This low feeling of civic obligation does not mean that becoming a bureaucrat is unpopular in Russia. The culture seems to favor a positive view of the bureaucratic career. Acquiring privilege may be a factor in this outlook. In 1995 an article on "Russia's new rulers" stated: "The privileges for the new nomenklatura include free medical care in the best hospitals, visits to nature preserves and vacation areas that had been reserved for the Soviet elite, access to exclusive grocery stores, special license plates and even preferred treatment in the cafeteria of the agency that is the successor to the K.G.B. . . . The infamous Russian bureaucracy is, if anything, more bloated than ever."[70] Also important for the organizational climate is the striking prevalence of informalist behavior, including "sloppiness," in governmental administration. As a Canadian observer has noted, "Although the [Russian] bureaucracy is labyrinthine and oppressive, it can also be whimsical and full of loopholes. Canadians view rules as rules, but Russians tend to see them as negotiating positions. It is possible to enter into your own private dialogue with authority, to bribe, or flatter, or trick officialdom into letting you slip through the net."[71]

Anyone who has dealt with Russians in an academic setting knows this to be true. Another observer speaks of the "pervasive dysfunctionality, lawlessness, and lack of accountability which characterize Russia's political system and public institutions." In 1996 a top-level Russian government official stated that Russian state mechanisms operated rather poorly and with little coordinative capacity, even if the presidential administration weighed in. Stephan Sestanovich has written of "the dangerous autonomy of the military, police and K.G.B.; the fact that constructive policy so often sinks in a sea of intrigue, special favors and incompetence." And that old Russian phenomenon of dualism is still with us, notably the "huge presidential bureaucracy" that "functions quite separately from the government."[72]

Another aspect of the Russian organizational climate is the lack of solid information and the consequent lurching from rumor to rumor. One specialist says that there is a "failure to replace Russia's tradition of mutual distrust and intragovernmental rivalry with a genuine willingness to collaborate in the formulation of policy."[73] The phenomenon of mistrust is easily noticeable in dealings among Russian academics, who often tell one not to tell another academic in their own department anything of what has been told. Apparently Russian professional life is replete with special and secret individualized deals and arrangements.

The Russian government is similar. The governor of a region in the Urals says, "So the enemies are the bureaucracy." Even if the president and the prime minister are "for" a proposal, the ministries can be "against." He continues, "Not a single issue can be settled legally in Moscow because all the officials are tied to one another. . . . Muscovites in the bureaucracy and administration are probably relatives tenfold; everyone fixes up with another a son-in-law, a son, a grandson—one's own people all around. You have only to arrive in Moscow and it's like being in a big village."[74]

Also evident in the Russian organizational climate is a certain "headstrongness" of action on the part of bureaucrats, a long-standing phenomenon. One is reminded of the generals who added territory to the empire in Central Asia without asking St. Petersburg for approval. And then there is the example of Russian bureaucrats in the nineteenth century insisting that Russia not buy rifles from abroad. She had to be self-sufficient. The result was that in the 1878 war with Turkey the latter had the better infantry weapons. The Soviet bureaucracy retained this quality partly because of the militarization brought about by the Civil War and also because Stalin filled the party with "hooligans who terrorized the populace."[75] Certainly the dangerous testing that led to the Chernobyl incident is a prime example of narrow-minded risk taking. "The Soviets take more chances than we do," says an American expert on nuclear energy. Or perhaps what we have here is a tendency toward disregarding reality and danger. Two Slovenian scholars' definition of bureaucracy seems most apt here: "an alienated power with the right to decide without consideration of reality."[76] They correctly see a tendency for "paperwork people" not to know the actual situation, a problem often noted in Soviet times.

In 1973 the chairman of the Uzbek Council of Ministers noted that "in some administrative organs the . . . workers frequently spend most of their time . . . on resolving current secondary matters [and] . . . filling out various forms." He also lamented the tendency for high administrative organs to try to resolve "all problems," instead of allowing them to be dealt with locally: "We still have officials who, gathering everything in their own hands, do not allow their subordinates to take even a single step, thus paralyzing their initiative and contributing to the weakening of individual responsibility." Tucker cites Gorbachev's complaint about the "persistent addiction to bureaucratic paperwork" that thwarted initiative and innovation from below. And then there is the report of 2000 from Moscow on the time-consuming need for accountants for private enterprises to file quarterly "six different reports with six different offices in six different parts of the city," a process with long lines. In typical Russian style, receipts are "awarded" to each "supplicant" one by one.[77]

Not to be forgotten is the presence among the top bureaucracy of representatives of the *gosudarstvenniki*, or "etatist-nationalists," who believe in the need for a strong and ubiquitous state. Such a predilection invites departures from reality. As Milosz once said, "The basis of all bureaucracy is the propaganda that passes from bottom to top. It is meant to soothe the conscience of those at the summit, assuring them beyond a doubt that they stand at the head of a mighty, smoothly run organization."[78]

A notable departure from reality is that of Gorbachev's Prime Minister Valentin Pavlov, who, when the economy was collapsing, drove away foreign investment with the ludicrous charge that Western investors wanted to destroy the Soviet economy.[79] A tragic example of Russian bureaucratic divorce from the realities of a situation is the insanely obtuse refusal of top Navy brass to deal consequentially with the sinking of the submarine *Kursk* in 2000 even though some members of the submerged sub's crew were still alive. Of course, Russian officers have long tended, with pride, to see their soldiers as expendable. During the visit of a U.S. president to the USSR a top officer at the airport said of the honor guard, "If we tell them to stay where they are they would let themselves be sucked into the engines." Scholars in Russia can now point out that if World War II had been fought more intelligently, fewer Russian combatants would have died.

Cultural Content: Western Examples

All countries' bureaucracies exhibit patterns of cultural behavior that are dysfunctional in terms of achieving formal goals. Crozier, writing of the French bureaucracy, notes the "extreme caution of the organization leaders and the frustrations and lack of initiative of the lower echelons," even though in France the permanent bureaucracy is fairly efficient.[80] U.S. examples can easily be cited, although overall the American national bureaucracy runs rather well. James Q. Wilson lists some of the routine successes of public administration in the United States and concludes by saying, "There are not many places where all this happens. It is astonishing it can be made to happen at all."[81] Still, there is a cultural element in American national bureaucracy, and sometimes it goes awry, just as it does in the Russian.

James D. Barber calls Washington, D.C., "this capital of political culture" and notes that its existence is based on "a set of inherited modes of belief and expectation" causing the government to work on "a set of mores—values thought natural—increasingly divergent from the country's common sense . . . a peculiar tribal ethic."[82] Here are just a few examples of culture as a problem in American government. In 1999 the Centers for Disease Control and Prevention used $8.8 million of the $22.7 million set aside by Congress for research on chronic fatigue syndrome for other research. Employees of the Veterans Administration have routinely denied veterans' claims for benefits simply because the employees wanted to accumulate work credits and qualify for bonuses. In addition, the agency shredded thousands of documents a judge had ordered turned over to a veterans association. Congressional investigators have found that the U.S. Postal Service suffers from a "dysfunctional organizational culture" of autocratic managers and adversarial employee unions. The U.S. Foreign Service has been said to have a "subtle subculture" shunting women officers into jobs from which promotion to policy-making positions is unlikely. The CIA seems to retain a culture that elevates the Directorate of Operations and its personnel above the rest of the members of the agency. Some have called it "a bureaucratic behemoth swathed in a half-holy mystique," with an "imperious attitude" of never being wrong wrapped in the "rites of a college fraternity." A leading observer of the Defense Department sees a "culture of procurement . . . that draws the military towards new weapons *because* of their great cost, not in spite of it." The Immigration and Naturalization Service (INS), now split into two agencies, has been charged with a "historic failure to hold its managers accountable for egregious wrongdoing," with a "good old boys' club" protecting them. There is even a cynical motto in the INS: "Screw up—move up."[83]

When the head of the District of Columbia's Human Resource Administration posed as a "client" of her own agency, she found that she suffered "numerous indignities": the loss of her documents, the bureaucratic runaround, and being "depersonalized."[84] And the private sector is not immune from cultural deficiencies in its workings. For example, customers, dealers, and suppliers of one of the big three automakers have described its operating attitude as "arrogant." Medical doctors have been accused of a culture of protectiveness and secrecy regarding medical errors. The director of a state health care administration has said of doctors, "There's a strong back current that keeps people from being entirely honest." A physician who discloses another physician's mistake faces "almost certain retribution."[85]

Russian Examples

Still, negative cultural behavior in the bureaucracy of the United States is very different in style and nature from that in Russia. For example, when a Soviet military pilot who had defected was shown American aircraft carrier operations he was "amazed that such large numbers of people are active in so many phases of flight deck handling of aircraft and that they work together in complete harmony without screaming or arguments." Anyone who has lived in Russia has observed the bad, even violent, relations among coworkers on the job. Ironically, the U.S. embassy in Moscow has been accused of being permeated with "Russian"-type behavior, suspiciousness and standoffishness, toward both Russians and Americans. In general, U.S. government dealings with the Russian government encounter a cultural predisposition that is often distinctive and a source of tensions in the relationship. For example, in 1995 a Russian government minister told an American diplomat that the United States tries to move much faster on issues than Russians deem proper or possible. And sometimes the Russians ask for things that the United States would never even consider giving. For example, also in 1995, Russian ministries wanted the U.S. Defense Conversion Committee to help them control all contacts of Russian defense enterprises and their employees with foreign businesses and governments and to be the sole vehicle for U.S.–Russian cooperation in all defense conversion, public or private. A U.S. position paper on this disagreement states, "It is important that the Vice President reaffirm our view that governments should play a limited, facilitating role in defense conversion and that the private sector must be the main engine of conversion cooperation," a very "American" cultural position.[86] In one meeting of a working group of the Gore–Chernomyrdin Commission in 1996 the Russians tried to co-opt the American side into agreeing to work through only one Russian central government agency, all directed toward trying to prevent American aid to private Russian firms and American linkages with regional governments.

Russian Tradition

These negative cultural aspects of Russian administration are not new. Russia has long been a land of many little but important pieces of paper, long lines, haughty officials, and the bureaucratic runaround, where unwritten rules were numerous and important. Because the rule of law has never been ingrained in Russian government decision making and operations and because communications were poor, the bureaucracy tended to do things its own way. Leading bureaucrats could often take "political" decisions, even working against policy, and minor functionaries could act as if they were in effect the tsar, lording it over a people who had no recourse but informal and careful avoidance. Given the vast power of the state, formal public opposition would bring, eventually, harsh retribution, even death: "The Tsarist bureaucratic tradition . . . left behind a legacy of condescension and disdain for the simple citizen. . . . Besides the usual bureaucratic difficulties he was greeted by rudeness and impatience. All this was also a reflection of both the sorry state of human relations in Russia and the absence of elementary cultural habits."[87]

Russian bureaucrats today are still looking to tsarist bureaucratic practices as a model for their own activities. This may be a source, for example, of the formalism, haughtiness, and "distance" common among Russian bureaucrats. They may confuse what they are doing with the life and style of the former Russian "leisure class aristocracy" or the Soviet elite. They have no or little knowledge of the practice of public administration and business in the West. Also important as a cultural model, because the present Russian bureaucracy was derived from the peasantry, may be the traditional Russian peasant's apparent drive for maximum output, not profit. This could have had a role in producing the industrial bureaucrat's fixated drive for the greatest amount of output irrespective of quality. (The Stalinist plan and the penalties for failure are no doubt also important.)[88]

Another possible effect of traditional Russian culture on administrative practices may well have been the Russian Orthodoxy of the peasant. This, too, could have had a role in producing "ceremonialist" and formalistic elitism among bureaucrats. In a way, the prerevolutionary Russian culture of the countryside took revenge on the Bolshevik Revolution and Marxism by taking root in central recesses, for example, the military and the state bureaucracy. Religious beliefs and practices could also have produced some of the "fetishist" love of routine and paperwork typical of the Russian bureaucracy. When I told a historian of Russia about two bureaucrats in an office of the Russian Ministry of Higher Education in 1977 doing crossword puzzles at 10 A.M., he exclaimed, "Why, it's like the nineteenth century!"

Another cultural continuity from the past is the practice of dualism in Russian administration. A particular function is rarely isolated in one agency. Usually it is performed by two or more. Blacker once noted that the Soviet economy was "two parallel systems, military and civilian, connected at certain key junctures, but essentially separate in form and function." And under Yeltsin, as Kagarlitsky points out, "alongside the old military-industrial complex, a sort of 'military-police' complex has come into being."[89] The latter may be made up of more personnel than the military possesses. The Chechen War of the early 1990s was fought, on the Russian side, largely with special forces of the Ministry of the Interior, not the Ministry of Defense.

Russian bureaucracy has long been characterized by a definite degree of unprofessionalism. One can even speak of sloppiness and sluggishness in action. This does not mean that many Russian administrators do not see themselves, as noted by Sternheimer, "chiefly as 'professionals' with a job to get done." However, Stalin's self-protective blockage of quick action combined with the cultural heritage of tsarism and "peasantism" created an "inveterate sluggishness" that hobbled and permeated the Soviet system and which still remains evident. The discovery that a Hungarian prisoner of war was kept for fifty-three years because it was assumed that his Hungarian speech was a sign of insanity is an egregious case of unprofessionalism. Although it can be seen as a deviant exception, it still "counts."

Often gift giving is necessary to make the bureaucracy work. American historians of Russia give gifts to archivists in order to be able to use the archives. A commentator notes that "the entire idea of archives as public domain is novel to a nation that has always regarded them as a tool for officials and bureaucrats. . . . Russian archivists still believe they are doing researchers a great favor by letting them in." A Russian sent to Moscow to get a minister's signature on a form found that it took him three days at the ministry just to find out whom to deal with. A gift of chocolates to a secretary was crucial. The minister signed the form without looking at it. During the Soviet period top administrators often had so much to do that they were forced into a type of patrimonialism: "The general director of the enterprise is a walk-around, face-to-face manager, a taskmaster and parent figure whose influence is felt everywhere, from the executive suite to the production floor." In Soviet industrial enterprises there was an "absence" of horizontal integration and networking because they violated the unwritten rules.[90]

The KGB was not immune to unprofessionalism. According to a defector from it, "The unwritten rule was that an intelligence officer could only be decorated after his boss had been. . . . So the intelligence service decorated either the wrong people, or the right people for the wrong reason, or the wrong people for the wrong reason, as operatives joked among themselves."[91] The same source reports that officers were exhorted to recruit U.S. citizens. However, because it was an unspoken assumption that this was unattainable, "as soon as an officer would report a glimmer of success in that department, he immediately became the object of grave suspicions." He sums up his frustrations: "Of course, there are honest and talented individuals in the ranks of the political and bureaucratic class, but the shots are invariably called by the incompetents."[92]

Russian sources also stress the unprofessionalism of today's Russian bureaucracy. Obolonskii notes a post-Soviet "decline in the level of professionalism" for two main reasons: the movement of the "most qualified and capable" bureaucrats "into commercial structures" and the "disappearance of the CPSU 'master.'"[93] Interviews with officials show that the "stability of officials' positions in the administrative apparatus" is determined by "loyalty to the heads of administration and the ability to maintain a relationship with 'essential people.' Civil servants consider professionalism and a prestigious education to be less important. Thus, at present the principle of professionalism does not dominate the civil service."[94]

A state senator from Massachusetts who spent some time in the Pskov area during the 1990s says that "the most simple decision becomes massive discussion and debate" with "constant chaos" surrounding decision making until the "chief person puts his foot down."[95] This person was often the "holdover in charge." I am reminded of the obstreperous and unfocused discussions at faculty meetings during 1977 at a *kafedra* of the Moscow University Law School that went on until the chair imposed a decision.

The thinking of Russian bureaucrats has puzzled and fascinated observers for some time. Joseph Conrad writes of "a display of bureaucratic stoicism in a Russian official's ineradicable, almost sublime contempt for truth." During the Soviet period there was a wealth of writing on the severe distortion and even outright falsification in reporting on plan outcomes. The Soviet economic bureaucracy also ran on an "engineering mentality" that gave what Gregory calls "technocrats" a great deal of influence over the decision making made by *khoziaistvenniki* and *apparatchiki*.[96]

Informalism and Formalism

Both informalism and formalism exist in Russian bureaucracy. Sternheimer notes that "effective informal communications are always underpinned by a set of unspoken rules dictating mutuality: *ty mne, a ia tebe* [you scratch my back, and I'll scratch yours] remains the governing principle of interpersonal interactions." Informal supply and trade arrangements involving the *tolkach*, almost the Pantagruel of writing on Soviet industrial management, were widespread during the Soviet period, and personal relations were very important in the running of the Soviet economy. A great deal of informal negotiating and implicit agreements also existed.[97]

At the same time, excessive formalism can frequently be seen in various forms. An American who negotiated with the Soviets in 1968 found that "Soviet diplomats and warriors seemed to have less routine interdepartmental contact with each other than did Americans. More of the exchanges of information between them appeared to occur only at the most senior levels." Signing paper seems to have great, though to an outsider unclear, significance. For example, Primakov, the prime minister appointed by Yeltsin in September 1998, said on NTV that the agreement between Yeltsin and the Parliament drafted in August 1998 to redistribute powers between president and Parliament had to be formally signed: "It can be updated . . . but it must be signed." This incident, having to do with "matters of state," may have justified such formalism. However, here is another example. A Polish novelist visiting Russia in winter 1990 as part of an official delegation lost the ticket for his "insignificant medium-sized man's hat" checked at a museum. The cloakroom attendant, an elderly woman, refused to give it up without the ticket, even when importuned to do so by the entire delegation, the interpreter, and a squad of soldiers. Finally a deal was worked out through the museum's administrative director: "A report was drawn up. It was signed by the director, the novelist, the cloakroom attendant and the interpreter, after which the hat was returned and the delegation departed in the 24 degree below zero weather."[98] Also germane here is the intense dislike Russian officials often express for each other. For example, in 1998 two high officials, one the minister of finance, got into a public mutual accusatory mode, and one actually filed suit against the other.[99]

Bureaucratic formalism in Russia can also be so intense and rigid that it becomes bureaucratic fetishism or makes bureaucratic process a quasi-religious, that is, "sacral," aspect of government. Bureaucratic forms are so rigidly observed that performance of function does not occur. This reveals the bureaucrat to be an integral symbol and part of the state, not just an instrument of the political system and a servant of the populace performing certain set and legally limited functions. Indeed, under both the tsarist and the post-Soviet systems bureaucrats have been so important that elected officials have sometimes been willing to give up their elected positions to be bureaucrats. This suggests that to Russians the symbolism of bureaucracy is more powerful than that of democracy. Sometimes this rigid approach to bureaucratic activity has had aspects of "cargo-cultism," that is, the bureaucrat acts out this role in a rigid and undeviating manner and, thus, a necessary system-strengthening "ceremony" is supposed to have occurred. The bureaucratic process becomes something akin to a Mass. The fundamental power of the overall system has thereby been demonstrated; it can do even absurd things and still survive and dominate.

Risk Avoidance

An unwillingness to take responsibility or risk may exist in all bureaucracies. "Those whose lives are heavily involved in the activities of the market welcome risk taking as part of the game; those who work in bureaucracies typically want to see risks managed in ways that correspond to their beliefs in rational organization" and possibly their control as well. The Soviet period saw numerous complaints about bureaucrats' unwillingness to change and their proclivity to resist orders to do so: "And they do not want the responsibility, they cannot overcome their own inertia, and in one way or another impede the introduction of the new method." Putin ran into it also. Putin's inability to maintain forward motion may have made the bureaucracy lose confidence in him and respond "in its usual manner—by simply failing to execute instructions."[100] Bukovsky suggests that denial of responsibility is a result of Stalin wiping out the early revolutionary zeal. The result is an apparatus

> growing more and more sclerotic, overtaken by . . . fear of responsibility, fear of superiors—and by bureaucratic indifference. It was overgrown with a tangle of laws, regulations, and decrees, and it wasn't always clear how to interpret them. Better just to pass the buck to your superiors and wait for instructions. At the top they were in no hurry to issue instructions. They much preferred to punish their subordinates for negligence, or to hand down new regulations and decrees, which all had to be interpreted and have their contradictions reconciled.[101]

Popular Preference

One fundamental fact of Russians' thinking on bureaucracy seems clear—many Russians want to be bureaucrats. We have seen this in Yeltsin's ability to get troublesome politicians out of his hair by, as the British might say, "translating" them to the bureaucracy. One reason for this "job preference" may be that Russian history has lacked certain other job choices common in the West, for example, business and other societal slots popular there but not prestigious or remunerative in Russia, such as law and medicine. And in Russia, given the powerlessness of the ordinary individual for so long, it probably was a good idea to acquire some power in order to create better "life chances" for oneself. Being a bureaucrat gave one some security and "insulation" from the arbitrariness of the state (although in Stalin's time all were in danger). No wonder the Russian bureaucrat has long been noted for arrogance, elitism, arbitrariness, and even cruelty.

Arrogance and Indifference

Russian bureaucratic arbitrariness and indifference are illustrated by the long-overdue return by Russia of some Japanese POWs of World War II to Japan only in 1998, when possibly dozens of others were still stuck in Siberia. Also pertinent are the stories of Americans in Russia not being able to return to the United Sates for fifty or more years. One of them, finally cleared to leave after forty years, got to the plane but was stopped, for ten years it turned out, supposedly because of a technicality involving his wife's visa.[102] The story of Dostoyevsky being lined up for execution and then, surprise, not being shot comes to mind. This experience alone must have had a role in creating Dostoyevsky as we know him. Who says Russian bureaucracy lacks significance?

Such bureaucratic qualities are also revealed by the practice in Soviet times of letting interethnic riots "burn themselves out." The way the *Kursk* sub disaster was handled highlights the "military culture of cruelty and disregard for human life, even of one's own servicemen."[103] Aslund has said that one of the things that distinguishes Russia from some other countries is that "its elite is particularly vicious." McDaniel says that Russia generally is distinguished by "antimodernism" or what he calls the "Russian idea." This would tend to justify or exaggerate certain premodern views and inclinations of the bureaucrats. McDaniel is on more visible ground when he speaks of "the traditional Russian pattern of a swollen, bureaucratized and unjust state . . . alien to the society."[104]

The elitist ways of thinking of Soviet bureaucrats can be illustrated by my experience with a functionary of the Soviet Ministry of Higher Education who would not allow me to extend my stay in the USSR even though my visa was good for the extra month. His argument was, "Your government has not given you permission for a longer stay." Luckily, I ran into him at a party given by the U.S. embassy, and, when I introduced him to an American diplomat who told him that the U.S. government did not mind if I stayed longer, he reluctantly agreed to an extension of my stay. He seemed to think that I was the "property" of my government, probably an age-old Russian bureaucratic view of ordinary people as "commodities." And then there is the explanation of egregious anti-American propaganda given by a Soviet functionary to an American: "It's for the peasants." A well-known American who writes on Russian themes once told me that getting the Soviet bureaucracy to do anything is like getting a crowd to squeeze a tube of toothpaste without any of them leaving a fingerprint on the tube. Certainly, Russian bureaucrats are preoccupied with serving their superiors rather than the population they ought to serve. A Russian political scientist said in 1995, "In our country, as soon as a person comes to power, 90 percent of his efforts are directed at his own problems."[105] This is a natural result in a society of poor people and a culture in which the state was long understood as the ancestral private property of the ruler.[106]

Perhaps the repressiveness and nastiness of Russian officialdom are also partly an unprincipled and somewhat desperate reaction to the common Russian feeling that everyone should be equal. The bureaucrat has to drive home his superiority every chance he gets in order to convince himself and others that he is indeed superior, in power at least, and in order to dampen down the potential rebellion and the popular tendency toward *uravnilovka* or leveling down. The result has long been a decided social distance of bureaucrats from the society at large and a tendency to lord it over people and also be pretty hard on them in the performance of bureaucratic functions. One observer in a "White" area in 1919 noted that bureaucrats taking delight in making difficulties for people was a "very characteristic example of Russian officialdom." The "catch-22" is not uncommon. In 1996 a U.N. legal officer in Moscow noted that "you can't get permanent residence registration unless you have refugee status. But you can't get refugee status without residence registration. It's a huge problem."[107]

Secrecy and Deception

Secretiveness combined with deceptiveness has long been a strongly held attitude among Russian bureaucrats. Almost any information can be considered a state secret. Both Remington and Huskey have noted the secretiveness of Russian bureaucratic agencies (as well as the making of rulings that "often take precedence over the law"). In 2000 the secretary-general of the Union of Russian Journalists declared, "The secretiveness of the authorities . . . is hurting every citizen" and said that the governments of all of Russia's eighty-nine regions restrict freedom of speech. The sinking of the *Kursk* saw a great deal of Russian bureaucratic secretiveness and deception in action. That old Russian fear of punishment was a factor. Felgengauer writes, "Russian admirals know too well that disclosing secrets to the West may easily land them in the clink, while risking the lives of sailors will not." Some of the secrecy and misinformation in the case of the *Kursk* seemed "designed to protect individual bureaucracies." *Izvestiia* wrote, "Lies and fear are the features of Russian authority." Many assessments and theories on the *Kursk* tragedy were offered without any facts to support them. Indeed, it has been said that Russian bureaucratic information giving expands the number of theories without attempting to eliminate any. The Norwegian admiral involved in the *Kursk* rescue attempt said that the Russian side "unleashed so much spurious and distorted information on us that it threatened the safety of our divers."[108]

Personal Networks

Informal personal networks are a significant feature of Russian administration—and of much else in Russia. Many people of prominence in and out of politics have a *komanda* or team made up of people they have established based on school and work. There is nothing particularly Russian about this, of course. Yet in Russia under Soviet and early postcommunist conditions these networks could be very important. In the USSR they influenced government policy and even the strength of the state. Brown, citing Rigby, says that "'the plethora of local cliques and patronage groupings which cut across formal structural boundaries' and in some cases subverted official norms and goals . . . constituted a 'shadow culture' in some ways analogous to the 'shadow economy.'" During the late 1990s it is said that outstanding individuals such as Gaidar and Chubais have influenced government policy through personal networks based in the bureaucracy and research institutes whether or not they themselves are in the government. And often "insiders," somewhat like American lobbyists, who know the key people and how to get through the labyrinthine bureaucracy to talk with them, are very important. One is reminded of the *tolkach*, mentioned above, of such crucial importance in Soviet industry.[109]

CORRUPTION

We now move on to the consideration of bureaucratic corruption, a Russian long-standing phenomenon in administration, as it manifests itself in the post-Soviet period.

Significance

"The first requirement of an administrator is that he prove trustworthy," said St. Paul in his First Letter to the Corinthians. Corruption, or what the *Oxford English Dictionary* defines as "the destruction or spoiling of anything, *esp.* by disintegration or decomposition," is a serious threat to good administration. This "misuse of public power and the public good for private profit" covers a number of activities from bribery, to influence peddling, to nepotism and kickbacks. In many countries it is the norm, not the exception, and sometimes "destroys all honest social life."[110]

Political or official corruption has a "long and rich heritage," with no age or place with incorruptible politics and government. Human greed has been as much a building block of political systems as has service to the national or public interest.[111] But because most corruption is clandestine, it is "notoriously hard to measure and empirical economic research on the question is fairly meager."[112] Yet public corruption is widespread: "Growing crime and corruption threaten not only Russia, but the entire world." Corruption has a number of deleterious economic and societal effects. Both the International Monetary Fund (IMF) and the World Bank now contend that corruption is an obstacle to economic development. As an IMF source puts the case, it discredits free markets, weakens the rule of law, impedes Western investment, and even results in nuclear proliferation and terrorism.[113] Another list of negative effects includes misallocation of talent, loss of tax revenue (certainly a problem in Russia), lowering the quality of the infrastructure and public services, and distortion of the composition of government expenditure. The World Bank lists corruption as a major cause of poverty. And corrupt politicians tend to choose investment projects not on the basis of inherent worth but on that of bribes and kickbacks.[114]

The problem is so significant worldwide that the United Nations has held several meetings, adopted various declarations on the issue, and issued a code of conduct for officials. During the 1990s "a wave of bribery scandals hit all parts of the world." The payoffs and thievery surrounding the French state-owned oil company shook the foundations of that republic and touched many of the leading figures in political life. Also, during the early 1990s "at least six heads of state, more than fifty cabinet ministers, scores of congressmen, and hundreds of business men have lost their jobs, their liberty, and even their lives on account of allegations of corruption."[115] Colleges and universities now teach courses about corruption, for example, "Corporate Deviance and Official Corruption." In mid-2000 a seminar on the theme "Corruption in Russia" was held in Golitsyno, near Moscow, by the Moscow School of Political Studies.[116] Corruption and politics have always gone closely together. How is corruption to receive scope and the security to exist without the collaboration and approval of the holders of state power? The public official unavoidably has private interests, as Marx recognized.[117] Under certain conditions, low pay, lax supervision, low morale, and so forth, the official may act to maximize those personal interests at public expense. Some, like Lord Acton, see power itself as the "hot-bed of corruption." Others say that "corruption is always endemic, and it is worse in the early stages of capitalism." Others might say that communism, by elevating the state to Olympian heights and equating criticism of the state to anticommunism, gave bureaucrats a license to be corrupt and protected them from the consequences of their actions. So much for "causes." Many could say, as did a British banker so bluntly, "The further east and south you go [in Europe], the more corruption."[118]

Corruption is now crucially salient and important for Russia's present and the course of its postcommunist transition. One commentator says, "A tidal wave of crime and corruption is sweeping Eurasia, threatening to bury the nascent and fragile democratic institutions in Russia and other countries in the region." Another asks if Russia will become a failed democracy or even a "new rogue"—a backsliding state "swamped by corruption and overwhelmed by the difficulties of state-building." Elsewhere, in apparent exasperation, he answers his own question, saying, "One of the most important advantages a country can have is a lean, flexible, honest civil service. The Russians not only don't have it; they don't get it."[119]

One big negative effect of today's Russian corruption is its exclusion of much-needed investment, both domestic and foreign. Indeed, it encourages capital flight: "Corruption and bureaucratic holdups are acting as a brake on investment." The "sad" experience of dealing with the Russian bureaucracy has resulted in a loss of faith in Russia, says Sergei Rogov, head of the USA Institute. According to William C. Potter, Western training "may be for naught" unless the "culture of bribes" is extinguished. *The Economist* has stated that "criminally minded officials, rather than hoodlums, are the biggest threat to corporate security in Russia." Corruption also prevents and undermines faith in the efficacy of democracy, which is seen more and more as a criminal and ineffective system. "Corruption also holds back economic reforms and the development of a true market economy from which the majority can benefit because the status quo is the one convenient to those reaping the profits of corruption," notes Donald Jensen, a former U.S. diplomat working in Moscow. He adds, "In sum, corruption corrodes a society. When nepotism replaces merit, when cunning and cheating replace trust and honesty, when force and murder triumph over the law and a sense of decency—then the threads binding together a civil society are weakened and eventually destroyed."[120]

The situation is serious. Russia's former minister of the interior notes that the Chechens who took over a Russian town in 1995 passed twenty-four checkpoints and were able to buy their way past all but two of them. A former justice minister of Ukraine points out that in Russia and elsewhere in the former USSR "the members of the nomenklatura are now the virtually uncontrolled arbiters of the distribution and use of state property." Russia has become like Palermo, in Sicily, during the nineteenth century, "where the social realities and the criminal and the political all intersected, where a man might be at once . . . an officer of the local police or national guard, the head of a criminal family and a leading political activist."[121] An émigré from Russia told me that his businessman father found that the "man to see" in his town's mafia was a professor.

There is voluminous documentation on corruption in other ex-communist countries.[122] However, here we need only note that ex-communist systems can be rather corrupt and that even the use of harsh measures, for example, executions in China, seem not to reduce the phenomenon much. In 2000 the prime minister of China said publicly that corruption, which some sources say began in the 1960s with the Cultural Revolution, was threatening to undermine the party's authority. The next year Li Peng, China's second-highest government official, warned that corruption could end Communist Party rule. In 1999, in only one province, Guangdong, almost five thousand officials were penalized for corrupt acts.[123]

The Tsarist Period

Corruption is nothing new in Russia, but post-Soviet conditions have given it scope and dimension much greater than it had in the past. Corruption, or illegal informalism, has long been a feature of Russian governmental administration. When the great historian Karamzin was asked by Alexander I to explain what bureaucrats do, he answered, "They steal" (one word in Russian—*voruiut*). Florinsky writes of the "self-seeking, corrupt, and inefficient bureaucracy" of imperial Russia, whereas Pushkarev says, "In addition to the usual bureaucratic vices, the Russian bureaucratic class . . . was renowned for its money-grubbing and extortionism." In 1998 Russia's procurator-general said, "The officialdom of Russia never was very law-abiding," and he added that today "corruption has spread to all levels of the state mechanism."[124]

One origin of corruption in Russian governmental administration may lie in the "routineness" of the governors, in the time of Ivan III and his son Vasilii (1440–1505 and 1479–1533), receiving food and services from the local population as pay. This is called *kormlenie* (lit. "feeding"). Documents of the sixteenth century show that these officials "abused their privileges shamelessly." Ivan IV's (1530–84) law code, the Sudebnik, "attacked the corruption of officials" in several of its articles. Nevertheless, some seventeenth-century state administrators exhibited "extraordinary venality."[125]

Another reason for bureaucratic corruption in Russia is that the country was long a "patrimonial" state, with the tsar acting, as in Pipe's definition, as both ruler and proprietor. There was no private sphere or civil society as it developed in the West. In tsarist Russia at one time the state controlled some profitable branches of commerce and industry and gave some of the nobility, who long made up the higher state administration, economic privileges in return for their support. Soviet communism can be seen as "an especially virulent form of patrimonialism." Although nominally private property did not exist, "in practice the state and party 'owned' virtually everything." In the post-Soviet period patrimonialism retained much of its vitality as a result of phony privatization benefiting bureaucrats, the loans-for-shares deals favoring insiders, and the state's use of "authorized" banks to handle its funds. As a result, "Russia's patrimonial heritage has ensured that corruption and lawlessness are . . . a systemic problem that is unlikely to go away soon." As Yeltsin once said, in very "Russian" fashion, "Corruption is like weeds. No matter how hard you try to get rid of them, they keep reappearing." As Hamilton points out, one of the continually recurring metaphors for the Russian state and government is "the public official as corrupt, immoral 'scoundrel.'"[126] Russians' particular attitude toward the law, a tendency to see it as to be used for one's own benefit, as reflected in various folk sayings, may help make corruption fairly common. As Chinyaeva puts it, "People demand strict laws against corruption, but tend to see any proposed regulation . . . as an irritating complication to the usual ways of resolving problems."[127] The Russian historian M. Shakhmatov, after analyzing old Russian chronicles and literature, has concluded that the Russian ideal of the state is one of equity or fairness (*gosudarstvo pravdy*), rather than a Western-type state of law (*gosudarstvo zakona*).

The Soviet Period

Despite the holdover of totalitarian means, corruption existed even during Soviet times, particularly toward their end. Indeed, one authority on Russia says that the Soviet elite was "completely corrupt." Even top military officers were involved, expecting and obtaining gifts when visiting or inspecting units.[128] Another says that the Soviet economy was "little more than a web of corruption." A scholar of Soviet society writes that it faced "an ethical malaise of serious proportions" and that corruption, "a fundamental dishonesty in social and economic relationships among people, does indeed permeate the system." An émigré lawyer from Russia writes, "The Soviet Union is infected from top to bottom with corruption."[129] In 1973, when an American scholar of Soviet literature returned from the USSR to the United States, she exclaimed, "Oh, how corrupt they have become!" Possibly, Andropov and Gorbachev feared that "corruption, if allowed to go unchecked, might . . . ultimately compromise the regime itself, as had clearly happened in Poland in the late 1970s and early 1980s."[130] But it would be wrong to see this corruption as the only Russian cultural continuity. There were times in Soviet existence when "a sense of greatness" allowed many members of society to rise above their personal interests and act selflessly for what seemed the good of all.

Soviet corruption can be explained at various intellectual levels. Kaminski goes back to some major philosophers to find causes. He cites the doubts expressed about the young Soviet experiment by both Max Weber and Gaetano Mosca. The former notes that the initially high standards of a revolutionary movement conceal a "trap," the base motives of many among the following, with, as Acton suggested earlier, power corrupting even the "pure souls." Mosca emphasizes that "the strictly logical application of any single principle" and the lack of opposing "organized social forces" result in a "natural tendency" of the leaders to "abuse their powers" and the eventual communication downward of absolutism's vices to the entire political structure. Kaminski also emphasizes that "in Lenin's idea of the dictatorship of the proletariat there were no generally accepted rules" and that Marx hardly distinguished between the public and private realms, thereby delegitimizing both: "When a state denies a place for the private realm, it leaves no place for the public one."[131] A more down-to-earth explanation is given by Sternheimer, who apparently sees corruption as more avoidance than acquisition, as stemming from "overly taut plan targets," and as "motivated less by a desire for personal gain and the amassing of wealth than by the need to acquire a post, maintain one's job, or, above all, to avoid suffering."[132]

Because examples of corrupt behavior by officials during the late Soviet period are too numerous to count, I shall only present some examples from the 1980s and only examples involving Russians, not members of other ethnic groups. Our categories include high-level corruption, improper use of authority, bribery, lying and distortion of information, nepotism, and smuggling. The phenomenon of Soviet corruption does not lack a literature, though here I refer mainly to individual reports of it.[133]

Corruption occurred at the highest levels of Soviet officialdom. It has been described by several sources, including Luba Brezhneva, a niece of Leonid Brezhnev, once the general secretary of the Communist Party of the Soviet Union. In 1988 *Pravda* reported that a Soviet first deputy interior minister, Yuri M. Churbanov, Brezhnev's son-in-law, was involved in a big bribery and corruption scandal. He was arrested along with the premier and top Communist Party officials of Uzbekistan. Nikolai Shchelokov, a minister of internal affairs under Brezhnev, spent 700,000 rubles of government money on luxury items for his family and acquaintances.[134]

Misuse of authority by bureaucrats was not uncommon, particularly against journalists and others trying to work honestly or expose the real state of things. The problem sometimes became the stuff of plays, as in "We the Undersigned," in which a major character says, speaking of bureaucratic higher-ups, "We have a real mafia here. . . . Not a mafia that murders people, like in Sicily. But to trample a man underfoot when he's in the way—they'll do it without blinking an eye."[135] Distorting production results and inventing successes were long a fundamental part of Soviet industrial managers' lives. As Schwartz says, "The managerial bureaucracy sought to produce by every possible means including informal behavior and outright illegalities."[136] Bribe taking occurred as well and as a "common" and "widespread" practice, according to a deputy interior minister. Bribery of the police was "commonplace." In the 1980s several top officials of the Construction, Foreign Trade, and Fishing Ministries were imprisoned for bribe taking.[137] Nepotism was common, even in universities and military academies (the Russian word for nepotism, *kumovstvo*, is derived from the word for godparent, *kum*). Yeltsin, as party leader of Moscow, revealed that most of the students at the USSR's two top diplomat-training institutions were children of Soviet officials and that this was a "gross violation" of norms of behavior. Émigrés report that students who failed entrance examinations to higher educational institutions could still get in if their fathers were high in the pecking order.[138]

Smuggling by officials could reach true heights of innovation. For at least ten years during the 1970s caviar was smuggled abroad in cans labeled as smoked herring, and the profits went into officials' secret bank accounts abroad. But something went wrong. One of the cans did not leave the USSR and was bought by a policeman. The case reached into the Communist Party Central Committee itself and resulted in the arrest of some two hundred people. Officials smuggling things into the country was also not uncommon. But perhaps the most surprising case occurred during the Gorbachev period. One of the new private companies got hold of some "extra" above-plan military tanks and tried to sneak them abroad. When I asked one of the entrepreneurs involved what his thoughts on this were, he answered, "Why should the government have a monopoly on arms sales?" As *Kommunist* put it in 1990, "Links of the state trade sector are becoming bases for organized crime and corruption."[139]

Corruption in the Soviet administration was so deeply ingrained that it was ineradicable. Neither Gorbachev's reformist government nor harsh punishments, including the death penalty, diminished it. Reports of punishment of corrupt officials are common. Expulsion from the party was routine in such cases, and imprisonment was not uncommon. One source says that during the year 1987 alone 9,000 persons were expelled from the police.[140] Andropov initiated an anticorruption campaign, and Gorbachev appears to have continued this and tried to begin some sort of general reform of the Soviet administrative system.[141] However, Gorbachev's program was necessarily so all-encompassing and transformational that it was impossible to follow through on the particular changes required while trying to cope with the reactions, domestic and foreign, as well as the secondary effects, that his moves engendered. Gorbachev was soon out of his depth.[142] As Molotov is supposed to have said, "If we change anything everything will change."

The Post-Soviet Period and "Bizness"

The term *post-Soviet* is sometimes more a purely terminological construct than one reflective of reality. White has pointed out in some detail the great amount of continuity in the Russian "transition" and that "it was striking, compared with East-Central Europe, how many members of the communist leadership had managed to retain a presence in the new regime," with about 75 percent of Yeltsin's presidential administration coming from the "former" communist *nomenklatura*.[143]

Although private enterprise would at first seem to be something truly post-Soviet, some, perhaps much, of the corrupt behavior of the Soviet period was a form of incipient, though underground, business activity. And sometimes it was so developed that it can hardly be called incipient. I shall not give any detailed picture of the new business environment in Russia. That has been done elsewhere by the enormous and often sensationalistic publicity given to it in the West, perhaps because Russian business often seems to lack considerations of morality or limits and because it has been associated with criminality (the "mafia" etc.) as well.[144] Here one need simply point out that when the planned economy ended and government became weak and lacked money, many government officials "adjusted" to the new situation—as they could hardly avoid doing so if they were to keep themselves and their families in food. I shall only summarize the situation of corruption as it relates to bureaucrat–business connections. Still, there is no doubt that Russian bureaucratic corruption has been increased by the new open and large-scale presence of private enterprise.

That bureaucrats might become involved in business was suggested by E. Mendel in 1984, and in 1990 Richard Mills said that how the bureaucracy interfaces with the privatized sector would be a good focus for research.[145] By the mid-1990s it was apparent that in Russia the state and its bureaucracy could not be seen separately from business and crime, particularly the organized variety, the *mafiya*. Russia had again, as she had done before, adopted but altered Western models in its own ways. As a result, "It is a mistake to see the flourishing of crime in Russia as a disintegration of the state. The state is hopelessly enmeshed with organized crime in Russia. In fact, the power of the state is, to a certain extent, criminal in Russia."[146]

He could have added that in Russia the state is now also "hopelessly enmeshed" with business, many of whose members were once part of the state apparatus. As a Russian source puts it, "the current Russian state machinery is making the market work in the interests of the bureaucracy," that is, of itself.[147] Again, Russia as a social system is unable to differentiate among the state, society, and the economy. But how can it? The Soviet monolith lasted generations and was built on the deaths of those who might have been able to create a Westernized Russia. Accordingly, the "uni-structural" Soviet pattern continues. "Socialist" scarcity gave rise to underground entrepreneurs who paid off bureaucrats and ran into criminals, often ex-functionaries, who took a cut. By the 1990s, criminals, businesspeople, and bureaucrats were working together to develop a new type of Russian capitalism. One Russian sees it as a "three-tiered edifice," with the bureaucrats on the first floor, the businesspeople on the second, and the gangsters on the third. Quite likely, "the roots of the current free-marketeers lie in the Soviet administrative class." Another Russian sees the result as inevitable. Decent elites are, he avers, "out of place in a poverty-stricken country where power is the surest path to personal enrichment."[148] Once the Communist Party of the Soviet Union and the KGB, the real Soviet state, were gone, the shadowy "players" of the Soviet period could really go to town. It was a kind of postcommunist only-in-Russia freedom in which those whom the Soviet system made ready, the bureaucrats, could be much freer than the rest. As the Polish playwright has a police sergeant put it, after a revolution makes him the new minister of state security, "All regimes need policemen" and other bureaucrats.

The times were ripe for exploitation. As one Russian ex-minister says of 1991 and 1992, "Russia was a Klondike. . . . It was a time of complete confusion. There were so many administrative controls, and there were just as many special privileges." The government and the security organs became decentralized and to some degree privatized—in a legal context lacking the legislation appropriate to a private enterprise economy. A Polish professor explained to me in 1994 that one reason for Russia's large-scale criminality lay in its formerly huge security and military apparatus, now on its own. Accordingly, it is no surprise that "corruption had exploded in the post-Soviet era." During 1991 and 1992 the present and former bureaucrats "tried to get their hands on whatever [state] assets they could or to position themselves for a form of privatization that would favor them." This "*nomenklatura* privatization" spread like wildfire. As a result, the former Soviet bureaucracy reconstituted itself as "the country's industrial and managerial elite" and formed political alliances with former party *apparatchiki* and "black-market crime bosses." As Handelman puts it, by late 1993 "it became harder and harder to tell gangsters apart from bureaucrats."[149] By 1994 "bureaucratic racketeering" was flourishing "all along the line—from registration, licensing and the obtaining of quotas to basic . . . inspection documents." The "turn to capitalism offered a singular opportunity for greedy civil servants. Suddenly, it was in their power to determine who could become a millionaire—or to become millionaires themselves."[150]

The effects were seen throughout society. "The Russian government itself became a major source of growing criminal activity," says a former American ambassador. "Organized crime has supplanted many of the functions of the state," notes Shelley. More and more Russians were turning to criminals in order to obtain "justice" (plus there were no forms or waiting in lines). As for taxes, some said that they were paying them to the *mafiya*. Official statistics were still not believable. "The state has been privatized," exclaimed Boris Kagarlitsky.[151]

The economy was negatively affected. "Businessmen are intertwined with government at every level," and business rivals are not defeated in business "but by the use of administrative power," writes *The Guardian*. Businesspeople inevitably were in a "vise," caught between "bribe-taking bureaucrats on one side and the racketeers on the other." There were numerous killings of economic figures. By 1999, more than half the economy was illegal or semilegal. Even the Ministry of Atomic Energy may have been partly privatized and criminalized, a real problem for U.S. efforts at proliferation control. In 2001 a Russian parliamentary official stated that the bureaucracy–mafia link may cost around $15 billion annually. Certainly normal economic development was dampened by this state–mafia "vise." Going to the state for permits to operate a business was costly in bribes and also an announcement to the mafia to take its cut. Poverty could not be reduced in this context, says the World Bank.[152] Clearly, the above facts show that today's Russian state is extraordinarily weak and is a major target of those who ought to be its servants: "Crime in Russia is . . . unusual in that the main target of organized crime is not the private citizen (who is too poor) but the state." Further, "organized crime has supplanted many of the functions of the state."[153]

Post-Soviet Corruption Overall

Leaving business as such behind we may now take a panoptic survey of Russian bureaucratic corruption today. The phenomenon is so generally accepted as being large in scale and serious in nature that one need only give some examples and the most significant statements by observers. The order of presentation is about the same as that used for Soviet-era corruption. I say little on nepotism as such because the new business environment offers many opportunities for "placement," and I say little on lying and distortion of information because the absence of a "planned" economy obviates the need to report false production. Still, the increase in the number of bureaucrats suggests nepotism may still be with us.

I add coverage of theft and sales of that stolen. Again, the presence of a market means that officials can sell what they steal from the state to private entities. Change of sorts has occurred. As General Lebed scornfully puts it, "State officials have always stolen in Russia. Except that previously they were obliged to steal carefully, like so many little moles. . . . Now, however, having seized power, the officials have destroyed the state for the sake of their own vested interests."[154] Another Russian observer also gives a hint of what is new. Today, "almost every Russian official has both an impersonal bureaucratic role and a personal profit-making role."[155] Others stress the present-day normalcy and routineness of bureaucratic corruption. Sergeyev sees a "deviant bureaucracy in which deviant behavior becomes a normal way of life" and "improper behavior" is a "normal feature" of the bureaucracy's operations. A Russian official speaks of corruption today as a "system-forming phenomenon, not an exception but a norm of life" and one basically "not separable from government." Zaslavskaya says that corruption "has deeply penetrated the state apparatus." One of the leading "oligarchs" adds that bribe taking and tax evasion "are considered almost acceptable behavior." Remnick sees corruption as routinized, with officials having little fear of punishment, and quotes a Russian banker who says that "government officials, who issue licenses and permissions of all sorts, 'practically have a price list hanging on the office wall.'"[156]

Certainly, Russia is rated as one of the most corrupt countries in the world. For example, the Corruption Perception Index for 2002 put Russia at 79 out of 102 countries rated, with 90 being the most corrupt. Russia has been at this "corruption level" for several years. In fact, in 1997 a survey of Western executives ranked Russia as the most corrupt country in the world.[157] Russians tend to agree. In 1998 more than 92 percent of the viewers of the TV program *Itogi* said that the Russian government was corrupt, and in 2000 16 percent of Russians polled cited corruption as the main cause of people's dissatisfaction with government. White found that trust in government was very low, at 8 percent—10 percent for courts and the police over the years 1993–98.[158] The nature and extent of Russian corruption are captured in the following quotation:

> For the United States to be like Russia today, it would be necessary to have massive corruption by the majority of members of Congress as well as by the Departments of Justice and Treasury, and agents of the F.B.I., C.I.A., D.I.A., I.R.S., Marshal Service, Border Patrol, state and local police officers, the Federal Reserve Bank, Supreme Court justices, U.S. district court judges, support of the various Organized Crime families, the leadership of the Fortune 500 companies, at least half of the banks in the U.S., and the New York Stock Exchange.[159]

The internal security forces (MVD) are corrupt. In 1995, as a test, the head of the service sent a vodka truck across Russia, and almost all security force checkpoints *solicited* bribes from the driver. A leading politician has said, "Today, to be successful, a Russian must be a close friend or relative of a high-ranking official." A TV journalist points out that a journalist never knows when an investigation into a story may prompt top officials to retaliate with deadly violence.[160] Hundreds of Russian journalists and also some politicians have been assassinated in recent years, with bureaucrats' involvement likely in some cases. Of course, as seven in ten government officials are said to be corrupt, this can be utilized for political purposes. A Russian president may find it easier to control corrupt officials than principled ones serving the country. And "corruption serves as a convenient brush with which to tar opponents. . . . When it suits the state, guilt can be manufactured on demand." *Kompromat* (compromising material), false or real, has ruined the careers of many officials, including honest ones. As in Gresham's Law, the bad drive out the good. The social context is one in which "average Russians . . . suffer abuse daily at the hands of the militia, the traffic police, and corrupt bureaucrats."[161]

Although all statistics are suspect in Russia today, we may be able to get some idea of the scale of official corruption from figures cited for arrests and prosecutions of bureaucrats. During three months of the year 2000 the main organized crime administration of the Interior Ministry exposed 1,022 crimes connected with corruption, instituting 324 criminal cases, with 102 going to trial. If these numbers are multiplied by four we get for the year the numbers 4,088, 1,296, and 408, but these are only indicators. The prosecutor-general has given the figure of 8,000 for cases of bribery and corruption considered by courts during 2000. In 1999 a former prosecutor-general said that about nineteen thousand cases of corruption were exposed during each of the previous three years, but he gave no breakdown of how many of these crimes were committed by officials or by persons trying to suborn or influence officials. The interior minister said that about 5,500 officials were under investigation for taking bribes during 1998.[162] In 1996 President Yeltsin said that 1,200 "senior officials" had been convicted of corruption but did not specify during what time frame. In 1997 he called corruption "Russia's most serious problem." He added that more than 2,500 officials were under investigation for corruption and criticized legislators for "not hurrying to adopt the necessary laws."[163]

"Corruption in Russia is a tree that has its roots at the top," says a former press secretary for President Yeltsin. A leading scholar of Russia argues that "those in power have little more than contempt for both Russia and its citizens and serve only the elite." He also quotes from Anatoly Chubais, the famous "privatizer," a former first deputy prime minister, and reputedly "the most hated man in Russia," who writes that the power elite views the Russian people as "simply an annoying, tiresome nuisance."[164] Charges of corruption have whirled about former President Yeltsin and members of his family and entourage. Reddaway says that the Yeltsin family was corrupted by the oligarch Berezovsky through money and expensive gifts. One of Yeltsin's sons-in-law became acting chairman of Aeroflot, in which Berezovsky was financially involved. A Swiss magistrate has said that a Swiss company gave $25 million in kickbacks to Yeltsin's Facilities Director Borodin. Then, in 1996, when Yeltsin faced a difficult election, the oligarchs provided large amounts of financial, media, and other support. An American scholar has said that IMF money may have gone to Yeltsin's 1996 campaign. It would not be surprising if the U.S. government secretly contributed additional money for the purpose. We have all heard the story of $500,000 in cash floating about the grounds of the Kremlin during the campaign. Corruption at the top is also indicated by the conviction of seventeen generals and admirals for corrupt acts in 1998.[165]

Reports of bribery of bureaucrats are easy to find. The statistics give numbers in the low thousands per year. However, a former finance minister has scornfully dismissed the official statistics, saying that the number of bribery cases for a year are more likely to be five million rather than five thousand. The causes of such rampant bribery, he added, include judicial shortcomings, unclear bureaucratic procedures, and the power of officials to issue required documents. Former Prosecutor-General Skuratov adds as a motive "insecure future after retirement" and says that "Russia's key manifestation of corruption is bribery." This assertion seems to be borne out by both public opinion and Western companies' experience. Forty percent of Russians "completely agree" that to rise "to the top" in Russia one has to give and take bribes, while 34 percent "largely agree." Only 8 percent disagreed. A study of Norwegian companies operating in Russia shows that although only three of thirty-eight paid off the mafia, one-third had bribed officials or business contacts. The study also reveals that Russian tax officials may be inclined to fine companies because the officials get commissions on such fines.[166] *Kormlenie* lives. Bribery is routinized in academic institutions. The going "price" for admission to the most prestigious universities in Moscow is now $10,000–15,000, with the price at provincial universities being $7,000–9,000.[167]

For many businesspeople in Russia the bureaucrats do more extortion than the mafia. For example, a private milk products company in Krasnodar "is harassed constantly by the sanitary and tax police." "They just try to get as much money out of you as possible," says a company manager. Another businessman says that although corruption used to be within some sorts of bounds, "today a bureaucrat won't stamp the forms you need for less than $100–200." All the security agencies, apparently, act in a self-serving manner. A lawyer called the MVD for his client, under investigation for a criminal offense, and was told that the charges could be dropped for $2,000. An ex-KGB general says that the Russian intelligence services provide information on competitors to businesspeople for pay. Accordingly, the "organs" can be said to have been privatized. According to the Russian media, the police and the mafia are increasingly cooperating with each other and "growing together" (*srashchivaiutsia*). Apparently 3,500 employees of the MVD were punished in 1996 for criminal offenses. Some employees of the State Statistical Committee acquired $30,000-plus per year for the sale of information. One top official received $1,200 per month. Using government funds to buy housing for top bureaucrats is not unknown. In Kemerovo $500,000 was used for this purpose. Corruption in the military is often reported. The generals made millions of dollars in illegal operations in arms, food, fuel, and real estate. In 1995 Yeltsin dismissed the head of a Defense Ministry agency for "gross financial violations."[168]

Theft of government funds and illegal sales of government property by bureaucrats are not unusual. A Russian journalist has said that bureaucrats tend to consider state property as theirs.[169] A Russian scholar notes that government "agencies seek to broaden their powers by various illegitimate means, including the disposal of state property, the manufacture of licenses and certificates." Another source notes: "Clerks from the State Food Corporation are not ashamed to steal million[s of] dollars of budget funds." Top managers of state fur enterprises "have used budget funds to improve their personal financial situation." In 1997 high-level tax officials used 6.6 billion rubles of the state for buying and renovating personal apartments. Two officials of the State Property Committee gave away twenty state apartments to benefit themselves. The Russian Coal Association, Rosugol, funneled 1.2 billion rubles through phony companies to unknown sources. Officials in the Ministry of Health were able to misappropriate more than three billion rubles.[170] As usual, the military did not hang back. Some high-ranking officers used money from the sale of government property to buy themselves Mercedes 500 SELs. (I wondered what was up as early as 1991 when I noticed large Mercedes painted in Moscow police colors.) Officers have also invested for their own benefit funds intended for their units. Others have taken money budgeted for soldiers' food or pay. One general took $3 million intended for officers' salaries, and in 2000 four generals embezzled the grand sum of $450 million, one-tenth of the entire military budget. Corruption "permeates every rank of the Russian military." The police are viewed negatively by over 60 percent of Russians, who perceive them as "dishonest and rottenly corrupt."[171]

Smuggling by corrupt border control personnel continues—and not just of cigarettes and liquor. Arms, nuclear materials, and money leave Russia illegally. Although there is no public knowledge of the illegal export of nuclear weapons, some Russian fissile material has been seized in Germany and elsewhere. But we do not know if all of it has been stopped. J. K. Galbraith once cleverly wrote of the "bezzle," the stolen money that still is not discovered. Several bureaucrats and military officers have been implicated in arms exports to "rogue" states. Russia loses most of the tax value of the goods that cross its borders. And at least $20–25 billion illegally leaves Russia every year.[172] More likely the figure is $40–55 billion. Russia sorely needs this money for investment.

Apparent attempts by both the Yeltsin and the Putin administrations to inhibit or reduce corruption may have been mere charades, perhaps for the consumption of Western lending agencies. Russia is, after all, the land of the Potemkin village. In any case, any attempts at mitigation, much less elimination, of what is institutionalized corruption face real limits. The mind-set of bureaucrats, and Russians in general, is a fundamental impediment to reform. A former interior minister has said that he does not consider bribery a form of corruption. The Accounting Chamber, the constitutionally mandated body of independent oversight over government, lacks a sufficient budget and does not have its own offices. "Law enforcement . . . is a bitter joke," says Remnick. Even President Putin, who because of his KGB background ought to know a thing or two about the realities of corruption and who is most into it, "is woefully lacking in tools to enforce anti-corruption standards." Russia's anticorruption legislation is "full of loopholes," with many forms of corruption simply not covered by the criminal code. No wonder both knowledgeable Russians and foreign observers see anticorruption moves as either purely for show or even less.[173]

Russian leaders have, however halfheartedly and ineffectively, tried to limit corruption. Both Yeltsin and Putin faced so many problems all at once that it is unrealistic to judge them harshly. Even Hercules would have found the Russian stable most "Augean." (It is doubtful that Hercules would take the job.) Yeltsin certainly spoke out on the seriousness of the problem, more than once. In his 1998 "State of the Nation Address" he said, "The problem of corruption in the government apparatus remains acute." The anticorruption theme was notable during his 1996 campaign. However, one commentator says that Yeltsin paid "scant heed" to the rampant corruption of his rule.[174] Still, Yeltsin tried, if only on paper, to make corruption both more difficult and formally illegal. In 1997 he introduced a requirement that top officials make declarations of income and provide information on their families' property. But the "devil is in the details" and in the culture. There was no operative mechanism to make these declarations public. He issued a decree to control widespread tax and customs exemptions, a major source of corruption.[175] Punishments aplenty for corrupt acts were handed out across the board but to little apparent effect given the general and overwhelming presence of the phenomenon. During 1996 more than twenty-two thousand police officials were supposedly sacked in "Operation Clean Hands." During the year 2000 thousands more police officers were dismissed, but crimes by the police had increased over the past year.[176]

Vladimir Putin has also spoken realistically about the pervasiveness and seriousness of corruption in Russia and the need to combat it. In early 2000 he said that the Security Council would focus on "the fight against corruption, money laundering and unlawful export of capital," and he appointed a high official of the tax police to the council. He also announced that he would form a trusted group of former KGB colleagues to tackle corruption. In an interview somewhat later he listed corruption along with poverty as the "main tasks" facing the Russian government. He even readily agreed with the American TV personality Larry King that corruption in Russia has made Western businesspeople "hesitant" to invest in Russia. However, as Putin's mentor, the now dead Anatoly A. Sobchak, states, "To this day the power structures of our country remain . . . in conflict with the new regime."[177] Only if those power structures are swept aside or fundamentally reformed might the fight against corruption begin to be successful. Still, even that would be woefully insufficient for success.

We must be realistic; Russia's corruption has no one cause and no one cure. Whatever happens, the problem will be with us for some time, perhaps for generations. The phenomenon does not yield itself to social science certainties: "Because corruption is, by design, covert, there is no real way of quantifying it."[178] Still, all Russians know it exists and, more, that it has greatly increased since the end of the USSR and that they have to deal with it in everyday life. This has long been true. As Voinovich puts it, "It must be combatted but it cannot be defeated. Three hundred years ago Peter the Great decided to eliminate everyone who took bribes. But, as his aide, Aleksandr Menshikov pointed out, 'If you do, Your Majesty, you risk not having a single subject left.' President Putin has less latitude than Peter." As a young Russian realistically states, "Russia is not only a 'struggling democracy'—it is a prospering 'mafiacracy.' It is a system where the line between stealing and earning, . . . business and crime, politicians and 'godfathers' is a line not only crossed, but one that ceased to exist some time ago."[179]

Causes

The "causes" or roots of corruption in Russia are many. Several people have "lists" or favorite explanations. My own begins with the practices of avoidance and petty accumulation allowed and fostered by the Soviet system in its last decades, described so well by Hedrick Smith in his *The Russians*, combined with the effects of the freedom that suddenly burst into people's lives when the Soviet system came to an abrupt and surprising end in 1991. The "freedom to be tricky and devious" was a natural outgrowth of Stalin's "Big Deal" of the 1930s. This has created a deeply engrained *mentalitet* favoring corruption as a fundamental Russian right.

It seems that most causal explanations of present-day Russian corruption come under the following headings: corruption is a developmental phase, the present weakness of the state, the state encourages it and prevents solutions, survival amid chaos demands it, morality and tradition, economic poverty, and insecurity. Interestingly, oil money is not cited. In the case of corruption in Nigeria, perhaps the most corrupt society in the world, oil revenues and "amoral familialism" stemming from the traditional culture are emphasized.[180] Why not in Russia? Russia is an oil exporter like Nigeria, and many attitudes from the peasantry have survived.

These explanations overlap. Jerry Hough says that Russians have been "rational actors responding to the incentive structure that was established for them. As Gordon Tullock emphasized . . . corruption is the rational response to anarchy. . . . It is irrational to buy an item if you can steal it."[181] This could also be called the "accepting" or "sophisticated" argument. There is also the related "there's no other way" argument. For example, the honest bureaucrat is locked into dealing with corrupt persons; accordingly, the honest administrator is a threat to the established order and will suffer for being honest and thus has to join the corrupt crowd. As a Russian academic puts it, "Everyone is stealing all the time. If a person is not sick, old or mentally ill, he wants to feed his family and will violate the law to survive."[182] This explanation is partly an economic one; the economy is in such bad shape that people lack alternatives to corrupt behavior. As a Russian prosecutor says, "We have to recognize that corruption is widespread, and it's because of the economic situation." The lack of well-off politicians is also cited, a sort of variant on Winston Churchill's argument that good politicians are not those who need to be paid: "Many here come to power simply to get rich." High taxes also encourage corruption, it is said.[183]

And then there is the weakness and the poor organization of the state. It is "a striking illustration of incapacity," notes Sperling. As a result, very few pay taxes. A Russian political consultant cites "the lack of clear demarcation among the various executive bodies" as making the whole administrative system "unstable," contributing to a "sense of insecurity among civil servants," and preventing any one agency from having clear responsibility in a particular sphere. "Such conditions are extremely favorable to corruption," he notes. Often one agency "combines regulatory, enforcement and supervisory functions, as well as managing property and providing services. The possibilities for corruption are obvious."[184]

Some see the cause as fundamentally a moral failing or a corruption-prone mentality. Satter says, "Russia's problem is not economic and it has never been economic; it is basically a moral problem" that must be solved before a normal market economy can take root there. A Russian poll on bureaucrats' attitudes shows that "only one-half of civil servants said that honesty was important" and "only one in four said it was important to respect civil rights and freedoms." It is laconically added, "The data seem to indicate that moral norms and prohibitions have lost their worth for a significant number of officials." Two main dangers are cited: a destructive effect on business and society as a whole and the "moral degeneration of the state apparatus . . . [and] a deterioration of its professional potential." The negative effects on morality of the brutal wars in Chechnya are also cited.[185]

CONCLUSION

To mitigate corruption in the Russian bureaucracy significantly a number of needs must be met. Some of these needs include a reforming government, making government transparent to and reachable by ordinary people, instituting a moral and behavioral code for civil servants, increasing their pay significantly, and developing an independent Parliament and judiciary. But none of this will be enough without the creation of a strong and active civil society that says resoundingly, as did Italian civil society several years ago, "Enough! No more corruption and graft!" There is as yet no sign of such a fundamental transformation of Russia, the creation of a new culture. It may come but only after generational change and at least a predictable if only mild prosperity. Also necessary will be the political will at the top to deal with corruption decisively.[186]

There is some realistic basis for hope that in the long term (by which time we shall all be dead) corruption in Russia can be significantly reduced. It seems to have happened in Italy through cultural and political change. Some speak of a "global rebellion against corruption" stretching "from France to the Philippines, from China to Colombia." Also, Putin knows that corruption has to be reduced. He has called for a strong Russian state but one that is "law based" and enjoying a "streamlined and corruption-free bureaucracy, a merit system for hiring and rewarding government workers." He also has said that "the authorities cannot fight corruption without developing the democratic institutions of civil society."[187]

But what might be done tellingly against corruption here and now? Various things would help, though there are "no silver bullet solutions." Rather, "individual reforms will tend to interact with and reinforce each other" over time.[188] As Talbott suggests, the state might intervene in the economy less and protect property rights and enforce the law more. Freedom House suggests that journalists band together in their increased coverage of corruption and that freedom of information laws be introduced and strengthened. Two writers in *Public Management Forum* have produced an excellent short list of practical measures, including financial disclosure requirements, disqualification from office of corrupt bureaucrats, the appointment of ombudsmen and senior officers within government departments who have the power to deal with reports of corruption, whistleblower protections, and telephone "hot lines" for reports of corruption. And, of course, an at least modest pay raise for administrators. Shelley adds that corrupt leaders ought not to receive support from the West and that the West needs a long-term policy of engagement on the issue.[189]

Given the breadth and depth of the historical and recent roots of corruption in Russia, any attempt to control and mitigate it, an attempt that must be made in order for Russia to have a chance at a decent future, will be long-drawn-out and difficult and will require time to have results. Process, too, must be changed to create a better, "Euro-American," administration and civil service. The bureaucracy will have to lose its sense of being a nonresponsible low-level "ruling class" and acquire a true sense of public service and a pride in fulfilling society's needs. Although we shall not see these transformative changes in the near future, this chapter is directed at providing a realistic understanding of Russian public administration—of what happens and why, how and to what effects, that is, of the process of administration.

NOTES

1. David Johnston, "Ex-Agent Bitter over Iran Affair," *New York Times*, 26 November 1989, 31.

2. See, for example, the excellent discussion of informalism in a chapter called "The Informal Structure of Bureaus" in Anthony Downs, *Inside Bureaucracy* (Boston: Little, Brown, 1967), 61–65. Downs here draws on Philip Selznick, "Foundations of the Theory of Organizations," *American Sociological Review* 13 (1948): 26–27, 30. See also the chapter on informalism in Wilbert Moore, *The Conduct of the Corporation* (New York: Random House, 1962).

3. George L. Yaney, "Law, Society and the Domestic Regime in Russia, in Historical Perspective," *American Political Science Review* 59, no. 2 (June 1965): 380; A. Agzamkhodzhayev, "Improving the Administration of Production Units," *Sovetskoe gosudarstvo i pravo*, no. 10 (1974): 39–46, in *U.S. Joint Publications Research Service* 64137 (20 February 1975): 19.

4. Selznick, "Foundations of the Theory of Organizations," 26–27, quoted in Downs, *Inside Bureaucracy*, 61–63.

5. John R. Kasich (R-OH), "Bloat, Failure, Doom Energy Department," *Daily Hampshire Gazette* (Northampton, Mass.), 13 July 2000, A10; Paul C. Light, "Bureaucracy Fumbles Nuclear Secrets," *Daily Hampshire Gazette* (Northampton, Mass.), 3 July 2000, A6. Light is the director of the Brookings Center for Public Service. The Department of Energy once failed to inform its political leadership of nuclear accidents at a plant in Savannah, Georgia. See Keith Scheider, "Energy Dept. Says It Kept Secret Mishaps at Nuclear Weapon Plant," *New York Times*, 4 October 1988, A1.

6. Stephen Sternheimer, "Information, Communications, and Decision-Making in the Soviet City," paper presented at the Annual Meeting of the American Association for the Advancement of Slavic Studies (AAASS), Philadelphia, November 1980, 36; Mark Kuchment, quoted in *New York Times*, 26 June 1984, C7.

7. James Feron, "Inside Egypt's High Councils," review of Mohamed Heikal, *The Road to Ramadan* (New York: New York Times/Quadrangle, 1976), *New York Times*, 12 February 1976.

8. Sergei Schmemann, *Echoes of a Native Land: Two Centuries of a Russian Village* (New York: Vintage Books, 1999), 50.

9. Peter Solomon, quoted in Jill A. Fraser, "The Great American Quadrennial Job Shuffle," *New York Times*, 21 February 1993, F22. Solomon also says, "In business process is irrelevant. Result is everything."

10. Charalambos Vlachoutsicos, lecture at Harvard University, 5 May 1986; Charalambos Vlachoutsicos and Paul Lawrence, "What We Don't Know about Soviet Management," *Harvard Business Review*, November–December 1990: 51–52, 56. Vlachoutsicos and Lawrence assert that one-person leadership was introduced into Russian public administration from the army by Tsar Paul I in the late 1700s ("What We Don't Know about Soviet Management," 58).

11. Sternheimer, "Information, Communications, and Decision-Making in the Soviet City," 5, 7, 15, 23–24, 28, 36.

12. U.S. Department of State, Department Notice, "Burn Bag Disposal Restrictions," 7 December 1995 (Office of Origin: A/OPR/FMSS/GS/BU).

13. Loren Graham, "He Saw the Future; It Didn't Work," review of *An American Engineer in Stalin's Russia: The Memoirs of Zara Witkin, 1932–1934*, ed. Michael Gelb (Berkeley: University of California Press, 1991), *New York Times Book Review*, 29 December 1991, 10; Joseph S. Berliner, "Continuities in Management from Stalin to Gorbachev, 1988," in *Soviet Industry from Stalin to Gorbachev*, ed. Joseph S. Berliner (Ithaca: Cornell University Press, 1988), 269–97; a U.S. government source, 1996.

14. Peter Passell, "Economic Scene—Moscow Gamble: Butter over Guns," *New York Times*, 9 August 1989, D2, citing Vladimir Ivanov, a Russian economist; "Joint Party–Government Letter Criticizes Economic Performance," *Radio Liberty Research*, 18 January 1978, 1.

15. Vladimir Voinovich, *The Ivankiad*, trans. David Lapeza (New York: Farrar, Straus and Giroux, 1977), reviewed in Anatole Shub, "Red Tape," *New York Times Book Review*, 7 August 1977, 10–11; Vladimir Bukovsky, *To Build a Castle* (New York: Viking Press, 1979), 272. *To Build a Castle* is a profound statement on the nature of the Soviet system.

16. Veronica Kutsyllo, "Scriveners of Sovereign's Orders," *Kommersant-Daily*, 8 June 1995, in *FBIS-SOV-95-112*, 12 June 1995, 23, 26; an unclassified U.S. Department of State cable from Moscow, 1996.

17. Esther B. Fein, "A Village Turns Tough, Not Wanting to Be Eaten," *New York Times*, 29 April 1991, A4; an *Informatsiono-Telgrafnoe Agentsvo Rossii–Telegrafnoe Agentsvo Sovetskogo Soiuza* (*ITAR-TASS*) dispatch, Moscow, 30 August 1998, from *Johnson's Russia List*, 30 August 1998. Sternheimer makes it quite clear that Russian bureaucrats think that public opinion is not to be heeded ("Information, Communications, and Decision-Making in the Soviet City," 8). The poll data are

in V. G. Smol'kov, "Bureaucratism," *Sotsiologicheskie issledovaniia*, no. 2 (1999): 40–43, in *Sociological Research* 39, no. 1 (January–February 2000): 8–9. For a general introduction to the study of elite political culture, see Bert A. Rockman, *Studying Elite Political Culture: Problems in Design and Interpretation* (Pittsburgh: University Center for International Studies, University of Pittsburgh, 1976).

18. Tea Petrin, *Restructuring the Yugoslav Economy through Entry of New Firms*, Occasional Papers Series, no. 19 (Amherst: University of Massachusetts, Program in Soviet and East European Studies, 1989), 21, 34; M. Timofeyev, "A General Scheme for the Management of the Timber Industry," *Planovoe khoziaistvo*, no. 9 (1975), in *U.S. Joint Publications Research Service* 65980 (22 October 1975): 29; V. Arpentyev, "To Strengthen State Discipline," *Sovetskaia Moldaviia*, 29 March 1973, 2, in *U.S. Joint Publications Research Service* 59151 (30 May 1973): 84; *Sovetskaia Latviia*, 13 August 1970, in *U.S. Joint Publications Research Service* 51442 (25 September 1970): 26; B. Shatilo, "The Results Have Been Summarized, the Task Set," *Finansy SSSR*, no. 5 (1972), in *U.S. Joint Publications Research Service* 56332 (22 June 1972): 3, 10.

19. "Sovershenstvovat' planovuiu rabotu" (editorial), *Pravda*, 5 January 1979, 1; Craig R. Whitney, "Soviet Officials Get Entangled in Their Tape," *New York Times*, 23 April 1980; Karl W. Ryavec, *Implementation of Soviet Economic Reforms* (New York: Praeger, 1975), 85–86 (see "Ministries versus Ministries"); Bukovsky, *To Build a Castle*, 38; Bill Keller, "Eclipsed," *New York Times Magazine*, 27 July 1999, 36; Leo Marks, *Between Silk and Cyanide* (New York: Free Press, 1999), reviewed in *New York Times Book Review*, 8 August 1999, 7.

20. *Trud*, 24 April 1980, 2, in *RFE/RL*, no. 9 (1980): 3; Serge Schmemann, "Soviet Seeks to Lay Blame for Ice Crisis," *New York Times*, 23 October 1983; *New York Times*, 14 September 1990, D4.

21. "Soviet Emerging as World Oil Power," *Wall Street Journal*, 9 June 1983, 37; *Literaturnaia gazeta*, no. 3 (1983): 13, in Andreas Tenson, "Soviet Agriculture Three Years into the Eleventh Five-Year Plan," *RL 457/83*, 7 December 1983, 7; *Pravda*, 9 August 1983, in *RL 374/83*, 6 October 1983, 3.

22. *Organizatsiia upravlenie v sisteme ministerstva* (Moscow: Izdatel'stvo Moskovskogo Universiteta, 1974), 181–82; *Kommunist* (Vil'nius), October 1974, in *U.S. Joint Publications Research Service* 64379 (21 March 1975): 26; N. Mamyrov and A. Semenov, "Improve the Work of Planning Organizations," *Narodnoe khoziaistvo Kazakhstana*, January 1974, in *U.S. Joint Publications Research Service* 62457 (12 July 1974), 65; Vlachoutsicos and Lawrence, "What We Don't Know about Soviet Management," table, "One Day in the Life of a SovTruck Factory Manager," 56.

23. Dusko Doder, "Andropov's Reforms Bring Little Change," *Washington Post*, 12 November 1983; *RL 213/88*, 20 May 1988, 5; G. P. van den Berg, *De Regering Van Rusland En De Sovjet Unie* (Leiden: G. P. van den Berg, 1977), 246, 256.

24. Coit D. Blacker, "Military Forces," in *After Brezhnev: Sources of Soviet Conduct in the 1980s*, ed. Robert D. Byrnes (Bloomington: Indiana University Press, 1983), 148; John W. Finney, "MIG-25 Found to Lag behind U.S. Aircraft," *New York Times*, 7 October 1976, 6; *RFE/RL*, 29 August 1997; information on reasons for production from Kosta Tsipis of MIT. See also John Barron, *MIG Pilot: The Final Escape of Lieutenant Belenko* (New York: Reader's Digest Press and McGraw-Hill, 1980).

25. Gen. Habiger, quoted in Maura Reynolds, "U.S. General: Russia Nukes in Safe Hands," *Associated Press* (Moscow), 7 June 1998. My remarks on the Cher-

nobyl disaster are based partly on the following: Serge Schmemann, "Refugees' Plight after Chernobyl Perplexes Soviet," *New York Times*, 26 May 1986, A1; and "Chernobyl Answers: New Questions," 21 July 1986, A3; Stuart Diamond, "U.S. Scientists Criticize Risk-Taking," 18 August 1986, A6 and "Moscow Reports A-Plant Workers Ignore Warnings," 16 August 1986, A1. Export controls are knowledgeably discussed in Gary Bertsch and Igor Khripunov, *Restraining the Spread of the Soviet Arsenal: Export Controls as a Long-Term Nonproliferation Tool*, Status Report (Athens: Center for International Trade and Security, University of Georgia, March 1996), 25.

26. For a case study of environmental politics in the USSR, see Donald R. Kelley, "Environmental Problems as a New Policy Issue," in *Soviet Society and the Communist Party*, ed. Karl W. Ryavec (Amherst: University of Massachusetts Press, 1978), 88–107. Major studies of the Soviet environmental situation and the agencies involved include Barbara Jancar, *Environmental Management in the Soviet Union and Yugoslavia: Structure and Regulation in Federal Communist States* (Durham: Duke University Press, 1987), particularly chap. 3, "The Environmental Agencies"; and Charles E. Ziegler, *Environmental Policy in the USSR* (Amherst: University of Massachusetts Press, 1987), especially chap. 5, "Soviet Environmental Administration."

27. Jancar, *Environmental Management in the Soviet Union and Yugoslavia*, 68–69, 121; Ziegler, *Environmental Policy in the USSR*, 117, 125, 132–33.

28. Interview with Vladimir Putin, *Izvestiia*, 14 July 2000, from *Johnson's Russia List*, 16 July 2000; results of a poll taken by Vserossiski Tsentr Izucheniia Obshchestnennogo Mneniia, in Yuri Levada, "*Homo Sovieticus* Ten Years On," *Russia on Russia*, no. 2 (June 2000): 17. The same article contains a poll result of 57 percent saying that they expect nothing from the state (Levada, "*Homo Sovieticus* Ten Years On," 18). See also a ROMIR poll announced by *Interfax*, 2 August 2002, discussed in *Johnson's Russia List*, 2 August 2002; D. J. Peterson, "The USSR—Coming to Terms with AIDs," *RFE/RL* 2, no. 25 (22 June 1990): 12; and *Brothers and Sisters*, a dramatization of Fyodor Abramov's trilogy, *The Pryaslins*. Finally, see John Freedman, "Before and After History Changed," *New York Times*, 9 July 2000, AR5, AR19; *New York Times*, 2 December 1977; and *RFE/RL* 2, no. 7 (31 January 1993): 7.

29. On computerization, see Erik P. Hoffmann, "Soviet Information Processing: Recent Theory and Experience," *Soviet Union* 2, no. 1 (1975): 22–49; D. A. Allakhverdyan, "Problems of National Economic Management at the Current Stage," *Finansy SSSR*, no. 11 (November 1972): 26–36, in *U.S. Joint Publications Research Service* 59684 (1 August 1973): 1–23, especially 11, 15, which states some of the limits to an automated control system, as done in "Cybernetics and Computers" in my *Implementation of Soviet Economic Reforms*, 269–72. See also V. E. Vishuyakov, "Interaction of Automated Control Systems and State Administrative Agencies," *Sovetskoe gosudarstvo i pravo*, no. 8 (1973), in *U.S. Joint Publications Research Service* 60329 (19 October 1973): 50, on the dangers of bureaucratized centralization. Personnel cuts in Belarus are mentioned in B. Shatilo, "The Results Have Been Summarized; the Tasks Set," *Finansy SSSR*, no. 5 (1972), in *U.S. Joint Publications Research Service* 56332 (22 June 1972): 10.

30. A. E. Lunev, "Coordination in Government Administration," *Soverskoe gosudarstvo i Pravo*, no. 11 (1971): 29; Nicolas Spulber, *Organizational Alternatives in Soviet-Type Economies* (Cambridge: Cambridge University Press, 1979), 89;

Berliner, "Continuities in Management from Stalin to Gorbachev, 1988," 277–85; Paul Gregory, *Restructuring the Soviet Economic Bureaucracy* (Cambridge: Cambridge University Press, 1990), 35, 52, 74, 76, 79.

31. I. Kyuttis, "The Economic Efficiency of Production in the Top Elements of the Economy," *Kommunist Estonii* (Russian ed.), no. 3 (1973), in *U.S. Joint Publications Research Service* 59233 (8 June 1973): 1; Peter F. Drucker, *Management* (New York: Harper and Row, 1974).

32. Official of Poland's Gosplan, lecture at Harvard University's Russian Research Center, 1971; Allan Kroncher, "Soviet Managers Voice Their Exasperation," *RL 366/80*, 7 October 1980, 2; Kyuttis, "The Economic Efficiency of Production in the Top Elements of the Economy," 8; the claim that 90 percent of administrative personnel are engaged in collecting information is from a book by D. Nechaev, 102 (rest of citation lost); Leonid Khotin, an editor, 2 May 1988, reported in Kennan Institute, *Meeting Report*, n.d.; Lunev, "Coordination in Government Administration," 27; M. Panfilov, *Leningradskaia Pravda*, 28 July 1972, 2, in *U.S. Joint Publications Research Service* 56923 (30 August 1972): 28.

33. I. Morev, "Problems of Intersectoral Specialization," *Kommunist Sovetskoi Latvii*, no. 6 (1973), in *U.S. Joint Publications Research Service* 60181 (2 October 1973): 25; Philip Hanson, "More Problems with Imported Western Technology," *RL 26/84*, 13 January 1984; "A Further Promotion for Brezhnev's Son-In-Law," *RL 102/80*, 5 March 1980; Vladimir Putin, *First Person: An Astonishingly Frank Self-Portrait by Russia's President Vladimir Putin*, trans. Catherine A. Fitzpatrick (New York: Public Affairs, 2000), 48–49.

34. *RFE/RL Research Report* 2, no. 2 (8 January 1993): 18.

35. "Ne podmeniat', a napriavliat'," *Pravda*, 5 July 1984, 1; a U.S. government source, 1995.

36. Quoted in Alexander Stille, "An Old Key to Why Countries Get Rich," *New York Times*, 13 January 2001, A19.

37. Lawrence E. Harrison, "Culture Matters," *The National Interest* (summer 2000): 55. Harrison, who directed U.S. Agency for International Development missions in five Latin American countries, points out that culture is only one of "several factors . . . that influence progress" ("Culture Matters," 64). Still, Harrison's lists of cultural obstacles to the economic development of Latin Americans and Africans overlap in some cases with Russian cultural characteristics ("Culture Matters," 60).

38. Lawrence E. Harrison and Samuel Huntington, eds., *Culture Matters: How Values Shape Human Progress* (New York: Basic Books, 2000). Margaret Mead once said that during the 1930s culture seemed about to become a general explanatory concept. Possibly, fascism's misuse of this variable engendered a reaction against it.

39. John Armstrong has warned of this in his "National Character and National Stereotypes," *Transaction: Social Science and Modern Society* 33, no. 2 (January–February 1996): 48–52.

40. Gottfried Leibnitz, quoted in B. H. Sumner, "Russia and Europe," in *Oxford Slavonic Papers*, vol. 2, ed. S. Konovalov; Marquis de Custine, *Journey for Our Time* (1843), trans. from French by Phyllis Penn Kohler (New York: Pellegrini and Cudahy, 1951); Maxim Gorky, *O Russkom Krestianstve* (Berlin: Izdatel'stvo Ladyzhnikova, 1922), 16–19, quoted in Stephan Courtois and Mark Kramer, *The Black Book*

of Communism, trans. Jonathan Murphy and Mark Kramer (Cambridge: Harvard University Press, 1999), 732.

41. These paragraphs are based on a section in my *United States–Soviet Relations* (New York: Longman, 1989), 241 and the following pages.

42. See Erica Goode, "How Culture Molds Habits of Thought," *New York Times,* 8 August 2000, D1, D4. Asians tend to pay more attention to context and relationship, whereas Americans seem to detach objects from their contexts and to avoid contradictions. It would be fascinating to see the results of a study that examines Russians too. A summary of the research was to be published in the journal *Psychological Review.*

43. Archie Brown and Jack Gray, eds., *Political Culture and Political Change in Communist States,* 2d ed. (New York: Holmes and Meier, 1979 [1977]), 1, quoted in Archie Brown, "Introduction," in *Political Culture and Communist Studies,* ed. Archie Brown (Armonk, N.Y.: M. E. Sharpe, 1985), 2.

44. Archie Brown, "Introduction," in *Political Culture and Communist Studies,* ed. Archie Brown (Armonk, N.Y.: M. E. Sharpe, 1985), 4.

45. Archie Brown, "Conclusions," in *Political Culture and Communist Studies,* ed. Archie Brown (Armonk, N.Y.: M. E. Sharpe, 1985), 150, 154, 181.

46. Brown, "Conclusions," 188.

47. Takako Kishima, "Japan's Plan for Transcending Modernity: Japan's Cultural Scheme for Social Transformations," lecture at the University of Massachusetts at Amherst, 2 December 1992. Kishima, with a Ph.D. from an Ivy League university, is also a Shinto priest. On Japanese administrative culture, see chap. 4 in Warren M. Tsuneishi, *Japanese Political Style* (New York: Harper and Row, 1966).

48. Alexander Leyfell, Harvard University, personal communication, 9 May 1986; Yugoslav cultural attaché, lecture at the University of Massachusetts at Amherst (probably in the 1970s).

49. Nikolai Sokov and Anna Vassilieva, "The Cultural Roots of Russian Behavior in Kosovo," *Los Angeles Times,* 16 June 1999, from *Johnson's Russia List,* 16 June 1999.

50. Laura L. Phillips, *Bolsheviks and the Bottle: Drink and Worker Culture in St. Petersburg, 1900–1929* (DeKalb: Northern Illinois University Press, 2000); Eugene Huskey, *Presidential Power in Russia* (Armonk, N.Y.: M. E. Sharpe, 1999), 9.

51. Peter J. Stavrakis, "Government Bureaucracies: Transition or Disintegration," *RFE/RL Research Report* 2, no. 20 (May 1993): 30; "Work: Russian Firms in Need of Revolution: Management: Simon Pirani on the Cultural Problems Besetting Business," *The Guardian* (U.K.), 2 April 2000, from *Johnson's Russia List,* 3 April 2000; Michael Wines, "At Russian Post Office, Check Isn't in the Mail," *New York Times,* 3 October 1998, A1, A6; Vladimir E. Boikov, "The Professional Culture of the Civil Service," *Sotsiologicheskie issledovaniia,* no. 2 (1999), trans. in *Sociological Research* 39, no. 1 (January–February 2000): 21. On this continuity of personnel, see also Gennadii P. Zinchenko's "Regional Civil Servants: Composition and Social Characteristics" (*Sociological Research* 39, no. 1 [January–February 2000]: 29–30), where it is stated that "a considerable segment of the 'new generation' of directors and specialists came from the old nomenklatura" (29).

52. Thomas B. Larson, *Soviet–American Rivalry* (New York: Norton, 1978), 29. For specific examples of continuity in administration, see T. H. Rigby, *Lenin's Government* (New York: Cambridge University Press, 1979).

53. Martin Malia, *Russia under Western Eyes* (Cambridge: Harvard University Press, Belknap Press, 1999), 183.

54. Leonid Radzikhovsky, "Why There Is No Opposition to Putin," *Segodnya*, 4 August 2000, from *Johnson's Russia List*, 4 August 2000.

55. Malia, *Russia under Western Eyes*, 142; Yevgenia Albats, "Power Play," *Moscow Times*, 27 April 2000, from *Johnson's Russia List*, 26 April 2000.

56. Anatoly Korolyev, "Habit of Blackening Authorities Poisons Russia," *Moscow Times*, 27 May 1998, from *Johnson's Russia List*, 27 May 1998. The author's main point appears to be that Russians substitute criticism of government for societal action.

57. Edward C. Banfield, *The Moral Basis of a Backward Society* (New York: Free Press, 1958), 9.

58. Wallace S. Sayre, "Bureaucracies: Some Contrasts in Systems," *Indian Journal of Public Administration* 10, no. 2: 11.

59. Michael T. Kaufman, "Polish Echoes—and Ironies," *New York Times Magazine*, 25 August 1985, 47.

60. E. O. Komarov, *Biurokratizm—na sud glasnosti!* (Moscow: Politicheskaia literatura, 1989), 43.

61. George Alexander Lensen, ed., *Revelations of a Russian Diplomat: The Memoirs of Dmitrii I. Abrikossow* (Seattle: University of Washington Press, 1964), 213.

62. Richard Henry Dana, *Two Years before the Mast* (New York: Grosset and Dunlap, 1927), 367–68.

63. See, for example, Desmond Graves, *Corporate Culture—Diagnosis and Change: Auditing and Changing the Culture of Organizations* (New York: St. Martin's Press, 1986); Terrence E. Deal and Allen A. Kennedy, *Corporate Cultures: The Rites and Rituals of Corporate Life* (Reading, Mass.: Addison-Wesley Publishing, 1982); and J. Steven Ott, *The Organizational Culture Perspective* (Chicago: Dorsey Press, 1989). M. E. Pacanovsky and N. O'Donnell-Trujillo, *Organizational Communication as Cultural Performance*, in Communication Monographs, no. 50, 126, quoted in Ott, *The Organizational Culture Perspective*, 49.

64. Ott, *The Organizational Culture Perspective*, 69.

65. Ott, *The Organizational Culture Perspective*, 55, 53 (a list of over seventy elements of organizational culture), vii, 42–43 and see figure 4-2, "How Culture Tends to Perpetuate Itself," 88.

66. See "One Company, Two Cultures," *Business Week*, 22 January 1996, 88. The company is Medtronic, the inventor of the pacemaker. The clash of cultures in mergers is discussed in two articles on the topic, one on the merger of Netscape and America Online in 1998 and the other on the sale of Seagram to Vivendi S.A. in 2000. See *New York Times*, 24 November 1998, and 21 June 2000, C1.

67. Ott, *The Organizational Culture Perspective*, 47.

68. Karl W. Ryavec, "The Soviet Bureaucratic Elite From 1964–1979, *Soviet Union* 12, no. 3 (1985): 322–45; John LeDonne, Harvard University, personal communication, 2 May 1986.

69. W. Bruce Lincoln, review of William H. Odom, *The Collapse of the Soviet Military*, the *Washington Post*, 17 January 1999. Lincoln's comments remind me of those of Mark Raeff lamenting the unwillingness of Russians to serve in the imperial government (lectures at Columbia University, fall 1959).

70. Alessandra Stanley, "Russia's New Rulers Govern, and Live, in Neo-Soviet Style," *New York Times*, 23 May 1995, A1, A8. The opinion that Russia's bureaucracy is even more numerous than it was in Soviet times is frequently expressed. On 25 September 2000 Russian Duma Deputy Oleg Nikolaevich Smolin, chair of the Committee on Education and Science, speaking at Amherst College, said, "The level of bureaucracy is higher than in the USSR." As to privilege, for a photograph of a state guest house, see Henry Kissinger, *Years of Upheaval* (Boston: Little, Brown, 1982), after 424.

71. Article in *Canadian Living Magazine*, from *Johnson's Russia List*, 5 May 1997.

72. "The Re-making of the President," Jamestown Foundation *Prism* 2, no. 2 (26 January 1996): 3; a U.S. government source, 1996; Stephan Sestanovich, "Russia's Election: Expect the Extremes," *New York Times*, 4 June 1996, A15, and 8 May 1995, A6.

73. Celestine Bohlen, "Dark Rumors and Official Contradictions Fuel Russia's Economic Crisis," *New York Times*, 16 August 1998, 12; Peter J. Stavrakis, "Government Bureaucracies: Transition or Disintegration?" *RFE/RL Research Report* 2, no. 20 (14 May 1993): 33.

74. Governor Eduard Rossel, quoted in *FBIS-SOV-95-170*, 1 September 1995, 32.

75. Walter Pintner, at a National Meeting of the AAASS, many years ago; Jacob Heilbrunn, "What Stalin Knew" (op-ed), *Wall Street Journal*, 3 August 1998.

76. The American expert is Philip R. Pryde. See *New York Times*, 1 May 1986, A12; Matjaz Mulej and Vlado Sauperl, a chapter in *Cybernetics and Systems '86*, ed. R. Trappl (Amsterdam[?]: D. Reidel Publishing Co., 1986), 543.

77. N. Khudayberdyyev, "On Improving the Style and Methods of Work in the Soviet State Apparatus," *Ekonomika i zhizn'* (Tashkent), no. 9 (1973): 7–16, trans. in *U.S. JPRS* 60820 (20 December 1973): 12, 11; Robert C. Tucker, *Political Culture and Leadership in Soviet Russia* (New York: Norton, 1987), 158; Sabrina Tavernese, "In Moscow, Lines of Unhappy Accountants Find Reform Elusive," *New York Times*, 7 November 2000, C1.

78. The translation of *gosudarstvennik* as "etatist-nationalist" was suggested by Vladimir Zhdanov, 26 March 1997; see also Czeslaw Milosz's autobiography, *Native Realm: A Search for Self-Definition* (Garden City, N.Y.: Doubleday, 1968), 187. Milosz is wrong, however, when he says that bureaucracy's "activities . . . do not shape matter directly."

79. See "Mr. Pavlov's Ruinous Reflexes" (editorial), *New York Times*, 15 February 1991, A34: the *Times* was correct in saying that Russia would be "forced to come knocking on Western doors for investment, expertise and help."

80. Michel Crozier, "French Bureaucracy as a Cultural Phenomenon," in *European Politics: A Reader*, eds. Mattei Dogan and Richard Rose (Boston: Little, Brown, 1971), 389, 492.

81. James Q. Wilson, *Bureaucracy* (New York: Basic Books, 1989), 378. On the cultural side of bureaucracy, see also Wilson, *Bureaucracy*, chap. 6, 301–12.

82. James David Barber, "Foreword," in *How Washington Really Works*, by Charles Peters (Reading, Mass.: Addison-Wesley, 1980), viii–ix.

83. Associated Press dispatch, "CDC Diverts Dollars Earmarked for Chronic Fatigue Syndrome," *Daily Hampshire Gazette* (Northampton, Mass.), 6 July 1999, A5; Robert Lindsey, "Court Told of U.S. Abuses in Denial of Veterans' Aid," *New*

York Times, 7 December 1986, A48; "Hostility Taints Postal Service, Study Says," *New York Times*, 28 October 1994, A24; Barbara Gamarekian, "Women Gain, but Slowly, in the Foreign Service," *New York Times*, 28 July 1989, B5; Tim Weiner, "The C.I.A.'s 'Old Boy' Camaraderie: Deeply Ingrained and Slow to Change," *New York Times*, 16 October 1994, 30; James Fallows, "America's High-Tech Weaponry," *The Atlantic Monthly* 247, no. 5 (May 1981): 29; Stephen Engelberg and Deborah Sontag, "Behind One Agency's Walls: Misbehaving and Moving Up," *New York Times*, 21 December 1994, A1, D22. The remarks on the CIA come from a former CIA director and an eight-year veteran of the Senate Intelligence Committee staff.

84. Alison Mitchell, "Posing as Welfare Recipient, Agency Head Finds Indignity," *New York Times*, 5 February 1993, A1.

85. Adam Bryant, "New Attitude, Not New Boss, the Key, G.M. Watchers Say," *New York Times*, 23 October 1992, D1; "Study Spurs Public and Private Push to Cut Medical Errors," *New York Times*, 26 December 1999, 14.

86. Chief of Naval Operations, message, classified Secret, 15 November 1976, released by Iran from the files of the U.S. embassy in Teheran (see *Documents from the Espionage Den* 47 [Teheran, 1985]); Allessandra Stanley, "Russians Grouse (at U.S. Embassy)," *New York Times*, 18 November 1994, A10; a U.S. government source, 1995; draft scope paper, *Defense Conversion Committee*, no. 2 (5 June 1995). For additional Russian–American organizational differences, see Paul Lawrence and Charalambos Vlahoutsicos, *Behind the Factory Walls: Decision-Making in Soviet and American Enterprises* (Cambridge: Harvard Business School Press, 1990).

87. Baruch Knei-Paz, *The Social and Political Thought of Leon Trotsky* (Oxford: Clarendon Press, 1978), 286.

88. See the explication of the model of A. V. Chayanov, *The Theory of Peasant Economy* (Madison: University of Wisconsin Press, 1986 [1925]), in Gang Deng, *The Premodern Chinese Economy* (London: Routledge, 1999), 343.

89. Coit D. Blacker, "Military Forces," in *After Brezhnev: Sources of Soviet Conduct in the 1980s*, ed. Robert D. Byrnes (Bloomington: Indiana University Press, 1983), 149; the source for the quotation from Boris Kagarlitsky (1997) has been lost.

90. Sternheimer, "Information, Communications, and Decision-Making in the Soviet City," 11; Erich Goldhagen, "The Ideological Beliefs of Mikhail Gorbachev," *Midstream*, February–March 1990, 3–9; *New York Times*, 1 August 2000, A7; *New York Times*, 26 April 1995, A10; the story about the gift of chocolates was told me by a Russian émigré; Vlachoutsicos and Lawrence, "What We Don't Know about Soviet Management," 52, 56, 59.

91. Yuri B. Shvets, *Washington Station* (New York: Simon and Schuster, 1994), 123.

92. Shvets, *Washington Station*, 196, 292.

93. Aleksandr V. Obolonskii, "Post-Soviet Officialdom: A Quasi-Bureaucratic Ruling Class," *Obshchestvennye nauki i sovremennost'*, no. 5 (1996), trans. in *Sociological Research* 36, no. 6 (November–December 1997): 68–69.

94. Gennadi P. Zinchenko, "Regional Civil Servants: Composition and Social Characteristics," a translation of "Gossluzhashchie regiona: Sostav I sotsial'nye osobennosti," *Sotsiologicheskie issledovaniia* 2 (1999), in *Sociological Research* 39, no. 1 (January–February 2000): 29–30.

95. Massachusetts State Senator Stanley Rosenberg, lecture at University of Massachusetts at Amherst, 10 March 1995.

96. Gregory, *Restructuring the Soviet Economic Bureaucracy*, 74.

97. Sternheimer, "Information, Communications, and Decision-Making in the Soviet City," 23–24; Gregory, *Restructuring the Soviet Economic Bureaucracy*, 99, 103, 110–11, 120. I call the *tolkach* "a living example of informalism in bureaucracy" and the "peripatetic 'representative' of the Soviet firm" whose milieu is the supply problem and whose métier is its solution (*Implementation of Soviet Economic Reforms*, 257).

98. Leslie H. Gelb, "What We Really Know about Russia," *New York Times*, 28 October 1984, 67; Reuters (Moscow), 13 September 1998, from *Johnson's Russia List*, 14 September 1998; Janusz Glowacki, "Of Mother Russia—and a Hat," *New York Times*, 27 March 1990, A27.

99. "Animosity between Vasilev, Zadornov Runs Deep," *RFE/RL*, 19 February 1998.

100. Langdon Winner, review of Mary Douglas and Aaron Wildavsky, *Risk and Culture* (Berkeley: University of California Press, 1982), *New York Times Book Review*, 8 August 1982, 8; *Zaria vostoka*, 8 July 1975, in *U.S. Joint Publications Research Service* 65722 (19 September 1975): 101; Jacob Heilbrun, "The First Steps from Authoritarianism to Civil Society," *Los Angeles Times*, 27 August 2000, from *Johnson's Russia List*, 27 August 2000.

101. Bukovsky, *To Build a Castle*, 32–33.

102. Nicholas D. Kristof, "Japan's Blossoms Soothe a P.O.W. Lost in Siberia," *New York Times*, 12 April 1998, 3; Seth Mydans, "51 Years Later, U.S. Expatriate Leaves Russia," 13 April 1985, 1. When I was living in Russia in 1977 I would run into some of the American expats who had arrived with their parents during the 1930s but had never been allowed to leave.

103. Jonathen Steele, "Battleship Indifference," *The Guardian* (U.K.), 25 August 2000, from *Johnson's Russia List*, 26 August 2000. My father, Louis Ryavec (Rijavec), the product of a poor mountainous rural Slavic environment who spent his entire long life in manual labor, said of the Russians, "The Russian are just too rough."

104. Anders Aslund and Timothy McDaniel, lectures at the Kennan Institute for Advanced Russian Studies, Washington, D.C., 13 February 1997, Meeting Report from *Johnson's Russia List*, 18 April 1997.

105. Suzanne Massie, the Russian Research Center, personal communication, 7 February 1986; Sternheimer, "Information, Communications, and Decision-Making in the Soviet City," 8; interview with Gennady Barbulis, then head of the Russian Strategy Center for Political Sciences, *Argumenty i fakty*, no. 28 (July 1995): 3, trans. in *FBIS-SOV-95-136-5*, 17 July 1995, 2.

106. A. V. Obolonsky, "Biurokratiia I biurokratizm," *Gosudarstvo I pravo* 12 (December 1993): 96.

107. P. D. Ouspensky, *Letters from Russia* (London: Arkana [Penguin], 1991), 53; Sarah Koenig, "Refugees Straining Patience in Russia," *New York Times*, 26 December 1996, A6.

108. Thomas F. Remington, *Politics in Russia* (New York: Longman, 1999), 224, citing Eugene Huskey; Igor Yakovenko, *ITAR-TASS*, 3 May 2000, cited in *RFE/RL*, 4 May 2000; "Old Habits Die Hard," *Washington Post*, 19 August 2000, e-mail version; Sharon LaFraniere, "False Russian Data Risked Divers, Norwegian Says," *Washington Post*, 6 September 2000, from *Johnson's Russia List*, 6 September 2000.

See also Michael Wines, "Norway Complains of Kremlin Meddling in Sub Rescue," *New York Times*, 25 August 2000, A10.

109. See Gerald M. Easter, *Reconstructing the State: Personal Networks and Elite Identity in Soviet Russia* (New York: Cambridge University Press, 1999); Archie Brown, review of T. H. Rigby, *Political Elites in the USSR: Central Leaders and Local Cadres from Lenin to Gorbachev* (Brookfield, Vt.: Edward Elgar, 1990), *Slavic Review* 52, no. 1 (spring 1993): 148; an e-mail from Ferry Philipsen in Russia on *Johnson's Russia List*, 19 November 1997; "Business Consultants Sharpen Hammer and Sickle," *New York Times*, 30 July 1989, 16; Andreas Tenson, "The Number One Problem in Soviet Industry: Ensuring the Supply of Materials and Equipment," *RL 94/80*, 3 March 1980.

110. "Fighting Corruption in the Polish Third Sector," Freedom House's *NGO News* 12 (spring 1999): 2; a Vatican document on liberation theology, "Instructions on Christian Freedom and Liberation," *New York Times*, 6 April 1986, 14.

111. Harvey G. Kebschull, "Political Corruption: Making It the 'Significant Other' in Political Studies," *PS: Political Science and Politics*, December 1992, 705–6. Kebschull cites a number of serious works on corruption, for example, Michael Clarke, ed., *Corruption: Causes, Consequences and Control* (New York: St. Martin's, 1983); and Robin Theobald, *Corruption, Development and Underdevelopment* (Durham: Duke University Press, 1990).

112. Paolo Mauro, *Why Worry about Corruption?* (Washington, D.C.: International Monetary Fund, 1997), 1.

113. Paul Lewis, "2 Global Leaders Use Leverage to Combat Corruption," *New York Times*, 11 August 1997, A4; Ariel Cohen, in the World Bank *TRANSITION* 6, nos. 5–6 (May–June 1995): 7–9.

114. Mauro, *Why Worry about Corruption?* 6–7; Ron Synovitz, "World Bank Report Blames Poverty on Governments, Vested Interests," End Note, *RFE/RL*, 26 September 2000; Vito Tanzi and Hamid Davoodi, *Roads to Nowhere: How Corruption in Public Investment Hurts Growth* (Washington, D.C.: International Monetary Fund, 1998), 1.

115. Herman F. Woltring and Ugljesa Zvekic, "Increased International Action against Corruption," *PMF (Public Management Forum)* 4, no. 4 (July–August 1998); John Brademas and Fritz Heimann, "Tackling International Corruption: No Longer Taboo," *Foreign Affairs* 77, no. 5 (September–October 1998): 18; Moises Naim, "The Corruption Eruption," *The Brown Journal of World Affairs* 2, no. 2 (summer 1995): 245. On the French Elf Aquitaine scandal, see David Ignatius, "A Crusade against Corruption," *Daily Hampshire Gazette* (Northampton, Mass.), 16 March 2001, reprinted from *Washington Post*.

116. Part of the proceedings were published in *Russia on Russia*, no. 4 (March 2001).

117. Jerrold Seigel, *Marx's Fate: The Shape of a Life* (Princeton: Princeton University Press, 1978), 93–94. Marx saw the bureaucrat as a prisoner of his own private interests driven to corruption by the defects of the bureaucratic role.

118. Gang Deng, *The Premodern Chinese Economy* (London: Routledge, 1999), 217 (however, Lord Acton said only that "power tends to corrupt"); Jerry F. Hough in *Johnson's Russia List*, 14 November 1997; Timothy Garton Ash, "The Puzzle of Central Europe," reprinted from *The New York Review of Books*, 18 March 1999, in

Minton Goldman, ed., *Global Studies: Russia, the Eurasian Republics, and Central Asia/Eastern Europe*, 8th ed. (Guilford, Conn.: Dushkin, 2001), 251. For a pertinent book, see William L. Miller, Ase B. Grodeland, and Tatyana Y. Koshechkina, *A Culture of Corruption: Coping with Government in Post-Communist Europe* (New York: Central European University Press, 2000).

119. Ariel Cohen, in the World Bank *TRANSITION* 6, nos. 5–6 (May–June 1995): 1; Thomas L. Friedman, "Altered States," *New York Times*, 27 June 2000, A31; Thomas L. Friedman, "Playing Russian Roulette," *New York Times*, 24 October 1999, WK15.

120. Interview with Sergei Rogov, *Pravda*, quoted in *Johnson's Russia List*, 25 June 1998; William C. Potter, quoted in *Johnson's Russia List*, 20 June 1998; "The Russian Mafia Means Business," *The Economist*, 4 July 1998; Donald Jensen, quoted in Askold Krushelnycky, "Corruption Destroys People's Faith in Democracy," from *Johnson's Russia List*, 7 September 2000.

121. Moscow *Interfax* (in English), *US FBIS-SOV-95-163*, 23 August 1995, 21; Joel Blocker, "Corruption among State Officials in Eastern Europe," *RFE/RL*, sometime in 1997; Peter Robb, review of James Fentress, *Rebels and Mafiosi: Death in a Sicilian Landscape*, *New York Times Book Review*, 7 January 2001, 23.

122. On corruption in ex-communist countries other than Russia, see, for example, Commission on Security and Cooperation in Europe, *Bribery and Corruption in the OSCE Region* (Washington, D.C.: U.S. Government Printing Office, 2000); Edward A. Gargan, "Widespread Fraud Reported in China," *New York Times*, 1 March 1988, A11; Seth Mydans, "Vietnam Awash in Graft Trials, but They Don't Clean Up Graft," *New York Times*, 25 May 1999, A5; Jane Perlez, "Rogue 'Wrestlers' Have an Armlock on Bulgaria," 12 January 1995, A4 ("wrestlers" are former security personnel engaged in crime); Scott Peterson, "A Decade of Graft and Decline in Post-Soviet Georgia," from *Johnson's Russia List*, 21 February 2001; and the corruption issue of *NGO News*, no. 12 (spring 1999).

123. Fox Butterfield, "China, for a Fortunate Few at the Top, Is Paradise of Privileges and Perquisites," *New York Times*, 2 January 1981, A6; Elizabeth Rosenthal, "China's Fierce War on Smuggling Uproots a Vast Hidden Economy" and "Beiching Gets a Scolding for Official Corruption, and Applauds," *New York Times*, 6 March 2000, A1 and A10; Elizabeth Rosenthal, "China: Corruption Warning," *New York Times*, 10 March 2001, A5.

124. Igor Zakharov, "Bookworm: A Russian Tradition: Officials Who Steal," *Moscow Times*, 6 June 1998, from *Johnson's Russia List*, 6 June 1998—"These words are still valid today," says Zakharov; Michael T. Florinsky, *Russia: A History and an Interpretation*, vol. 2 (New York: Macmillan, 1960), 1088; Sergei Pushkarev, *The Emergence of Modern Russia: 1801–1917*, trans. Robert H. McNeal and Tova Yedlin (New York: Holt, Rinehart and Winston, 1963), 27; Procurator-General Yuriy Skuratov, at a press conference in Moscow, 2 July 1998, from *Johnson's Russia List*, 8 July 1998.

125. Robert O. Crummey, *The Formation of Moscovy: 1304–1613* (New York: Longman, 1987), 107, 150, 237. Ironically, the derivative term *kormushka* or "feeding trough" also means "sinecure" colloquially.

126. Donald N. Jensen, "Patrimonialism in Post-Soviet Russia," *RFE/RL*, 17 February 1997 (Jensen was then the associate director of Radio Free Europe/Radio

Liberty's Broadcasting Division); Anne Wing Hamilton, "Bureaucrat-Bashing in Russia and the United States," paper presented at the Annual Meeting of the AAASS, Philadelphia, November 1994, 12.

127. Elena Chinyaeva, "Tackling Corruption Isn't as Exciting as in the Movies," *Transitions Online*, 9–15 October 2000, from *Johnson's Russia List*, 17 October 2000. Two of the Russian sayings she quotes are "If it is prohibited but you want it badly, then it is allowed" and "The law is like a horse-steering lever—you turn it your own way."

128. See, for example, Kimberly Marten Zisk, "Institutional Decline in the Russian Military: Exit, Voice and Corruption," in *Russia in the New Century: Stability or Disorder?* eds. Victoria E. Bonnell and George W. Breslauer (Boulder: Westview, 2001), 78–100.

129. Anatol Lieven, quoted in Scott Peterson, "A Decade of Graft and Decline in Post-Soviet Georgia," *Christian Science Monitor*, 21 February 2001, from *Johnson's Russia List*, 20 February 2001; Gennady Andreev-Khomiakov, *Bitter Waters: Life and Work in Stalin's Russia* (Boulder: Westview, 1997), quoted in an ad for the book; Leon P. Baradat, *Soviet Political Society*, 3d ed. (Englewood Cliffs, N.J.: Prentice-Hall, 1992), 392; Konstantin Simes, *USSR: The Corrupt Society* (New York: Simon and Schuster, 1982), 297.

130. Stephen White, *Russia's New Politics: The Management of a Postcommunist Society* (Cambridge: Cambridge University Press, 2000), 12.

131. Antoni Z. Kaminski, *An Institutional Theory of Communist Regimes* (San Francisco: ICF Press, 1992), 121–22, 131–33.

132. Sternheimer, "Information, Communications, and Decision-Making in the Soviet City."

133. See, for example, William A. Clark, *Crime and Punishment in Soviet Officialdom* (Armonk, N.Y.: Sharpe, 1993); Maria Los, *Red-Collar Crime: Elite Crime in the USSR and Poland*, Occasional Paper, no. 216 (Washington, D.C.: Kennan Institute for Advanced Russian Studies, 1986); Lydia S. Rosner, *The Soviet Way of Crime* (South Hadley, Mass.: Bergin and Garvey, 1986); Charles L. Schwartz, "Economic Crime in the USSR: A Comparison of the Khrushchev and Brezhnev Eras," *International Comparative Law Quarterly*, March 1981, 281–96; Konstantine Simis, *USSR: The Corrupt Society* (New York: Simon and Schuster, 1982); Hedrick Smith, *The Russians* (New York: Quadrangle Press, 1976); Steven J. Staats, "Corruption in the Soviet System," *Problems of Communism* 21, no. 1 (January–February 1992): 40–47; Victor Yasmann, "The Russian Civil Service: Corruption and Reform," *RFE/RL Research Report* 2, no. 16 (16 April 1993).

134. Luba Brezhneva, *The World I Left Behind: Pieces of a Past* (New York: Random House, 1995), reviewed in Katrina vanden Heuvel, *The New York Times Book Review*, 30 July 1995, 7–8; "Soviet Implicates Officials in Bribes," *New York Times*, 24 January 1988, 4; "Report Says Shchelokov Embezzled 700,000 Rubles," *RL 213/88*, 20 May 1988, 12.

135. Anthony Austin, "Soviet Writer Rebuked for Deviation in Hit Play," *New York Times*, 12 May 1981. And on suppression of investigative journalists, see "New First Secretary in Voroshilovgrad Oblast," *RL 85/87*, 27 February 1987, 15.

136. Harry Schwartz, *The Soviet Economy since Stalin* (Philadelphia: Lippincott, 1965), 23. Government ministries engaged in the same behavior. See *RL 464/87*, 13 November 1987, 9, citing *Pravda*, 12 November 1987.

137. Deputy Interior Minister Demidov, quoted in "Bribe-Taking Said to Be Widespread in USSR," *RL 414/87*, 16 October 1987, 2; Baradat, *Soviet Political Society*, 198; "Soviet Deputy Minister Jailed for Corruption," *RL 340/85*, 11 October 1985; "Corruption in the USSR Ministry of the Fish Industry," *Arkhiv Samizdata 4629*, early September 1981, in *RL 242/82*, 15 June 1982, 4; "Former Minister and His Wife Jailed for Bribe-Taking," *RL 232/87*, 19 June 1987.

138. Walter Laqueur, *The Dream That Failed: Reflections on the Soviet Union* (New York: Oxford University Press, 1996), 61; R. W. Apple Jr., "Bribes Help Soviet Officials Enjoy Life," *New York Times*, 22 November 1980; "Moscow City Boss Attacks Diplomats' Training Institution," *RL 286/86*, 25 July 1986, 2; a paper by a former student based on interviews with ex-Soviets living in the United States.

139. "Red-Herring Operation Involving Soviet Ministry Officials Discovered," *RL 154/80*, 23 April 1980; Craig R. Whitney, "Moscow Consumed by Rumors of a Caviar Scandal in the Highest Places," *New York Times*, 21 April 1980; "Deputy Minister's Arrest in Smuggling Scandal Confirmed," *RL 321/86*, 27 August 1986, 12; V. Volkonskii, "'Kul'turnyi torgash' sredi nac," *Kommunist*, no. 1 (January 1990): 62.

140. "Two Soviet Trade Officials Executed," *RL 402/85*, 29 November 1995, 7; USSR Minister of Internal Affairs A. Vlasov, *RL 203/88*, 27 May 1988, 14.

141. Seth Mydans, "Corruption Campaign in Soviet Takes Its Toll," *New York Times*, 8 February 1985, A1, A10; "Pravo I rezhim ekonomii" (editorial), *Kommunist*, 24 September 1985, 1. And see "Soviet Interior Ministry Is Being Purged," *RL 28/87*, 11 January 1987, 3.

142. Baradat points out that Gorbachev's anticorruption campaign engendered extremely negative reactions among some ethnic groups, raising new problems of governance (see *Soviet Political Society*, 339).

143. White, *Russia's New Politics*, 263, 267–68.

144. For example, see Joseph R. Blasi, Maya Kroumova, and Douglas Kruse, *Kremlin Capitalism: Privatizing the Russian Economy* (Ithaca: ILR Press, 1997); Rose Brady, *Kapitalizm: Russia's Struggle to Free Its Economy* (New Haven: Yale University Press, 1999); Roman Frydman, Kenneth Murphy, and Andrzej Rapaczynski, *Capitalism with a Comrade's Face* (Prague: Central European University Press, 1998); Roman Frydman, Cheryl W. Grey, and Andrew Rapaczynski, eds., *Corporate Governance in Central Europe and Russia*, 2 vols. (Prague: Central European University Press, 1996); Thane Gustafson, *Capitalism Russian-Style* (Cambridge: Cambridge University Press, 1999); Stephen Handelman, *Comrade Criminal: Russia's New Mafiya* (New Haven: Yale University Press, 1995) and "The Russian 'Mafiya,'" *Foreign Affairs* 73, no. 2 (March–April 1994): 83–96; Valery Kryukov and Arild Moe, *The New Russian Corporatism: A Case Study of Gazprom*, Post-Soviet Business Forum paper (London: Royal Institute of World Affairs, 1996); Peter Reddaway and Dmitri Glinski, *The Tragedy of Russia's Reforms: Market Bolshevism against Democracy* (Washington, D.C.: U.S. Institute of Peace Press, 2001); Peter Rutland, *Business and the State in Contemporary Russia* (Boulder: Westview Press, 2000); Victor M. Sergeyev and Ake E. Andersson, *The Wild East: Crime and Lawlessness in Post-Communist Russia* (Armonk, N.Y.: M. E. Sharpe, 1997); Yuri Shchekochikhin, "Where Does the 'Mafiya' Come From?" *Demokratizatsiya* 2, no. 2 (spring 1994): 191–93; Louise Shelley, "Post-Soviet Organized Crime," *Demokratizatsiya* 2, no. 3

(summer 1994): 341–58 (note, the entire issue is devoted to organized crime in Russia); J. Michael Waller, "Organized Crime and the Russian State," *Demokratizatsiya* 2, no. 3 (summer 1994): 392–411; and Janine R. Wedel, *Collision and Collusion: The Strange Case of Western Aid to Eastern Europe* (New York: Palgrave for St. Martin's Griffin, 2001). This last book shows that Russian state–business crime affected Western aid institutions (see Wedel, *Collision and Collusion*, especially 203).

145. Ernest Mendel, "What Is the Bureaucracy?" in Tariq Ali, *The Stalinist Legacy* (New York: Penguin, 1984), 86; Richard Mills, personal communication, 4 May 1990.

146. David Satter of the Hudson Institute, speaking on a panel "Dealing with Putin's Russia," on Voice of America's "On the Line," from *Johnson's Russia List*, 7 April 2001.

147. *Segodnia* (Moscow), 13 October 1995, 2, in *FBIS-SOV-95-201*, 18 October 1995, 11.

148. G. L. Ulmen, "Socialist Corruption" (letter), *New York Times*, 10 August 1998, A26; Shchekochikhin, "Where Does the 'Mafiya' Come From?" 192; Donald N. Jensen, statement in *Johnson's Russia List*, 7 November 1996; Shvets, *Washington Station*, 292.

149. Vladimir Lopukhin, who was the minister of fuel and energy in 1991–92, quoted in Sabrina Tavernise, "Pardoned Fugitive Said to Be in Talks on Russian Deal," *New York Times*, 7 February 2001, W1; Brady, *Kapitalizm*, 148; Blasi, Kroumova, and Kruse, *Kremlin Capitalism*, 37; Handelman, *Comrade Criminal*, 7, 10.

150. Andrei Neshchadin, "'Shadow' Economy's Role in a Criminalizing Society," *Izvestiia*, 21 September 1994, in *Current Digest of the Post-Soviet Press* 46, no. 38 (19 October 1994): 6; Paul Starobin, "Why Putin Has to Bust the Bureaucrats," *Business Week*, 14 August 2000, from *Johnson's Russia List*, 3 August 2000.

151. Ambassador Jack F. Matlock, "Russia: The Power of the Mob," *The New York Review of Books*, 13 July 1995, 13; Shelley, "Post-Soviet Organized Crime," 344; Michael R. Gordon, "Moscow Statisticians Accused of Aiding Tax Evasion," *New York Times*, 10 June 1998, A3; Boris Kagarlitsky, quoted in *The Exile* (Moscow), 11 March 1998, from *Johnson's Russia List*, 11 March 1998.

152. Jonathan Steele, "Keeping It in the Family," *The Guardian* (U.K.), 13 August 1999, from *Johnson's Russia List*, 12 August 1999; Celestine Bohlen, "Graft and Gangsterism in Russia Blight the Entrepreneurial Spirit," *New York Times*, 30 January 1994, 12; White, *Russia's New Politics*, 167; Paul Goble, "The Long Shadow of the Second Economy," in *RFE/RL*, 27 September 1999; Ludmila Foster, writing in *Johnson's Russia List*, 17 October 2000; United Press International, Moscow, in *Johnson's Russia List*, 29 January 2001; interview with Alexei Arbatov, in *FOCUS* 3, no. 1 (January 1996): 2; Ron Synovitz, "World Bank Report Blames Poverty on Governments, Vested Interests," in *RFE/RL*, 26 September 2000.

153. Victor M. Sergeyev, "Organized Crime and Social Instability in Russia: The Alternative State, Deviant Bureaucracy, and Social Black Holes," in *Russia in the New Century: Stability or Disorder*, eds. Victoria E. Bonnell and George W. Breslauer (Boulder: Westview Press, 2001), 158; Louise Shelley, briefing of the Commission on Security and Cooperation in Europe, Washington, D.C., 10 June 1994, 3.

154. Interview with General Alexander Lebed, *La Repubblica* (Rome), 12 November 1995, 10, in *US FBIS-SOV-95-220*, 15 November 1995, 5.

155. Charles Fairbanks Jr., "The Feudalization of the State," *Journal of Democracy* 10, no. 2 (1999): 49, quoted in Valerie Sperling, "Introduction: The Domestic and International Obstacles to State-Building in Russia," in *Building the Russian State: Institutional Crisis and the Quest for Democratic Governance*, ed. Valerie Sperling (Boulder: Westview Press, 2000), 11.

156. Sergeyev, "Organized Crime and Social Instability in Russia," 163; Sergei Karaganov and other officials, press conference, 14 April 2000, from *Johnson's Russia List*, 17 April 2000; Tatyana Zaslavskaya, "The Russian Population," *Segodnya* (Moscow), 2 August 1995, 3, in *U.S. FBIS-SOV-95-171-S*, 5 September 1995, 21; Alfa Bank President Petr Aven, an article in *Kommersant-Daily*, 29 February 2000, in *RFE/RL*, 1 March 2000; David Remnick, "Can Russia Change?" *Foreign Affairs*, January–February 1997, 36, quoting Mikhail Smolensky, head of Moscow's Stolichnyi Bank.

157. The only countries scoring lower than Russia in 2000 were Angola, Azerbaijan, Cameroon, Indonesia, Ukraine, and Yugoslavia (Serbia). Transparency International's Corruption Perception Index is based on surveys of businesspeople, the general public, and country analysts (see *RFE/RL Newsline*, 15 September 2000). The 1997 survey that placed Russia as the most corrupt country was conducted by Control Risks Group in Britain and was based on Western managers' perceptions of Russian officials (see *New York Times*, 6 November 1997, A8).

158. Michael Wines, "Surprising Russian Stir on . . . Corruption," *New York Times*, 3 November 1998, A3; *Nezavisimaia gazeta*, trans. in *Johnson's Russia List*, 6 March 2000; White, *Russia's New Politics*, table 8.1, 270.

159. Note, this is less than half the quotation from Maureen Orth, "Russia's Dark Master," *Vanity Fair*, September 2000, from *Johnson's Russia List*, 5 September 2000.

160. A U.S. government source, 1995; Gregory Yavlinsky, "Shortsighted," *New York Times Magazine*, 8 June 1998, 66; Yevgenii Kiselyev of NTV, on C-Span, 13 January 1997.

161. Jeffrey Tayler, "Russia Is Finished," *The Atlantic Monthly*, May 2001, 48, 50. Although this article may be wrong in its thesis, it is correct in its facts.

162. *ITAR-TASS* (Moscow), 23 April 2000, from *Johnson's Russia List*, 23 April 2000; *RFE/RL Newsline*, 12 February 2001; *Interfax* (Moscow), 5 March 1999, from *Johnson's Russia List*, 6 March 1999; Associated Press report, *New York Times*, 4 November 1998, A11.

163. *OMRI* report, 16 February 1996; *RFE/RL*, 26 September 1997.

164. Pavel Voshchanov, quoted in *New York Times*, 14 October 1999, A6; Peter Reddaway, quoted in *Johnson's Russia List*, 11 June 1998.

165. Peter Reddaway, testimony and writing discussed in an *RFE/RL* report, 4 September 2000, from *Johnson's Russia List*, 4 September 2000; Peter Stavrakis, speaking at the Annual Meeting of the AAASS, Boston, 14 November 1996; *RFE/RL*, 13 March 1997, 2 July 1999, and 14 September 2000.

166. Boris Fedorov, quoted in *OMRI*, 28 February 1995; Yuriy Skuratov, quoted in *ITAR-TASS*, 2 July 1998, from *Johnson's Russia List*, 8 July 1998; Lyudmila Khakhulina, "Inequality and Social Justice," *Russia on Russia*, no. 2 (June 2000): 66; the Norwegian company study was publicized by Reuters on 18 July 1996 and sent to me via e-mail.

167. *Izvestiia*, 20 June 2001, in *RFE/RL*, 21 June 2001.

168. "Moscow's Raid on Sin Leaves the Biggest Stones Unturned," *New York Times*, 30 July 1996, A6; *New York Times*, 13 November 1995, A7; Michael Dobbs, "What Russians Call Democracy," *Washington Post*, 16 June 1996, C2; a U.S. government source, 1996; retired KGB General Oleg Kalugin (author of *First Directorate*, a memoir), on C-Span, 4 March 2001; Peter Reddaway in *Johnson's Russia List*, 24 January 1998; *OMRI* reports, 19 June 1996 and 20 January 1997; *Komsomolskaia Pravda*, 16 June 1998, from *Johnson's Russia List*, 11 July 1998; *Eastview Press Survey*, 23 February 1998; Steven Erlanger, "Scandals Put Russian Defense Chief on the Defensive," *New York Times*, 2 November 1994, A3; a U.S. government source, 1995 (referencing an *ITAR-TASS* report).

169. Elena Ardabatskaia, article in *Komsomolskaia Pravda*, no. 80 (21814) (in early 1998), in *Eastview Press Survey*, 29 April 1998. The author says that officials tend to consider even the local people as theirs.

170. Mikhail Krasnov, "Corruption as a Consequence of Bad Government," *Russia on Russia*, no. 4, "Corruption in Russia" (March 2001): 17; *Moskovskii Komsomolets*, no. 12 (17770) (January 1998), from alex@ipres.ru, 22 January 1998; *Izvestia*, 13 January 1998, 5; *Argumenty I Fakty*, January 1997, from *Johnson's Russia List*, 20 January 1997; *RFE/RL*, 26 March 1998; *Izvestia*, 1 August 1996, in *OMRI*, 23 July 1996; a U.S. government source, 1995.

171. Eva Busza, "State Dysfunctionality, Institutional Decay and the Russian Military," in *Building the Russian State: Institutional Crisis and the Quest for Democratic Governance*, ed. Valerie Sperling (Boulder: Westview Press, 2000), 120, 122; *Rossiiskaia gazeta*, 6 June 2001, in *REF/RL*, 11 June 2001; *Kommersant Daily*, 23(?) February 1998, in *Eastview Press Survey*, 23 February 1998; stratfor.com report, 9 August 2000, from *Johnson's Russia List*, 9 August 2000; a 2002 survey by the Central European Research Group Foundation, in *Mark H. Rodeffer's Daily Report*, 28 August 2002.

172. John Kenneth Galbraith, *Economics and the Art of Controversy* (New Brunswick, N.J.: Rutgers University Press, 1955); U.S. government sources, 1995; *Kommersant*, no. 92, in *Eastview Press Survey*, 26 May 1998; *Novaia gazeta*, in *Eastview Press Survey*, 23 February 1998; *ITAR-TASS*, 2001, in *RFE/RL*, 26 March 2001.

173. Louise Shelley has used the apt term *institutionalized corruption* (see testimony before the Commission on Security and Cooperation in Europe, hearing, 21 July 1999 [Washington, D.C.: U.S. Government Printing Office, 2000], 17); former Interior Minister Vladimir B. Rushailo, quoted in Patrick E. Tyler, "In High-Level Shake-Up Putin Replaces Russia's Defense, Interior and Nuclear Energy Chiefs," *New York Times*, 29 March 2001; Yury Boldyrev, "Russian Progress Thwarted by Conspiracy of Silence," *St. Petersburg Times*, 12–18 May 1997, from *Johnson's Russia List*, 12 May 1997; David Remnick, "The Hangover," *The New Yorker*, 22 November 1993, 57; Patrick E. Tyler, "In a Russian Region Apart, Corruption Is King," *New York Times*, 5 April 2000, A10; Deborah Seward, "Putin Seeks to Root Out Corruption," Associated Press (Moscow), from *Johnson's Russia List*, 28 March 2000; *Obshchaia gazeta*, no. 46 (1996), in *RFE/RL*, 25 November 1996. More recently Marshall I. Goldman has correctly said, "There is little indication that anything is being done to clean up the corruption" (letter, *New York Times*, 20 January 2000, A22).

174. Reuters (Moscow), 2 December 1998, from *Johnson's Russia List*, 2 December 1998; Patrick E. Tyler, "How Yeltsin Nearly Scuttled Democracy in Russia," *New York Times*, 8 October 2000, 4.

175. "State Officials to Declare Incomes," *Interfax* (in English), 9 May 1997, on Presidential Decree no. 484, from *Johnson's Russia List*, 13 May 1997; Jonas Bernstein, "Another Battle in Russia's Phony War on Corruption," *Washington Post*, 29 June 1997, from *Johnson's Russia List*, 30 June 1997; Steven Erlanger, "Bowing to I.M.F., Yeltsin Takes New Steps to Fight Spending and Corruption," *New York Times*, 2 March 1995, A10.

176. See *RFE/RL*, 26 February 1996, 30 May 1997, and 30 November 2000.

177. Tyler, "In High-Level Shake-Up Putin Replaces Russia's Defense, Interior and Nuclear Energy Chiefs"; Michael R. Gordon, "Putin Will Use Ex-K.G.B. Men to Battle Graft," *New York Times*, 24 March 2000, A1; *ITAR-TASS* (Paris), 6 July 2000, from *Johnson's Russia List*, 6 July 2000; *Larry King Live*, transcript from *Johnson's Russia List*, 9 September 2000; Anatoly A. Sobchak, quoted in Michael Wines, "What Putin Portends for Russia," *New York Times*, 1 January 2000, 6.

178. Naim, "The Corruption Eruption," 247.

179. Interview with a small group of Russians, born in Russia but resident in the United States, carried out in 2000 in Massachusetts by Chris Kenney, a student at the University of Massachusetts; Vladimir Voinovich, "Russia's Blank State," *New York Times*, 30 March 2000, from *Johnson's Russia List*, 31 March 2000; a term paper by Nikita Zakharov, "United States Aid to Russia," 17 May 2001, 6.

180. See, for example, Oladimeji Aborisade and Robert J. Mundt, *Politics in Nigeria*, 2d ed. (New York: Longman, 2001), 73–76, 188. The authors' description of police checkpoints set up to extort money sounds like Russia (*Politics in Nigeria*, 73). In 2000 some American students in Moscow, to avoid arrest, had to hand over all their money to policemen just because one of them did not have his visa with him (personal communication).

181. Jerry F. Hough, in *Johnson's Russia List*, 22 January 1999, in response to another posted item. This seems an argument similar to the one that corruption is unavoidable in developing countries. See Ronald Wraith and Edgar Simpkins, *Corruption in Developing Countries* (London: George Allen and Unwin, 1963).

182. Adam Tanner, "Russia's Economic Crisis Fosters Endemic Corruption," *Reuters*, 9 November 1998, from *Johnson's Russia List*, 8 November 1998.

183. Tanner, "Russia's Economic Crisis Fosters Endemic Corruption."

184. Sperling, "Introduction," 12–13 (see also Valerie Sperling, ed., *Building the Russian State: Institutional Crisis and the Quest for Democratic Governance* [Boulder: Westview Press, 2000], 92, 108); Krasnov, "Corruption as a Consequence of Bad Government," 18–19.

185. David Satter of the Hudson Institute, report, "The Rise of the Russian Criminal State," at a meeting of the Kennan Institute for Advanced Russian Studies, 9 November 1998; Boikov, "The Professional Culture of the Civil Service," 20; Oleg Moroz, "Will We Return to a Police State?" *Literaturnaia gazeta*, 5 July 1995, in *US FBIS-SOV-95-143*, 26 July 1995, 21. The war continues at this writing in 2003.

186. Boikov, "The Professional Culture of the Civil Service," 21; Krasnov, "Corruption as a Consequence of Bad Government," 19; Naim, "The Corruption Eruption," 247; Keith Henderson, "Corruption: What Can Be Done about It?"

Demokratizatsiya 6, no. 4 (fall 1998): 690–91 (issue on corruption in Russia and Ukraine); Pavel Felgengauer, "Defense Dossier," *Moscow Times*, 2 March 2000, from *Johnson's Russia List*, 2 March 2000.

187. David Ignatius, "A Crusade against Corruption," *Daily Hampshire Gazette* (Northampton, Mass.), 16 March 2001, possibly drawn from the *Washington Post*; Vladimir Putin, possibly not a direct quotation, in Wines, "What Putin Portends for Russia," 6; interview with Vladimir Putin, Paris, 6 July 2000, from *Johnson's Russia List*, 6 July 2000.

188. Brademas and Heiman, "Tackling International Corruption," 21.

189. Strobe Talbott, speech at the 50th anniversary of the Harriman Institute, 29 October 1996, from *Johnson's Russia List*, 30 October 1996; Freedom House, *NEWS*, 10 June 1999; Woltring and Zvekic, "Increased International Action against Corruption"; Boris Nemtsov, in *RFE/RL*, 14 April 1997; Shelley, testimony before the Commission on Security and Cooperation in Europe, 16.

4

⚜

Power, Politics,
and Resistance

The bureaucracy controls the state as its own possession. . . . It is its private property.

—Attributed to Karl Marx

Russia has become a bureaucratic state, where official power has destroyed all spontaneous and natural growth in the relations of public life.

—Georg Brandes, *Impressions of Russia*

Organizations have . . . no conscience, no esthetic taste, no sense of humor, no sense of justice. . . . Virtue can only be said to be possessed by individuals. God's grace is not dispensed at group rates.

—Garrison Keillor, "Toasting the Flag"

Make way for me; I am a cog in the mighty machine of state.

—Marquis de Custine, *Letters from Russia* (on a Russian bureaucrat)

*B*y *power* I mean the ability to make things happen and not happen, or happen differently than intended, in government operations and public policy. The fundamental argument for the power of the Russian bureaucracy is given in chapter 2—the security of office and the implementation of policy give bureaucrats various forms of power. They can come to see themselves as the real government; they can distort and remake policy as they implement, or pretend to implement, it; and they can resist those who are supposed to be the "policymakers" in these and many other ways. They can, for example, enter the political arena and acquire "protectors" among the politicians or, in democracies, the public. They can even refuse to act, citing difficulties of one sort or another. The political power of bureaucrats is a well-covered theme in writings about administration in the West.[1] Given the background above, in this chapter I flesh out and concretize bureaucratic power in the Russian context and show how it is political in nature. One way I shall do this is to show how bureaucrats play politics and power with each other under the tent of government. Another way is to show how bureaucrats resist "leaders'" attempts at organizational change and reform and also deter such attempts. Nothing shows power as much as resistance to governmental authority and other power. In any case, power is so central to politics, particularly in a bureaucratized state like Russia, that it can hardly be overexamined. And, as Pipes says, in Russia "politics has meant administration."[2]

Russian culture is highly conscious, wary, and critical of the state bureaucracy in various ways. For example, in August 1968 the Moscow Puppet Theater devoted half of one show to the problem of bureaucracy. Every time a "bureaucrat" puppet was hit with a stick it would split into two—into an identical "clone" with a stentorian "Soviet" voice. The bureaucrats could not be eliminated, we were being shown. A Russian novelist has depicted the committee of bureaucratic types that attempted a coup against Gorbachev and Yeltsin in 1991 as men with "ugly thuggish faces, thick-voiced, with corruption written all over them, like ill-fitting false teeth."[3] In 1989 a Russian sociologist found a "strong negative attitude" toward the bureaucracy. In a poll the same year nearly 40 percent of the respondents said that the bureaucracy was the number one enemy.[4] In a 1993 survey of Russians' preferences regarding backgrounds of candidates, government officials came in third after educators and entrepreneurs. In a 1997 poll 34 percent said that they feared corrupt officials (and for the main principle they wished would underlie Russian society, law and order came in first at 27 percent, while 24 percent listed democratic rights and freedoms). Also in 1997, 61 percent of Russians said that they did not trust the Russian government (only 12 percent said they trusted it).[5]

My 1998 interview with a Russian woman academic (age thirty-five) shows that the ranks of the bureaucracy are seen as growing (this is a general feeling in Russia); that any problem requires interaction with the bureaucracy and much paperwork and that this is "normal"; and that although many bureaucrats behave like "kings," some try to be helpful, particularly the younger ones, who are less power conscious. I got the impression that the nature of the individual bureaucrats and how they relate to their power is the key variable for their behavior. Of course, if this is true, then the vaunted Russian tendency toward personalizing relationships would be commonly present in persons' relations with the state bureaucracy. Carnaghan's recent study shows that many Russians think that they have little if any influence on officials: "As far as they [her respondents] could tell, the people sitting in government offices were essentially the same people who had always been there and who cared as little about the people's opinions as they ever had." Russians also are "highly unsatisfied with the police. They considered them corrupt and unprofessional, no one you would want to meet on a dark street." Indeed, they "are generally disappointed with the accomplishments of those who govern them."[6]

If the standard view of bureaucrats as mere clerks or tame implementers of policy made by the "political leaders" is accepted, they have little power. But who are the "political leaders"? In the Soviet Union "the full members of the Politburo" is not a bad answer. Today, one could say the "members of the presidential staff and the cabinet ministers." Yet many, perhaps half or more of the people in these groupings, rose mainly through the state, not the party, apparatus.

Bureaucracies everywhere affect policy, unavoidably in its implementation but also through the provision of advice, often done selectively in the bureaucracy's interests, to the "leaders" or ruling politicians and sometimes by "statizing" them, that is, bringing one or more of them into the bureaucrats' perspective. The putative policy maker, then, can even become the tool of the bureaucracy, partly made up of "permanent politicians," a situation portrayed humorously in the British television show *Yes, Minister*. It is part of the Russian political tradition that bureaucracy has a certain independence of the political leaders and is able to act against their ostensible ideology and larger purposes in particular instances. Russian bureaucrats have never been merely "citizens with government jobs" but, rather, beings of superior status and power at a decided social distance from the population at large and with a tendency to lord it over people and also be pretty hard on them in performing bureaucratic functions. Russian bureaucracy has always acquired an "aristocracy-like" status as the privileged servant of the powerful rulers.[7] In addition, top bureaucrats can either become top politicians and policy makers (notable historical examples include Witte, Andropov, and Putin) or come to make decisions of strategic and political importance. An American negotiating arms control with General Secretary Brezhnev recounts the case of Brezhnev being unable to make a specific decision, probably because he lacked the requisite specialized knowledge; a top defense bureaucrat was called in and made the decision at once—but not without expressing annoyance, in Brezhnev's presence, at being disturbed in his work.[8] Though Kissinger was skeptical of the claim, he recounts that "Dobrynin [long-term Soviet ambassador to the United States] was infinitely inventive in developing variations on the theme of a beleaguered Brezhnev assailed on all sides by fractious colleagues" and limited in his actions by the generals and the Ministry of Defense.[9] Perhaps it is true that the USSR was governed not by "fiendishly clever ice-cold brains" but by "a cumbersome, ill-informed, mutually suspicious, apprehensive, and dimly improvising elite" dependent, to some degree, on the bureaucrat specialists.[10]

SIGNIFICANCE

No special lengths have to be covered to find Russians emphasizing the importance of the bureaucracy today. One Russian commentator sees the strangling of democracy by the "giant, monstrous bureaucratic machinery, incomparable even to what we had during the stagnation period. . . . A machinery which, in accordance with Parkinson's laws, is working not to the benefit of Russia, but to the benefit of bureaucrats. Bureaucracy, uncontrollable and corrupt, is the real power which has risen above us and is managing us."[11] Solzhenitsyn says that the "bureaucracy . . . is powerless to manage the country effectively but . . . is very tenacious in defending its own prerogatives." A post-Soviet former mayor of Moscow has said, speaking of the reformers, "In fact we never took power. We found ourselves in a coalition with the reformist wing of the senior state bureaucracy. . . . And in that coalition we would never be leaders."[12]

Russians ascribe great political importance to the state bureaucracy. For example, an academic of the Financial Academy of the Russian government begins an article by saying: "The basic function of political power is, as is known, administration, the direction of society as a whole. . . . [B]ureaucracy is the indispensable element of the state apparatus of administration."[13] The chairman of the State Duma has pointed out the importance of bureaucrats: "To prevent confusion in Russia each time there is a change in government, there should be first deputy ministers. They are supposed to be pure bureaucrats, people who are outside all parties and political groupings." One is reminded of the old French saying, "Governments come and go, but the civil service remains."[14] The comparable Russian saying may be: "Times change, but the authorities [*nachal'stvo*] remain."[15]

Unfortunately, today's Russian government is unable to act fully as a government. A high-level Polish politician said in 1998 that "the core of Russia's troubles is not the turbulence in its financial markets or the fallout from the Asian crisis, but [governmental] mismanagement." An American academic points to "the cancerous growth of bureaucracy, layer after stifling layer," which has grievously weakened the Russian state, leading to its "spreading inefficiency and incompetence," including its inability to collect taxes or wage war effectively. This theme of a weak and incompetent state is emphasized by many current observers of Russia and suggests that a serious break in the Russian political tradition has occurred. For example, Weigle says that "the state itself is very weak and has a limited capacity to govern the country." The generals cannot control their troops in Chechnya. That bureaucracy that was so powerful an arm of the state no longer functions as it did. (This is not to say that the Russian bureaucracy was ever efficient.) Michael McFaul is correct in seeing Russia as undergoing an unusual and undesired, yet real, "revolution."[16] By 1993 Western experts tended to agree that much of Russia's hunger and poverty was more the result of disorganization than of shortages. Apropos of revolution, it is worth remembering that in 1917, too, the Russian bureaucracy lost the ability to manage.

Russians' consciousness of the weight of bureaucracy upon them was very evident during the Soviet era as well. A female Moscow internist said that "our bureaucratic apparatus has deep roots. It will take a long time to pull up these roots." A "low-level defector," the wife of a Soviet diplomat, points out, "What was missing in my life was the ability to make choices, to make my own decisions . . . simply not possible in the highly regulated, bureaucratic Soviet society." She adds that because "the Soviet bureaucracy is vast . . . the only way to get anything done is to find a way around it," something Russians learned so well that they are still doing it. Returning to the USSR was, for her, impossible because of "the bureaucracy, where everything sinks as if in quicksand." Another, "higher level" defector, a diplomat at the United Nations, writes aptly of "the circuitous evasiveness so characteristic of Soviet bureaucrats" and the dismal experience of working in an organization in which "there was no praise or encouragement, only occasional reprimands" and never any feedback on reports or why a suggestion had been rejected and where there was a real and continuous fear of being demoted "for something, no matter how trivial." An even higher level personage, the one-time director of the prestigious USA Institute, peopled by men in tweed jackets reminiscent of the former "uniform" of American college professors, though emphasizing that he was never a dissident but, indeed, one who "willingly" served the Soviet system, rails at "the double-dyed bureaucracy" by which "all decisions were taken at the very top, but the top could not make a single decision properly." In addition, he laments, the Soviet economy was not run, as claimed, by any economic laws of socialism but, rather, "by Parkinson's Law—in accordance with the selfish interests of government agencies and the bureaucracy." He notes that "the number of ministries and agencies grew constantly. . . . One side of Kalinin prospect was completely taken over by them." And high officials constituted "something akin to an aristocracy—a life peerage associated with honors, with a higher standard of living . . . and a good assortment of privileges (from the cradle to the grave)."[17]

The memorable remarks of a nineteenth-century visitor in Russia, the Marquis de Custine, show that the problem of overbureaucratization may have been historically endemic:

> Government in Russia is military discipline in place of civil order, a state of siege which has become the normal state of society. [The Yugoslav ambassador made the same observation in the 1950s.] As a result, a wealth of unnecessary and petty precautions here engenders a whole army of clerks, each of whom carries out his task with a degree of pedantry and inflexibility, and a self-important air solely designed to add significance to the least significant employment. He refrains from speaking, but you can see him thinking . . . "Make way for me; I am a cog in the mighty machinery of state."[18]

How Soviet as well as timelessly Russian this image is.

BUREAUCRATIC BASES OF POWER

Tradition determines much in all systems. Soviet socialism was bureaucratized and probably hyperbureaucratized, a land of thousands of little pieces of paper issued by government bureaucrats. This would be obvious even if Trotsky had never lived to call attention to it. Hirszowicz sees its origins in Lenin's authoritarian "organization-man" personality; the postrevolutionary growth of the state, caused partly by tsarist predilections; the need to defend the system against "capitalist encirclement" and Stalinism and its massive but primitive industrialization; the upward mobility of segments of the working class; and the rise of the secretarial and security apparatuses. "All these factors . . . were consolidated *before* the horrors of the 1930s," she notes, thereby ascribing less than a central role to the great purges and perhaps to the natural propensities of any Russian governmental arrangement at the time.[19] As Mandel points out, there was a "total lack of understanding of the bureaucratic phenomenon" by most Bolsheviks. Whether, as he suggests, Soviet history could have been different if the problem had been properly understood early on is impossible to know.[20] And Stalin eliminated the formal study of administration flourishing during the 1920s. The bureaucrats in the economy had an especially important power base, for "political power is concerned with power over the process of production and distribution of the product."[21]

The post-Stalin relaxation, at least for the functionaries, under Brezhnev certainly let the problem of bureaucratization deepen and proliferate. Colton says that "Leonid Brezhnev and his Politburo . . . swore by what they termed 'trust in personnel,' believing that their interests were usually best served by letting established agencies get on with their jobs with a minimum of interference from without."[22] And the Brezhnev Politburo eventually became something of a "cabinet," divided by the opposing institutional interests of its members and limited to a degree by the "diffusion of power" within it. Bialer notes that in Brezhnev's time "all major specialized hierarchies of the Soviet Party-state have their chief executives represented in the Politburo."[23] It was possible to ask if the leader of the Soviet Union was only "the administrator of the [bureaucratic] maze, himself lost in it."[24] Dyker points out that one factor giving bureaucrats power is that although they do not control the creation of plans, they have a big say in plan implementation, a factor often emphasized in studies of bureaucracy: "In practice . . . the ministries . . . have exercised a great deal of effective control over small- and medium-sized investments."[25] But the "really significant" factor giving bureaucrats such power was the "absence of a private propertied class."[26] This continues to hold true. Yes, the "oligarchs" and tens of thousands of other businesspeople now exist, but they lack the security that the rule of law and a pro-business culture would give them. In short, bureaucrats and their institutions are not mere instruments of the political elite but, in fact, forces in their own right.

Bureaucrats also know their interests and act as best they can to defend them from the "leadership" and other agencies. It is the bureaucrats, and not their political leaders, who have the specialized knowledge, the "expertise," and as Max Weber told us, the "files," the documentation and "memory" of the government. They are also present at the "barricades" of governmental presence and action and get to decide how to act and react "on the spot." They have some discretionary power. A Western businessman resident in contemporary Moscow says, "The laws are just written in gray. The same rule looks different in the hands of each . . . official."[27] And, after all, the "emperors" are far away and tied up with their purely political games much of the time. Accordingly, the bureaucratic "mice" have quite a lot of room for play. Also, the bureaucrats are the ones who make things "happen" and make things "work." As Karl Marx is reputed to have written, "The bureaucracy controls the state as its own possession. . . . It is its private property."[28]

The privilege automatically associated with anyone connected with the Russian state is also a factor in the bureaucracy's power base. "They are the state" in the eyes of the general populace. During Soviet times there was a "material gap" between the bureaucratic elite and the general populace.[29] Today the bureaucrats have the power to re-create that material gap. The postcommunist systems have all been dependent on the functionaries left over from the former communist systems. I am reminded of once meeting with a young "reformist" member of the St. Petersburg Duma. A friend, a former vice rector of a university who is now in business, said after the meeting, "A nice fellow, but he and his kind don't know how to get things done." (My friend had had the difficult job of finding food for his university, a task requiring a great deal of ingenuity, effort, and the making of countless deals.)

Numbers are always an important indicator. Russia has a great many bureaucrats, and the number is increasing. (All sources say this is so; no one is saying that the numbers are decreasing.) One source says that the number increased by 14 percent between 1995 and 1998. A recent source says there were 1,340,000 people in the "state apparatus" at the beginning of 2000 and that the number went up by "tens of thousands" during the first half of 2001 alone. Possibly the cost of this bureaucracy increased by a factor of ten between 1995 and 2001, from 4.4 billion to 40.7 billion rubles.[30] The increase in numbers may indicate that a sort of "buy off" or "pay off" is taking place, a new "Big Deal," with the political leaders having made a decision, perhaps finding that there was no alternative, to raise the number of bureaucrats even in these difficult times. This is always a tendency for insecure regimes. The new federalism may also be one of the reasons for this. But even in the Soviet period, as Matthews has noted, "the increase in top bureaucratic posts wildly outstripped the increase in the population."[31]

THE COMMUNIST PARTY AND THE STATE BUREAUCRACY

And what of the Communist Party during the Soviet period? Wasn't it in charge? It was—to a degree and in a sense. But it never, after Stalin, attacked the functionaries in any significant sense. To have done so would have meant raising the danger of a runaway purge that would have endangered the party itself. Even Khrushchev's *sovnarkhoz* scheme was only a short-lived problem for the bureaucracy, with many of its structures and personnel surviving it intact.[32] Mikoyan is reported once to have quickly objected to the suggestion by a fellow Politburo member that a certain number of people be arrested immediately. Mikoyan replied pointedly that he was the last surviving member of a Politburo in which a similar suggestion had been acted on.

There were a number of problems, or "contradictions," in the nature of the Communist Party of the Soviet Union (CPSU) and its relationship to politics and administration. The fundamental problem was, as Rosa Luxemburg predicted to Lenin at the Second Congress of the Russian Social-Democratic Labour Party in London almost a century ago, that the party became an organization. It ceased to be a free alliance or community of like-minded radical people in a common belief system and instead became an ordered "army" with a top-down chain of command, a "führer," and a system of discipline. It was also transformed by becoming a government, even if it pretended that it was not. (Stalin once claimed that he was a "private citizen.") The vanguard party of Lenin lost ground to the "vanguard bureaucracy" or party-state system developed so strongly and personalistically by Stalin. Theen says that the CPSU was then "politically eclipsed by the government bureaucracy."[33] Having achieved "success," the party suffered from its effects, particularly the influx of countless persons seeking status, power, and social and material advancement. And destroying the upper and middle classes and the church removed some sense of morality that might have limited the worst effects of this "careerism." But that went with the ideology and the great hatred of conventional society that suffused, enveloped, and drove Marxism almost everywhere. Contemporary writers, lacking living old Marxists to talk to, often do not know that hatred was a major element in modern socialism. (British socialism contained "more Methodism than Marxism," yes, but some other countries were not so fortunate.)

The Soviet pattern of rule linked Marxist language and perspective to state-centered culture and action—in a tradition of a highly powerful, centralized, and bureaucratic state. This itself was a major contradiction. Yet Stalin forced Marxism and administration together in a unique system that existed for decades and came to have many defenders. It became, after all, what everyone in the USSR was accustomed to. Most people are accepting, even enthusiastic, prisoners of the systems in which they live. The Communist Party itself became highly bureaucratized. Certainly, Marxist rhetoric and inclination interacted with administrative and political needs in a creative tension of contradictions that made the Soviet system "work" in its own peculiar way. Yet there were better ways in which it might have worked. The Marxist–bureaucratic "marriage" often made for extremely complicated, even convoluted, thinking, policy, and action. So much that needed to be done for the sake of people and efficiency could not be done because no "Marxist" justification or administrative procedure could be found for it. The system became trapped in its own net. Neither Marxist ideology nor administrative necessity won, but both were in tension and often in conflict with one another. Statism and leftist radicalism were the two faces of the Janus-like Soviet Union.[34] The CPSU's main function became coping with the problems caused by the CPSU. So the Soviet leadership, all the way to Gorbachev and the system's end, was trying to control the state bureaucracy with its own, compounding problems. This was a major issue and contradiction. There were others. Because the party was ultimately responsible for what was done and not done, its functionaries and ordinary members tended to rush in and take over administrative work that was not going well, pushing aside the state functionaries. The political leadership continually spoke against such *podmena* (substitution) but also encouraged and condoned it in various ways. One Soviet-era commentator says that party officials "bury themselves" in problems brought to their attention, neglecting their "proper duties" of ideological guidance and strategizing. He continues: "It is easier to usurp and duplicate the functions of others than to organize, create and show initiative. Unfortunately, the Party apparatus still has many officials who erroneously assume that the more they interfere in the work of the economic agencies and of their managers, the better it is, so they say, for the cause." And the upshot is that it is sometimes difficult even to differentiate between the party apparatus and the Soviet or economic apparatus. He goes on to give the result: "Independence and initiative are suppressed, and the sense of responsibility declines."[35]

The author might have been giving some unnamed corollary of Parkinson's Law—instead of doing no harm, top administrators tend to try to do something too concrete for them, claiming it as an accomplishment whatever the result. *Podmena* occurred because the party's rewards depended on the bureaucracy's results. Accordingly, there was an unspoken but unambiguous symbiosis between the party and the state bureaucracy even though there was supposed to be some clear demarcation between them. No one was fooled. Commentators spoke of the two hierarchies as being part of the same "bureaucratic ruling class."[36] Members of the two groupings made compromises with each other so that both could look good. Locally, "family circles" sprang up to isolate and protect the local operatives, both party and state, from the higher-ups. Some state functionaries must have felt close to the party, of which they were often members, and shared the party's concern with externalities, but others were inevitably drawn into their own technical and other concerns. Accordingly, there were splits and disagreements between party and state functionaries on generalist versus technical grounds.[37] And often state cadres had interests of their own to protect from the party's overall views. If the Soviet Union had lived long enough to have had a "long run," then these splits might have become open, political, "party" differences. Hugh Seton-Watson, as early as 1956, pointed to the bureaucratic "state bourgeoisie" as a basis for eventual democratic-type transformation of the country.[38] It was, in effect, a basis of a future civil society and a business class.

What else about the party apparatus separated it from the state bureaucracy? An excessive but strongly defended sense of importance? One writer speaks of "party headquarters, where there are clocks, portraits, corridors, and everywhere an endless pretense of seriousness." An academic sees party officials as "firemen running from one fire to another in disorderly fashion." One could be reminded of the Russian Orthodox Church in imperial times, an organization fixated on ceremonial observances but somewhat neglecting morality.[39] But the "party" was itself divided, as many point out. Yanov sees the party as "an unstable coalition, a bloc . . . of various embryonic political parties with different and even opposing interests," with, for example, the central party administration with, perhaps, an interest in reform opposed by local party leaders intent on protecting their and other local interests.[40] This, of course, gave the bureaucrats plenty of opportunity to pursue their own interests.

It is possible that sometimes the members of the party apparatus were different sociopsychological types than many of the state officials. Ploss once said that there was a "firm and definite difference" between the kinds of people in the party apparatus and those in the state bureaucracy. Hirszowicz sees the party types as "men on the move" who sought power and importance. Their functions were different, others say. Hill sees them as "adjudicators" between ideology and societal demands. Hazard says that the party elite was on the way to becoming "an inner cabinet or elite of the Administrators." One could also see the apparat as a "general specialization" within the Soviet ruling elite or as the "Ministry of Policy" in the Soviet system. Khrushchev apparently wanted the apparat to get into the thick of administration and production, whereas, later, Gorbachev wanted to pull it out of economic affairs to concentrate on ideology and mass organization.[41] Some people spent time in both hierarchies, but "generally, Party work took place during the early or 'late early' part of [state bureaucrats'] careers," suggesting that it may have sometimes served as a "stepping-stone" or "proving ground." Yet clearly, "party apparatus work was not necessary for the attainment of high rank in the state bureaucracy." In one sample 63 percent of high-level state bureaucrats had not been in party work.[42]

Despite the differences between the party and the state bureaucracy, many see them as essentially the same or as equal parts of a larger whole. Mandel sees the party apparatus as "heavily integrated into the state apparatus." Brown says, "The party institutions were . . . themselves part of the state structure." A Russian judge says that the "CPSU . . . was fitted into [*vmontirovana*] the state system."[43] Certainly, the Soviet Party elite used the state apparatus as one of its main means of controlling society, and accordingly the party elite had statist interests similar to those of the state cadres. And party supervision (*kontrol'*) must have tended to give party people a "ministerial" viewpoint. To a degree ideology became management—and not for the first time. "Christianity as a troubling secret society . . . gradually changed into something like a branch of the Civil Service," writes Rebecca West.[44]

The party apparat's political supremacy depended on the state bureaucracy. The apparat could only select the chief bureaucrats, periodically scrutinize one of their spheres of operations, bring pressure on them through the party-controlled media and party mass membership, and occasionally remove a few of them. But the bureaucracy was fundamentally secure. Any onslaught on it or even a serious reorganization or "reform" of it would have threatened the industrial base of Soviet power and its global position as a seemingly modern society and great power. Even Gorbachev's campaign against bureaucratic business as usual and for economic revitalization presupposed keeping a strong state economic bureaucracy and, thus, was limited in its means and possibilities. The party apparat was perhaps more successful in blocking our view of bureaucratic influence and power over processes ("process power"?) than in actually controlling the bureaucrats. The party's need for and dependence on the bureaucrats was indicated by its lavish honorings of state bureaucrats by prizes, orders (which carried monetary stipends), and high salaries and significant perquisites. Someone once aptly called the Soviet union a "medal society."[45]

Now to focus on the power of the state bureaucrats over policy and governmental action. Hammer sees "at least three ways" in which bureaucrats can influence policy: policy consultation, policy initiation, and policy implementation. In the first case bureaucrats get their views on policy before the leadership. In the second instance the bureaucrats raise issues and call for actions. In the last case, perhaps even if they have lost in the other two cases, the bureaucrats can change policy while they implement it. All three ways of affecting policy are found in most political systems. Hammer adds that bureaucrats can also distort (and prevent) information going to the leadership, resulting in the "leakage of authority," a process that "tends to be cumulative."[46] All this is correct, and I welcome his saying, "The [Soviet] regime's effort to control the bureaucracies through the mechanism of the party apparatus has not been entirely successful." However, I take issue with Hammer when he says, "Bureaucratic politics . . . is not a struggle for power but a struggle for resources." Yes, as he says, bureaucracies "are not opposition groups" that want to gain full, open, and formal control of government. However, as he himself also says, much policy making in the USSR has been done secretly. In such an environment the role of the bureaucracy in policy and politics is unavoidably magnified.

Rigby has correctly shown that Soviet politics was often "cryptopolitics" or "conflicts of interest and articulation . . . denied a special political sphere of operation [that] tend to give a political coloration to processes ostensibly executive and administrative in character."[47] In a dictatorship the stakes and potential of bureaucratic action are much greater than in a democracy. Also, Soviet bureaucrats were part of the ruling party and of the state, not mere neutral civil servants with a limited governmental role. Their role was elastic to a real degree. Bureaucrats were also protected from popular views and actions. As Aron says, "A classless society leaves the mass of the population without any possible means of defence against the elite."[48] And this special elevated and protected status allowed the bureaucrats to be high-handed and even harsh toward the populace and its potential general interests. As Tatu says, even if the "steel eaters" cannot dictate policy, they are "still strong enough to prevent other groups from reaching their goals." And, as *Pravda* once complained, "party organizations of ministries . . . cannot directly influence the work of the enterprises and institutions under the jurisdiction of these ministries."[49] Certainly, the heads of major governmental organizations "are themselves political actors" and tend to advance the interests of the agencies they head.[50] The local party organizations were at a disadvantage versus top ministerial officials. Hough, in a study of local party organs, emphasizes the independent power of the ministerial elite: "The top Soviet industrial officials . . . remain very formidable opponents in bureaucratic struggles on planning and technical questions." He points out that the local party–higher state administrator interaction "is that of a supplicant–superior relationship" with the local party organ the supplicant. Hough also raises the crucial question of "whether the use of specialized personnel in the Party's Central Committee apparatus has not meant the penetration of the values of the bureaucratic elite into the political leadership as much as or more than the enhancement of political control over the policy process."[51] Matsuzato has called local bureaucracies highly politicized local political parties—"administrative parties."[52]

Gregory makes similar points in a study based primarily on interviews: "The evidence suggests that ministerial status places one in the inner sanctum of the Soviet ruling elite." He also echoes Hough by saying that ministers had "an important advantage over local party officials" through their ability to deal directly with other central bureaucratic institutions.[53] It is also to be noted that 25 percent of the top ministerial officials in one sample were members of the party Central Committee, a high status that had to give them significant access to the political leaders and implicit license to do a great deal in their institutions' interests.[54] Note that in 1987 six, twice as many as in 1983, members of the party Politburo had governmental duties. Some of this power and status must have "trickled down" to lower level bureaucrats, at least as encouragement to "push a little" now and then.

THE STATE BUREAUCRACY AND POLITICS

Bureaucrats and politics often go hand in hand. In Germany, for example, 173 civil servants were members of the lower house of the parliament, the Bundestag, in 1981. This was 33 percent of the membership. And this was prior to reunification and does not refer to the upper house, or Bundesrat, where all of the members are civil servants. At the time the

Sozialdemokratischen Partei Deutschlands, the main socialist party, was "increasingly developing into a civil service party in parliament."

American presidents and other "superiors" have found it difficult to fire certain civil servants. For example, President Carter had to give up the idea of firing a deputy head of an agency when he found out that the man was a political associate of "Tip" O'Neill, the House leader and crucially important for Carter's influence in Congress. Nixon would "exile" offending civil servants to Detroit or other undesirable duty stations in lieu of firing them. And then there are the cases of J. Edgar Hoover, who died in office as the director of the FBI, and Admiral Hyman Rickover, who was kept in his post for years by special acts of Congress every two years despite the Navy top brass's desire to fire him. Eventually, he retired with great honors. The American president had advantages over the Soviet general secretary. If the president was determined to act against a bureaucrat, then he could rely on his constitutional powers. Truman fired General MacArthur. But in the USSR all power was based on politics, and constitutional power was unavailable to the general secretary. And, of course, in the USSR "heaven is high and the emperor is far away"; the bureaucratic managers had "considerable leeway in which to perform." In any case, "bureaucrats are always semi-administrators and semi-politicians."[55]

The state bureaucracy has affected leadership politics in the USSR more than once. Certainly, one reason Khrushchev had to go was that he had attacked the stability and privileges of the bureaucracy.[56] Khrushchev's policies were an extreme aggravation to many. Valenta calls Brezhnev, Khrushchev's successor, "a skillful bureaucrat playing the role of General Secretary of the CPSU" whose "stand on many political issues is probably to be explained largely in terms of bureaucratic politics" and his work in various parts of the Soviet bureaucracy.[57] Andropov, Brezhnev's successor, though a member of the Politburo, was fundamentally a state functionary, the head of the KGB, an organization of great importance and probably comfort for the elite as a whole. Certainly, "Andropov's accession seems to have been based on the support of the major state institutions represented in the Politburo." His brief tenure as "GenSec" was marked by a "covert political struggle" involving "an established and largely corrupt machinery impervious to reform."[58] Gorbachev, the last Soviet leader, was clearly a reformer of significance and drive but was unable to bring about significant change in the nature of either the party or the state bureaucracy. He was ultimately overwhelmed by the contradictions inherent in the Soviet system and by the "party," which was unable to relate positively to Gorbachev's idealism.

Soviet bureaucratic politics is well displayed in the perennial interbureaucratic conflict of the times. This occurs everywhere. When I served in the U.S. government, the commandant of the U.S. Marines decided that he had to have his office in the Pentagon. Fine, said the Army and the Air Force, but do not expect any space from us; you have got to get it all from the Navy. Disputes over space are common within agencies as well. Frank von Hippel has written that "the greatest consumer of energy at the upper levels of government is fighting over turf. . . . This leads to incessant warfare."[59] Janos Kornai has said that bureaucratic boundaries are like property boundaries, as one U.S. bureaucrat learned: "I gave away a water fountain and lost a whole floor and 400 employees." Members of the U.S. Arms Control and Disarmament Agency (ACDA) have accused officials of the State Department of lying. The National Security Council was supposed to solve such problems but rarely could. Conflicts between the secretary of state and the president's national security adviser, the director of the CIA, and the secretary of defense are always assumed to exist, whether or not they do.[60]

In the Soviet system, too, ministries and other agencies were often in conflict with one another. They also failed to cooperate and coordinate. For example, technological advances and new equipment of one branch were not transferred to others. As one top official lamented: "We are faced once again with the tendency to 'create one's own preserve.'" Ministries were even known to sabotage the production efforts of other ministries.[61]

This problem has continued into the post-Soviet period. For example, in 1995 the Ministry of Science, the Academy of Sciences, and the Fund for Fundamental Research were engaged in a naked rivalry over how a proposed national computer network was to be run. The Ministry of Science wanted to run it on its own. Issues of weapons trade also brought out interagency conflict.[62]

THE POST-SOVIET BUREAUCRACY AND POLITICAL ISSUES

The post-Soviet government contains many of the same people who made up the Soviet government. Continuity of personnel is high. Unlike the case in postfascist Germany and postimperial Japan, there has been no supreme force or directing reformist entity available to vet the bureaucracies and select persons willing to change the ethos of the system for at least the key positions. The Soviet system may have fallen, but it was never defeated and replaced. And now the personnel have much more freedom than in the Soviet period. As before, there is no accountability to the people. But new is the "democracy for bureaucrats" of no control from above. As Rogov puts it, "Individual bureaucrats control considerable power. Such bureaucrats have largely determined distribution of capital and property since the move away from a command economy."[63] Some of

the "power ministries," and perhaps others, "act outside of executive control, thus limiting the capacity of the Russian state to act."[64] Most of
Yeltsin's prime ministers were ex-bureaucrats. Chernomyrdin, for example, did serve the party apparatus for about ten years, but after 1982 he
clearly became a state bureaucrat, helping run the vast oil and gas industry of the USSR, a position that may have made him enormously wealthy.
By 1996 the new government team was made up mainly of industrial bureaucrats, and in 1993 we could note that more than half the candidates
running for seats in the Duma came from government structures. A political analyst has written of an equilibrium in politics existing "between the
three large groups of bureaucrats": the "new clerks" on the presidential
staff, the "top-ranked civil servants" with their own "domains," and the
"scribes," intellectuals outside the inner circle who try to exert pressure
on the president through their writings and consultations with key persons. Yavlinsky, head of the Yabloko Party, has spoken of the need to "de-
bureaucratize Russia," a worthy and necessary goal to achieve a prosper-
ous and modern Russia but not one that can be accomplished in only one
or two decades.[65]

An example of free-floating bureaucracy in action and one that was
very significant for the United States and a big irritant in U.S.–Russian relations is that of Minatom, the Ministry of Atomic Energy, viewed in
Washington with great suspicion and some trepidation. For it is Minatom
that can let the Russian nuclear genie out of the bottle and convey it to the
so-called rogue states that, whether it is justified or not, are such a concern
within the American government. An American diplomat once called the
ministry "a very desperate and self-serving organization that is trying
very hard to survive" and which the U.S. government tried to circumvent
so that it could bring its nuclear concerns directly to President Yeltsin. The
ministry was a seemingly free-floating entity oriented toward profit making and the retention of its employees at full strength and driven by an
ideology that saw nuclear energy and materials as necessary and inher-
ently benign. The president removed Viktor Mikhailov, the minister of
atomic energy in 1998, but it seems that the ministry continued on its
semi-independent course after that.[66]

CHANGE, REFORM, AND RESISTANCE

Bureaucratic reform, or a significant change in culture and activity,
though often announced, has never occurred in Russia, either in the Soviet period or since, except perhaps as a "treadmill of reforms," amount-
ing to little. The word is used in Russian political history, perhaps with
some justification there, though those reforms were swept away by the

Russian Revolution and Stalinism, which did change Russia in many significant ways.

Perhaps three general positions can be taken in regard to a bureaucracy (and its reform): using it as it is and accepting most of its idiosyncrasies and deficiencies (the "realistic" position), trying to purge it of its problems and making it work well and "humanly" (the "optimistic" position), and defeating it and replacing it with an alternative or even eliminating it (the "transformative-humanistic" position). Note that some "hard" conservatives might also adopt this third position, though suffusing it with a conservative ideology. In most governments the first option prevails most of the time.[67] There is often skepticism associated with reform. As the political humorist Mark Russell has put it, "Streamlining the government is like painting racing stripes on an arthritic camel."[68]

Occasionally a variant of the third option, elimination or "sunset," is actually realized. For example, in 1996 three or so U.S. government agencies went out of existence as part of Vice President Al Gore's "Re-inventing Government" program. One was the 108-year-old Interstate Commerce Commission, the oldest regulatory agency in Washington.[69] Others were the Bureau of Mines and a tea-tasting board. However, that old dinosaur, the Bureau of Indian Affairs, somehow survived. Of course, unanticipated consequences, that old bugaboo, can attend even elimination of a bureaucracy. For example, in the late 1990s Senator Jesse Helms succeeded in getting the Clinton administration to eliminate two foreign affairs agencies. One of them was the U.S. Arms Control and Disarmament Agency, which was merged with the Department of State. Ironically, ACDA personnel were so numerous that they swamped the few arms control people in the State Department, and two new, highly paid undersecretary positions were created—not what Helms had in mind with his "reorganization," accepted by the White House in order to free up some funds for State being "sat upon" by the senator. According to interviews, the incorporation of ACDA into State had its ups and downs for the arms controllers. On the plus side, everyone in Washington knows what State is, so now telephone calls are returned and there is favorable response to requests. However, on the down side, employees now see their superiors only once or twice a week and only in formal settings. Yet top ex-ACDA people now get to talk with top people in State, including the secretary.[70]

Apparently some U.S. government programs have been successfully transformed. In 1995 the Ford Foundation gave $100,000 to each of fifteen U.S. government programs for successful innovational change.[71] Reorganizations may be able to go further faster in private enterprise, but this cannot be stated with certainty because I have done no research on private business. Still, nongovernmental entities in a capitalist economy can fire people, and the remaining employees can be moved about at will (they

cannot appeal successfully to politicians). There is a considerable literature on business reorganization and revitalization.[72] Even so, as a professor of business says, "Trying to transform these big corporations, really
making a fundamental change in the way they do things, is very difficult." A management consultant says that "the heart of changing any big
company . . . is transforming the inbred culture." A "turnaround specialist" who became chief executive of an American corporation says that
what is essential for real change is to "get rid of the people who represent
the old culture, or they will fight you . . . and you have to get rid of all the
old symbols."[73] In government one usually cannot drop the "old symbols" except through revolution, a rather drastic and rare way to effect organizational change.

Exactly because the Russian Revolution and Stalinism did occur, the history of governmental reform in Russia is not encouraging. Many reforms
were begun in imperial Russia, and some of them, for example, the creation of the *zemstva* and trial by jury and the allowance of unions (for a
time), seemed to presage eventual democratization. But the progress of
these reforms was seriously inhibited by the desire of those in administration (not really bureaucrats) to maintain their personal relationships and
what they saw as "our thing." As LeDonne notes, "Reform and adherence
to abstract principle disturbs personal networks and the power of key people in the bureaucracy."[74] Even in Soviet times reforms were begun that
had real potential for significant change in administration, for example, the
introduction of Taylorism in the 1920s and the Liberman or Kosygin reforms of industrial management in the 1960s.[75] A number of minor reforms
with significance for administration were also begun.[76] This is not to say
that any proposed reforms of the Soviet period were fundamental. One can
see all of them as having a partial, even a "Potemkin" nature, in which
eliminations of structures and removals of persons "have often been more
apparent than real."[77] In the latter years of the Soviet Union "management
training" became the vogue, with the leadership appearing "to see in management science a means to assert greater control over its clumsy administrative apparatus" with particular enthusiasm shown for systems theory.
But its impact was far less than hoped for. Still, "business schools" have
popped up all over the former Soviet Union (FSU in Washingtonese).[78] The
early post-Soviet period saw the "500 Days" plan of reform, announced in
September 1990, intended to abolish most agencies that regulated industry.
What it gave us, however, was rampant inflation and *"nomenklatura* capitalism," in which dynamic persons and groups of the Soviet bureaucracy
and political class seized control of much of the worthwhile parts of the
economy. The state withered and became a "weak state," but the bureaucrats, and certain others, including former members of the security apparatus, flourished and battened on the people as a whole.

Briefly, why didn't reform and reorganization work in the Soviet period? Fundamentally, as Alec Nove once pointed out, bureaucracy is inherent in Marxism, which assumes all is simple.[79] Another important reason is that part of the party elite feared that limited reform would snowball and change the entire system to its disadvantage and possibly even destroy the Soviet Union. Molotov, Stalin's right-hand man for so long, is supposed to have said, "If we change anything, everything will change." So much for communist confidence and belief in Soviet power. (Would that more Western Sovietologists had understood how fragile the Soviet system was.)

There was also serious, entrenched, and cleverly used resistance to change by top-level bureaucrats and by many others as well. Often resistance was simply following "SOP," "standard operating procedure." Work-to-rule is the surest form of sabotage. Conyngham says that a "classical approach to formal organization . . . has imposed rigid limits on the application of innovative methods of management."[80] The Soviet bureaucratic class was locked into a variant of the "military at war" approach to administration, a lasting result of the experience of the Civil War set into "cement" (the title of a Soviet novel) by Stalinism. Liberman writes of "the old bureaucratic ills—inflexibility, irresponsibility and lack of initiative, reliance upon the formality of issuing orders."[81] Keith Bush writes of the resistance to the Kosygin reforms, of "bureaucratic inertia as perhaps the most formidable obstacle . . . in the path of the reforms . . . [and] resistance to change by Soviet officials at all levels and in all branches."[82] A 1980 German analysis of the problems of Soviet administration emphasizes "the growing importance of bureaucratic politics" and the fact that "the Party itself to a large extent has become integrated into the administrative system . . . at the expense of its 'statesmanlike' . . . role."[83] Gorbachev, too, faced bureaucratic resistance to his attempt to implement perestroika. Brown writes of "ministerial encroachment" on even those enterprises authoritatively allowed some independence in an economic experiment. Gorbachev once spoke of the Ministry of Finance "editing the experiment" contrary to the government's decisions.[84] Perhaps if Gorbachev had understood his own Soviet system better, then his reforms might have gone further. He also ought to have maintained the value of the ruble and the output level of goods most desired by the population. As one Russian observer says, the first reform attempts made by Gorbachev destroyed the few great strengths of the Soviet economic system. As a result of him allowing the money supply to get out of hand, "no one has any initiative to do anything if they are going to be paid in rubles."[85] Gorbachev understood imagery but not economic-political reality.

Just because the "big cheese" orders something, there is no guarantee that his order will be followed. While I was speaking at the CIA of Gorbachev's (the "boss's") problems in convincing his bureaucrats that he was serious, one of the old hands of the agency responded with a laugh and said, "We're still waiting to see if our boss is serious." Ronald Reagan had already been president for five years. Zbigniew Brzezinski, President Carter's national security adviser, once said that "much of policy is determined by the deliberate distortion of decisions."[86] John Stuart Mill once noted the limited power of the tsar vis-à-vis his "own" bureaucracy: "The Czar himself is powerless against the bureaucratic body: He can send one of them to Siberia, but he cannot govern without them or against their will. On every decree of his they have a tacit veto, by merely refraining from carrying it into effect."[87] There is no end to specific statements on how "Gorby's" policies were stonewalled and limited by the Soviet bureaucracy. In 1991 Anders Aslund saw the bureaucrats' power center in an association of the directors of big industry, the Scientific-Industrial Union. Abraham Brumberg, quoting a Soviet newspaper in 1989, says that "hardly a week passes without a news story about how Soviet *chinovniks* (officials) are conspiring to sabotage Gorbachev's reforms." He quotes from Alexander Bovin, a prominent commentator, who says with apparent exasperation that "even those things that are really and truly permitted are continuously obstructed by our command-and-administer system." The *New York Times*, citing the economist Ed A. Hewitt, writes of "sabotage by bureaucrats who have remained firmly in control."[88] And so Gorbachev passed into history—with a little more help from bureaucrats and from a former construction engineer named Yeltsin.

YELTSIN

The Soviet Union is no more, yes, but it is not dead. It still lives on in various senses: first, a numbing memory so many share of the way things "ought" to be done; and second, in personnel politics, in the bureaucracy, and throughout the institutions of society. Authoritarian regimes leave their mark on societies even after they have been formally overthrown because such regimes eliminate independent groupings and institutions and habits of independence.[89] Such a situation can hardly give quick birth to a Western-type civil society free of the state and willing to stand up to it. The now-deceased mayor of St. Petersburg said in 2000, "To this day, the power structures of our country remain, according to the method of work and the personnel that they have, in conflict with the new regime."[90]

No one political leader could be expected to overcome this post-Soviet incubus, particularly an ex–construction engineer from a closed city who was beset by the limitations of health problems and a Soviet-induced lack of understanding of the Western-type "polyarchy" toward which he was trying to head. Boris Yeltsin was crucially important for putting an end to the coup against both him and Gorbachev and then ending the Soviet Union in the same year, 1991. He also had an expansive and relaxed view of Russian citizenship, speaking of it as a status for all who lived in Russia, not just ethnic Russians. As the party first secretary of Moscow, he was repelled by the cronyism and corruption of the Moscow elite and tried to bring it to an end, but Gorbachev, ever the weaver and dodger, removed Yeltsin from the post, publicly degraded him, and thereby set the stage for his own eventual removal and the extinction of the USSR.[91] But, despite Yeltsin's merits and strengths, by allowing prices to float in an oligopolistic economy and never creating for the new state the power to tax, he set Russia to sliding into a near-anarchy in which only the most clever, dynamic, and ruthless people could live well. This made democracy, as well as the United States, unpopular. If what Russia has is democracy, who would want it?

Yeltsin had definite antibureaucratic views, acquired during his years in the Soviet economy and party. He later said, for example, "If people wanted to . . . even . . . build a school . . . they had to go begging to Moscow hat in hand for money from the ministers." He probably had it in for the ministries. "Economic decentralization means gradual liquidation of the ministries," he said in 1989. Note that when he served in Moscow "all the ministers belonged to the Moscow Party organization," and he encountered a great deal of bureaucratic sabotage of his efforts there.[92] He himself admitted that he got the "shakes" when he realized he would be taking over the "enormous Soviet Russian bureaucracy." He writes of the "coup plotters" of 1991 as a "whole platoon of government bureaucrats whom the system had turned into cogs and stripped of any human traits."[93] He has often singled out bureaucratization as a severe, even crippling, problem for Russia. In 1986 he "called on the public to fight against bureaucracy." In 1989 he said that even the Communist Party of the Soviet Union "had become a bureaucratic administrative structure, rather than a political party." In 1988 he went so far as to say, "We have stifled man spiritually. He has been under the pressure of exaggerated authorities, orders, unceasing instructions, an infinite number of decrees."[94] He made a number of other strong statements on the problems of bureaucracy during his presidency. And they seem to show where he wanted to stand, politically, if he only could. In a speech at the Russian Civil Service Academy in 1995 he stated that "the civil service . . . continues to be in a state of crisis."[95] In the same year he railed against crime and corruption in the bureaucracy and stated that his first priority was the "enhancement of state power." On the same occasion, he said that the lack of preparedness in the Army was the cause of human rights violations in Chechnya. Also in 1995, he lashed out at state bureaucrats, saying that they impede reforms, and urged "serious changes in the state service and the personnel policy of Russia."

Two of his stronger statements were made in 1994 and 1999. In the former he said that he had ordered his aides to "purge" the bureaucracy of
corrupt practices. In the 1999 statement he exclaimed, "We need to burn
out" the bureaucracy, "and that's what we intend to do." In his 1998
"State of the Union" speech he spoke of his intent to reform the state machinery. It was to be "shaped in a new fashion. . . . The goals of the reform
are to make the state machinery more compact, effective and controllable
by society. We will be advancing toward this objective."[96] In 1997 he ap-
pealed to elected authorities of Russia, and his prime minister, to appoint
more young people to responsible positions because of "the novelty of
their decisions, the boldness of their approaches, and the originality of
their ideas" and because they "do not have time for intrigues."[97]

Strong talk, but what did he do? Here we have a sad failure. No case
can be made that the Russian state administration was improved during
Yeltsin's eight years as president. As is often true in politics, what is said
or promised is not backed up by deeds while in office. But Yeltsin had inherited a system that he could change only at the top and perhaps a bit at
the margins. "Most of the bureaucracy was unchanged from the Soviet
past," and, as Yeltsin's young (age thirty-five) reformist finance minister
said, the people in his ministry "promise exactly the policies I have been
fighting against." All the reformers, those "happy few," were grossly out-
numbered. And the reformers must not be seen as all democrats. Huskey
describes well the unique features of "fragmented power" blocking
change in Russia, where governmental divisions were "quite different"
from the ones seen in the West:

> There [in Russia] the members of the Government limit the authority of the
> prime minister not by political interventions during cabinet meetings but by
> carving out for themselves a broad measure of autonomy in their own ad-
> ministrative portfolios. In Russia, a minister is more likely to influence pol-
> icy through bureaucratic intrigue—by sabotaging the drafting or implemen-
> tation of an initiative—than through cabinet debates. Thus . . . the Russian
> government is an unwieldy coalition of ministers, most of whom are devoted
> first and foremost to their own institutional interests.[98]

Under such conditions Yeltsin did well, indeed, very well, to hang onto
his position and to prevent a formal, wholesale reversion to a "USSR II" or
some sort of authoritarianism run either by the old crew of the Soviet state
that filled the government's offices or the authoritarian-nationalist
opposition—or both, the much mentioned "Red–Brown coalition." However, this significant success was seriously marred by the lack of other successes, the prevalence of many painful problems for so many Russians, and
the negative features of Yeltsin's own rule. He introduced a highly bureau-

cratized "superpresidentialism," a "partially democratic regime," with a huge apparatus of executive power, which, among other negative effects, promoted "unaccountable, irresponsible behavior on the part of officeholders in the executive branch."[99] These officeholders were quite numerous. Possibly Yeltsin's staff numbered 3,500 officials (*otvetstvennye rabotniki*) in late 1993, after the use of force against the Duma. This staff may have soon increased to 5,500 officials plus a force of about twenty thousand to protect the president. One U.S. government report says that the staff "increasingly appears to rival the government ministries in power, if not size."[100]

Most of Yeltsin's tenure in office was a political balancing act. He made the most of his special constitutional position to stay in power and keep at bay all the oppositions he faced. He soon dropped Gaidar, his first reformist prime minister, and replaced him with Chernomyrdin, the veteran bureaucrat from the state energy industry.[101] Now we saw a continual drift to more conservative figures to run the government but with Yeltsin always retaining, and sometimes using, an ultimate veto power exercised from his besieged and entrenched pinnacle of power. By 1994 Yeltsin brought the "power ministries" and the security services under his direct control. This process did not reduce bureaucratic power and capabilities. As Buzgalin says, "The Chernomyrdin bloc was created in the classic nomenklatura-bureaucratic mold: a herd of bureaucrats, holding a wide variety of political views, crowded into it, mostly out of careerist considerations but also under pressure 'from above.' . . . [S]upport for the government was their only credo."[102]

Yeltsin eventually came to be trapped in his heavily protected Kremlin and enveloped in excess and somewhat meaningless, even ridiculous, bureaucracy of his own creation. He became an inveterate issuer of decrees that were ignored and appointer of powerless "plenipotentiaries." He even issued decrees on decrees. Yet he survived and found a successor to protect him in his retirement, a real success in terms of "pure politics."

Yeltsin's actions faced a great deal of public criticism, allowed in Russia's defective or limited democracy, but the opposition to Yeltsin was too fragmented, disillusioned, and unwilling to cooperate for any effective countermovement to arise. And Yeltsin had shown that he was able to react with force in any crisis of his rule. He was a "sleeping bear" of a "tsar" but one who stayed alert to his political surroundings. Gennadi Barbulis, one of Yeltsin's close aides, said of Yeltsin's political methodology, "It is our history and it is very much Yeltsin's style. He is creating a dynamically tense complex of power where each person is capable of something important but none has the independence needed to act alone. . . . This bizarre structure will guarantee that he remains the real power."[103]

Other criticisms and explanations were common. Andrei Piontkowsky once said, "After all, Yeltsin is an old Communist Party secretary, and this is his style—to apply administrative methods." Anatolii Sobchak has said that Yeltsin retained people in important posts "who were not democrats" and let the Russian government become "too large and complicated," with a level of disorganization such that documents were "frequently lost." Barbulis criticizes Yeltsin for his "lack of resistance to old bureaucratic structures which boycotted reforms" and his failure to build "civilized relations" with the members of Parliament. One Russian newspaper notes that Yeltsin had imposed security standards on Kremlin employees that were so similar to those of the communist era that Soviet questionnaires could probably be used.[104] Continuity again.

Yeltsin did make a few moves apparently intended to attain some control over the bureaucracy. For example, several high-level federal and regional officials were dismissed in 1996 for misusing federal funds, and several others were sanctioned for various offenses and administrative failures. Also in 1996, an attempt was made to create some oversight regarding the actions of officials in the executive branch. In 1997 Kremlin cadres were ordered to disclose their incomes and property holdings. However, the order had too many loopholes to be effective. (Property in relatives' names did not count.) Dozens of personnel were dismissed from the Federal Security Bureau (FSB) in 1999.[105]

This had little effect. I have recounted above the fact that Yeltsin's orders to the Customs Service had no lasting effect; they were each obeyed only once. Kozyrev, one of Yeltsin's foreign ministers, spoke of the "revenge of the apparatus," in discussing the resistance of the bureaucracy to the Yeltsin government. American consulting firms or investors found that the bureaucracy would always refer them only to Russians and Russian organizations and businesses connected with the given agency. It was widely assumed that any attempt by the government to change the tax system would not be obeyed by the State Tax Service, showing a wide gulf between policy and implementation and a clear lack of respect for or fear of the government by the bureaucracy. Attempts at governmental reorganizations tended to fail.[106] On top of all this failure vis-à-vis the bureaucracy, the Yeltsin team was devoting great energies to "pre-empt and block the further development of the grassroots democratic movement." Everyone and anyone was seen as an enemy. The result was great power moving to "oligarchical clans that came mostly from the former Soviet establishment." Civil society was "thrown backward" in its development as a result of the hyperinflation and the wiping out of the middle class's savings.[107]

PUTIN

Everyone knew that at some point the elderly, ill Yeltsin would go, through death, incapacitation, or removal (either peacefully or otherwise). Few thought he would voluntarily resign, and no one thought he would pick as his successor an obscure, formerly low ranking (one could easily say nonranking), much younger man who once served in the KGB in East Germany (and that this person would be elected president of Russia soon afterward). As late as 1995, and even later, Putin's name was not mentioned as a possible successor to the old bear from the Urals.[108] Russia will often surprise us—a fact all of us who study and observe that northern colossus should have engraved in gold and carry with us at all times.

Putin is dealt with here only briefly because we are interested only in what he has said and done vis-à-vis state administration and what significance he may have for it. But it is still early days in Putin's presidency, and much about him has to be conjecture. In many ways he is still an unknown quantity. It is impossible to predict his future accomplishments and failures. A leader's historical fate depends not only on himself and his own thinking and efforts but also on a whole series of unforeseen factors independent of the leader's, and our, reach and wishes. As yet Putin has accomplished little of consequence. True, the economy is doing slightly better, but a part of that is because of higher energy prices alone.

To a real degree Putin is a product of Yeltsin, perhaps mainly of his dislikes and fears. Other potential successors apparently unduly raised Yeltsin's sense of competitiveness and acute sense of concern for the future, only natural in the Russian political context. Yeltsin and his family wanted to find a successor who would protect them and their property and interests. They found him in Vladimir Putin, an ex–security bureaucrat and the fifth premier for Russia in seventeen months. Yeltsin has said that he was looking for a young prime minister. Putin was still in his forties. But what was crucial in his selection is that Putin had broken the law to save his former mentor, Anatoly Sobchak, the first post-Soviet mayor of St. Petersburg, from prosecution. Putin got Sobchak out of the country.[109] Putin looked like a man who expresses loyalty to former mentors in concrete ways. Yeltsin's judgment of Putin was not misplaced. Putin's first act as acting president was to sign a decree granting Yeltsin a series of legal immunities and a generous allowance for the rest of his life.[110] This certainly looks like a "quid pro quo" of the kind so often denounced in American politics.

A key fact making Putin highly significant for our topic is that he is a former bureaucrat. Indeed, many see him as still a bureaucrat. This has various possible implications. Putin may think and act as a typical bureaucrat. Shevtsova says, "Mr. Putin is at his core a bureaucrat who wants to make the system work and not to revolutionize it."[111] He favored other bureaucrats in making appointments, particularly individuals from the former KGB and its successor agencies, to important positions. And the rise of a bureaucrat to the top political position tells us something about Russia or reinforces it—bureaucrats can be very important there. The longer Putin stays in office, the stronger the case made here for the special importance of bureaucracy in Russia.

Various observers have suggested that Putin is one bureaucrat in a historical progression. His similarity to Stolypin has been noted—"both maintained close ties to the special services, focused on domestic affairs, opposed both the left and the right, . . . were 'conservative liberals' and patriots, and both had few close confidants." However, there is one major difference: "Above Stolypin was the tsar; above Putin are only the will of the elites and the patience of the people." Another observer, commenting on Putin's background in the security services, says, "The secret police, while playing its murderous role, has also been a source of innovative thinking, or 'modernism' in the specified sense of anti-Western modernization *a la russe*." But, he concludes significantly, the secret police always failed to save the system.[112] Although Putin has said that his work in the German Democratic Republic was carrying on liaison with the Staasi, a few sources have claimed that he worked for an arm of the KGB charged with eliminating dissent in the USSR.[113] Others have pointed out that an advantage of Putin being in the "catbird seat" of Russian politics is that "he understands the bureaucracy from the inside, having himself climbed the ladder from the bottom rung to the top. . . . [H]e knows firsthand the Russian bureaucrat and the rules of their games."[114] But still others consider Putin as part and parcel of the state bureaucracy—and in the worst senses. For example, it is asserted that Putin is backed by the "bureaucratic bourgeoisie," which came out of the Soviet *nomenklatura* but acquired capital by privatizing all the state property it could get hold of.[115]

The tragic and probably avoidable sinking of the submarine *Kursk* in 2000 was not one of Putin's finer moments. McFaul says that the crisis showed Putin acting "like a bureaucrat, not a leader." Gessen says that his statements and behavior at the time suggest that he "sees himself as a bureaucrat who should keep to his place, not a leader who should go where the trouble is" and that they show that Russia cannot afford to have a Soviet-era bureaucrat in charge.[116] Certainly, Putin is promoting security types to high positions, but in his case this is perfectly normal, whatever effects it may have, as is his appointment of people from St. Petersburg, where he has worked. These are the people he knows and is comfortable with. In 2001, for example, Putin promoted his friend, the director of the FSB, Putin's old job under Yeltsin, to full general, ostensibly "in connection with his 50th birthday."[117] Naturally, given Putin's background, there are voices speaking of "authoritarian reform" as being in store for Russia.[118] Ironically, President George W. Bush, who met Putin in mid-2001, spoke of him sympathetically as being apart from the state bureaucracy and as facing in it an opposing "anti-American bureaucracy" that is a "hangover" from the Cold War.[119] Eventually, it will be clear which of these views is the correct one.

Meanwhile, Putin's popularity remains high, despite the fact that none of the problems existing when he came into office has been solved. Why this popularity? There are various theories. One Russian journalist says that Putin fits perfectly into the old Russian myth of "a tsar fighting the boyars." In addition, Putin also fits right into the Russian classical historical cycle or rhythm, "attention–rest–attention." A Russian pollster sees Putin's popularity as based on the hopes that so many Russians have that "a young and vigorous leader would be able to tackle the problems that President Yeltsin . . . could not. After a year and a half, Putin still preserves that symbolic 'resource of hope.'"[120] But for how long will Putin have the benefits of "that little bird which sits in the soul," as Emily Dickinson so touchingly put it? It may fly away at some point.

Putin has made statements indicating that he is highly cognizant of the problems of the Russian state bureaucracy and of Russian government in general. He has said realistically that "Russia has from the very start developed as a super-centralized state. . . . It is part of its genetic code, its tradition, the mentality of its people."[121] He has also called for "demilitarizing Russia's public life" through sweeping governmental reforms.[122] Militarization has long been a feature of Russian society. Peter the Great may have started it, and Stalin certainly carried it to its limit. Putin has also met with senior members of the government to discuss the "debureaucratization of the economy" in order to make life easier and predictable for businesspeople and to increase foreign investment.[123]

An excellent source of his statements in this regard is his interview of mid-2000 with *Izvestiia*. Here he expresses some understanding of the difficulties Russian bureaucracy poses for ordinary Russians:

> The creation of a strong and effective state cannot entail the violation of civil freedoms. . . . [I]t is really bad when certain officials perceive the entire state line aiming to establish law and order as a chance for greater bureaucratic arbitrary rule, that is, when customs officers, tax inspectors or border guards treat people with disrespect, also insulting their human dignity and causing them trouble with all sorts of unjustified fault-finding remarks and suspicions.[124]

In the same interview Putin also spoke against state mechanisms that "impose all sorts of bans and restrictions upon society," in favor of all state agencies having "clear-cut responsibilities" and of raising the professional standards of state officials. He also said that he could act "only in the boundaries of constitutional space" and that a state must be ruled by law. However, the "constitutional space" left to him by Yeltsin's constitution is a bit "roomy."

His statements are all to the good in terms of Russia's needs concerning its state administration. However, Putin also speaks often of creating a stronger state and one with fewer internal disagreements—for example, "The current tug-of-war inside the Russian state power system must be stopped."[125] According to Marshall Goldman, Putin has said, "The stronger the state, the freer the individual" and has commented that one cannot get anywhere without secret agents. In his inaugural address Putin stated, "We must know our history . . . and always remember that those who created the Russian state championed its dignity and made it a great, powerful and mighty state." This state orientation is a typically Russian position. In his first national address Putin emphasized that restoring strong central power is the key to making Russia again a great power on the world scene. He has also called for letting government ministers make independent decisions, a tricky suggestion given Russian bureaucrats' proclivities.[126]

Although any concluding judgments on Putin have to be tentative, it is clear that at this stage of his presidency he is engaged in centralization and strengthening federal power—and this means weakening the power of the regional leaders and that of any independent societal-economic institutions, notably the media and the business elites, including some of the so-called oligarchs. Much of this has already, by mid-2003, been accomplished. Yet it is also clear that no new authoritarian political system has been established, so far. Russia is a very large country, and any such "grand design," if it exists, will take many years to implement. However, there are indications that the bureaucratic old guard has been encouraged by Putin's existence and his efforts. What it will do under this circumstance, if anything, we do not yet know. Can Putin master the state bureaucracy and then remake it into one befitting a democracy? There will be no democracy without a new bureaucracy. My judgment of Putin is that he is "half" a Westerner. He knows what conditions businesspeople need to create a good economy and is trying to bring about those conditions. He also knows what is wrong with the state administration and why it is the way it is. However, as a Russian and ex-bureaucrat who wanted to join the KGB from a young age, he also seems to believe that harsh measures are sometimes needed.[127] The political nature of his advisers may be crucial for the "historical Putin" we are yet to see. What is also important for this is whether the Russian economy revives and people's living standards rise. If they do, then Putin can afford to govern "lightly" and to maximize his better half.

CONCLUSION

This chapter has attempted to show, by example and weight of evidence, that the Russian state bureaucracy is an important political factor in its own right. Russia has long been, and remains, a state-oriented society to a great extent. In such a sociopolitical context the state administration and its personnel cannot help but be politically important and, more than that, have what can intelligently be called political power. We have covered much of the necessary ground to realize this effort: the Soviet Communist Party, its nature, and its relationship with the state bureaucracy; the issues facing the post-Soviet bureaucracy; and the statements and actions, as they relate to bureaucracy, of Yeltsin and Putin. However, the opinion of Putin presented here is still open because he is still a struggling political figure in the early stages of his presidency. But assuredly, the "ride" to come will be both interesting and crucially important for Russia, its state, and its people.

NOTES

1. A few good representative works include James W. Fesler and Donald F. Kettl, *Politics of the Administrative Process*, 2d ed. (Chatham, N.J.: Chatham House, 1991); Morton Halperin, *Bureaucracy, Politics and Foreign Policy* (Washington, D.C.: Brookings Institute, 1974); David C. Kozak and James M. Keagle, eds., *Bureaucratic Politics and National Security* (Boulder: Lynne Rienner, 1988); David Nachmias and David H. Rosenbloom, *Bureaucratic Government USA* (New York: St. Martin's Press, 1980); G. Guy Peters, *The Politics of Bureaucracy*, 4th ed. (New York: Longman, 1995); Robert Reich, *Locked in the Cabinet* (New York: Knopf, 1997); Francis E. Rourke, *Bureaucracy, Politics, and Public Policy*, 4th ed. (Boston: Little, Brown and Co., 1984); and Ezra N. Suleiman, ed., *Bureaucrats and Policy Making* (New York: Holmes and Meier, 1985).

2. Richard Pipes, "Russia's Past, Russia's Future," *Commentary*, June 1996, 36.

3. Ludmila Ulitskaya, *The Funeral Party*, trans. Cathy Porter (New York: Schocken Books, n.d. [2001?]), 86–87.

4. Yuri Levada, lecture at the Harriman Institute, Columbia University, 13 February 1990, summarized in *At the Harriman Institute* 3, no. 13: 1.

5. Sarah Oates, "Elected Officials, Political Groups and Voting in Russia," *RFE/RL Research Report* 2, no. 33 (20 August 1993): figure 5, 64; the two 1997 polls were reported in *Johnson's Russia List*, 14 November 1997 and 18 July 1997.

6. Ellen Carnaghan, "Thinking about Democracy: Interviews with Russian Citizens," *Slavic Review* 60, no. 2 (summer 2001): 358, 360, 362.

7. Here I have drawn on two of my unpublished writings: "The Soviet State Bureaucratic Elite, 1964–84: Statement of Significance and Some Suggestions for Research," paper prepared for the Conference on Elites and Political Power in the USSR, University of Birmingham (U.K.), 1–2 July 1987; and "Russian Bureaucratic Continuities," paper prepared for the panel "Bureaucracy in Post-Soviet Russian Politics," at the 30th National Convention of the American Association for the Advancement of Slavic Studies (AAASS), Boca Raton, Fla., 24–27 September 1998.

8. I have been unable to find a source for this incident, which I remember as being related by Henry Kissinger in his memoirs.

9. Henry A. Kissinger, *Years of Upheaval* (Boston: Little, Brown and Co., 1982), 269. Kissinger writes, "To argue that the General Secretary of the Soviet Communist party required a pretext to participate in Soviet bureaucratic decisions was to elevate chutzpah into an art form" (*Years of Upheaval*, 269). Perhaps Kissinger was overestimating Brezhnev's power and underestimating that of the bureaucracy.

10. Conor Cruise O'Brien, "Odd Man Out," review of Arkady N. Shevchenko, *Breaking with Moscow* (New York: Knopf, 1985), *The New York Review of Books*, 11 April 1985, 3. O'Brien also calls the Soviet political system "an absurd and ramshackle structure," close to my characterization of "criminal absurdity" after having lived in the USSR for a semester in 1977.

11. Alexander Bovin, "Power Crisis," *Izvestiia*, 30 December 1997, from *Johnson's Russia List*, 12 December 1997. Gorbachev once said of Parkinson, in effect, "Parkinson is alive and lives in the USSR."

12. Alexander Solzhenitsyn, article in *Obshchaia gazeta*, quoted in *Johnson's Russia List*, sometime in 1996; regrettably, my notes with the quotation from Gavriil Popov do not allow an exact citation.

13. A. Karamysheva, "Biurokratiia i texhnologiia vlast'," in *Tekhnologiia vlast' i upravleniia v sovremennom gosudarstve* (Moscow: "Universitetskii gumantarnyi litsei," 1999), 122.

14. Chairman of the State Duma Ivan Rybkin, quoted in *Moskovskiy Komsomolets*, 2 November 1995, 2, in *U.S. FBIS-SOV-95-214*, 6 November 1995, 39.

15. Quoted in V. Bozhanov, "'Bolevye tochki' v rabote apparata," *Kommunist*, no. 18 (1989): 37. Bozhanov worked for the Minsk *obkom*.

16. Grzegorz W. Kolodko, "Russia Should Put Its People First" (op-ed), *New York Times*, 7 July 1998, A23; report on Allen Lynch, "The Crisis of the Russian State," *The International Spectator* (Rome), April–June 1995, in Association for the Study of Nationalities, *Analysis of Current Events* 7, no. 7 (March 1996): 5; Marcia Weigle, book review, *Slavic Review* 60, no. 1 (spring 2001): 190; Patrick E. Tyler, "Russian General Says His Troops Were 'Lawless' in Chechen Towns," *New York Times*, 12 July 2001, A1; Michael McFaul, "Refocusing American Policy toward Russia," *Demokratizatsiya* 6, no. 2 (spring 1998): 326–46.

17. Alexandra Costa, *Stepping Down from the Star: A Soviet Defector's Story* (New York: G. P. Putnam's Sons, 1986), 15, 61, 144; Arkady N. Shevchenko, *Breaking with Moscow* (New York: Knopf, 1985), 136, 229, 230; Georgi Arbatov, *The System: An Insider's Life in Soviet Politics* (New York: Times Books [Random House], 1992), v, 217–18, 222, 225. Arbatov was clearly part of the Soviet "aristocracy." I met him in spring 1997 in connection with the visit to Moscow of an emissary of the U.S. Senate.

18. Marquis de Custine, *Letters from Russia*, trans. and ed. Robin Buss (London: Penguin, 1991), 44, 28–29.

19. Maria Hirszowicz, *The Bureaucratic Leviathan* (Oxford: Martin Robertson, 1980), 81. I reviewed this book in *Slavic Review*.

20. Ernest Mandel, "What Is the Bureaucracy?" in *The Stalinist Legacy*, ed. Tariq Ali (New York: Penguin, 1984), 76.

21. J. Kuron and K. Modzelewski, *An Open Letter to the Party*, International Socialism Publication (1968), quoted in David Lane, *The End of Inequality? Stratification under State Socialism* (Harmondsworth, England: Penguin Books, 1971), 43.

22. Timothy J. Colton, "Perspectives on Civil–Military Relations in the Soviet Union," in *Soldiers and the Soviet State*, eds. Timothy J. Colton and Thane Gustafson (Princeton: Princeton University Press, 1990), 26.

23. Pointed out, for example, by Bruce Parrott in his "Political Change and Civil–Military Relations," in *Soldiers and the Soviet State*, eds. Timothy J. Colton and Thane Gustafson (Princeton: Princeton University Press, 1990), 51; Seweryn Bialer, "The Soviet Political Elite and Internal Developments in the USSR," in *The Soviet Empire: Expansion and Detente*, ed. William E. Griffith (Lexington, Mass.: Lexington Books, 1976), 31.

24. Timothy Garton Ash, "The Hungarian Lesson," *The New York Review of Books*, 5 December 1985, 5. Although Ash is referring to Hungary, the question is germane to the USSR also.

25. David A. Dyker, "The Power of the Industrial Ministries," paper presented at the Conference on Elites and Political Power in the USSR, University of Birmingham (U.K.), 1–2 July 1987.

26. David Lane, *The End of Inequality? Stratification under State Socialism* (Harmondsworth, England: Penguin Books, 1971), 69.

27. General Director Jeff Franks, Petrol Complex, a chain of gas stations in Russia, quoted in Sabrina Tavernise, "A Success for BP in Moscow," *New York Times*, 4 July 2001, W1.

28. Karl Marx, quoted in Anatoly Sobchak, *Khozhdenie vo vlast'* (Moscow: Novosti, 1991), 159. Sobchak was a post-Soviet mayor of St. Petersburg who died in early 2000. He once employed Vladimir Putin.

29. Mervyn Matthews, *Privilege in the Soviet Union* (London: George Allen and Unwin, 1978), 8. Matthews notes: "The very existence of the privileges described above removes much of the social justification for the Bolshevik Revolution"; and "although elitism in the Soviet Union may have been for some periods reduced, it has never been removed" (*Privilege in the Soviet Union*, 185).

30. Svetlana Babaeva, article in *Izvestiia*, no. 68 (25168), cited in *Eastview Press Review*; *Novaia gazeta*, 2 July 2001. I am indebted to Vladimir Zhdanov for the latter item. Although all statistics in Russia today merit questioning, these figures must be considered seriously.

31. Matthews, *Privilege in the Soviet Union*, 247. Matthews provides few statistics on numbers of bureaucrats, but he does state that enterprise managers or directors, *rukovoditeli*, then numbered "about 300,000 persons" (*Privilege in the Soviet Union*, 31).

32. Note the example of a deputy chairman of Gosplan remaining in Moscow during the *sovnarkhoz* interlude and becoming a minister after Khrushchev was ousted. See Karl W. Ryavec, "The Soviet Bureaucratic Elite from 1964 to 1969," *Soviet Union* 12, no. 3 (1985): 340–41.

33. Rolf H. W. Theen, "Party and Bureaucracy," in *Public Policy and Administration in the Soviet Union*, ed. Gordon B. Smith (New York: Praeger, 1980), 23.

34. This dialectical perspective is suggested by a statement on Soviet policy in Africa: "The key to the process is the initiatory role of the state sector, which is in effect equated with the vanguard party" (R. Craig Nation, "Soviet Engagement in Africa," in *The Soviet Impact on Africa* [Lexington, Mass.: Lexington Books, 1984], 30).

35. P. Yelistratov, "Organize Rather than Usurp," *Pravda*, 17 February 1966, 2, in *Current Digest of the Soviet Press* 18, no. 7 (9 March 1966): 27.

36. Vassily Aksyonov, "Success and the Soviet Writer," *New York Times Book Review*, 10 March 1985, 34.

37. I am indebted to Fred Kramer, my colleague in public administration, for reminding me of the generalist–technical bifurcation that can afflict government. During my work for the U.S. Arms Control and Disarmament Agency I observed several such examples of this sort of division within the government. Administrations have political needs that conflict with those of the agencies.

38. Referred to in George Breslauer, "In Defense of Sovietology," *Post-Soviet Affairs* 8, no. 3 (1992): 208.

39. Paul R. Gregory, review of Peter Rutland, *The Myth of the Plan: Lessons of Soviet Planning Experiences* (La Salle, Ill.: Open Court, 1985), *Slavic Review* 46, no. 2 (summer 1987): 320; Mackenzie Wallace, *Russia* (New York: Henry Holt, 1877), 307. I am reminded of the experience of a colleague who, about to leave the university administration building, asked an administrator, "What do all these people do?" He replied, "I have no idea."

40. Alexander Yanov, *Detente after Brezhnev: The Domestic Roots of Soviet Foreign Policy* (Berkeley: Institute of International Studies, University of California, 1977), 33.

41. Sidney Ploss, comments at the National Meeting of the AAASS, 7 November 1980; Hirszowicz, *The Bureaucratic Leviathan*, 188; Ronald J. Hill, "Party–State Relations and Soviet Political Development," *British Journal of Political Science* 10 (1988): 161; John N. Hazard, personal communication, 2 August 1981; Seweryn Bialer, comments at a seminar at the Harriman Institute, Columbia University, 9 November 1988, reported in *At the Harriman Institute* 1, no. 6 (January 1989): 2.

42. Ryavec, "The Soviet Bureaucratic Elite from 1964 to 1979," 337.

43. Mandel, "What Is the Bureaucracy?" 82; Archie Brown, *The Gorbachev Factor* (Oxford: Oxford University Press, 1997), 313; B. Pugachev, "KPSS byla ne partiei, a prestupnoi gosudarstvennoi strukturoi," *Izvestiia*, 5 May 1992. Pugachev was then a member of the Constitutional Court. The verb *vmontirovat'* could also be translated as "mounted onto" or "added onto." A scholar of the East German party says that by the late 1970s a shift of power had resulted toward more state influence within the party. Also, the party oriented itself toward the state as the body that regulated the social context. See Marlies Menge, "Political Scientist Analyses Shifts in GDR Power Structure," *Die Zeit*, 6 April 1979, in *German Tribune*, 22 April 1979, 4, reviewing Gero Neugebauer, *Partei und Staatsapparat in der GDR* (Opladen: Westdeutscher Verlag, 1979).

44. Rebecca West, "St. Augustine," in *Rebecca West: A Celebration* (New York: Viking, 1977), 165.

45. Matthews, *Privilege in the Soviet Union*, 37, 40, 120, and the following pages; Ryavec, "The Soviet Bureaucratic Elite from 1964 to 1979," 339. As for medals, Soviet men wore ribbons representing them on their civilian suits. Once, in a Moscow barbershop, I went ahead of a man who had two rows of ribbons. Two rows meant nothing; it simply did not count. On another occasion I took the time to watch a touching scene, in Moscow's main military department store, of old men happily having their ribbons redone.

46. Darrell P. Hammer, *The USSR: The Politics of Oligarchy*, 2d ed. (Boulder: Westview Press, 1986), 236–38.

47. T. H. Rigby, "Crypto-politics," *Survey*, no. 50 (January 1964): 183.

48. Raymond Aron, "Social Structure and Ruling Class," *British Journal of Sociology* 1 (pt. 2), no. 2 (1950): 131, quoted in David Lane, *The End of Inequality? Stratification under State Socialism* (Harmondsworth, England: Penguin Books, 1971), 51.

49. Michel Tatu, *Power in the Kremlin* (New York: Viking, 1970), 431; *Pravda*, 25 August 1971, 2, in *Current Digest of the Soviet Press* 23, no. 34 (21 September 1971): 1.

50. Robert Darst, "Unitary and Conflictual Images in the Study of Soviet Foreign Policy," in *Analyzing the Gorbachev Era* (Berkeley and Stanford: Berkeley–Stanford Program in Soviet Studies, 1989), 145.

51. Jerry F. Hough, *The Soviet Prefects* (Cambridge: Harvard University Press, 1969), 69, 79, 102. See also Jerry F. Hough and Merle Fainsod, *How the Soviet Union Is Governed* (Cambridge: Harvard University Press, 1979), 387–88, 447.

52. Kimitaka Matsuzato, lecture at the Kennan Institute for Advanced Russian Studies, Washington, D.C., 19 March 1996. Matsuzato was speaking of the Soviet period.

53. Paul R. Gregory, *Restructuring the Soviet Economic Bureaucracy* (Cambridge: Cambridge University Press, 1990), 131, 134.

54. Ryavec, "The Soviet Bureaucratic Elite from 1964 to 1979," 339.

55. Volker Jacobs, "Social Portrait of Bundestag Reveals Little Change," *Saarbrucker Zeitung*, 18 August 1981, trans. in *German Tribune*, 30 August 1981; Franz Schurmann, "Some Propositions on the Political Economy of the Socialist Countries," paper prepared for the Conference on Soviet and Chinese Communism, Lake Tahoe, 13–17 June 1965, 42; Fred W. Riggs, "Bureaucratic Politics in Comparative Perspective," paper prepared for the Annual Meeting of the American Political Science Association, Washington, D.C., 2–7 September 1968, 14.

56. See, for example, William Hyland and Richard W. Shryock, *The Fall of Khrushchev* (New York: Funk and Wagnalls, 1968); and the remarks years later of a Soviet economist, Soltan Dzarov, cited in *RL 55/88*, 5 February 1988, 8.

57. Jiri Valenta, "Bureaucrat in the Kremlin," *Problems of Communism* 24, no. 5 (September–October 1975): 71, 73. Memorable in this vein is Zbigniew Brzezinski, "Victory of the Clerks," *The New Republic*, 14 November 1964, 15–18. Three major events occurred on the same date in October 1964: Khrushchev's ouster, the election of a Labour government in the United Kingdom, and the detonation of China's first atomic bomb. The Labour victory probably would not have occurred if either of the other two events had taken place a day or more earlier.

58. Peter Taylor, "Romanov's Promotion: A Boost for Andropov?" *RL 288/83*, 29 July 1983, 5; Dusko Doder, "Kremlin Politics," *Washington Post Weekly Edition*, 26 August 1985, 7.

59. I have a memo on "space requirements," especially regarding division conference rooms, U.S. Arms Control and Disarmament Agency, 23 June 1995; see also Frank von Hippel, "Big Government and Little Analysts," *Physics Today*, June 1995, 51—this article produced a noticeable amount of "huffiness" among U.S. government bureaucrats, particularly the use of the sentence, "They must have been smart once too" regarding "some career bureaucrats." Von Hippel served in the White House Office of Science and Technology Policy from 1993 through 1994.

60. On the Carter administration, see, for example, Robert Pear, "The Policy Wars," *New York Times*, 28 July 1987; on the Reagan administration, see, for example, "Schultz Angrily Tells Inquiry That He Was Repeatedly Misled by Casey and Others over Iran," *New York Times*, 24 July 1987, A1; for an academic discussion of interagency conflict seen as an aspect of the politics of allocation, see Matthew Holden, "'Imperialism' in Bureaucracy," *American Political Science Review*, December 1966, 943–51.

61. See, for example, the section "Ministries versus Ministries," in Karl W. Ryavec, *Implementation of Soviet Economic Reforms* (New York: Praeger, 1975), 85–86.

62. A U.S. government source, 1995. On the arms trade disputes see, for example, "Arms Sale Hopes Bring Ministries into Conflict," *Current Digest of the Soviet Press* 44, no. 28 (1992): 8–11; and "Ministries Seen Differing on Caspian Oil Issue," *Segodnia* (Moscow), 19 July 1995, 2, in *FBIS-SOV-95-140*, 21 July 1995, 11–12.

63. Sergei Rogov, lecture at the Foreign Policy Research Institute, Philadelphia, 10 March 1997, from *Johnson's Russia List*, 11 March 1997. He spoke of the Russian political system as "an authoritarian system without authority."

64. Marcia A. Weigle, review of Neil Robinson, ed., *Institutions and Political Change in Russia* (New York: St. Martin's Press, 2000), *Slavic Review* 60, no. 1 (spring 2001): 190.

65. Steven Erlanger, "Kremlin's Technocrat," *New York Times*, 15 December 1992; a U.S. government source, 1996; *New York Times*, 3 December 1993 and 8 December 1993, A3 (on Duma candidates); Vladimir Razuvayev, article in *Nezavisimaia gazeta*, 10 January 1997, 2, trans. in *Johnson's Russia List*, 10 January 1997; *OMRI* report, 15 February 1995.

66. Some pertinent sources are *New York Times*, 23 November 1994 and 5 May 1995; an article in *Moskovskie novosti*, no. 61 (4–11 December 1994): 14, trans. in *Current Digest of the Soviet Press* 46, no. 48 (28 December 1994): 17; Michael R. Gordon, "Russia Names Atomic Chief, and the U.S. Is a Little Wary," *New York Times*, 5 March 1998, A12; and Steven L. Taylor, *Directory of Nuclear Related Enterprises and Companies of the Former Soviet Union* (Livermore, Calif.: Lawrence Livermore National Laboratory, November 1995).

67. An extreme example is the comment made by Iran's security chief about the killing of four dissidents by rogue agents in 1998. The killings were "insignificant mistakes," he asserted in 2001, not mentioning the eighty or so killings of dissidents by the security service during the 1990s. See "Iran Plays Down Killings in 1998," *New York Times*, 23 July 2001, A2.

68. *Mark Russell Show*, public TV, 15 September 1993.

69. David E. Sanger, "A U.S. Agency, Once Powerful, Is Dead at 108," *New York Times*, 1 January 1996, A1.

70. Interviews in the U.S. Department of State, July 1999.

71. "Six Federal Programs That Really Work," *Washington Post Parade Magazine*, 22 October 1995, 18. One such program was the "reinvention" of the Bureau of Water Reclamation in the Department of the Interior. At the time there was an Innovations in American Government Program at the JFK School of Government in Cambridge, Mass.

72. For example, Howard W. Oden, *Transforming the Organization* (Westport, Conn.: Quorum Books, 1999); and Gerald R. Pieters and Doyle W. Young, *The Ever-changing Organization* (Boca Raton, Fla.: St. Lucie Press, 1999).

73. Steven Lohr and James Bennet, "Lessons in Rebounds from G.M. and I.B.M.," *New York Times*, 24 October 1994, D1, D4; Glenn Collins, "Tough Leader Wields the Ax at Scott," *New York Times*, 15 August 1994, D1, D8.

74. John LeDonne, remarks at the Russian Research Center, Harvard University, 12 March 1986.

75. See, for example, Zenovia Sochor, "Soviet Taylorism Revisited," *Soviet Studies* 33, no. 2 (April 1981): 246–64; and Yevsei Liberman, "The Soviet Economic Reform," *Foreign Affairs*, October 1967, 53–62.

76. For example, in 1986 a "sweeping reorganization" of the construction industry was announced, and in 1987 a reform of the health system and the allowance of bankruptcy were declared. See *RL 313/86*, 15 August 1986, 8; *RL 482/87*, 27 November 1987, 12; and *RL 139/87*, 10 April 1987, 3. See also Susan J. Linz and William Moskoff, eds., *Reorganization and Reform in the Soviet Economy* (Armonk, N.Y.: M. E. Sharpe, 1988); and Barbara Ann Chotiner, *The 1982 Reorganization of Agricultural Administration in the Soviet Union*, Carl Beck Paper, no. 907 (Pittsburgh: University of Pittsburgh Center for Russian and East European Studies, 1992).

77. Matthews, *Privilege in the Soviet Union*, 146–47.

78. Mark R. Beissinger, "Soviet Factory Directors Go to Business School," *Wall Street Journal*, 2 November 1981, 26. A book from the early 1990s on the topic is Sheila M. Puffer, ed., *The Russian Management Revolution: Preparing Managers for the Market Economy* (Armonk, N.Y.: M. E. Sharpe, 1992).

79. Alec Nove, "The Economics of Feasible Socialism," lecture at the Russian Research Center, Harvard University, 16 April 1986. Although I did not put quotation marks around these words in my notes, I believe that they are the exact words Nove used.

80. William J. Conyngham, *The Modernization of Soviet Industrial Management: Socioeconomic Development and the Search for Viability* (Cambridge: Cambridge University Press, 1982), 266.

81. Liberman, "The Soviet Economic Reform," 62.

82. Keith Bush, "The Reforms: A Balance Sheet," *Problems of Communism* 16, no. 4 (July–August 1967): 41. Bush points out how limited the Kosygin or Liberman reforms were ("The Reforms," 31).

83. Astrid von Borcke, *Vor Reformen in Sowjetsystem?* (Koln: Bundesinstitut fur Ostwissenschaftliche und Internationale Studien, 1980), 17–18 (this is labeled 42-1980 of December 1980).

84. Archie Brown, "Change in the Soviet Union," *Foreign Affairs* 64, no. 5 (summer 1986): 1056–57.

85. Andrei Pokrovsky, "The Problems and Pitfalls of Soviet Economic Reforms," a course paper, 16 December 1990, 7, 11. Pokrovsky is an immigrant from Russia. He also notes that Gorbachev's reforms lacked a comprehensive approach and that they were intended to increase Soviet state power, not the individual well-being of the citizens, thereby denying the reforms a chance for popular legitimacy.

86. Zbigniew Brzezinski, quoted in *New York Times*, 22 April 1981.

87. John Stuart Mill, quoted in Marshall I. Goldman, "Even the Czar Faced Anchor-Draggers," *New York Times*, 26 June 1987, A35.

88. Anders Aslund, "Moscow's New Power Center," *New York Times*, 19 April 1991, A27; Abraham Brumberg, "Moscow: The Struggle for Reform," *New York Review of Books*, 30 March 1989, 37, quoting *Moscow News*, no. 1 (1989); "Moscow's Reforms: Turning Radical" (editorial), *New York Times*, 4 April 1990, probably referring to Ed A. Hewitt, "Prognosis for Soviet Economy Is Grave, but Improving," *New York Times*, 25 March 1990, E3.

89. See, for example, Gretchen Casper, *Fragile Democracies: Legacies of Authoritarian Rule* (Pittsburgh: University of Pittsburgh Press, 1995). Although this book deals with the Philippines and Latin America, some of its findings may be generally true, certainly for a dictatorial system like that of the USSR, so much more strict and isolated than most others.

90. Anatoly A. Sobchak, quoted in Michael Wines, "What Putin Portends for Russia," *New York Times*, 1 January 2000, 6.

91. For a vivid account of Yeltsin's bout with the Moscow party bosses, see the report on an interview given by Mikhail Poltoranin, an associate of Yeltsin at the time, in Kevin Devlin, "Soviet Journalist Describes El'tsin's Struggle against Party 'Mafia,'" *RL 206/88*, 20 May 1988.

92. "Boris Yeltsin at Columbia," transcript of a lecture at Columbia University, 11 September 1989, 8–9; Devlin, "Soviet Journalist Describes El'tsin's Struggle against Party 'Mafia,'" 2–4. Although Yeltsin used the term *apparatus* for his opposition, the term includes government officials and ministers ("Boris Yeltsin at Columbia," 6).

93. Boris Yeltsin, *The Struggle for Russia*, trans. Catherine A. Fitzpatrick (New York: Times Books [Random House], 1994), 19, 56 (this book was edited by Peter Osnos, once of the *Washington Post* and later the publisher of Public Affairs Press).

94. John Morrison, *Boris Yeltsin: From Bolshevik to Democrat* (New York: Dutton, 1991), 53, 84, 91.

95. Vladimir Polozhentsev, "Yeltsin Addresses Academy of Civil Service," Moscow Russian Public Television, 6 September 1995, in *FBIS-SOV-95-173*, 7 September 1995, 28.

96. Boris Yeltsin, "State of the Union Speech," *Rossiiskaia gazeta*, 18 February 1998, from *Johnson's Russia List*, 19 February 1998.

97. Steven Erlanger, "Yeltsin Blames Army for Failures," *New York Times*, 17 February 1995, A12; "Yeltsin Attacks Civil Servants, Urges Reforms," *Informatsiono-Telgrafnoe Agentsvo Rossii-Telegrafnoe Agentsvo Sovetskogo Soiuza* (Moscow), 6 September 1995, in *FBIS-SOV-95-172*, 6 September 1995; Alessandra Stanley, "Yeltsin Prods Government on Economy," *New York Times*, 11 June 1994, 3; Oleg Shchedrov, "Yeltsin Says Back on Form, Looks for Allies," Reuters, 20 April 1999, from *Johnson's Russia List*, 20 April 1999; *RFE/RL*, 24 April 1997.

98. Boris G. Fyodorov, quoted in Steven Erlanger, "Russia Finance Chief Tells of Enemies Within," *New York Times*, 4 June 1993, A6; Eugene Huskey, *Presidential Power in Russia* (Armonk, N.Y.: M. E. Sharpe, 1999), 103. One is reminded of the cynical view of American members of Congress—the district comes above all else, even party, ideology, or common sense.

99. M. Steven Fish, "The Executive Deception: Superpresidentialism and the Degradation of Russian Politics," in *Building the Russian State: Institutional Crisis*

and the Quest for Democratic Governance, ed. Valerie Sperling (Boulder: Westview, 2000), 179, 188 (the concept is covered over 178–91).

100. Peter Reddaway and Dmitri Glinski, *The Tragedy of Russia's Reforms: Market Bolshevism against Democracy* (Washington, D.C.: U.S. Institute of Peace Press, 2001), 442; "Yeltsin Again Reorganizes Staff," *U.S. FBIS Trends*, 23 August 1995, 1.

101. Serge Schmemann, "Yeltsin Abandons His Principal Aide to Placate Rivals," *New York Times*, 15 December 1992, A1.

102. Alexander Buzgalin, "Russia Is Our Home," Jamestown Foundation *Prizm* 4, no. 1 (9 January 1998), from *Johnson's Russia List*, 11 January 1998. Buzgalin adds that the wide diversity of bureaucrats in the group created a great deal of disagreement and even confrontation within it.

103. Gennadi Barbulis, quoted in Michael Specter, "Yeltsin's Kremlin: A Mystery Wrapped in a Riddle," *New York Times*, 18 July 1996, A3.

104. Andrei Piontkowsky, quoted in Jonas Bernstein, "Yeltsin to Crack Whip on Bureaucrats," *St. Petersburg Times*, 30 December–5 January 1997, from *Johnson's Russia List*, 2 January 1997; interview with Anatolii Sobchak, *Komsomol'skaia pravda*, 3 March 1992, in *RFE/RL Research Report* 1, no. 11 (13 March 1992): 78; interview with Gennadii Barbulis, *Rossiiskie vesti*, 7 September 1993, in *RFE/RL News Briefs* 2, no. 37 (6–10 September 1993): 5; *Moskovskie novosti*, no. 54 (1995), in Jamestown Foundation *Monitor* 1, no. 26 (17 August 1995): 2.

105. "Yeltsin Sacks Senior Officials," *OMRI*, 22 February 1996; Mikhail Berger, "Yeltsin Approves Control by Chubais' Iron Hand," *St. Petersburg Times*, 18–24 November 1996, from *Johnson's Russia List*, November 1996; David Filipov, "Kremlin Appears Resistant to Yeltsin's Brand of Cleaning," *Boston Globe*, 22 July 1997, from *Johnson's Russia List*, 22 July 1997; "Yeltsin Reshuffles Personnel at FSB," *RFE/RL*, 6 April 1999.

106. Interview with Foreign Minister Kozyrev, *Izvestiia*, 30 June 1992, 3, in *RFE/RL* 1, no. 46 (20 November 1992): 27; "Bureaucrats Sap Energy from Western Assistance Programs," *Surviving Together*, autumn 1994, 37–38; Steve Liesman, "Yeltsin Moves to Cut Business Taxes," *New York Times*, 26 May 1994, D7.

107. Reddaway and Glinski, *The Tragedy of Russia's Reforms*, 628.

108. For example, in Robert C. Tucker's conclusion in a book on post-Soviet leadership, he mentions seven "younger leaders" who might succeed Yeltsin but does not cite Putin, who at that time was completely out of the national picture. See Timothy J. Colton and Robert C. Tucker, *Patterns in Post-Soviet Leadership* (Boulder: Westview Press, 1995). Accordingly, Putin as president was almost a "bolt out of the blue."

109. Yeltsin's thinking here is drawn from his memoir, *Midnight Diaries* (New York: Public Affairs Press, 2000). See Patrick E. Tyler, "How Yeltsin Nearly Scuttled Democracy in Russia," *New York Times*, 8 October 2000, 4.

110. See, for example, Reddaway and Glinski, *The Tragedy of Russia's Reforms*, 610–19.

111. Lilia Shevtsova, quoted in *New York Times*, 8 May 2000, A3.

112. An article in *Nezavisimaia gazeta*, 22 February 2001, quoted in *RFE/RL*, 23 February 2001; Laurent Murawiec, "Putin's Precursors," *The National Interest*, summer 2000, 52.

113. *Repubblica* (Rome), 11 July 2001, quoted in *RFE/RL*, 12 July 2001.

114. Sergei Chugayev, "Conducting the State," *Moscow Times*, 28 February 2001, from *Johnson's Russia List*, 27 February 2001.

115. Alexander Tarasov, "Who Is Behind Putin," *Novaia gazeta*, no. 38 (2000), from *Johnson's Russia List*, 15 August 2000. Tarasov, a sociologist, notes, "This class is split into several warring clans."

116. Michael McFaul, "Kremlin Man Fails the Test," *Sunday Times* (U.K.), 27 August 2000, from *Johnson's Russia List*, 27 August 2000; Masha Gessen, "Comrade Putin, Taken at His Word," *New York Times*, 12 August 2000, A27.

117. *RFE/RL*, 12 July 2001.

118. The International Institute for Strategic Studies issued such a forecast in May 2000. See a Reuters report, 4 May 2000, in *RFE/RL*, 4 May 2000.

119. Peggy Noonan, "A Chat in the Oval Office," *Wall Street Journal*, 25 June 2001.

120. Leonid Radzikhovsky, "Why There Is No Opposition to Putin," RIA Novosti, *Segodnia*, 4 August 2000, from *Johnson's Russia List*, 4 August 2000; Yuri Levada, "The Year of 'Symbolic Order,'" *Russia on Russia*, no. 5 (June 2001): 6.

121. Oleg Shchedrov, "Central Power in Russia's Genes, Putin Says," Reuters (Moscow), 13 March 2000, from *Johnson's Russia List*, 13 March 2000.

122. Reuters (Moscow), 28 March 2001, from *Johnson's Russia List*, 28 March 2001.

123. *Interfax* report, in *RFE/RL*, 5 February 2001.

124. Interview with Vladimir Putin, "Putin Says No Threat of Police State," RIA Novosti, *Izvestiia*, 14 July 2000, from *Johnson's Russia List*, 16 July 2000. This is a lengthy statement of Putin's responses to a variety of questions (fifteen pages).

125. Putin, "Putin Says No Threat of Police State."

126. Marshall I. Goldman, "Recent History Suggests Putin Has Not Shaken His Totalitarian Roots," *Boston Globe*, 28 June 2000, A15; Putin's inaugural address, 7 May 2000, trans. Reuters and *BBC Monitoring*, in *New York Times*, 8 May 2000, A3; Putin's first national address, *Agence France Presse*, 8 July 2000, from *Johnson's Russia List*, 9 July 2000; Ana Uzelac, "President Putin Prepares Cabinet Revamp," *Moscow Times*, 2 April 2001, from *Johnson's Russia List*, 2 April 2001. Putin served in the KGB for fifteen years, then as an assistant to the first post-Soviet mayor of St. Petersburg, and then, under Yeltsin, as director of the KGB's main successor agency, the FSB, before becoming prime minister and then acting president.

127. I have based this judgment on my reading of Vladimir Putin, *First Person: An Astonishingly Frank Self-Portrait by Russia's President Vladimir Putin*, trans. Catherine A. Fitzpatrick (New York: Public Affairs, 2000), a book of interviews.

Conclusion

[One goal of legislation should be] transforming our country from a Russia of bureaucrats to a Russia of citizens.

—Ivan Rybkin, chair of the Russian Duma, 1995

Everything is possible in Russia, except reform.

—attributed to Oscar Wilde

"You know what, let's go to Russia," says Maika ("T-shirt" or "Teesh") to her mother, who is from Russia.

"Yes, we'll go, definitely, only let's wait for them to get sorted out a bit first."

"Get what sorted?"

"You know, wait for things to settle down a bit, whatever."

"But Alik said if things ever settled down it wouldn't be the same country. . . ."

"Don't worry, things will never really settle down there. . . ."

—Ludmila Ulitskaya, *The Funeral Party*

The most fundamental point of this book is that Russia's state bureaucracy remains both very important for Russia and a serious problem for Russia's citizens and its democratization. Russia cannot be a democracy in the fullest sense unless that bureaucracy changes significantly. This book attempts several tasks: first, making a case for the political and systemic importance of the state bureaucracy in Russia across three political systems, the tsarist or imperial, the Soviet (which

saw three or four significant variations of the system during its existence), and the post-Soviet.[1] In a sense, time has been held constant, no
doubt a very "un-American" act. Americans make too much of tempo-
ral and generational "differences." Here I have shown that in Russia
time has not done very much in some senses, for example, to the central importance and power of the state bureaucracy or to its predilections. This, for a long time, has been the Russian way of things, the Russian normality. Time changes things, if it does at all, at very different
speeds in different cultures.

Second, many statements and facts about the Russian state bureaucracy
from "diverse sources" have been brought together systematically under
various headings for the first time. This gathering of facts and statements
shows that the topic has a "pedigree" of some age and size and, in effect,
many advocates or boosters. If large numbers of people say that something has importance, then it does—certainly in politics, where what is
true is to some degree what people say is true. Of course, Russians necessarily see bureaucracy as much more significant than do Americans, who
live not only in a different country but in a different context across the
board.[2] What is called "the state," of which the bureaucracy is a central
part, exists on a grand scale in Russia, and Russians know it does and often lament or curse this fact, but the concept of the state is still rather
vague, and rarely used, in the American context.[3]

Third, a case has been made for the importance and significance of the
state bureaucracy in Russia's past, present, and future, thereby giving us
a more realistic and better grounded sense of Russia's politics and government. In short, the place and power of bureaucracy in Russia are not
going to go away, for a variety of reasons. At best bureaucracy might be
transformed into a body or institution that gibes better with democracy,
and supports it more, than the Russian bureaucracy of history and the
present does. This, of course, would be, if begun, a labor of decades—and
perhaps of Hercules as well—and would require not just change or reform but transformation, something difficult to imagine for Russia: "The
more things change. . . ." Yes, globalization is indeed taking place. However, the result will probably not be uniformity. Each country will still be
unique, though it will have more similarities with other countries.

Fourth, some experience of American bureaucracy has been brought to
this endeavor. I have been a bureaucrat two or three times during my life,
as an officer of the U.S. Navy, as a U.S. government functionary, and as a
minor bureaucrat in an American state university. I have seen some of
what is often decried in Russian bureaucracy in the United States as well.
This shows that some Russian bureaucratic behavior is not "Russian" but
just extreme bureaucratic normality or possibility ("bureaucratism" or
"bureaupathology"). The frequent citation of American and other non-

Russian bureaucratic experience above shows us to what extent non-Russian bureaucratic patterns and behavior apply to the Russian.

ISSUES

The survival of Russia, up in the air for a time, now seems assured, though it will probably survive as a country of less population, a pattern that is the present European norm. Look at Germany, for example. But then again, one out of every seven people in the world lives in a country other than the one in which he or she was born. There is plenty of room in Russia for newcomers. They may well come. At a conference in Washington, after I mentioned how much unused land there is in Russia, I was invited to the Chinese embassy for a chat on the topic. Still, this survival will find Russia walking "a thin line between authoritarianism and democracy" until a new system of politics and rule is consolidated.[4] And Russian survival will continue to see threats and pressure, both real and imagined.

Russia is stuck in a nineteenth-century realist calculus without the ability to influence outcomes. It feels threatened by American activity in Europe, and its leaders can for the moment employ only rhetoric to make their desires known. It is fractured internally and currently lacks the ability to control events even within its own borders.[5]

Yet, with the number of nuclear weapons Russia possesses, its rhetoric has a certain importance. Witness the need for President George W. Bush to meet with Russia's President Putin twice in the first half of 2001. Ironically, Bush, whose positions are opposed by most American allies, was actually helped, at least on the surface, by Russia's Putin.

In any case, Russia has been in difficult, even desperate, straits several times in its history and always rebounded in national power (if not in the power of its inhabitants as individuals). Russia has been a political entity for 600 or more years, but we are now still only a decade into the post-communist era. It was terribly weak after World War II, but it recovered to challenge the United States and Western Europe in a "fierce arms race." President Nazarbayev of Kazakhstan reminds us: "Despite the post-Soviet squalor, it would be wrong to count Russia out."[6] As the historian Hosking correctly points out, Russia is "durable." This inner Eurasian "state commanded a zone so extensive, so strategically placed, and so abundantly endowed with resources that its rulers and subjects could survive almost indefinitely." At times it overreached and then imploded: "In that respect the period since 1989 is not unprecedented."[7] True, "in its administrative structures it has been an Asian empire, building upon or adapting the practices of China and the ancient steppe empires" with "a cumbersome official class for administration and the mobilization of re-sources" operating through a "network of interlocking patron–client rela-tionships."[8] Much written in this book tells the same tale in detail, from imperial times to Putin's time.

Today Russia faces a host of problems in her attempt to resurrect her-self. The Central Intelligence Agency has grouped these problems under the headings demography, health, intellectual capital, and physical infra-structure. But the bureaucratic or organizational factor is unavoidably mentioned more than once, for example, the "high resistance" of certain government agencies to reform.[9]

In chapter 2 I deal with the issue of the present Russian "weak state." Solving this problem is discussed there in a somewhat dialectical manner. Although once it seemed necessary to make the Russian state smaller, to-day it is also necessary to strengthen and improve it and to make it one that supports democracy and free enterprise, and efficiently so, without grating against people's sensibilities or reducing their rights. And when all this is done, the Russian state will need to be a very different one, and the bureaucracy will still have to be strong but use its strength sparingly and in a focused and democratic manner. More time is required. A deputy prime minister said in 2001, "In ten years . . . we have been unable to cre-ate an effective state which is capable of ensuring stable economic growth." This admission suggests that some at the top know "what is to be done." But, of course, there is no easy formula for curing the ills of a weak or semifailed state and making it one that supports the rule of law, with an honest civil service exhibiting real energy in a constructive manner.[10]

Russia's needs are many. Most of them require a revivified and much improved state administration. Some of the requirements for this could be labeled "structural-institutional." Others connected with, and just as im-portant for, better administration could be categorized as "psychological-cultural." The former are easier and quicker to bring about than the latter. A predictable legal, fiscal, and administrative environment has been men-tioned by many. Also required are "a new system of social security [one not based just on place of employment], an effective retirement system, a wel-fare program, a jobs training program . . . [and] a system of unemployment compensation."[11] Only such a social safety net would give the Russian la-bor market the necessary modern flexibility it needs. The ability to collect taxes is crucial. A state cannot run on politics and words alone.

Among the structural-institutional needs pertinent to Russian adminis-tration are a smaller, higher quality, and better trained bureaucratic staff; a rational system of tax collection and a central bank that manages debt and money to the benefit of the state and the economy; and a whole series of changes in the way the bureaucracy operates: transparency of activity, accessibility, accountability, avoidance of conflict of interest, the existence of independent monitors, and, of course, the maintenance of the rights of individuals.[12] Perhaps an analogy of what needs to be done structurally is to imagine the needs of a family that, over the generations, has gone from living in a log cabin to living in a castle, but a castle with Intercontinental Ballistic Missile silos in the keep and computers in the west wing but still drafty and without hot water and other modern amenities. To live well today the castle has to be completely rebuilt or even torn down and a new type of structure erected in its place.

More difficult to create are the psychocultural requirements of improved Russian administration. As Ehrmann says about the limits of constitutional changes in France, "Institutional changes will remain fragile . . . as long as they are not backed by a change in mentality," a word that has powerful resonance in today's Russia.[13] It is clear that what has been a major problem besetting Russian government has been a mind-set or attitude among the bureaucrats encouraging them to act as if they themselves, even individually, constitute the state. Historically, Russian rulers have engaged in development, and, after disasters, putting Russia "back on track," through the use of the state administration. Putin today is attempting the same thing. But the inner nature of the bureaucrats' mentality needs to be different this time because of the demands of the present sense of European and international "normalcy." For "without civilized institutions, human nature is naked and raw."[14] One requirement of a transformed Russian administration is the infusion into it of people who do not think of themselves as "little gods." One serious problem of Russia, I believe, is that too many people have gone into the military and into science and engineering. There have been fewer "good people" to help run things. And too many people have been allowed into administration. It has been much larger than needed. As a senior Russian researcher puts it, "We have an excessively large but incompetent army of bureaucrats, a considerable part of whom are incapable of doing their work."[15] And just possibly, in terms of bureaucratic attitudes, Russia has suffered from some problem inherent in its families, upbringing, or education. But I know no way to ascertain the truth of the matter. There has long been a feeling, even in Russia, that there are too many engineers and that engineering education is much too narrow. (Once I had dinner, by chance, with a young Russian who was studying to be an engineer who designed locomotives—and nothing else.) Only if the sorts of Russians who have produced Russia's magnificent "high culture" go into politics and administration is there a chance that the problems of Russian bureaucracy will be worked out well. Possibly, the current emphasis on business may draw away from administration a lot of people who do not belong there. (In France at present applications to the prestigious Ecole nationale d'administration are noticeably down. There are good opportunities elsewhere.)[16]

But government service, to attract good people, must offer challenging and rewarding work and the opportunity for personal growth in a decent and predictable environment in which bureaucrats are treated well by their superiors. This means changing the work environment in a big way.[17] As Boris Fedorov, one of the big names in Russian administration today, puts it, since most of the "young and energetic reformers were kicked out" of government during the government reshuffle of 1994–96, young people have experienced a "loss of confidence in the authorities." He continues, "Clearly, many talented and strong people were left outside government. Why are they not involved in government? . . . They cannot remain silent when their bosses are making mistakes, they are too independent, and they do not want to serve numerous 'influence groups.'"[18] In other words, what Russian government and its constituent parts need is an effective participatory citizenship, a benefit that will not be forthcoming without major changes. Lewin has emphasized that real change in Russia and the solution of its current crisis require a "practicing democracy" with new and vital societal institutions, for example, an effective opposition, powerful trade unions, organized political parties, and churches. Also required, he says, is a new political culture, that necessary new "mentality" that I have mentioned, whereby ordinary citizens will be able to understand what government does, to choose and support political leaders, and to monitor their behavior: "This assumes that citizens have a degree of confidence in the system, that voters and their elected representatives basically agree on a code of ethics, and that governors and governed share a set of principles and ideals."[19]

This is, yes, all necessary, but it is a tall order for now. Maybe it can be brought about in two or three decades. And, of course, the rule of law is necessary. Summers has called this the "most important" requirement for Russian transformation, "so there can be reliance on secure property rights, confidence in contract enforcement and the general set of measures to go with an effective commercial system."[20] Many of these changes require a functioning and strong democracy in Russia, also something that will be a bit of time yet in arriving. Technique and gimmickry alone will not do the trick, as Roy Medvedev pointed out years ago.[21]

But to do all this correctly requires that the result is still recognized and accepted broadly within Russia as "Russian." A real, native, natural Russia has to arise to provide a comfortable base for any new Russian governmental and bureaucratic arrangement and any real Russian civil society. We have no means or "methodology" for determining how close to, or how far from, this sociocultural normalcy we are at this "point in time." A truly Russian future has to be created at the same time as a better future is being built. Voices in Russia call out for this. They are not all to be criticized for being "right wing" or "fascistic." For example, as one such Russian voice states, "Only by re-establishing its own natural identity—by restoring itself as a unique civilization that has something of Europe, something of Asia, and much more that is entirely its own—can Russia assume its rightful place in the global community." We shall probably wonder for some time still "in what shape and form the eternal spirit of Russia . . . [will] be reborn."[22]

NOTES

1. These variations could be labeled Leninist, Stalinist, Khrushchevite, and Brezhnevite. Whether Gorbachev actually produced a new variation on the Soviet theme, broke away from it, or just ran down the Brezhnevite variation is open to debate.

2. I have fond memories of Isaac Deutscher saying more than once at Columbia University during the 1960s in response to questions, "I cannot answer that question in this context."

3. It is common in Russia to speak of "the Russian state," but the usage "the American state" is rare and "fringy" and possibly has a leftist connotation. Although American right-wingers lambaste "government" and do not use the term *state*, that is probably what they mean.

4. Marcia A. Weigle, book review, *Slavic Review* 60, no. 1 (spring 2001): 190. Weigle makes the good point that until "informal networks cease to undermine institutional integrity" there will be no consolidation of Russian institutions.

5. Stephen Hadley, "Defining the Path to a Peaceful, Undivided and Democratic Europe," *U.S. Institute of Peace Special Report*, 20 June 2000, 2. In August 2001 Hadley was the deputy assistant to the president on national security affairs.

6. President Nursultan A. Nazarbayev, quoted in Judith Miller, "Kazakhs Take Strong Issue with Bush's Missile Project," *New York Times*, 21 May 2001, A6. See also Steven Merritt Miner, a review of two books on Russia, *New York Times Book Review*, 8 July 2001, 15.

7. From chap. 1 in Geoffrey Hosking, *Russia and the Russians: A History* (Cambridge: Harvard University Press, Belknap Press, 2001), from *Johnson's Russia List*, 9 July 2001.

8. Hosking, *Russia and the Russians*, chap. 1.

9. U.S. CIA, "Russia's Physical and Social Infrastructure: Implications for Future Development," December 2000, from *Johnson's Russia List*, 11 May 2001 (six pages). This study specifically lists problems with the Ministries of Health and Education and the Academy of Sciences.

10. Russian Deputy Prime Minister Aleksey Kudrin, speaking at the seminar "The Role of the State in the 21st Century," the World Economic Forum, at Davos, Switzerland, 27 January 2001, reported by *Informatsiono-Telgrafnoe Agentsvo Rossii–Telegrafnoe Agentsvo Sovetskogo Soiuza*, from *Johnson's Russia List*, 28 January 2001; the sentence that follows was suggested by Thomas L. Friedman, "Code Red," *New York Times*, 30 March 2001, A23.

11. Michael McFaul, "Why Russia's Politics Matter," *Foreign Affairs*, January–February 1995, 95.

12. From a list of "historically important" state institutions given in David Calleo, book review, *New York Times Magazine*, 25 March 2001, 9; and a list of administrative requirements for democratic government given in Elaine Ullman, Institute for Training and Development (Amherst, Mass.), lecture at Smith College, 26 April 2001. All of these have been lacking in Russian administration.

13. Henry W. Ehrmann, *Politics in France*, 4th ed. (Boston: Little, Brown and Co., 1983), 341. This may have been the leading English-language textbook on French politics in its time.

14. Victor Brombert, book review, *New York Times Magazine*, 24 January 1999, 7.

15. Yuri Rozenbaum, "Bureaucratic Expansion," *Nezavisimaia gazeta*, 8 May 1997, from *Johnson's Russia List*, 12 May 1997. Rozenbaum adds that the bureaucracy operated "much quicker" in tsarist times than it does now, even though it lacked modern communications.

16. See *New York Times*, 9 July 2000, 3.

17. The U.S. civil service faces similar needs for change. See Paul C. Light, "The Empty Government Talent Pool: The New Public Service Arrives," *Brookings Review* 18, no. 1 (winter 2000): 23.

18. Boris Fedorov, "Budennovsk, Armavir, Piatigorsk—Where Next?" *Rossiiskie vesti*, 7 May 1997, from *Johnson's Russia List*, 13 May 1997.

19. Moshe Lewin, "A Country Falling Apart: The Collapse of the Russian State," *Le Monde Diplomatique*, November 1998, from *Johnson's Russia List*, 11 November 1998. A Russian article on the connection between culture and bureaucracy is A. I. Demidov, "Political Culture as a Means of Struggle against Bureaucracy," *Sovetskoe gosudarstvo i pravo*, no. 7 (1988): 32–40.

20. U.S. Secretary of the Treasury Lawrence Summers, statement at the United Nations, 5 July 2000, reported by *Reuters*, in *Johnson's Russia List*, 6 July 2000. Perhaps things have improved a bit in this regard recently. In mid-2001 the British firm BP was able to regain control over a Russian company in which it had invested half a billion dollars. See Sabrina Tavernise, "BP Prevails in Struggle for Company in Russia," *New York Times*, 2 August 2001, W1.

21. Roy Medvedev, quoted in George Breslauer, *Five Images of the Soviet Future: A Critical Review and Synthesis* (Berkeley: Institute of International Studies, University of California, 1978), 51. Medvedev said, "There is only . . . one acceptable alternative to bureaucracy, and that is genuine democratization."

22. The phrase "point in time" is Watergate-era bureaucratic language. Vladimir Krasnov, *Russia beyond Communism: A Chronicle of National Rebirth* (Boulder: Westview, 1991), 304; Janusz Glowacki, "Of Mother Russia—and a Hat," *New York Times*, 27 March 1990, A27 (Glowacki is a Polish playwright).

Selected Bibliography

Afanas'ev, Yuri. "Russian Reform Is Dead." *Foreign Affairs* 73, no. 2 (March–April 1994): 21–26.

———. "Russian Imperial Policy: Tsars—Bolsheviks—Primakov." *Perspective* (e-mail version) 9, no. 4 (March–April 1999).

Aktual'nye problemy politiki i politologii v Rossii. Moscow: RAGS, 1999.

Albats, Yevgenia. *The State within a State: The KGB and Its Hold on Russia*, trans. Catherine A. Fitzpatrick. New York: Farrar, Straus and Giroux, 1994.

Altshuler, Alan A. *The Politics of the Federal Bureaucracy.* New York: Dodd, Mead, 1968.

Anderson, Perry. *Lineages of the Absolutist State.* London: Verso, 1979.

Arbatov, Georgi. *The System: An Insider's Life in Soviet Politics.* New York: Times Books (Random House), 1992.

Armstrong, John A. "Tsarist and Soviet Elite Administrators." *Slavic Review* 31, no. 1 (March 1972): 1–28.

Bakhrakh, D. N. "Administrativnaia vlast' kak gosudarstvennoi vlasti." *Gosudarstvo i pravo*, no. 3 (March 1992): 13–20.

Banfield, Edward C. *The Moral Basis of a Backward Society.* New York: Free Press, 1958.

Baradat, Leon P. *Soviet Political Society*, 3d ed. Englewood Cliffs, N.J.: Prentice-Hall, 1992.

Barnard, Chester I. *The Functions of the Executive.* Cambridge: Harvard University Press, 1938.

Beissinger, Mark R. *Scientific Management, Socialist Discipline, and Soviet Power.* Cambridge: Harvard University Press, 1988.

Berg, Gerard Pieter van den. *De Regering Van Rusland En De Sovjet Unie.* Leiden: G. P. van den Berg, 1977.

Berliner, Joseph S. "Continuities in Management from Stalin to Gorbachev, 1988." In *Soviet Industry from Stalin to Gorbachev*, ed. Joseph S. Berliner. Ithaca: Cornell University Press, 1988.

————. *Factory and Manager in the USSR*. Cambridge: Harvard University Press, 1957.

Blau, Peter M. *The Dynamics of Bureaucracy*, 2d rev. ed. Chicago: University of Chicago Press, 1963 [1955].

Blau, Peter M., and Marshall W. Meyer. *Bureaucracy in Modern Society*. New York: Random House, 1971.

Blazyca, George. "The Politics of Economic Transformation." In *Developments in Central and East European Politics*, eds. Stephen White, Judy Batt, and Paul G. Lewis. Durham: Duke University Press, 1998.

Blondel, Jean. *Government Ministers in the Contemporary World*. Beverly Hills, Calif.: SAGE, 1985.

Boikov, Vladimir E. "The Professional Culture of the Civil Service." *Sotsiologicheskie issledovaniia*, no. 2 (1999), trans. in *Sociological Research* 39, no. 1 (January–February 2000): 13–23.

Boilard, Steve D. *Russia at the Twenty-first Century*. Fort Worth: Harcourt Brace, 1998.

Bondarenko, T. S. *Sindrom nepogreshimosti: Kak s nim borot'sia?* Moscow: Politizdat, 1989.

Bova, Russell. "Democratization and the Crisis of the Russian State." In *State Building in Russia*, ed. Gordon B. Smith. Armonk, N.Y.: M. E. Sharpe, 1999.

Brady, Rose. *Kapitalizm: Russia's Struggle to Free Its Economy*. New Haven: Yale University Press, 1999.

Brovkin, Vladimir. "Fragmentation of Authority and Privatization of the State." *Demokratizatsiya* 6, no. 3 (summer 1998): 504–17.

Brown, Archie, and Jack Gray, eds. *Political Culture and Political Change in Communist States*, 2d ed. New York: Holmes and Meier, 1979.

Brym, Robert J., and Vladimir Gimpelson. *The Size, Composition, and Dynamics of the Russian State Bureaucracy in the 1990s*, October 2002.

Brzezinski, Zbigniew K. *Between Two Ages*. New York: Viking, 1970.

————. *The Grand Failure*. New York: Scribner's, 1989.

————. *Out of Control: Global Turmoil on the Eve of the Twenty-first Century*. New York: Scribner's, 1993.

Bukovsky, Vladimir. *To Build a Castle*. New York: Viking Press, 1979.

Busza, Eva. "State Dysfunctionality, Institutional Decay and the Russian Military." In *Building the Russian State: Institutional Crisis and the Quest for Democratic Governance*, ed. Valerie Sperling. Boulder: Westview Press, 2000.

Cerny, Philip G., and Martin A. Schain, eds. *French Politics and Public Policy*. New York: Methuen, 1981.

Chodok, Symon. *The New State: Etatization of Western Societies*. Boulder: Lynne Rienner, 1989.

Clark, William A. *Crime and Punishment in Soviet Officialdom*. Armonk, N.Y.: Sharpe, 1993.

Cocks, Paul. "Rethinking the Organizational Weapon." *World Politics* 32, no. 2 (January 1980): 228–57.

Cohen, Harry. *The Demonics of Bureaucracy: Problems of Change in a Government Agency*. Ames: Iowa State University Press, 1965.

Cohen, Stephen F. "Brezhnev and the Reign of Conservatism." In *Sovieticus*. New York: Norton, 1986.

Colton, Timothy J. *Transitional Citizens: Voters and What Influences Them in the New Russia.* Cambridge: Harvard University Press, 2000.

Commission on Security and Cooperation in Europe. *Bribery and Corruption in the OSCE Region.* Washington, D.C.: U.S. Government Printing Office, 2000.

Conrad, Joseph. *Under Western Eyes.* Garden City, N.Y.: Doubleday, 1924.

Costa, Alexandra. *Stepping Down from the Star.* New York: Putnam, 1986.

Creel, H. G. "Chinese Bureaucracy and the Modern State." Paper prepared for the Annual Meeting of the American Society for Public Administration, Washington, D.C., 8–11 September 1965.

Crozier, Michel. *The Bureaucratic Phenomenon.* Chicago: University of Chicago Press, 1967.

Crummey, Robert O. *The Formation of Moscovy: 1304–1613.* New York: Longman, 1987.

Custine, Astolphe Marquis de. *Letters from Russia*, trans. and ed. Robin Buss. London: Penguin, 1991.

Deal, Terrence E., and Allen A. Kennedy. *Corporate Cultures: The Rites and Rituals of Corporate Life.* Reading, Mass.: Addison-Wesley Publishing, 1982.

Demidov, A. I. "Political Culture as a Means of Struggle against Bureaucracy." *Sovetskoe gosudarstvo i pravo*, no. 7 (July 1988): 32–40.

Djilas, Milovan. *The New Class: An Analysis of the Communist System.* New York: Praeger, 1957.

Downs, Anthony. *Inside Bureaucracy.* Boston: Little, Brown, 1967.

Drakulic, Slavenka. *How We Survived Communism and Even Laughed.* New York: Norton, 1991.

Dunham, Vera. *In Stalin's Time: Middleclass Values in Soviet Fiction.* Durham: Duke University Press, 1990.

Dunmore, Timothy. *The Stalinist Command Economy: The Soviet State Apparatus and Economic Policy, 1945–1953.* London: Macmillan, 1980.

Dyker, David A. "The Power of the Industrial Ministries." Paper presented at the Conference on Elites and Political Power in the USSR, University of Birmingham (U.K.), 1–2 July 1987.

Edeen, Alf. "The Soviet Civil Service: Its Composition and Status." In *Revolutions: Theoretical, Comparative, and Historical Studies*, 2d ed., ed. Jack Goldstone. Fort Worth: Harcourt Brace, 1994.

Ehrmann, Henry W. *Politics in France*, 4th ed. Boston: Little, Brown, 1983.

Fainsod, Merle. *How Russia Is Ruled*, rev. ed. Cambridge: Harvard University Press, 1963.

Farmer, Kenneth C. *The Soviet Administrative Elite.* New York: Praeger, 1992.

Finifter, Ada W., ed. *Political Science: The State of the Discipline.* Washington, D.C.: American Political Science Association, 1983.

Fischer, David Hackett. *Albion's Seed: Four British Folkways in North America.* New York: Oxford University Press, 1989.

Fish, M. Steven. *Democracy from Scratch: Opposition and Regime in the New Russian Revolution.* Princeton: Princeton University Press, 1995.

Fletcher, Joseph. "The Mongols: Ecological and Social Perspectives." *Harvard Journal of Asiatic Studies* 46, no. 1 (June 1986): 11–50.

Florinsky, Michael T. *Russia: A History and an Interpretation,* vol. 2. New York: Macmillan, 1960.

Gerth, H. H., and C. Wright Mills, eds. *From Max Weber: Essays in Sociology.* New York: Oxford University Press, 1946.

Glassman, Ronald M., William H. Swatos Jr., and Paul L. Rosen, eds. *Bureaucracy against Democracy and Socialism.* New York: Greenwood Press, 1987.

Goldman, Marshall I. *Lost Opportunity: Why Economic Reforms in Russia Have Not Worked.* New York: Norton, 1994.

Goldstone, Jack A., ed. *Revolutions: Theoretical, Comparative, and Historical Studies,* 2d ed. Fort Worth: Harcourt Brace, 1994.

Gore–Chernomyrdin Commission. "Waiting for the Taxman." Scope paper of the Gore–Chernomyrdin Commission, U.S. government, 11 January 1996.

Gorer, Geoffrey, and John Rickman. *The People of Great Russia.* New York: Chanticleer Press, 1950.

Graves, Desmond. *Corporate Culture—Diagnosis and Change: Auditing and Changing the Culture of Organizations.* New York: St. Martin's Press, 1986.

Gregory, Paul R. *Restructuring the Soviet Economic Bureaucracy.* Cambridge: Cambridge University Press, 1990.

Gustafson, Thane. *Capitalism Russian-Style.* Cambridge: Cambridge University Press, 1999.

Halperin, Charles J. "George Vernadsky, Eurasianism, the Mongols, and Russia." *Slavic Review* 41, no. 3 (fall 1982): 477–93.

Hamilton, Anne Wing. "Bureaucrat-Bashing in Russia and the United States." Paper presented at the Annual Convention of the American Political Science Association, Philadelphia, November 1994.

Hammer, Darrell P. *USSR: The Politics of Oligarchy,* 2d ed. Boulder: Westview Press, 1986.

Handelman, Stephen. *Comrade Criminal: Russia's New Mafiya.* New Haven: Yale University Press, 1995.

Harrison, Lawrence E., and Samuel Huntington, eds. *Culture Matters: How Values Shape Human Progress.* New York: Basic Books, 2000.

Hazard, John N. *The Soviet System of Government,* 5th ed. rev. Chicago: University of Chicago Press, 1980.

Heller, Mikhail, and Aleksandr M. Nekrich. *Utopia in Power.* New York: Summit, 1986.

Hingly, Ronald. *The Russian Mind.* New York: Scribner and Sons, 1977.

Hirszowicz, Maria. *The Bureaucratic Leviathan: A Study in the Sociology of Communism.* Oxford: Martin Robertson, 1980.

Hodges, Donald C. *The Bureaucratization of Socialism.* Amherst: University of Massachusetts Press, 1982.

Hodnett, Grey. "Soviet Succession Contingencies." *Problems of Communism* 24, no. 2 (March–April 1975): 1–21.

Hollander, Paul. "Politicized Bureaucracy: The Soviet Case." *Newsletter on Comparative Studies of Communism* 4, no. 3 (May 1971): 12–23.

———. Paper on Soviet bureaucracy at the Annual Meeting of the American Political Science Association, New York, 9 September 1996. Reprinted in *The Many Faces of Socialism.* New Brunswick, N.J.: Transaction Books, 1983.

Holmes, Stephen. "Cultural Legacies or State Collapse? Probing the Postcommunist Dilemma." In *Post-Communism: Four Perspectives*, ed. Michael Mandelbaum. New York: Council on Foreign Relations, 1996.

Hough, Jerry F. *The Soviet Prefects: The Local Party Organs in Industrial Decision-Making*. Cambridge: Harvard University Press, 1969.

Huang, Yasheng. "The Statistical Agency in China's Bureaucratic System." *Communist and Post-Communist Studies* 29, no. 1 (March 1996): 55–75.

Huskey, Eugene. "Institutional Design in Russia." Unpublished MS.

Huskey, Eugene, ed. *Executive Power and Soviet Politics*. Armonk, N.Y.: M. E. Sharpe, 1992.

———. *Presidential Power in Russia*. Armonk, N.Y.: M. E. Sharpe, 1999.

Jay, Antony. *Management and Machiavelli*. London: Hodder and Stoughton, 1967.

Johnson's Russia List, e-mail subscription service, Lanham, Md.

Kamanyshev, A. "Biurokratiia i tekhnologiia vlast'." In *Tekhnologiia vlast i upravleniia v sovremennom gosudarstve*. Moscow: Universitetskii gumantarnyi litsei, 1999.

Kaminski, Antoni Z. *An Institutional Theory of Communist Regimes*. San Francisco: ICF Press, 1992.

Kantor, Vladimir. "Our Need for Bureaucracy." *Sociological Research* 36, no. 6. (November–December 1997): 83–92. Trans. from Russian "I neobkhodimosti u nas biurokratii," *Svobodnaia mysl'*, 1996, no. 12: 79–85.

Kapuscinski, Ryszard. *The Soccer War*. New York: Vintage, 1992.

Kebschull, Harvey G. "Political Corruption: Making It the 'Significant Other' in Political Studies." *PS: Political Science and Politics* 25, no. 4 (December 1992): 705–9.

Khasbulatov, R. I. *Biurokraticheskoe gosudarstvo*. Moscow: Megapolis-Takom, 1991.

Khotin, Leonid. "The Soviet Enterprise Director" (lecture). Kennan Institute *Meeting Report*, 2 May 1988.

Khudokormov, A. G. *Ekonomicheskie korni biurokratizma*. Moscow: Ekonomika, 1998.

Kissinger, Henry. *Years of Upheaval*. Boston: Little, Brown, 1982.

Knei-Paz, Baruch. *The Social and Political Thought of Leon Trotsky*. Oxford: Clarendon Press, 1978.

Komarov, E. I. *Biurokratizm—Na sud glasnosti!* Moscow: Political Literature, 1989.

Kosiakov, V. M., and O. A. Mitroshenkov. "Biurokraticheskoe proiavleniia i metody bor'by s nimi." *Sovetskoe gosudarstvo i pravo*, no. 6 (June 1985): 20–27.

Krasnov, Mikhail. "Corruption as a Consequence of Bad Government." *Russia on Russia* 4 (March 2001).

Krasnov, Vladimir. *Russia beyond Communism: A Chronicle of National Rebirth*. Boulder: Westview, 1991.

Lane, David. *The End of Inequality? Stratification under State Socialism*. Harmondsworth, England: Penguin, 1971.

———. "Soviet Elites, Monolithic or Polyarchic?" In *Russia in Flux*, ed. David Lane. Aldershot, England: Edward Elgar, 1992.

Lane, David, and Cameron Ross. *The Non-nomenklatura: The Personnel of the Government Bureaucracy in the USSR*. Unpublished MS, circa 1992.

LaPalombara, Joseph, ed. *Bureaucracy and Political Development*. Princeton: Princeton University Press, 1963.

Lawrence, John. *A History of Russia*. New York: Mentor (New American Library), 1962.

Lawrence, Paul, and Charalambos Vlahoutsicos. *Behind the Factory Walls: Decision-Making in Soviet and American Enterprises*. Cambridge: Harvard Business School Press, 1990.

LeDonne, John. *Ruling Russia*. Princeton: Princeton University Press, 1984.

Lenin, V. I. *On the Soviet State Apparatus*. Moscow: Progress, 1977.

———. *The State*. Peking: Foreign Languages Press, 1970.

Lensen, George Alexander, ed. *Revelations of a Russian Diplomat: The Memoirs of Dmitrii I. Abrikossow*. Seattle: University of Washington Press, 1964.

Leonhard, Wolfgang. *The Kremlin since Stalin*, trans. E. Wiskemann and M. Jackson. New York: Praeger, 1962.

Lewin, Moshe. "The Collapse of the Russia State." *Le Monde Diplomatique*, March 1998. Excerpts reproduced in *Johnson's Russia List*, 11 November 1998.

Lieberthal, Kenneth, and Michel Oksenberg. *Policy Making in China*. Princeton: Princeton University Press, 1988.

Lieven, Anatol. *Chechnya: Tombstone of Russian Power*. New Haven: Yale University Press, 1998.

Lieven, Dominic. *Russia's Rulers under the Old Regime*. New Haven: Yale University Press, 1989.

Lincoln, W. Bruce. *The Great Reforms: Autocracy, Bureaucracy, and the Politics of Change in Imperial Russia*. DeKalb: Northern Illinois University Press, 1990.

———. *Nikolai Miliutin: An Enlightened Bureaucrat of the 19th Century*. Newtonville, Mass.: Oriental Research Partners, 1977.

Loewenstein, Karl. *Max Weber's Ideas in the Perspective of Our Time*. Amherst: University of Massachusetts Press, 1966.

Los, Maria. *Red-Collar Crime: Elite Crime in the USSR and Poland*, Occasional Paper 216. Washington, D.C.: Kennan Institute for Advanced Russian Studies, 1986.

Lovell, David W. *Trotsky's Analysis of Soviet Bureaucratization*. London: Croom Helm, 1985.

Lukacs, John. "The Soviet State at 65." *Foreign Affairs* 65, no. 1 (fall 1986): 21–36.

Lustig, Michael W. *Trotsky and Djilas: Critics of Communist Bureaucracy*. New York: Greenwood, 1989.

Lynch, Allen. "The Crisis of the Russian State." In *The International Spectator* (Rome), April–June 1995. Quoted in Association for the Study of Nationalities. "The Institutionalization of the Mismanagement of the Russian State." Association for the Study of Nationalities. *Analysis of Current Events* 7, no. 7 (March 1996).

Malia, Martin. *Russia under Western Eyes*. Cambridge: Harvard University Press, Belknap Press, 1999.

Mandel, Ernest. "What Is the Bureaucracy?" In *The Stalinist Legacy*, ed. Tariq Ali. Harmondsworth, England: Penguin, 1984.

Marx, Karl. "On Bureaucracy." In *Karl Marx: Selected Writings*, ed. David McClellan. London: Oxford University Press, 1997.

Matthews, Mervyn. *Privilege in the Soviet Union*. London: Allen and Unwin, 1978.

Mauro, Paolo. *Why Worry about Corruption?* Washington, D.C.: International Monetary Fund, 1997.

McAuley, Mary. *Soviet Politics: 1917–1991.* Oxford: Oxford University Press, 1992.

McDaniel, Tim. *The Agony of the Russian Idea.* Princeton: Princeton University Press, 1996.

Medish, Mark. "Building the New Russian State" (lecture). Kennedy School of Government, 9 January 1998 (text distributed by the U.S. Information Agency).

Meyer, Alfred G. *The Soviet Political System.* New York: Random House, 1965.

Millar, James R., and Sharon L. Wolchik. *The Social Legacy of Communism.* Cambridge: Cambridge University Press, 1997 [1994].

Miller, William L., Ase B. Grodeland, and Tatyana Y. Koshechkina. *A Culture of Corruption: Coping with Government in Post-Communist Europe.* New York: Central European University Press, 2000.

Mironov, Boris. "Bureaucratic- or Self-Government: The Early Nineteenth Century Russian City." *Slavic Review* 52, no. 2 (summer 1993): 233–55.

Moore, Wilbert. *The Conduct of the Corporation.* New York: Random House, 1962.

Mosse, Werner E. "Russian Bureaucracy at the End of the *Ancien Régime*: The Imperial State Council, 1897–1915." *Slavic Review* 39, no. 4 (December 1980): 616–32.

Murray, Donald. *A Democracy of Despots.* Boulder: Westview Press, 1996.

Nachmias, David, and David H. Rosenbloom. *Bureaucratic Government USA.* New York: St. Martin's, 1980.

Nagy, Piroska Mohacsi. *The Meltdown of the Russian State: The Deformation and Collapse of the State in Russia.* Williston, Vt.: Edward Elgar, 2000.

Nove, Alec. *The Soviet System in Retrospect*, Fourth Annual Harriman Lecture, Columbia University, 17 February 1993.

———. *Stalinism and After.* London: Allen and Unwin, 1975.

Obolonsky, A. V. "Biurokraticheskaia deformatsiia sosnanii i bor'ba s biurokratizmom." *Sovetskoe gosudarstvo i pravo*, no. 1 (January 1987): 52–61.

———. "Biurokratiia i biurokratizm." *Gosudarstvo i pravo*, no. 12 (December 1993): 88–98.

———. "Post-Soviet Officialdom: A Quasi-Bureaucratic Ruling Class." *Obshchestvennye nauki i sovremennost'*, no. 5 (1996).

———. "Russian Politics in the Time of Troubles: Some Basic Antinomies." In *Russia in Search of Its Future*, eds. Amin Saikal and William Maley. Cambridge: Cambridge University Press, 1955.

Odom, William E. "Soviet Politics and After: Old and New Concepts." *World Politics* 45, no. 1 (October 1992): 66–98.

Organizatsiia upravlenie v sisteme ministerstva. Moscow: Izdatel'sto Moskovskogo Universiteta, 1974.

Orlovsky, Daniel T. "Recent Studies on the Russian Bureaucracy." *Russian Review* 35, no. 4 (October 1976): 448–67.

Ostrowski, Donald. "The Mongol Origins of Muscovite Political Institutions." *Slavic Review* 49, no. 4 (winter 1990): 525–42.

———. *Moscovy and the Mongols: Cross-Cultural Influences on the Steppe Frontier, 1304–1589.* Cambridge: Harvard University Press, 1998.

Ott, J. Steven. *The Organizational Culture Perspective.* Chicago: Dorsey Press, 1989.

Ozernoy, Maryanne. "A Political History of the Russian State: The Basis for Bureaucratic Power." *Soviet and Post-Soviet Review* 23, no. 1 (1996): 1–14.

Parkinson, C. Northcote. *Parkinson: The Law*. Boston: Houghton Mifflin, 1980.

Peters, G. Guy. *The Politics of Bureaucracy*, 4th ed. New York: Longman, 1995.

Petro, Nicolai N. *Russian Democracy: An Interpretation of Political Culture*. Cambridge: Harvard University Press, 1995.

Pierre, Jon, ed. *Bureaucracy in the Modern State: An Introduction to Comparative Public Administration*. Aldershot, England: Edward Elgar, 1995.

Pintner, Walter M. "The Social Characteristics of the Early Nineteenth-Century Russian Bureaucracy." *Slavic Review* 29, no. 3 (September 1970): 429–43.

Pintner, Walter M., and Don Karl Rowney, eds. *Russian Officialdom: The Bureaucratization of Russian Society from the Seventeenth to the Twentieth Century*. Chapel Hill: University of North Carolina Press, 1980.

Pipes, Richard. *Russia under the Old Regime*. New York: Scribner's, 1974.

——. "Russia's Past, Russia's Future." *Commentary* 101, no. 6 (June 1996): 30–38.

Popov, Gavriil. *Blesk i nishcheta administrativnoi sistemy*. Moscow: PIK, 1990.

Pushkarev, Sergei. *The Emergence of Modern Russia: 1801–1917*, trans. Robert H. McNeal and Tova Yedlin. New York: Holt, Rinehart and Winston, 1962.

Putin, Vladimir. *First Person: An Astonishingly Frank Self-Portrait by Russia's President Valdimir Putin*, trans. Catherine A. Fitzpatrick. New York: Public Affairs, 2000.

Radio Free Europe/Radio Liberty. See either *Research Reports* or *Newsline* (the latter is an e-mail service).

Raeff, Marc. "Seventeenth-Century Europe in Eighteenth-Century Russia?" *Slavic Review* 41, no. 4 (winter 1988): 611–19.

——. *Speransky: Statesman of Imperial Russia, 1772–1839*. The Hague: Martinus Nijhoff, 1969.

——. *Understanding Imperial Russia*, trans. Arthur Goldhammer. New York: Columbia University Press, 1984.

Reddaway, Peter, and Dmitri Glinski. *The Tragedy of Russia's Reforms: Market Bolshevism against Democracy*. Washington, D.C.: U.S. Institute of Peace Press, 2001.

Remington, Thomas F. *Politics in Russia*. New York: Longman, 1999.

Rigby, T. H. "Crypto-politics." *Survey*, no. 50 (January 1964): 183–94.

——. "The Government in the Soviet Political System." In *Executive Power and Soviet Politics*, ed. Eugene Huskey. Armonk, N.Y.: M. E. Sharpe, 1992.

——. *Lenin's Government: Sovnarkom, 1917–1922*. Cambridge: Cambridge University Press, 1979.

——. "Politics in the Mono-organizational Society." In *Authoritarian Politics in Communist Europe*, ed. Andrew C. Janos. Berkeley: Institute of International Studies, University of California, 1976.

Rizzi, Bruno. *The Bureaucratization of the World*, trans. Adam Westoby. New York: Free Press, 1985.

Romanyuk, V. "How an Ordinary Bureaucrat Blocked a Decision of the USSR President." *Izvestia* 5 (July 1990), in *Current Digest of the Soviet Press* 42, no. 27 (1990).

Rossiia v zerkale reform. Moscow: Russian Independent Institute of Social and National Problems, 1995.

Rourke, Francis E. *Bureaucracy, Politics, and Public Policy*, 4th ed. Boston: Little, Brown and Co., 1984 [1976].

Rueschmeyer, Dietrich, and Peter B. Evans. "The State and Economic Transformation: Toward an Analysis of the Conditions Underlying Effective Intervention." In *Bringing the State Back In*, eds. Dietrich Rueschmeyer, Peter B. Evans, and Theda Skocpol. Cambridge: Cambridge University Press, 1985.

Russia on Russia: Administrative and State Reforms in Russia, no. 5 (June 2001).

Rutland, Peter, and Natasha Kogan. "Corruption and the Russian Transition." Paper presented at the Annual Meeting of the American Political Science Association, Boston, 2–6 September 1998.

———. *Business and the State in Contemporary Russia*. Boulder: Westview Press, 2000.

Ryavec, Karl W. *Implementation of Soviet Economic Reforms: Political, Economic and Social Processes*. New York: Praeger, 1975.

———. "Russo-Soviet Bureaucratism: Recent Russian Views." *The Soviet and Post-Soviet Review* 23, no. 1 (1996): 67–84.

———. "The Soviet Bureaucratic Elite from 1964 to 1979." *Soviet Union/Union Sovietique* 12, no. 3 (1985): 322–45.

———. "Soviet Industrial Managers, Their Superiors and the Economic Reform: A Study of an Attempt at Planned Behavioural Change." *Soviet Studies* 21, no. 2 (October 1969): 208–29.

———. *United States–Soviet Relations*. New York: Longman, 1989.

———, ed. *Soviet Society and the Communist Party*. Amherst: University of Massachusetts Press, 1978.

Sayre, Wallace. "Bureaucracies: Some Contrasts in Systems." *Indian Journal of Public Administration* 10, no. 2 (April–June 1964): 219–29.

Schecter, Jerrold L. *Russian Negotiating Behavior: Continuity and Transition*. Washington, D.C.: U.S. Institute of Peace Press, 1998.

Schmemann, Sergei. *Echoes of a Native Land: Two Centuries of a Russian Village*. New York: Vintage Books, 1999.

Schurmann, Franz. *Ideology and Organization in Communist China*, 2d ed. enlarged. Berkeley: University of California Press, 1968.

Scott, John. *Behind the Urals*. Bloomington: Indiana University Press, 1973.

Sergeyev, Victor M. "Organized Crime and Social Instability in Russia: The Alternative State, Deviant Bureaucracy, and Social Black Holes." In *Russia in the New Century: Stability or Disorder*, eds. Victoria E. Bonnell and George W. Breslauer. Boulder: Westview Press, 2001.

Service, Robert. *A History of Twentieth-Century Russia*. Cambridge: Harvard University Press, 1997.

Shelley, Louise. Testimony before the Commission on Security and Cooperation in Europe, hearing, 21 July 1999. Washington, D.C.: U.S. Government Printing Office, 2000.

Shelley, Louise R. "The Challenge of Crime and Corruption." In *Russia's Policy Challenges: Security, Stability, and Development*, ed. Stephen K. Wegren. Armonk, N.Y. and London: M. E. Sharpe, 2003.

Shevchenko, Arkady N. *Breaking with Moscow*. New York: Knopf, 1985.

Shevtsova, Lilia. *Yeltsin's Russia: Myth and Reality*. Washington, D.C.: Carnegie Endowment, 1999.

Silverman, Bertram, and Murray Yanowitch. *New Rich New Poor New Russia*. Armonk, N.Y.: M. E. Sharpe, 1997.

Simes, Konstantin. *USSR: The Corrupt Society*. New York: Simon and Schuster, 1982.

Sinyavsky, Andrei. *Soviet Civilization: A Cultural History*, trans. Joanne Turnbull and Nikolai Formozov. New York: Arcade, 1990.

Skilling, H. Gordon, and Franklyn Griffiths, eds. *Interest Groups in Soviet Politics*. Princeton: Princeton University Press, 1971.

Skocpol, Theda. "Old Regime Legacies and Communist Revolutions in Russia and China." In *Revolutions: Theoretical, Comparative, and Historical Studies*, 2d ed., ed. Jack A. Goldstone. Fort Worth: Harcourt Brace, 1994 (originally published in *Social Forces* 55, no. 2 [December 1976]).

Smith, Gordon B., ed. *State-Building in Russia*. Armonk, N.Y.: M. E. Sharpe, 1999.

Smith, Hedrick. *The Russians*. New York: Quadrangle Press, 1976.

Smith, Raymond F. *Negotiating with the Soviets*. Bloomington: Indiana University Press, 1989.

Solnick, Steven L. *Stealing the State: Control and Collapse in Soviet Institutions*. Cambridge: Harvard University Press, 1998.

Sperling, Valerie, ed. *Building the Russian State: Institutional Crisis and the Quest for Democratic Governance*. Boulder: Westview Press, 2000.

Stavrikis, Peter J. *Shadow Politics: The Russian State in the 21st Century*. Carlisle Barracks, Penn.: Strategic Studies Institute, U.S. Army War College, 8 December 1997.

Sternheimer, Stephen. "Information, Communications, and Decision-Making in the Soviet City." Paper presented at the Annual Meeting of the American Political Science Association, Philadelphia, November 1990.

Stillman, Richard D., II. *The American Bureaucracy*. Chicago: Nelson-Hall, 1987.

Stojanovic, Svetozar. *Between Ideals and Reality: A Critique of Socialism and Its Future*, trans. Gerson S. Sher. New York: Oxford University Press, 1973.

Suleiman, Ezra N. *Bureaucrats and Policy Making*. New York: Holmes and Meier, 1985.

———. *Elites in French Society: The Politics of Survival*. Princeton: Princeton University Press, 1978.

Suny, Ronald Gregor. *The Soviet Experiment*. Oxford: Oxford University Press, 1998.

Sutherland, Sir Iain. Lecture. Harvard University, 11 March 1986.

Szamuely, Tibor. *The Russian Tradition*. New York: McGraw-Hill, 1974.

Talbott, Strobe. *Endgame: The Inside Story of SALT II*. New York: Harper and Row, 1979.

Tanzi, Vito, and Hamid Davoodi. *Roads to Nowhere: How Corruption in Public Investment Hurts Growth*. Washington, D.C.: International Monetary Fund, 1998.

Taranovski, Theodore. "Alexander III and His Bureaucracy: The Limitations on Autocratic Power." *Canadian Slavonic Papers* 26, nos. 2–3 (June–September 1984): 207–19.

———. "The Imperial Bureaucracy in the Reign of Alexander III." Mimeographed paper prepared for the Central Slavic Conference of the American Association for the Advancement of Slavic Studies, St. Louis, Mo., November 1971.

Tatu, Michel. *Power in the Kremlin*, trans. Helen Katel. New York: Viking, 1970.

Taubman, William, and Jane Taubman. *Moscow Spring*. New York: Summit Books, 1989.

Theen, Rolf H. W. "Party and Bureaucracy." In *Public Administration in the Soviet Union*, ed. Gordon B. Smith. New York: Praeger, 1980.

Thompson, Victor A. *Modern Organization*, 2d ed. Tuscaloosa: University of Alabama Press, 1977.

Treisman, Daniel. "Russia's Taxing Problem." *Foreign Policy*, no. 112 (fall 1998): 55–66.

Trotsky, Leon. *The Revolution Betrayed*. New York: Merit, 1965.

Tsuneishi, Warren M. *Japanese Political Style*. New York: Harper and Row, 1966.

Tuchman, Barbara W. *The Proud Tower: A Portrait of the World before the War*. New York: Macmillan, 1966.

Tucker, Robert C. *Political Culture and Leadership in Soviet Russia*. New York: Norton, 1987.

———. *The Soviet Political Mind*. New York: Norton, 1971.

Urban, Michael E. *The Ideology of Administration: American and Soviet Cases*. Albany: State University of New York Press, 1982.

Venturi, Franco. *Roots of Revolution: A History of the Populist and Socialist Movements in Nineteenth Century Russia*. New York: Grosset and Dunlap, 1960.

Vogel, Ezra. F. "Politicized Bureaucracy; Communist China." In *Communist Systems in Comparative Perspective*, eds. Leonard J. Cohen and Jane P. Shapiro. Garden City, N.Y.: Anchor Books, 1974.

von Mises, Ludwig. *Bureaucracy*. Cedar Falls, Iowa: Center for Futures Education, 1983.

Waller, Michael. *The End of the Communist Power Monopoly*. Manchester: Manchester University Press, 1993.

What Is the State? Moscow: Progress Publishers, 1986.

White, Stephen. *After Gorbachev*. Cambridge: Cambridge University Press, 1993.

———. *Russia's New Politics: The Management of a Postcommunist Society*. Cambridge: Cambridge University Press, 2000.

White, Stephen, Alex Pravda, and Zvi Gitelman, eds. *Developments in Soviet Politics 4*. Durham: Duke University Press, 1997.

White, Stephen, Richard Rose, and Ian McAllister. *How Russia Votes*. Chatham, N.J.: Chatham House, 1997.

Wilson, James Q. *Bureaucracy: What Government Agencies Do and Why They Do It*. New York: Basic Books, 1989.

Woll, Peter. *American Bureaucracy*. New York: Norton, 1963.

———. *American Government: Readings and Cases*, 12th ed. New York: Harper Collins, 1995.

Wright, Vincent. "The Administrative Machine: Old Problems and New Dilemmas." In *Developments in French Politics*, eds. Peter A. Hall, Jack Hayward, and Howard Machin. New York: St. Martin's, 1994.

Yaney, George L. "Law, Society and the Domestic Regime in Russia, in Historical Perspective." *American Political Science Review* 59, no. 2 (June 1965): 379–90.

———. *The Systemization of Russian Government*. Urbana: University of Illinois Press, 1973.

Yasman, Victor. "The Russian Civil Service: Corruption and Reform." *RFE/RL* 2, no. 16 (16 April 1993).

Yeltsin, Boris. "Address to the Civil Service Academy," 6 September 1995. In *FBIS-SOV-95-173*, 7 September 1995.

———. *The Struggle for Russia*, trans. Catherine A. Fitzpatrick. New York: Times Books, 1994.

Yergin, Daniel, and Thane Gustafson. *Russia 2010*. New York: Random House, 1993.

Zaionchkovskii, P. A. *Pravitel'stvennyi apparat samoderzhavnoi Rossii v XIX v.* Moscow: Mysl', 1978.

Zverev, A. F. "Biurokratiia v zerkale sotsiologii." *Gosudarstvo i pravo*, no. 8 (August 1992): 115–22.

Suggested Reading

RUSSIAN BOOKS ON ADMINISTRATION AND BUREAUCRACY: A SAMPLE

Administrativnoe zakonodatel'stvo Rossiiskoi Federatsii: Sbornik normativnykh aktov. 2 vols. Vladikavkaz: Vladikavkazskii in-t upravleniia, 2000.

Afanas'ev, M. N. *Praviashchie elity i gosudarstvennost' posttotalitarnoi Rossii.* Moscow: Institut Prakticheskoi Isikhologii, 1996.

Aktual'nye problemy administrativnogo prava Rossii. Omsk: Ministerstvo vnutrennikh del Rossiiskoi Federatsii, Omskii Iuridicheskii Institut, 1999.

Aktualnye problemy politiki I politologiii v Rossii. Moscow: Izdatel'stvo RAGS, 1999.

Ankudinov, Iu. A. *Organizatsiia i stil' raboty rukovoditelia predpriiatiia.* Moscow: Ekonomika, 1976.

Arkhipova, T. G., M. F. Rumiantseva, and A. S. Senin. *Istoriia gosudarstvennoi sluzhby v Rossii XVIII–XX veka.* Moscow: Ros. Gos. Gumant. Un-t, 1999.

Bakhrakh, D. *Administrativnoe pravo Rossii: Uchebnik dlia vuzov.* Moscow: Norma, 2000.

Borodkin, F. M., and N. M. Koriak. *Vnimanie: Konflikt!* Novosibirsk: Nauka, Sibirskoe Otdelenie, 1983.

Dorskaia, A. A. *Istoriia gosudarstvennykh uchrezhdenii Rossii do 1917g.* St. Petersburg: Izdatel'stvo RGPU im. A. I. Gertsena, 1998.

Dzodziev, Viktor. *Problemy stanovleniia demokraticheskogo gosudarstva v Rossii.* Moscow: Ad Marginem, 1996.

Ekonomicheskaia reforma: Poisk reshenii. Moscow: Izdatel'stvo Politicheskoi Literatury, 1990.

Ezhov, V. A. *Gosudarstvennoe upravlenie SSSR posle Velikoi Otechestvennoi Voiny (1945–1950 gg.): Uchebnoe posobie.* St. Petersburg: Nestor, 1999.

269

Garniuk, Sergei D., ed. _Sovet narodnykh komissarov, sovet ministrov, kabinet ministrov SSSR, 1923–1991._ Moscow: MOSGORARKHIV, 1999.

Gerber, Rikhard, and Gerbert Iung (Herber, Richard, and Herbert Jung). _Kadry v sisteme sotsialisticheskogo upravlenie._ Moscow: Progress, 1970 (a translation of _Kaderarbeit im Sistem sozialistischer Fuhrungstatigkeit_).

Gimpel'son, E. G. _Sovetskie upravlentsy: 1917–1920 gg._ Moscow: Rossiiskaia Akademiia Nauk, 1998.

Gosudarstvennaia sluzhba. Moscow: Delo, 1999.

Gosudarstvennaia sluzhba Rossiiskoi Federatsii: Pervye shagi i perspektivy. Moscow: Izdatel'stvo RAGS, 1997.

Gosudarstvennaia vlast' SSSR: Vysshie oragny vlasti i upravleniia i ikh rukovoditeli 1923–1991, istoriko-biograficheskii spravochnik. Moscow: ROSSPEN, 1999.

Gosudarstvennoe upravlenia i gosudarstvennaia sluzhba v transformiruiushchemsia obshchestve. Moscow: RAGS, 2001.

Grazhdanin i apparat upravleniia v SSSR. Moscow: Nauka, 1984.

Grazhdanskie initsiativy i predotvrashchenie korruptsii. St. Petersburg: Norma, 2000.

Isikhologiia i upravlenie. Leningrad: Leningradskogo Universiteta, 1979.

Ispolnitel'naia vlast' v Rossiiskoi Federatsii: Problemy razvitia. Moscow: Iurist', 1998.

Ivkin, V. I., ed. _Gosudarstvennaia vlast' SSSR: Vysshie organy vlasti i upravleniia i ikh rukovoditeli, 1923–1991. Istoriko-biograficheskii spravochnik._ Moscow: ROSSPEN, 1999.

Karpunin, M. G. _Stil' rukovodstva i khoziaistvennaia perestroika._ Moscow: Ekonomika, 1988.

Khasbulatov, R. I. _Biurokraticheskoe gosudarstvo._ Moscow: Megapolis-Takom, 1991.

Khudokormov, A. G. _Ekonomicheskie korni biurokratizma._ Moscow: Ekonomika, 1988.

Korzhikhina, T. P. _Sovetskoe gosudarstvo i ego uchrezhdeniia: Noiabr' 1917–Dekabr' 1991 g._ Moscow: Rossiiskii gosudarstvennyi gumanitarnyi universitet, 1995.

Kotandzhian, G. S. _Sotsial'no-isikhologicheskie faktory upravleniia kollektivom._ Erevan: Aiastan, 1983.

Levin, B. D., and M. N. Perfil'ev. _Kadry apparata upravleniia v SSSR._ Leningrad: Nauka, 1970.

Markov, Marko. _Sotsializm i upravlenie._ Moscow: Ekonomika, 1973 (a translation from the Bulgarian [Sofia, 1971]).

Martynov, S. D. _Professionaly v upravlenii._ Leningrad: Lenizdat, 1991.

Maslennikov, M. Ia. _Rossiiskii administrativnyi protsess._ Tver: Tver State University, 2001.

Mukhin, A. _Korruptsiia i gruppy vliiania._ Moscow: SPIK-Tsentr, 1999.

Nastol'naia kniga gosudarstvennogo sluzhashchego. Moscow: "Ekonomika," 1999.

Obolonskii, A. V. _Biurokratiia dlia xxi veka? Modeli gosudarstvennoi sluzhby: Rossiia, SShA, Angliia, Avstraliia._ Moscow: "Delo," 2002.

Obolonskii, A. V., and V. D. Rudashevskii. _Metodologiia sistemnogo issledovaniia problem gosudarstvennogo upravleniia._ Moscow: Nauka, 1978.

Osnovy upravleniia: Uchebnik dlia vuzov. Moscow: Vysshaia Shkola, 1986.

Paramonov, I. V. _Uchit'sia upravliat'._ Moscow: Ekonomika, 1977.

Peregudov, S. P., N. Iu. Lapina, and I. S. Semenenko. _Gruppy interesov I Rossiiskoe gosudarstvo._ Moscow: Editorial URSS, 1999.

Politicheskie aspekty gosudarstvennogo upravleniia: Federal'nyi i regional'nyi opyt. Moscow: Rossiiskaia Akademiia Gosudarstvennoi Sluzhby pri Presidente Rossiiskoi Federatsii, 1997.

Politicheskoe upravlenie: Teoriia i praktika. Moscow: RAGS, 1997.

Popov, Gavriil. *Blesk i nishcheta administrativnoi sistemy.* Moscow: PIK Nezavisimoe Isdatel'stvo, 1990.

———. *Problemy teorii upravleniia.* Moscow: Ekonomika, 1970.

Popov, L. L. *Upravlenie, grazhdanin, otvetstvennost'.* Leningrad: Nauka, 1975.

Regional'noe upravlenie: Opyt i problemy. Kiev: Naukova Dumka, 1984.

Rossiiskaia akademiia gosudarstvennoi sluzhby pri Presidente Rossiiskoi Federatsii. *Ezhegodnik '98.* Moscow: Izdatel'stvo RAGS, 1999.

Rossiiskaia gosudarstvennost': Traditsii, preemstvennost', perspektivy. Moscow: Izdatel'stvo Gosudarstvennogo Gumantarnogo Universiteta, 1999.

Rossiiskaia vlast' v litsakh: Biograficheskii spravochnik. Moscow: Tsentr "Panorama," 2001.

Salishcheva, N. G. *Administrativnii protsess v SSSR.* Moscow: Iuridicheskaia literatura, 1964.

Shepel', V. M. *Upravlencheskaia isikhologiia.* Moscow: Ekonomika, 1984.

Shepelov, L. *Chinovnyi mir Rossii: XVIII-nachalo XX vv.* St. Petersburg: Iskusstvo-SPb, 1999.

Shilov, D. *Gosudarstvennye deiateli Rossiiskoi imperii, 1802–1917: Bibliograficheskii spravochnik.* St. Petersburg: Dmitrii Bulanin, 2001.

Sistema raboty s kadrami upravleniia. Moscow: Mysl', 1984.

Slovar' adminsitrativnogo prava. Moscow: Fond Pravovaia Kul'tura, 1999.

Smirtiukov, M. S. *Sovetskii gosudarstvennyi apparat upravleniia,* 2d ed. Moscow: Politicheskaia Literatura, 1984.

Sobchak, Anatolii. *Khozhdenie vo vlast'.* Moscow: Novosti, 1991.

Sotsial'nye aspekty upravleniia. Moscow: Ekonomika, 1981.

Sovet narodnykh komissarov, sovet ministrov, kabinet ministrov: 1923–1991, entsiklopedicheskii spravochnik. Moscow: "MOSGORARKHIV," 1999.

Spiridonova, V. I. *Biurokratiia i reforma.* Moscow: Institut Filosofii, Rossiiskaia Akademiia Nauk, 1997.

Struktury gosudarstvennoi vlasti: Telefonyi spravochnik. Moscow: Agentsvo "Bisnes-Press," 2002.

Sungurova, A. Iu., ed. *Grazhdanskie initsiativy I predotvrashchenie korruptsii.* St. Petersburg: NORMA, 2000.

Tekhnologiia vlasti i upravlenie v sovremennom gosudarstve. Moscow: Universitetskii Gumantarnyi Litsei, 1999.

Tenevaia ekonomika. Moscow: Ekonomika, 1991.

Tikovenko, A. G. *Nachal'nik i podchinennyi.* Minsk: Nauka I Tekhnika, 1984.

Tkachenko, A. A. *Territorial'naia obshchnost' v regional'nom razvitii i upravlenii.* Tver: Tverskoi gosudarstvennyi universitet, 1995.

Upravlenie i problema kadrov. Moscow: Ekonomika, 1972.

Vlast': Pravitel'stvo Rossii. Moscow: Institut Sovremennoi Politiki, 1997.

(For articles, see the journal *Gosudarsto i pravo,* formerly *Sovetskoe gosudarstvo i pravo.*)

Index

About the Author

Karl W. Ryavec is professor emeritus of political science at the University of Massachusetts, Amherst. He is the author of several books, including: *Implementation of Soviet Economic Reforms: Political, Organizational, and Social Processes* (1975); *The Soviet Ministerial Elite, 1964–1979: A Representative Sample* (1981); *United States–Soviet Relations Today: The Reluctant Rivals* (1987); and *United States–Soviet Relations* (1989). He is also the editor of two books: *Soviet Society and the Communist Party* (1978) and *A Scholar's Odyssey/Ferenc A. Váli* (1990).